The Impossibility
of Religious Freedom

The Impossibility
of Religious Freedom

WINNIFRED FALLERS SULLIVAN, 1950-

PRINCETON UNIVERSITY PRESS

PRINCETON AND OXFORD

Published by Princeton University Press,
41 William Street, Princeton, New Jersey 08540
In the United Kingdom: Princeton University Press,
3 Market Place, Woodstock, Oxfordshire OX20 1SY

Second printing, and first paperback printing, 2007
Cloth ISBN-13: 978-0-691-11801-7
Cloth ISBN-10: 0-691-11801-9
Paperback ISBN-13: 978-0-691-13058-3
Paperback ISBN-10: 0-691-13058-2

The Library of Congress has cataloged the cloth edition of this book as follows

Sullivan, Winnifred Fallers, 1950–
The impossibility of religious freedom / Winnifred Fallers Sullivan.
p.   cm.
Includes bibliographical references and index.
ISBN 0-691-11801-9 (hardcover : alk. paper)
1. Warner, Maria—Trials, litigation, etc.   2. Boca Raton (Fla.)—Trials, litigation,
etc.   3. Cemeteries—Law and legislation—Florida.   4. Freedom of religion—United
States.   I. Title.
KF228.W353S85 2005
342.7308'52—dc22   2004058685

British Library Cataloging-in-Publication Data is available

This book has been composed in Janson

Printed on acid-free paper. ∞

pup.princeton.edu

Printed in the United States of America

3   5   7   9   10   8   6   4

For my mother

Contents

Acknowledgments   ix

Note on Sources   xi

List of Illustrations   xiii

INTRODUCTION   1

CHAPTER ONE   Outlaw Religion   13

CHAPTER TWO   The Trial: The Plaintiffs   32

CHAPTER THREE   The Trial: The Other Witnesses   54

CHAPTER FOUR   Legal Religion   89

CHAPTER FIVE   Free Religion   138

APPENDICES

APPENDIX A: Relevant Law: Excerpts from U.S. and Florida Constitutions,
RFRA, FRFRA, and Rules and Regulations of
Boca Raton Cemetery   161

APPENDIX B: Expert Reports of Broyde, Katz, McGuckin, Pals,
and Sullivan   179

APPENDIX C: Ryskamp Opinion   219

Notes   245

Bibliography   269

Index   281

Acknowledgments

In the preparation of this book, my many debts to the following are both professional and personal: Jeremy Biles, Alexandra Brown, Spencer Dew, Sandy Dowler, Margaret Fallers, Susan Gilles, Hillel Gray, Philip Hamburger, Stanley N. Katz, Hans Kippenberg, Beth Lamanna, Cynthia Gano Lindner, Martin E. Marty, Heather Miller, Helen Scharbach Newlin, M. Sandford Norbeck, Kay Read, Frank Reynolds, Richard A. Rosengarten, Barry Sullivan, George Sullivan, Lloyd Sullivan, Brigitta van Rheinberg, James Boyd White, Robert Yelle, and the anonymous reviewers. But, most importantly, my friend, colleague, and teacher, Frank Reynolds. I am very grateful to all of them for their counsel and support. I am also grateful to Washington and Lee University and the University of Chicago for the institutional support they have provided.

Further, I owe a posthumous debt, personal and professional, to Philip B. Kurland, who saw earlier than most, and with greater clarity, the issues with which this book is concerned.

Note on Sources

All of the materials used in the preparation of this book are a matter of public record.

Illustrations

(Following page 31)

1. Grave of the wife of Mr. Karram (1999)
2. Grave of the wife of Mr. Karram (2004)
3. Grave of the brother of Ms. Monier and Ms. Cavedoni (1999)
4. Grave of the brother of Ms. Monier and Ms. Cavedoni (2004)
5. Grave of the son of Mr. and Mrs. Payne (1999)
6. Grave of the son of Mr. and Mrs. Payne (2004)
7. Grave of the son of Ms. Davis (1999)
8. Grave of the son of Ms. Davis (2004)
9. Grave of the father of Ms. Riccobono (2004)
10. New section of Boca Raton Cemetery (2004)
11. Old section of Boca Raton Cemetery (2004)
12. Grave-digging equipment (2004)
13. Example of Jewish grave with stones left by mourners (2004)
14. Other nonconforming graves (2004)
15. Other nonconforming grave (2004)
16. Other nonconforming grave (2004)
17. Other nonconforming grave (2004)
18. Other nonconforming grave (2004)
19. Other nonconforming grave (2004)
20. Other nonconforming grave (2004)

Note: All of the photographs dated 2004 were taken by the author. The photographs taken in 1999 were entered into evidence at the trial.

The Impossibility
of Religious Freedom

So Rachel died, and she was buried on the way to Ephrath (that is, Bethlehem), and Jacob set up a pillar upon her grave; it is the pillar of Rachel's tomb, which is there to this day.

—Genesis 35:20 (RSV)

Woe to you! For you are like graves which are not seen, and men walk over them without knowing it.

—Luke 11:44 (RSV)

[S]now was general all over Ireland . . . faintly falling . . . upon all the living and the dead.

—James Joyce, "The Dead"

The sovereign sphere is the sphere in which it is permitted to kill without committing homicide and without celebrating a sacrifice, and sacred life— that is life that may be killed but not sacrificed—is the life that has been captured in this sphere.

—Giorgio Agamben, *Homo Sacer*

Introduction

This book is about the impossibility of religious freedom. Many laws, constitutions, and international treaties today grant legally enforceable rights to those whose religious freedom is infringed. Stories of the conflict between the demands of religion and the demands of law are daily news items all over the world, and take a familiar patterned form. Schoolgirls in France seek permission to wear the *hijab* to school. Sikhs in Britain seek exemption from motorcycle helmet laws. Muslim women seek civil divorces in India on the same ground as their Hindu and Christian neighbors. The Jehovah's Witnesses seek the right to be a recognized religious organization in Russia and to be exempt from patriotic exercises in Greece. Native Americans seek repatriation of religious items in the cases of U.S. museums. In each of these cases a court or a legislature or an administrative official must make a determination as to whether the religious practice in question is legally religious. In other words, in order to enforce laws guaranteeing religious freedom you must first have religion.

The impossibility of religious freedom is not obvious, nor is the advocacy of such a position popular. A commitment to religious freedom is a taken-for-granted part of modern political identity in much of the world. Certainly this is so in the United States. Even most of those whose own personal stance is fiercely secular would include the right to religious freedom among those rights fundamental to a free democratic society. Indeed, Americans who may be able to agree on little else agree that religious freedom is one of the shining achievements of the United States, one that they are often anxious to export around the world.[1] Nowhere, as Americans understand it, is religion so strong and so free. Not in Europe, which is believed to be pervasively and irredeemably atheistic, and where new religious movements are persecuted. Not in the Muslim world, where it is believed that adherence to Islam is enforced by authoritarian regimes and non-Muslims are discriminated against. Not in China, where it is believed that all religion is suspect. But there is a very real sense in which religious freedom is turning out to be impossible to realize, even in the United States. Drawing a line around what counts as religion and what does not is not as easy as periodically recommitting ourselves politically to religious freedom. Defining religion is very difficult, particularly at the beginning of the twenty-first century. Who is to say what is the authentic way for an American to be Christian or Jewish or Muslim or Inuit or Daoist or . . . ?

This book tells two stories. First, it tells the story of how a motley group of ordinary Americans buried their dead in one cemetery in a small Florida city in the 1980s and 1990s, in defiance of local regulation, and then challenged the federal courts to enforce their right to the free exercise of their religion. Second, in light of the sometimes heroic effort of this group of ordinary American Protestants, Catholics, and Jews to explain what they did and why they did it to a group of ordinary American lawyers and judges and city officials, it tells the story of the impossibility of religious freedom today. The story of the trial itself is a small but moving local tale of a dispute that is now in its second decade. The implications of these local events are, however, arguably of wider significance.

Warner v. Boca Raton (hereinafter the *Warner* case)[2] was brought on behalf of a group of Florida residents who sought to prevent the forced removal of the numerous statues, plantings, crosses, Stars of David, and other individually crafted installations that, with the tacit permission of city officials, they had placed on the individual graves of their deceased relatives over the course of ten to fifteen years (see photographs between pp. 31 and 32). The suit sought a statutory and constitutional free-exercise-of-religion exemption from local cemetery regulations that limit the size and placement of memorials to small flat metal plaques, flush with the ground, giving only names and dates, and that can be easily mowed over. The principal issue at trial was whether the nonconforming memorial arrangements assembled by plaintiffs were an "exercise of religion," and therefore protected by the relevant statutes and constitutional provisions.

The burial practices of the *Warner* plaintiffs belong to a grouping of religious beliefs and practices that one might call "lived religion," or "folk religion," that is, religion that takes place beneath the radar of religious officials and institutions. These practices, as with the familiar impromptu memorials constructed at the side of the road at the site of automobile accidents or at places of national tragedy such as that of the Oklahoma City bombing, reflect U.S. religious diversity, immigrant piety, political idealism, and a do-it-yourself style of religious ritual and iconography. This kind of religion is, for the most part, local and family-centered—but it is also linked in important ways to international and transnational religious communities and traditions.

The lived religion of the *Warner* plaintiffs, as represented by the Boca Raton cemetery memorials, will be seen in the context of this trial as resistant to, and yet shaped in fundamental ways by the larger U.S. religious and legal history and landscape of which they are a part. But the religious practices described in this book and the conditions set by the legal context in which they find themselves are not exclusive to the U.S. context; with some local shading, they are common throughout the world. We live increasingly in a world of diaspora religious communities in which all religions are everywhere, in which all religions everywhere are governed by secular legal regimes, and in which all religions everywhere are being reinvented by their adherents to suit new circumstances. The *Warner* trial provides a case study for how and whether, given these conditions, law anywhere today can do what it is being asked to do: guarantee freedom of religion. Courts need some way of deciding what counts as religion if they are to enforce these laws. Is it possible to do this without setting up a legal hierarchy of religious orthodoxy? And who is legally and constitutionally qualified to make such judgments? Can "lived religion" ever be protected by laws guaranteeing religious freedom?

Religion and law today speak in languages largely opaque to each other. When they intersect, whether in the work of academics or in the public square, it is usually in one of several familiar ways: in debates concerning certain issues of public policy—such as abortion, homosexuality, cloning, and euthanasia—or in the high-profile stories of the asserted denial of religious freedom mentioned above, such as prohibitions against Islamic veiling in France and Turkey, or of government funding of faith-based initiatives in the United States. These debates and these stories, for the most part, focus on the political questions and assume an unproblematic understanding of secular law, its history, and how it works today. They assume that, given the political will, laws—and courts—can do the work of enforcing the rights of religion. Less attention is given to how and whether law affects religion in these cases—to the actual encounter in courtrooms today between the religious lives of ordinary people and secular legal regimes. How can courts fairly assess evidence about religious practice? How can courts determine what counts as religious for the many laws all over the world that give persons whose actions are religiously motivated special privileges in law?[3]

This book is, then, on the smallest scale, about what counts as religion, legally, in Boca Raton, Florida, at the beginning of the twenty-first century. The book will consider the *Warner* case itself in some detail, but I will first put the case, and my own involvement in it, in a somewhat larger legal context.

On the fifth and final day of the trial, in March 1999, just before giving his ruling from the bench, the Honorable Kenneth L. Ryskamp, U.S. district judge for the Southern District of Florida, announced: "I must admit that I enjoyed the four days immensely. I mean it's not very often where you can spent [*sic*] four days in court and talk theology all day. And I happen to enjoy that. And I thought it was interesting. It's an experience unlike anything I've had in 13 years on the bench."[4] It should come as a surprise—to Americans at least—that a federal judge would describe a four-day trial as "talking theology all day." "Talking theology," we might think, is something that properly happens in churches and seminaries, or—at the very least—among private citizens. It is certainly not something that a federal judge should be doing while on the bench. It is not something that the government should be doing at all—if, by "talking theology," we mean talking about God.[5]

Characterizing all Americans is certainly almost as difficult as defining religion; but American attitudes toward religion are the product of a distinctive history, and Americans, on the whole, tend to be quite fastidious about the line between religion and government. Europeans, while often more secular in their personal orientations, are much more used to living with a lingering religious "establishment" of sorts and consequently less squeamish about public displays of religion and public involvement of religion in the life of the community and governmental involvement in the operations of religious communities. Religious freedom is often understood in Europe not to be incompatible with public funding of religion, for example.[6] Some Americans might be more tolerant of generalized religious references and more comfortable with ceremonial religiosity than others; but most would recoil at the idea that a federal judge should be deciding in a federal court, for the purposes of secular law, what does and what does not count as real religion—what counts as what we might call "legal" religion. When Judge Ryskamp speaks of "talking theology" he is referring to his efforts to determine exactly what counts as religion for the purposes of law.

The *Warner* case does not seem at first blush to have the marks usually associated with important legal cases in this country. It is not yet a Supreme Court case. It is not regarded as a landmark case in the legal literature. It seems now unlikely to be widely cited or discussed in legal circles. Furthermore, protection of the practices at issue in this case were not necessary for the survival, or even central to the identity, of a religious community, as was the case in many of the well-known American judicial decisions about religion: cases concerning Jehovah's Witnesses proselytizing, Mormon polygamy, Amish educational practices, or Native American sacred lands, to mention just a few.[7]

4

The practices for which protection was sought in the *Warner* case are more modest and more typically mainstream American. The *Warner* plaintiffs are not members of a religious elite. They are ordinary Americans attending to the most critical events of their lives—the deaths of their children, spouses, and parents. They are ordinary Americans seeking to create a place for mourning within the spaces set out by city, state, and federal laws, and by the cemetery industry. But if the religious activities at these graves are seen as unimportant and as not deserving of protection, legally speaking, then statutes guaranteeing religious freedom may be accomplishing just the reverse of their stated intent. These laws may be harming rather than fostering freedom of religion. In the important area of defining legal religion and legally protecting religious freedom, the *Warner* case provides, I believe, a valuable example.

Those "talking theology" in federal court with Judge Ryskamp in this trial in March 1999 included the plaintiffs (relatives of those whose remains were buried in the cemetery), city officials and managers of the cemetery, a financial analyst, two experts on the cemetery industry, five experts on religion, the lawyers, and the judge. I was the third of the three religion experts hired by the plaintiffs' lawyers. The other two expert witnesses for the plaintiffs were a priest and a rabbi, both also academics. The City hired two religion scholars as experts. The testimony of all of those testifying at this trial was often at cross-purposes. As with many religion cases in the American courts, to read the testimony and the legal arguments in the *Warner v. Boca Raton* case with the eye of a scholar of religion is to wade into a murky mixture of half-remembered childhood teachings (whether at the knee of one's grandmother or in formal religious instruction), ideas promoted in the popular literature of spirituality, fragments of Supreme Court opinions, the demands of the politics of identity, academic theories and opinions, and genuine, if often uninformed, fascination and concern. Indeed, one could say that the process of the trial itself, not just the ultimate decision, was somehow at times indecent, however unintentionally, in its ignorance about religion and in the resulting harassment of the plaintiffs. Certainly by bringing suit the plaintiffs consented, in some sense, to intrusive questioning—but did they consent to ill-informed and sometimes humiliating badgering about their religious beliefs and practices? And to what purpose?

The *Warner* case, in its very modesty, nicely illustrates the modern legal conditioning and predicament of religion. And it does so in the context of the peculiarly American conjunction between a strict separationist political ideology and a widespread evangelical style of religiosity, a conjunction further distinguished by the very American sense that everyone is an expert when it comes to religion. The United States is, as many have observed, at once a profoundly secular and a profoundly religious society. "Separation of church and state" means that there is no established authority. A reformed evangelical piety means that each person is enthusiastically open to new religious experience, his or her own and everyone else's. Together, these conditions produce a religious field both diverse and uniform. Throughout the *Warner* trial Judge Ryskamp inhabited this American double consciousness, at once separationist and evangelical, uneasily, I think, not sure how to resolve it. He confidently asserted the entire and complete right of every American to believe as she or he chooses while at the same time thoroughly enjoying arbitrating among competing views. This practice of his, his arbitration among views, was what he called "talking theology." Biblically literate in a lay sense, Ryskamp felt no hesitation in openly preferring his own reading of the Hebrew Bible to that of the rabbi. He also felt no compunction about preferring his own version of church history to that of the church historian. Religion appeared to be judged in his courtroom according to the fabled "I know it when I see it" standard.[8]

Judge Ryskamp is like many Americans, I think, both in his obvious pleasure in "talking theology" and in his self-confident evaluation of the available evidence about religion. He *was* interested in religion and he was entirely democratic, if often uninformed, when debating authoritative sources. Religious authority was located for him in the individual, not in the religious community. Summarizing his reaction to the plaintiffs' testimony in the *Warner* case, he revealed his own very American brand of broadmindedness when it comes to religion:

> I would say at the outset, of all the plaintiffs who testified and the depositions that I've read, I believe that all of them have sincere religious beliefs. This does not require any testimony of orthodoxy, because orthodoxy is not an issue. . . . In listening to the testimony, the views expressed weren't necessarily my views but I recognize them as all valid religious beliefs that are entitled to protection under the law. I'm sure that if I express my religious views some people would say that's very weird and that's very strange, you know, I can't agree with that. That's unorthodox. And that's what makes up religion, is that we all have the right in this country to have whatever religious views we choose to have. So I would say as a blanket matter at the beginning that I recognize all of these views that have been expressed as sincerely held religious views.[9]

"Sincerity" is the only standard, he says here.[10] Each person is entitled to his or her own beliefs. Yet, legally defined orthodoxy, not sincerity, was the final standard used in the *Warner* trial.

The case before him demanded that Judge Ryskamp make a decision about what counts as religion. Where else was he to look for authority, other than his own judgment? The five expert witnesses on religion in the *Warner* case, of which I was one, did not have an obvious place in the conversation. We did not speak out of his largely individualistic and self-taught evangelical epistemology. We spoke of history and culture and tradition. Ryskamp was suspicious about our claims to authority and reluctant to credit our testimony. Our claims of authority, whether scholarly in a religious or in a secular sense, were un-American. A federal judge has a great deal of power. Academic expertise can be impotent in such a place, particularly, perhaps, if the expertise is about religion. In the end Ryskamp drew back from the implications of the embracing antiauthoritarianism expressed above, falling back on his own authority as a federal judge and as a religious American.

Religious freedom and the legal disestablishment of religion, as political ideas, find their origin in the early modern period in Europe.[11] With other markers of modernity identified by scholars—the rise of the nation state, the maturing of an international market, the invention of modern warfare, the advent of printing and literacy, the emergence of a middle class, among others—a new relationship of religion to political governance was created with the breakup of the monopoly of the Roman Church.[12] For perhaps the first time since Constantine, religious affiliation in Europe began to be detached again from political identity. National and religious identity no longer necessarily went hand in hand. To be sure, at first, new national religious establishments were created to take the place of the continental monopoly of the Roman Catholic Church, but over the centuries religion was both consciously and unconsciously remodeled to accommodate the new secular political order and new ideas of citizenship. Religion was thereby politically and legally divided into modern and antimodern, long before the reappearance of "fundamentalism" in the 1970s.[13] The precondition for political participation by religion increasingly became cooperation with liberal theories and forms of governance.[14]

As a result, the modern religio-political arrangement has been largely, although not exclusively, indebted, theologically and phenomenologically, to protestant reflection and culture.[15] Particularly in its American manifestation. "Protestant" is here spelled with a small "p." I use "protestant" not in a narrow churchy sense, but rather loosely to describe a set of political ideas and cultural practices that emerged in early modern Europe in and after the Reformation; that is, I refer to "protestant," as opposed to "catholic," models of church/state relations. (According to this use, Protestants can be "catholic" and Catholics can be "protestant.") Religion—"true" religion some would say—on this modern protestant reading, came to be understood as being private, voluntary, individual, textual, and believed. Public, coercive, communal, oral, and enacted religion, on the other hand, was seen to be "false." The second kind of religion, iconically represented historically in the United States, for the most part by the Roman Catholic Church (and by Islam today), was, and perhaps still is, the religion of most of the world. Indeed, from a contemporary academic perspective, that religion with which many religion scholars are most concerned has been carefully and systematically excluded, both rhetorically and legally, from modern public space. Crudely speaking, it is the first kind—the modern protestant kind—that is "free." The other kind is closely regulated by law. It is not incidental that most of the plaintiffs in the *Warner* case, the case considered in this book, are Catholic.

This book, to reiterate, is about the impossibility of religious freedom. Not the impossibility of societies in which persons are free to believe what they want and to associate themselves freely with others who believe in similar ways. Or in which persons are free to speak of religious matters openly and freely. Or in which government is prohibited from disfavoring one group of citizens for invidious reasons. These are rights that belong to all peoples. What is arguably impossible is justly enforcing laws granting persons rights that are defined with respect to their religious beliefs or practices. Forsaking religious freedom as a legally enforced right might enable greater equality among persons and greater clarity and self-determination for religious individuals and communities. Such a change would end discrimination against those who do not self-identify as religious or whose religion is disfavored. It might also force religious groups to fend for themselves politically, economically, and philosophically in a new world of radical normative pluralism.[16]

In this book I will, as I have said, describe one trial in detail. I intend by so doing to provide "ethnographic"[17] evidence from which to question the received wisdom that legal guarantees of religious freedom are logically, or even morally, necessary elements of the emerging international legal order. A detailed look at one trial permits the fine-grained texture of this problem to emerge—in a way impossible, I would argue, in larger-scale studies of modern religion and law or politics, whether historical, sociological, or philosophical. The *Warner* case is not unusual. I see it as typical. Philosophers may consider the metaphysical underpinnings of human rights from above.[18] Here I intend a bottom-up look at the problem. A careful reading of the words and actions of the participants in the *Warner* trial—the witnesses, the lawyers, and the judge—shows a fragile and complex religious life unreachable by legal enforcement of the rights of religion.

The religious practices at issue in this case concern death. They are burial and mourning practices. If religion is anything, it could be said to be about what human beings do in relation to their mortality. Indeed prehistoric peoples are understood to be religious on the basis of the evidence of their burial practices. If these practices do not fall within the scope of protected religion under the most recent American statutes designed to protect religion from government burdens, how can such laws be rationally defended?

In October 1998, about six months before the *Warner* trial, I received a telephone call from Jim Green, one of the lawyers for the plaintiffs in the *Warner* case, a call in which he asked me to serve as an expert witness in the case. Jim found me because I had served as an expert witness in an earlier religion case concerning the impact of Wisconsin state-prison regulations on the prisoners' exercise of religion.[19] Our telephone conversation followed what I have since come to see, after a number of such conversations, as a fairly typical pattern. I am sitting in my office. Out of the blue, a lawyer calls me, asking me to testify at a trial. He wants me to testify that a certain religious group believes certain things, or does certain things. I am usually asked to testify in one of two ways, depending on whether the case is a "free exercise" or an "establishment"-clause case, in American constitutional parlance:[20] In the first kind of case, a "free exercise" case, I am asked to testify that, if required to conform to laws that impinge on or prohibit a particular religious practice, the religious lives of the members of the group performing such a practice will, in some sense, be "substantially burdened"; in the second kind, an "establishment" case, I am asked to testify that if a particular law were to continue to be enforced, the government, through the legal favor shown to a particular religious group, would be "endorsing" one religion while discriminating against other religious groups, as well as against individual believers and nonbelievers with different religious commitments or orientations. Other scholars of religion also receive these calls with some frequency. Lawsuits in which religion is at issue occur with regularity in state and federal courts all over the United States, either because an individual's religious practice conflicts with the requirements of law or because government is seen, in some sense, to be unconstitutionally benefiting a particular religious point of view or religious practice. Religion scholars and anthropologists regularly testify as to the authenticity of the religious views and practices in question in these cases.

I am almost always uncomfortable with the way the lawyer poses the question to me in these telephone calls (as are other experts, I am sure). I find myself explaining to him that religion does not work that way. I say that religion, particularly American religion, fits uneasily into a legal scheme that demands such categories and such expert certainty. Rationalizing religion in the ways proposed by courts and legislatures in this country fails to capture the nature of people's religious lives at the beginning of the twenty-first century, maybe of any century. Such rationalization also asks the government to be the arbiter of religious orthodoxy. My instinct in these phone calls is to say that these issues do not belong in courts—that "law" in a modern secular society ought not to be occupied with "religion" in any way, but certainly not in such a way as to put courts in the position of defining which religious belief or practice is authentic, and therefore legally significant. And yet these cases are often poignant: cases of ordinary Americans going about their lives, often in very modest ways, and coming up against legal regulation and legal ignorance of various sorts. I have served, and am serving, as an expert in several cases, including the case considered in this book. In each case I have, perhaps arrogantly, perhaps naively, thought that I could be helpful in educating the court about religion, helping to put the parties' actions into contexts in which they might be understood as religious, or not. I am concerned about the way the line between religion and not-religion is being drawn in this country and elsewhere.

Courts, legislatures, and other government agencies judge the activities of persons as religious or not, as protected or not, based on models of religion that often make a poor fit with religion as it is lived. In the phone calls I have with lawyers, I tell them what I think I can say that might be helpful, and I conclude with a warning that I have written academic articles—and now this book—suggesting that legal protection for religion is certainly theoretically incoherent and possibly unconstitutional. But—I think to myself—cases continue to be brought, and surely education is better than ignorance.

This book is about one particular case in which I happened to be involved, but there is a sense in which it could be about almost any case regarding religion in a country in which a secular state polices religion. In the United States recent cases have included the following occasions in which religion and law have come in conflict: An inmate in a Wisconsin prison wants, contrary to prison regulations, to wear a cross; Indians want, contrary to the regulations of the National Park Service and in competition with park visitors, to use land sacred to their ancestors; evangelical chaplains in the navy want equal opportunity to promotion with chaplains of other Christian denominations; a county in Georgia, in a gesture arguably favoring Christianity and Judaism, depicts the Ten Commandments on its seal; a prison, also arguably favoring Christianity, funds an Evangelical Christian prison fellowship administering a program in an Iowa prison.[21] There are hundreds, perhaps thousands, of such cases, here and in other secular jurisdictions. The word "religion" or "religious" appears over 14,000 times in state and federal statutes and regulations in the United States alone.[22] What can these words mean, in law?

I did not choose this case. It chose me. I was asked, as I have said, to serve as an expert witness for the plaintiffs in this case. I agreed, with some uncertainty about the extent of my expertise on the matter in question and with some concerns about the effect on the plaintiffs' case of my published skepticism concerning the kinds of legal claims being made. I first made a rather limited commitment, carefully circumscribing what I believed I could do to be of use to the plaintiffs and what I believed I could do with integrity, given my views. The City, the defendant in the *Warner* case, had argued that what the plaintiffs had done was not an "exercise of religion." I thought that I could comfortably testify that what the plaintiffs had done would be considered religion by most religion scholars. What people do with respect to death is at the heart of religion, I thought. I wrote a short report summarizing my opinion and was scheduled to fly in for a short appearance at the trial.

Expert witnessing takes a peculiar form in U.S. courts. Expert witnesses are hired by the parties and are examined and cross-examined in an adversary context, both in depositions and at trial.[23] There are studies that show that in the United States, juries certainly, and perhaps judges as well, regard expert witnesses, whatever their expertise, with a somewhat jaundiced eye and tend to discount their testimony, viewing it as bought and paid for.[24] The dubious evidentiary value of such witnessing is compounded by the professional and ethical challenges faced by the experts themselves, some peculiar to religious studies, but many shared by all academic experts. The legal process demands a level of certainty with which most academics are justifiably very uncomfortable. A number of academics who have served as expert witnesses have written about the moral and professional ambiguities raised by serving as an expert.[25] These are unquestionably serious issues, and I acknowledge and honor those who have written eloquently about the impossibilities of achieving the kind of scholarly objectivity and certainty demanded by the courts.[26]

I do think, however, that scholars have a public-service obligation to offer their expertise, when it can be helpful, conscious of the dangers of making the situation worse, and that the experience can have a kind of bracing honesty about it, one that challenges academics to come to terms with how the words they use may have direct effect on people's lives.[27]

Over the course of the time of trial preparation during which I had periodic telephone conversations with the plaintiffs' lawyers, I was gradually drawn in and came to think that I could be of some real help in a case I consider a valuable exemplar for those promoting religious freedom in this country and elsewhere. I came to believe that there were discrimination issues—that there were issues of justice and fairness. I was pressed into service as consultant to the plaintiffs' lawyers for the whole trial,[28] an exhilarating experience for a former litigator. I found that questions I had been thinking about for years gained a certain urgency and clarity when considered in connection with the very real lives of people accidentally made visible by the legal system.

I will not use my own participation in this trial as a central organizing principle for this book. In a real sense I was a bystander. I hope that the fact of my presence does not distract from the argument here. I did not personally interview any of the participants. Everything here described and interpreted, with the exception of my own experience of being there, is a part of the public record in the case. I have not sought the permission of either the plaintiffs or the plaintiffs' lawyers in the publication of this book, but have tried faithfully to represent their public actions and words as I experienced them. These are my reflections on this case, and not a brief on their behalf. I will try to describe my own role accurately, as I will the other expert witnesses' at trial, but this book is not about me . . . and other stories could be told about these events.

Outlaw Religion

THE EVENTS LEADING UP TO the trial in the *Warner* case took place in the City of Boca Raton, which is located in the southern Florida county of Palm Beach. Boca Raton, or *Boca Ratones*, Spanish for "the rat's mouth" (or perhaps "the pirates' cove," describing a natural harbor on the southeastern coast of Florida in which Spanish ships may have taken shelter during the sixteenth and seventeenth centuries),[1] was, like much of southeastern Florida, a swampy backwater until the twentieth century. Only sixty years ago, Boca Raton had a population of nine hundred and was dominated by a recently built air base. Today Boca Raton is a flourishing city of 75,000 residents, boasting a federal courthouse and a university: Florida Atlantic University.

The first modern development[2] of that part of southern Florida, about forty-five miles north of Palm Beach, began at the end of the nineteenth century. First came the railroad and then, for a short time, there was a dream of big agricultural business. Led by Joseph Sakai, an enterprising young Japanese American from New York and a graduate of New York University, a group of Japanese farmers emigrated to Boca Raton in the early twentieth century with a view to establishing pineapple plantations. They called their settlement Yamato.[3] Disease and bad weather dashed their plans, and the town remained a small agricultural community through the first decades of the twentieth century. The City of Boca Raton was formally incorporated in 1925 but remained economically dependent on local farming and tourism until midcentury. In the 1960s IBM led the development of light industry in the town.

Both before and after World War II, Boca Raton has also been a seasonal destination for northern industrialists seeking luxurious resort-style living, as well as for ordinary Americans on vacation. Addison Mizner, a New York society architect of the 1920s who designed many of the architecturally significant buildings in Palm Beach, purchased 17,000 acres of land and designed a private hotel and residence complex for Boca Raton. His plans, which would have made Boca Raton a posh private resort town, were never fully realized because of the Depression. An exclusive resort community was eventually built, however, and Mizner's design and vision persist in the Mediterranean-style architecture that dominates Boca Raton today.[4]

In addition to polo and golf, attractions for the rich, Boca Raton has also been the home of a briefly successful safari park, Africa USA (1953–1961) and a nationally known evangelical conference center, Bibletown USA (originally established in 1950 and whose successor today is Bibletown Community Church),[5] both of which brought visitors to town. Bibletown USA was sued in 1963 by the city of Boca Raton and by Palm Beach County for violating the conditions of its tax exemption. In a 1968 ruling appealing the granting of summary judgment, the court quoted the lower court's order: "The point is accented by repeating: Because of the nature of its solicitation for patronage it was impossible to determine whether people were in attendance for religious purposes, or as tourists in search of entertainment offered, or as investors."[6] According to a former mayor from the1980s (the husband of one of the plaintiffs in the *Warner* case), Boca Raton today has more golf courses per capita than anywhere else in the world.[7] Until the 1960s, then, Boca Raton was a small town with a seasonal and at times socially prominent resort community. There was also a small black community, known as Pearl City.[8]

The 1970s brought a real estate boom across South Florida. Since then, Boca Raton has developed into a largely wealthy enclave with strict zoning and gated communities, dominated by neo–Spanish colonial architecture. In 2003 its website boasted:

> Boca Raton is known nationally and internationally as an originator in the area of comprehensive zoning. Both the low density, i.e. dwelling units per acre, character of the City and the innovative Park of Commerce Industrial Park have influenced development around the country. The sign code, which was initiated in the late 1960's, gives the City a unique look with minimal commercial intrusion into landscaping and streetscapes. . . . Because of its initiative, the city has reaped the benefits of effective land use planning—a stable tax base with increasing property values.[9]

The City spent $1 million in the late 1970s unsuccessfully defending a growth cap intended to protect its carefully nurtured character.[10]

The *Warner* case arguably concerns Boca Raton's effort to extend its aesthetics, its strict zoning laws, and its concern for property values to the city cemetery, the cemetery with which the *Warner* case is concerned. The cemetery, now almost ninety years old, originated in 1916, on one acre near the water, land that was purchased specifically for the purpose of the foundation of a cemetery. It was later moved twice before being established at its present site. The first move was because of development of the land for the Boca Raton Resort in the 1920s. The second move, in 1944, was to accommodate the building of a runway for an army air base established for training radar officers. The second move also displaced residents of Japanese descent and poor black families.

The moving of a cemetery is not uncommon in the United States. Cemeteries have a more peripatetic life and less legal protection than might be expected. One must abandon any notion that bodies lie permanently in consecrated ground. Dead bodies, like living ones, are on the move, perhaps particularly in Florida.[11] Since the second move of the Boca Raton Cemetery and the closing of the army base, the City has grown up around the originally suburban location.[12] The cemetery is now located in a residential section of Boca Raton.

The present Boca Raton Cemetery is approximately 21.5 acres in size. It can accommodate more than 10,000 "in-earth" burials.[13] The cemetery lies next to the St. Joan of Arc Catholic Church, founded in 1956, and is close to a well-frequented highway. The older part of the Boca Raton Cemetery, that part which has been moved twice, contains upright stone monuments of various sizes and shapes shaded by large trees. A photograph of this part of the cemetery is featured on the city website.[14] The newer part of the cemetery, that part with which the *Warner* case is concerned, has small lots placed closer together to maximize income and the efficient use of the space for the growing city.

The newer part of the cemetery was designed as a "memorial garden," that is, a cemetery with markers laid flat on the ground and without vertical monuments, consistent with contemporary practice as described by industry experts during the trial. In such memorial gardens, and in the Boca Raton Cemetery since 1961, "monuments" may consist only of small flat identifying markers, or plaques, flush with the ground. These plaques are often constructed with detachable flower vases that, when inverted, fit into a hole in the marker designed for that purpose. The expectation is that the flower vase will be used only on anniversaries and holidays. Except when the flower vase is in use, the grave site would be entirely flat, and invisible from a distance.

The memorial-garden style of cemetery, the style of the newer section of the Boca Raton Cemetery, is popular for both aesthetic and practical reasons. The clean, uncluttered sightlines of such cemeteries are attractive to some. Death is anonymous, euphemized, and blurred. The grave, in such a setting, is also understood to be "natural," that is, it is understood to be continuous with the natural setting, facilitating "reconciliation with the natural environment."[15] Furthermore, it is claimed that cemetery workers can more easily mow the lawn and maneuver both digging and mowing equipment as graves are dug, filled, and maintained. (Graves in the cemetery are dug with a backhoe, after which a legally required concrete or metal liner weighing up to two tons is installed before the burial. The liners preserve the structural integrity of the cemetery, in part for the safety of the cemetery workers.)

Olan Young, sexton[16] of the Boca Raton Cemetery during the 1980s, testified concerning the reason for limiting the memorials to flat monuments:

> All modern cemeteries are into flat markers because it's so much more cost effective and it's safer. They can run mowers over an open field of grass very easily. . . . The way they're doing it now with the flat markers and everything cut down low you can mow over the whole works, even over the markers . . . and that's the way all modern cemeteries are designed. You go out to the other cemeteries you won't find anything sticking out from the ground. It looks kind of cold but that's the way these cemeteries are.[17]

Experts at the trial testified that the industry standard today is the memorial garden.[18]

For the short period of the *Warner* trial, this rather mundane and common enough space, a small undistinguished cemetery beside a well-frequented city thruway, was the subject of heated debate. On one side were advocates of a modern, clean, secular aesthetic and the convenience and efficiency of city management. On the other side was a modestly flourishing resistance, a protest demanding room for another kind of religion and another kind of government, one that the city's experts and lawyers, as well as the judge, quaintly termed "cemetery anarchy."

The Boca Raton Cemetery is managed by the City Parks Department, but sales are handled by the Boca Raton Mausoleum Company, a private outfit that has built the mausoleums in the cemetery and gives a percentage of its revenue to the city. Testimony at trial showed that the cemetery has annual sales of about $1 million and an annual budget of approximately $500,000. Cemetery rules provide that the purchaser of burial rights in the cemetery receive a certificate of title and a list of regulations. (A copy of the Boca Raton Cemetery Rules and Regulations is reproduced in Appendix A and available on the city website.) The Boca Raton purchaser, as is typical in U.S. cemeteries, does not own the property but owns only the "exclusive right of burial of the human dead in that certain parcel of land."[19]

The right of burial in the Boca Raton Cemetery acquired by a purchaser of one of its plots is subject to the following limitations:

1. That the burial right herein granted will be used only in conformity with the Cemetery Rules and Regulations as they may be from time to time adopted or amended.
2. That the property herein described shall forever remain under the exclusive control of the [the City] for the purposes of care and maintenance.[20]

Burial lots are 3′ 2″ by 8′ 2″ and cost approximately $1,100 in 1999. A "marker" is defined in the Boca Raton Cemetery regulations as:

A memorial which does not extend vertically above the ground and is constructed of approved metal or stone containing *names, dates, or other engraved lettering* used in identification of one or more persons and placed at the head of a lot or plot [emphasis supplied].[21]

The regulations further provide:

(2) Restrictions on Above Ground Memorials and Monuments: No memorials, monuments, or enclosures shall be permitted above ground in any section of the Cemetery grounds except in Section A [the older section, now filled]. Stone or bronze markers are allowed in all other sections provided that they are level with the ground surface.[22]

Testimony at trial established that the standard size of these flat markers was twenty-four inches by fourteen to sixteen inches. Although not apparently permitted by the definition of a "marker" in the regulations, which explicitly limit identification on the marker to "names, dates, or other engraved *lettering* [emphasis supplied]," the City has consistently permitted the engraving of religious and other identifying symbols on the markers, as mentioned above.

If you went to the Boca Raton Cemetery today, you would see that the new section of the cemetery, Section B, is, in fact, not flat and uncluttered, nor has it been for some time. It is filled with objects that rise above the level of the grass. It is those objects that are at issue in this case. Notwithstanding the regulations limiting memorialization to flat plaques, a practice grew up in the Boca Raton Cemetery over the course of a number of years from the mid-1980s to the mid-1990s in which individual owners decorated graves above the ground with various objects that did not conform to the regulations. Over that time, almost five hundred such "grave shrines" were constructed. The *Warner* case was a class action brought on behalf of the owners of these graves.

There were eleven named plaintiffs in the *Warner* case:

- Caridad Monier and her sister, Barbara Cavedoni, are Cuban immigrants. They had buried their brother, who had committed suicide, in the cemetery. The two sisters testified that they pray almost daily at their brother's grave on which they have placed a statue of the Sacred Heart.
- Marina Warner and her son, Richard Warner, had erected stone memorials engraved with Stars of David and planted ground cover on the graves of deceased family members: Marina's husband and her other son.
- Maria Riccobono's gregarious father was buried in the cemetery with a statue of the resurrected Jesus to watch over him.
- Souhail Karram, a Lebanese immigrant and self-styled "born-again" Christian, had buried his wife in the Boca Raton Cemetery under a four-foot oak cross covered with silk lilies, which he made by hand.
- Ian and Bobbie Payne had commissioned a stone Star of David for the grave of their son, who had died tragically young. They had also purchased an adjoining grave on which they had placed a small stone bench.
- Joanne Davis arranged a group of small statues of children on the grave of her infant son who had died in a beach accident.
- Emile and Eleanor Danciu mourned the death of her father buried in the cemetery and watched over by a statue of the Virgin Mary.

These plaintiffs in the *Warner* case, although previously unknown to one another, came to know each other during the protests over enforcement of the cemetery regulations that preceded the filing of the lawsuit (photographs of these graves can be found following this chapter).

The nonconforming grave decorations at issue in this case were not professionally manufactured monuments, for the most part, but rather handmade and privately assembled collections of statues, crosses, Stars of David, candles, fences, plantings, and marble chips. Many of these were purchased at garden centers. The aesthetic, as I said, reminds one of the memorials one sees by the side of the road for the victims of automobile accidents, or those that, on a larger scale, are created spontaneously at the sites of various tragedies, such as the destruction of the World Trade Center. They are at once private and public, individual and communal, kitschy and profoundly moving. They are expressions of what we might call "outlaw" religion.

The City was nervous and defensive at trial about the charge that its regulations excluded religion from its cemetery. City representatives indignantly and repeatedly insisted that symbols noting religious affiliation were permitted on the flat markers, so that what the lawyers called "religious expression" was not, in fact, prohibited by the City. At his pretrial deposition

Sexton Young described the symbols, religious and otherwise, that appeared on the flat markers:

> There was a limit of two symbols for any single marker. They could have two symbols of their choice, religious symbols or any type of symbol. If a guy was a doctor, he could put the doctor's emblem on there. If he was a member of the Masonic order, they'd have the Masons on there, Knights of Columbus or whatever. And if he was a minister he'd have something on there, a Bible, an open Bible on there. Any emblem that they would desire. With a limit to two to a single marker. . . . The manufacturing company that made the markers recommended that because if you got too many emblems on there, it would look too congested and make the marker look too gaudy.[23]

The small flat markers, in a very compressed space, are meant to serve as a canvas for personal biography, identity, and religious and professional affiliation—even good taste. Religion is reduced to one among many possible identifying standardized symbols, similar in size and design.

At the time of the publishing of the decision in the *Warner* case in the fall of 1998, a Palm Beach reporter described the Boca Raton Cemetery as follows:

> If you're lucky enough to be buried on Section A on the west side of Boca Raton's Municipal Cemetery, you might eternally lie beneath the broad shade of two colossal banyan trees or, at the very least, rest among speckled granite and monochromatic color schemes. You could rest amid city pioneers and other noted townsfolk. This section boasts another bonus: exemption from cemetery rules which prohibit memorials, monuments, or enclosures aboveground everywhere else in the cemetery. Panning across the west end reveals further evidence of its privileged status: pricey polished crosses, marble columns, and even a ten-foot-high hulking monument honoring Boca's World War II vets.
>
> The east side of the cemetery lacks that kind of history but makes up for that lack with devout diversity. Virgin Mary statues gaze over gravesites; red-robed Jesuses extend forgiving hands toward heaven, their Sacred Hearts almost glowing from their chests. There are also Sabbath candles, Stars of David, and other stuff exhibited on the east side that one might find in any Miami botanica or Judaica shop. But this ain't Miami. It's Boca. One might think that a city often blasted for its homogeneity would welcome a chance to embrace ethno-religious icons in its public cemetery and that its rules should apply to all plots, regardless of size or

location. Maybe a moneyed city like Boca Raton shouldn't meddle with one's constitutional right to freedom of expression or the way families honor their dead.[24]

The *Death Care Business Advisor*, a cemetery industry trade publication, quoted Boca Raton city officials, speaking about the cemetery regulations: "[T]he rule must be enforced because of complaints from some of the plot owners that the grave decorations are 'garish.' City officials also said opponents have indicated that they bought into the cemetery specifically because it is not cluttered, and wouldn't be in the future."[25] On a small scale, the Boca Raton Cemetery has become an experiment in living with pluralism.

Most of the plaintiffs claimed in the Complaint instituting the *Warner* case and at trial that they were unaware of the regulations prohibiting the installation of any grave decorations other than the flat plaques. Most also testified that the city workers explicitly gave permission, in apparent contravention of the regulations, for their installation. The City, while it admitted to inconsistent enforcement of the regulations, claimed that all of the plaintiffs had received copies of the regulations and were therefore on notice as to the restrictions concerning aboveground memorials. The City also denied giving permission for the nonconforming items.

It was not entirely clear at the trial why the nonconforming practices were so promiscuously permitted. Partly, it seems, lax enforcement was the result of genuine sympathy on the part of the sexton and his assistants. They hesitated to discomfit bereaved people, but they also, in some sense, found the decorations appropriate. A number of the plaintiffs testified that city workers at the cemetery, far from being hostile to their activities, admired and actually assisted them in constructing the memorials. Indeed, throughout the controversy with the city, which has lasted more than ten years, officials, both at the City Council level and those directly involved in management of the cemetery, seem to have been of mixed minds, both because of fear of adverse publicity and because of a genuine desire to accommodate grieving citizens. And as the City hesitated to insist on enforcement, the practice grew and attracted others who wished to decorate their graves in a similar manner. The continued presence of the decorations encouraged new purchasers to believe that they were permitted.

Beginning in the early nineties, the City decided to start enforcing the regulations. Various reasons have been asserted for the change of heart. At the trial, the City asserted only safety and economic reasons. Some of the plaintiffs commented that there were also aesthetic and class issues: the grave decorations were said to be "not Boca"; there were said to be complaints from other owners. Whatever the reason or reasons, in August 1991 the City sent notices to owners of graves that were in noncompliance requesting that the graves be brought into compliance within thirty days. Some owners complied. Others did not. A second notice was sent in July 1992. Again there was partial compliance. Petitions were brought by the nonconforming owners to the City Council, which, in response, formally agreed to postpone enforcement until the matter could be resolved.[26]

In July 1996 and June 1997, the City Council met in public session to consider the situation. Some of the *Warner* plaintiffs, as well as city councilors and members of the public, spoke, offering a wide range of views and expressing concern about religious freedom, aesthetic considerations, freedom of expression, and expense. In the 1996 meeting, Joe Cogley, then deputy director for the Recreational Services Department (the City department responsible for the cemetery), asked the City to relax the rules to give the managers some flexibility in dealing with grief-stricken people. The Cemetery Rules and Regulations were subsequently revised to permit decorations for a period of sixty days after a burial and on certain anniversaries and holidays.[27]

After the Council meeting in 1996, and in response to the controversy, the City commissioned a survey of plot owners in the cemetery that was conducted by researchers at Florida Atlantic University (located in Boca Raton). The survey concluded as follows:

> The results of this survey have revealed that the majority of the plot owners, regardless of the time length of plot ownership, location (east or west) of plot, or frequency of visitation, believe that the July 23, 1996 Rules and Regulations should be followed by all plot owners as required by the City of Boca Raton. They believe that contributions to a Tree Legacy landscape beautification program is a much higher priority than allowing plot owners to decorate plots without limitations. They believe that the regulations should apply to all current owners and to future owners.[28]

In June 1997 the City Council, emboldened by the results of the survey, passed a resolution requiring that all cemetery decorations be brought into compliance within ninety days. A story appeared in June 1997 in the *Palm Beach Post* describing the dispute:

> A survey of cemetery plot owners and relatives shows fierce opposition to the fancy shrines that litter the city's graveyard. Opponents say the hodgepodge of items makes the place look like Coney Island. But some plot owners say the memorials are the only way they can honor the

departed. The items spread across the cemetery include pink flamingos, pinwheels, Japanese lanterns, wind chimes, rock and flower gardens, fences and benches.[29]

Letters were subsequently sent to owners of the plots by the City asking them to remove nonconforming items before January 15, 1998, or the City would remove them. Suit was filed fifteen days after the deadline.

On January 30, 1998, the American Civil Liberties Union, on behalf of a class of local residents whose family members were buried in the Boca Raton Cemetery, those who had installed nonconforming memorials, brought an action against the City of Boca Raton and against certain city councilors individually.[30] The suit was filed in Florida state court, the Fifteenth Judicial Court in and for Palm Beach County.

The City chose to remove the case to the local federal district court, the U.S. District Court for the Southern District of Florida, presumably because they hoped to receive a more favorable hearing in a federal court.[31] On June 17, 1998, the plaintiffs filed an Amended Complaint in the removed case. It is this Complaint that defined the plaintiffs' case at trial. The plaintiffs' claim for injunctive relief in the Amended Complaint asserted violations by the City of the relevant provisions of the U.S. and the Florida Constitutions,[32] and the then newly enacted Florida Religious Freedom Restoration Act, referred to here as the Florida RFRA, discusssed below. (The relevant constitutional provisions as well as the relevant provisions of the federal and Florida RFRAs and the rules and Regulations of the Boca Raton Cemtery at the time of the trial are reproduced in Appendix A.) The *Warner* plaintiffs claimed that the Boca Raton Cemetery Regulations, both as written and as enforced, were an unconstitutional and illegal burden on the exercise of religion. The plaintiffs sought an injunction prohibiting enforcement of, and invalidating, the City's regulations limiting decorations in the City's cemetery.

While the plaintiffs asserted both U.S. and Florida constitutional claims, at trial the most promising legal claim on behalf of the plaintiffs, by common consent, and for reasons discussed below, was that made on the basis of the Florida RFRA. The Florida RFRA, then newly passed, provides, in part, as follows:

(1) The government shall not *substantially burden* a person's *exercise of religion*, even if the burden results from a rule of general applicability, except that government may substantially burden a person's exercise

of religion only if it demonstrates that application of the burden to the person

(a) is *in furtherance of a compelling governmental interest;* and

(b) is the *least restrictive means* of furthering that compelling governmental interest [emphasis supplied].[33]

It is worth taking some time to understand the Florida RFRA. Such statutes exist in many states and are quite recent.[34] These new laws are controversial and significantly expand the rights of religiously motivated persons to demand exemptions from government regulation. RFRA statutes have also produced considerable litigation.

The words of the Florida RFRA prohibit *all* government entities in Florida from "substantially burdening" a person's "exercise of religion," unless the government entity in question can show that its action is both "in furtherance of a compelling governmental interest" and is "the least restrictive means of furthering that governmental interest." A person who claims to be "substantially burdened" in the exercise of his religion by any government entity in Florida may bring an action to require the government to exempt him from an obligation to conform to the requirements of that government action. The plaintiff in such a case must prove only that she or he was engaged in the "exercise of religion" and that the government has "substantially burden[ed]" that exercise of religion. If the plaintiff is able to offer such proof, the burden of proof shifts at trial to the government. The government then, in order to prevail, must show that the regulation in question, even though it resulted in a substantial burden to the plaintiff's exercise of his or her religion, is "in furtherance of a compelling governmental interest" and that "the least restrictive means" was employed to implement that interest. These last two conditions, which constitutional lawyers call the "compelling interest" test and the "least restrictive means" standard, are familiar tools, known together as "balancing tests," for determining the constitutionality of governmental restrictions of rights. These tests are used by courts in other constitutional cases, not just in religion cases.

Unlike the federal RFRA and some other state RFRAs, the Florida RFRA also provides, in the "definitions" section of the Act, that an "exercise of religion" is "an act or refusal to act that is substantially motivated by a religious belief, whether or not the religious exercise is compulsory or central to a larger system of religious belief."[35] The legislative history of the Florida RFRA, discussed below, shows that this provision was added in reaction to the many restrictive judicial readings of the federal RFRA statute that had limited coverage of the statute to an exercise of religion that was shown to have been either "compelled by or central to" a particular religious community.[36]

The *Warner* case was the first case to be filed in Florida in which a court was asked to enforce the Florida statute.[37] There was, therefore, at the time of trial, no prior Florida precedent to assist the judge in interpreting the words of the statute. At various times during the trial, Judge Ryskamp expressed his awareness of being the first judge to interpret the statute.

The Florida RFRA, like the other state RFRAs, was enacted as one end result of a dramatic struggle in the 1990s between the U.S. Congress and the U.S. Supreme Court concerning interpretation of the free exercise clause of the First Amendment to the U.S. Constitution. There are a large number of judicial decisions interpreting the religion clauses of the First Amendment, and an enormous amount has been written by legal scholars about those clauses.[38] I will sketch here the contours of the most recent decisions on the subject, with a particular focus on how that interpretation resulted in the creation of RFRA laws.

The First Amendment to the U.S. Constitution provides:

> *Congress shall make no law respecting an establishment of religion, or prohibiting the free exercise thereof;* or abridging the freedom of speech, or of the press; or the right of the people peaceably to assemble, and to petition the government for a redress of grievances [emphasis supplied, relevant law is also reproduced in Appendix A].

The First Amendment religion clauses (the first sixteen words of the First Amendment) are, as enacted in 1789, usually understood to have been intended principally to provide jurisdictional limitations on Congress's capacity to enact legislation concerning religion. Such regulation was left to the states.[39]

Today the religion clauses are understood to authorize two kinds of actions in which citizens can challenge the activities of all government—local, state, and federal. Under what is known as the "establishment" clause, persons may bring actions against the government to challenge the government's actions as unconstitutionally favoring or "establishing" religion. The "free exercise" clause governs those cases in which persons complain that actions of the government are preventing them from fulfilling their religious obligations.

Many cases have both "establishment" and "free exercise" aspects. Indeed, one might say, as many have said, that the two "clauses" are two sides of the same coin. However, cases are usually styled as one or the other, depending on the original claim in the case, and different traditions of interpretation have developed in the two lines of cases.[40] The *Warner* case is a "free exercise" case, a case brought against the government on behalf of litigants asserting governmental burden on the free exercise of religion. "Establishment" issues lurk in the *Warner* case, though, as in other "free exercise" cases. If the *Warner* plaintiffs were to win eventually on the First Amendment claim, and religiously motivated persons were thereupon given an exemption from the Boca Raton Cemetery Regulations, the resulting favoring of religion over not-religion could arguably constitute an unconstitutional "establishment of religion," as prohibited by the First Amendment. All First Amendment cases and all RFRA cases present this potential catch-22.

Until 1940, the religion clauses were rarely interpreted by the Supreme Court.[41] The First Amendment, beginning as it does with the words, "*Congress* shall make no law . . ." was, until then, understood to restrict only the activity of the federal government. Most laws affecting religion are, and always have been, state laws governed by state constitutions, state constitutions that have also guaranteed freedom of religion. In 1940, in *Cantwell v. Connecticut*,[42] a case brought by Jehovah's Witnesses to challenge laws prohibiting proselytizing, the U.S. Supreme Court explicitly held for the first time that the First Amendment religion clauses had been "incorporated" into the Fourteenth Amendment through its "due process" clause. "Incorporation" meant that, as of 1870, the date of the adoption of the Fourteenth Amendment (reproduced in Appendix A), the religion clauses should be understood to limit the actions of the state governments as well as those of the national government. The Supreme Court, in *Cantwell*, was following its own rather recent decision to understand the post–Civil War Reconstruction amendments (Amendments 13, 14, and 15), particularly the Fourteenth Amendment, as having extended to citizens of the states some of the rights enumerated in the Bill of Rights. This doctrine is known as the Incorporation Doctrine.[43]

After the Supreme Court's 1940 decision in *Cantwell*, then, the religion clauses of the First Amendment should be understood to begin: "[*Neither Congress nor the states*] shall make any law. . . ." U.S. Supreme Court religion clause jurisprudence begins, in a very real sense, in 1940 with the *Cantwell* decision and its extension of the prohibitions of the religion clauses to the state governments. The timing of that decision and the political and cultural context of the post–World War II period, particularly the Supreme Court's concern with equality of persons, significantly affected the Court's subsequent interpretation of the religion clauses. The Court's opinions in that period, reflecting their preoccupation with racial equality, reveal an increasing concern with equality among religions and between religion and not-religion.[44]

The history of the Religious Freedom Restoration Acts begins in 1990, fifty years after incorporation, with the Supreme Court's decision in *Employment Division v. Smith*,[45] the most important of the Court's recent decisions concerning the meaning of the free exercise clause. The *Smith* case had been brought to federal court in Oregon by two members of the Native American Church.[46] The two plaintiffs in *Smith*, Alfred Smith and Galen Black, challenged the refusal of the Oregon Department of Human Resources to pay them unemployment compensation as being in violation of the First Amendment "free exercise" clause. Smith and Black, counselors in a state-run substance-abuse facility, had been fired because of their religious use of peyote, the hallucinogenic fruit of a cactus plant and then a controlled substance under Oregon narcotics law. Unemployment compensation was unavailable to them, they were told, because under Oregon law employees who had been fired "for cause," in this case illegal activity, were not entitled to the benefit of unemployment compensation.

In their suit against the state of Oregon, Smith and Black cited a line of Supreme Court opinions interpreting the free exercise clause of the First Amendment to require exemption from the law, under certain circumstances, for persons whose religious practice was burdened by state regulation. Smith and Black made this claim of constitutional exemption on the basis of the precedent of *Sherbert v. Verner*,[47] a 1963 unemployment compensation case, as well as subsequent cases following the *Sherbert* decision. *Sherbert* and those cases that followed, they argued, established the rule that the government may not "substantially burden" the exercise of religion unless the state demonstrates a "compelling interest" in doing so. Their use of peyote, Smith and Black argued, was not recreational but was an "exercise of religion" because it had been within the sacramental context of the Native American Church.[48] They also argued that the state lacked a compelling interest in enforcing the law in their cases. Smith and Black won in the Oregon courts.[49]

The Supreme Court of the United States, in a dramatic 6-3 decision, reversed the decision of the supreme court of Oregon in the *Smith* case.[50] In a rhetorically skillful but widely criticized ruling, Justice Antonin Scalia, writing for the majority, reinterpreted the line of cases relied on by Smith and Black and by the lower courts in the *Smith* case. According to Scalia, those cases, properly understood, were founded in hybrid constitutional claims in which other constitutional rights, such as freedom of speech, were asserted. It was those other rights, he said, that had compelled the results in those cases. Bypassing *Sherbert* and the line of cases following it and returning to the holding of the Court in a nineteenth-century Mormon polygamy case, *Reynolds v. U.S.*,[51] Scalia wrote: "we have never held that an individual's religious beliefs excuse him from compliance with an otherwise valid law prohibiting conduct that the state is free to regulate."[52]

Justice Scalia's opinion in *Smith* further stated that religious exemptions should be made by legislatures, not by courts:

> Values that are protected against government interference through enshrinement in the Bill of Rights are not thereby banished from the political process. Just as a society that believes in the negative protection accorded to the press by the First Amendment is likely to enact laws that affirmatively foster the dissemination of the printed word, so also a society that believes in the negative protection accorded to religious belief can be expected to be solicitous of that value in its legislation as well.[53]

Justice O'Connor, in her concurring opinion in *Smith*, responded:

> [T]he Court today suggests that the disfavoring of minority religions is an "unavoidable consequence" under our system of government and that accommodation of such religions must be left to the political process. . . . In my view, however, the First Amendment was enacted precisely to protect the rights of those whose religious practices are not shared by the majority and may be viewed with hostility. The history of our free exercise doctrine amply demonstrates the harsh impact majoritarian rule has had on unpopular or emerging religious groups such as the Jehovah's Witnesses and the Amish. Indeed, the words of Justice Jackson in *West Virginia State Bd. of Ed. v. Barnette* (overruling *Minersville School Dist. v. Gobitis*, 310 U.S. 586 [1940]) are apt: "The very purpose of a Bill of Rights was to withdraw certain subjects from the vicissitudes of political controversy, to place them beyond the reach of majorities and officials and to establish them as legal principles to be applied by the courts. One's right to life, liberty, and property, to free speech, a free press, freedom of worship and assembly, and other fundamental rights may not be submitted to vote; they depend on the outcome of no elections." 310 U.S., at 638.[54]

In *Smith* O'Connor, consistent with her actions in other religion cases, voted with the majority but wrote a separate concurring opinion giving her own reasons for the decision.[55] The Supreme Court since the *Smith* decision has held that a religiously motivated actor *may* have a free exercise claim against the government if he can show that a particular law was not really a law "of general applicability," but was designed specifically to target the religious activity of a particular group.[56]

The Supreme Court's decision in *Smith* was heard as a wake-up call by a coalition of religious activists across the political and religious spectra. *Smith* was seen to reinforce the Court's earlier decision in the *Lyng* case to reject a free exercise claim by Native Americans who objected to the federal government's construction of a logging road in the high country in California, land sacred to Indian tribes.[57] Indeed many representatives of religious groups understood the *Smith* decision to reflect a more generalized hostility to religion on the part of government, particularly on the part of the federal courts. These activists saw the decision in *Smith* as typifying a hostility common in the hypersecularized consciousness of the time. Joined in a Coalition for the Free Exercise of Religion, they took their cause to Congress, which explicitly undertook, in the federal Religious Freedom Restoration Act of 1993,[58] to reverse the Supreme Court's interpretation of the free exercise clause of the First Amendment as announced by the majority in *Smith*.

The federal RFRA, which moved rapidly through Congress and received broad bipartisan support, was explicitly designed to restore the possibility of constitutionally mandated legal exemptions for certain religious actors, by reinstating the *Sherbert* balancing test. The federal RFRA was thus specifically designed to reverse the Court's decision in *Smith* that religiously motivated actors could not claim an exemption from "neutral laws of general application."[59] When signing the bill, President Clinton observed:

> We all have a shared desire here to protect perhaps the most precious of all American liberties, religious freedom. Usually the signing of legislation by a President is a ministerial act, often a quiet ending to a turbulent legislative process. Today this event assumes a more majestic quality because of our ability together to affirm the historic role that people of faith have played in the history of this country. . . . [O]ur laws should not impede or hinder but rather should protect and preserve fundamental religious liberties.[60]

President George W. Bush has made similar statements about the importance of protecting religious liberty.[61]

The Supreme Court reacted decisively to the enactment of RFRA. In a 6-3 1997 ruling in *Boerne v. Flores*,[62] the Supreme Court held that the federal RFRA act was unconstitutional. Congress, the Court said, had no power to overrule the Court's interpretation of the Constitution.[63] The *Boerne* case concerned the decision of the Boerne City Council that resulted in the designation of one of the Catholic churches in Boerne, Texas, as a historic landmark, preventing its demolition and replacement with a more functional structure. Justice Kennedy, writing for the majority, concluded: "Broad as the power of Congress is under the Enforcement Clause of the Fourteenth Amendment, RFRA contradicts vital principles necessary to maintain separation of powers and the federal balance."[64] (A new law, the Religious Liberty Protection Act [RLPA],[65] designed with the hope of curing the constitutional defects of RFRA, was passed by the House of Representatives in 1999, but failed to be passed by the Senate. A successor to RLPA, the Religious Land Use and Institutionalized Persons Act (RLUIPA),[66] which prohibits government land-use regulation that imposes a substantial burden on a person's religious exercise, was signed into law by President Bush early in 2004.)

After the decision in the *Boerne* case, the pro-religion lobbyists, architects of the now essentially defunct federal RFRA, took their case to state legislatures, arguing that the states could do what Congress could not. The states, they said, were not inhibited by the limits of the Fourteenth Amendment grant of congressional power. A series of state, or "mini," RFRA's followed.[67] The Florida version, the statutory basis for the claims made by the plaintiffs in the *Warner* case, was passed in 1998.

While state and federal constitutional claims were also made by the plaintiffs in the *Warner* case, all parties seemed to be operating at trial on the assumption that because of the *Smith* decision's contraction of the reach of the First Amendment free exercise clause, it was the Florida RFRA claim that had the strongest possibility of success. *Smith* and *Boerne* seemed to have conclusively established that no exemptions were required by the First Amendment free exercise clause to laws that were facially neutral, that is to laws that applied to everyone, regardless of religious affiliation. It was the applicability and interpretation of the Florida RFRA, then, that received the most attention at the *Warner* trial, although the plaintiffs continued to press the constitutional claims.

A fundamental definitional ambiguity inheres in all religion cases. Whatever law is being applied in a particular case, whether statutory or constitutional, all religion cases in the United States require a finding that the activity in question qualifies as "religion." Such cases put courts in a difficult position. On the one hand, they are required by the use of the word "religion" in statutes and in the Constitution to inquire into its meaning, to draw lines between "religion" and not-"religion." On the other hand, there is much law in the United States saying that judges cannot enter into disputes regarding religious orthodoxy. The definition of religion for legal purposes in this country remains, as a result, profoundly unsettled.[68] The word is defined differently for different purposes and differently by different government agencies. Unlike in many European countries where religious communities must register with the government, no limits are placed in the United States on the creation of new religious communities. Only when the group seeks a legal benefit or legal exemption must it explain itself to the government. The resulting confusion undermines the fairness of all sorts of laws, including the tax code, prison rules, zoning provisions, and so forth.

The meaning of "substantial burden" has also been unsettled. During the period in which the federal RFRA was in force (1993–1997), before the *Boerne* decision, a debate grew up among federal courts as to the meaning of the statutory requirement of a "substantial burden" on the exercise of a person's religion. Did that requirement mean simply that the challenged prohibition must substantially burden only that particular individual's religious exercise, or did the prohibition have to prohibit an action that was significant for an entire religious community? In the federal courts this debate focused on whether a RFRA violation could only be found where the religious activity in question was "central to or compulsory to" the particular individual's religious tradition. For example, in *Mack v. O'Leary*,[69] the Seventh Circuit Court of Appeals considered an appeal in a prisoner's case. The allegation was that the defendant prison officials refused to accommodate the religious needs of Mack and the other Muslim inmates of Stateville prison during Ramadan. Judge Richard Posner, writing for the Seventh Circuit Court, began by observing that "[t]he Fourth, Ninth, and Eleventh Circuits define 'substantial burden' as one that either compels the religious adherent to engage in conduct that his religion forbids (such as eating pork, for a Muslim or Jew) or forbids him to engage in conduct that his religion requires (such as prayer). . . . The Eighth and Tenth Circuits use a broader definition: action that forces religious adherents 'to refrain from religiously motivated conduct,' . . . or that 'significantly inhibits or constrains conduct or expression that manifests some central tenet of a [person's] individual beliefs,' . . . imposes a substantial burden on the exercise of the individual's religion. The Sixth Circuit seems to straddle this divide, asking whether the burdened practice is 'essential' or 'fundamental.'"[70] Posner concluded: "We hold, therefore, that a substantial burden on the free exercise of religion, within the meaning of the Act, is one that forces adherents of a religion to refrain from religiously motivated conduct, inhibits or constrains conduct or expression that manifests a central tenet of a person's religious beliefs, or compels conduct or expression that is contrary to those beliefs."[71] This diversity among federal courts of appeal provides little guidance for judges interpreting state RFRAs.

While the Florida RFRA tracked the federal RFRA almost word for word, the definitions section of the Florida statute was an explicit effort to address the "error," as Judge Ryskamp would term it, in the federal courts' application of the federal statute: the judicial contraction in the courts of appeals of the coverage of the federal RFRA such that it protected only religious exercise that was "central to or compulsory to" a particular religious community. The definition of "exercise of religion" given by the Florida RFRA was "an act or refusal to act that is substantially motivated by a religious belief, whether or not the religious exercise is compulsory or central to a larger system of religious belief." The task presented to Judge Ryskamp was to decide exactly what the Florida definition meant and exactly how a court was to determine when an "exercise of religion" was "substantially burdened." Did the *Warner* plaintiffs' actions in the Boca Raton Cemetery constitute an "exercise of religion"? And was that "exercise of religion" "substantially burdened" by the City of Boca Raton?

The stage was set for the *Warner* trial.

1. Grave of the wife of Mr. Karram (1999)

2. Grave of the wife of
Mr. Karram (2004)

3. Grave of the brother of Ms. Monier and Ms. Cavedoni (1999)

4. Grave of the brother of Ms. Monier and Ms. Cavedoni (2004)

5. Grave of the son of Mr. and Mrs. Payne (1999)

6. Grave of the son of Mr. and Mrs. Payne (2004)

7. Grave of the son of Ms. Davis (1999)

8. Grave of the son of Ms. Davis (2004)

9. Grave of the father of Ms. Riccobono (2004)

10. New section of Boca Raton Cemetery (2004)

11. Old section of Boca Raton Cemetery (2004)

12. Grave-digging equipment (2004)

13. Example of Jewish grave with stones left by mourners (2004)

14. Other nonconforming graves (2004)

15. Other nonconforming grave (2004)

16. Other nonconforming grave (2004)

18. Other nonconforming grave (2004)

17. Other nonconforming grave (2004)

MICHELLE D. O'DONNELL
SEPT. 16, 1954
MARCH 1, 1995

19. Other nonconforming grave
(2004)

20. Other nonconforming grave (2004)

The Trial: The Plaintiffs

THE *WARNER* CASE was tried over the course of one week in March 1999 in the federal courthouse in Boca Raton before the Honorable Kenneth L. Ryskamp. Judge Ryskamp is a graduate and member of the board of trustees of Calvin College. His legal training was at the University of Miami Law School. After a successful career as a practicing lawyer in Florida, Ryskamp was appointed to the bench by President Reagan in 1986. Ryskamp is an active churchman, a member of the Coral Ridge Presbyterian Church in Fort Lauderdale, Florida.[1] He drafted the legal documents for the Florida churches of the Presbyterian Church in America, for which he serves as moderator. He is also a trustee of Palm Beach Atlantic University, a Christian liberal arts college in Palm Beach.[2]

The trial began on Monday and concluded on Friday. Virtually all of the named plaintiffs attended the trial every day, filling the jury box and the front row of the courtroom. They had come to know one another over the course of the controversy about the cemetery and appeared a cohesive and mutually supportive group. Representatives of the City sat at the table with the City's lawyers. Local news organizations attended and local TV news camera teams waited outside the courthouse at the conclusion of each day's proceedings.

The principal trial lawyers provided a nice contrast. Bruce Rogow, attorney for the city, teaches constitutional law at Nova Southeastern University Shepard Broad Law Center in Fort Lauderdale. Rogow is a well-known local lawyer, having argued a number of cases in the U.S. Supreme Court, and having attained modest local notoriety for representing the rap group 2LiveCrew in a free speech case in the Supreme Court in 1994.[3] A tall, handsome man, he appeared each day in a dark suit and starched white shirt. James Green, representing the plaintiffs, is a solo practitioner, a successful high-profile litigator who volunteers some of his time for the ACLU. Green's most recent case at the time the *Warner* trial started was a suit on behalf of sugarcane workers who, it was alleged, had been systematically cheated of their pay by sugar producers.[4] His courtroom demeanor reminded me of Colombo, the television detective. His wash-and-wear suits were crumpled. Also like Colombo, he only *appeared* disorganized, dropping pages while he cross-examined witnesses, and only *seemed* to forget what questions he was asking.[5] Both Rogow and Green were well pre-pared, experienced, and highly effective. Each was accompanied by associ-ate lawyers. All the lawyers and the judge knew one another from other trials. Previous encounters provided a subtext for those in the know.[6]

Among the many ironies of the *Warner* case, the plaintiffs, those seeking an injunction protecting their religious practices, were represented by the American Civil Liberties Union. The ACLU, as the judge pointed out dur-ing the trial,[7] more commonly finds itself challenging rather than promot-ing public religious expression. Indeed, the presumed negative ideological stance of the ACLU and other similar organizations with respect to reli-gion, public and private, has been one factor in the passing of new laws protecting religion. The ACLU, like many advocates of civil rights, is un-comfortable with religion. They are torn between a fear of the specter of established religion and a genuine desire to fight discrimination and preserve individual liberty. Jim Green, in his closing argument before the judge on the last day of the trial, related that the ACLU had been very di-vided about whether to take on the *Warner* case:

> [T]his was a hotly debated case within the ACLU. There are some in the ACLU who say, well, cemeteries should be secular. There are others who say we have a Free Exercise Clause. And that clause has to mean some-thing and if it means anything it should have meaning in this context. And there was a long hard debate. And we decided to take this case. And we decided to take this case because this does involve a cemetery, these are people who are expressing themselves through religious symbols.[8]

The director of the Florida chapter of the ACLU at the time of the trial, Howard Simon, was quoted in the *Palm Beach Post*, further explaining the ACLU's motivation in taking the case: "There aren't any exceptions in the Constitution [if religious expression] is too cluttered or too messy or not in good taste. That's a form of religious intolerance."[9] Judge Ryskamp, ad-dressing Mr. Green after giving his ruling and invoking the kissing-cousin relationship between "establishment" and "free exercise" cases, said: "Just do one thing. Don't file suit by the ACLU next week alleging an establish-ment clause violation for having religious sermons and symbols on public land." Mr. Green assured him that he would not.

Talking about religion was unfamiliar territory for the ACLU—and also, I think, for Bruce Rogow. Both Green and Rogow often spoke of the issues in the *Warner* case, particularly before the trial, by analogy with those in free speech cases. They spoke frequently of the need for freedom of religious "expression." The focus seemed to be on the individual's right to express himself, not so much on the religious content or larger religious context of that expression. For Judge Ryskamp, on the other hand, religion was familiar ground.

The trial began with opening arguments. Jim Green, for the plaintiffs, spoke of the expectation that religious "expression" will be found in a cemetery:

> It may well be difficult to draw a bright line around what is religion and what is not religion in some cases. This case, however, does not involve a fringe or marginal religious practice. . . . The evidence will show that a cemetery is a place where religious expression is to be expected. The City does not have to be in the cemetery business at all. But once it gets into that business, once it provides a municipal cemetery it must operate the cemetery constitutionally or not at all. In other words, the City must freely acknowledge and protect religious expression and practice that is foreseeable in a cemetery. As your Honor noted in his footnote to the order granting in part and denying in part the motion to suppress, the only kind of, virtually the only kind of expression that is foreseeable in a cemetery is religious.[10]

Bruce Rogow, for the city, balanced empathy with the need for law and order. He concluded:

> The City is completely empathetic and sympathetic to the plight of people who have lost loved ones and come to the cemetery. It is a difficult time. The testimony through cemetery sextons is going to be it's not a time when people are listening to details. They want to buy a plot, they want to bury a loved one. It's a very difficult time. But they were told there were rules and the rules had to be abided by.[11]

Openings were brief because there was no jury.

As a general rule in American courts, in a civil case, after opening arguments, the plaintiffs first present the evidence for their case, followed by the defendants. The plaintiffs then, after presentation of the defendants' evidence, have an opportunity to present rebuttal evidence concerning any new factual issues that have arisen in the defendants' case. And so on. Back and forth. Because there was no jury, this formal practice was somewhat relaxed in the *Warner* case. Witnesses were sometimes taken when available, out of order. In this chapter and the next I will present the affirmative evidence offered by the two sides, in turn, each in its entirety, roughly, although not strictly, following the order of evidence presented at trial. The following chapter, chapter 4, will take another look at the evidence with a view to considering the various models of religion that were used in the trial, as well as the role of the expert witnesses.

The plaintiffs, in order to prevail, were required by the Florida statute to prove that the City's regulations effectively prohibiting "vertical" memorials had "substantially burdened" the plaintiffs' "exercise of religion." At the same time, the plaintiffs also aimed to refute the City's claim that it had a compelling governmental economic interest in restricting memorials to horizontal plaques and that it had used the least restrictive means to accomplish this goal. A subsidiary issue concerned the knowledge that the plaintiffs had of the regulations. The City argued that in some sense the plaintiffs had deliberately flaunted the regulations while the plaintiffs argued that they either had not known about the regulations or had explicitly been given permission to create memorials in violation of the regulations. Any such knowledge turned out to be legally irrelevant. If the regulations as applied to the plaintiffs violated the Florida RFRA, it did not really matter whether they knew or did not know about the regulations. But the skirmishing around this issue helped to define the shifting relations among the plaintiffs and various city employees and to display the plaintiffs' bona fides.

The City's position was that the plaintiffs were not substantially burdened by the regulations because the memorials they had erected were not religiously important beyond the individual choices of the plaintiffs and their families, and therefore did not require accommodation under RFRA. While the City's lawyers repeatedly said that the City believed the plaintiffs were sincere about their religious beliefs, the City also argued that the particular actions the plaintiffs took—those that resulted in what the City termed "vertical" expressions of their religion—were the result of "purely personal preference," not of religion. What plaintiffs chose to do at these gravesites, the City argued, was personal, rather than religious, because the particular actions were not compulsory—that is, they were not specifically demanded of them by their religions and they were not central to the identity of their religious traditions. The City implied that the plaintiffs' actions were, in effect, decorating choices, not religiously motivated activity. Religiously motivated activity, as the City understood it, would be authoritatively prescribed and defined from above, not improvised from below.

In thus insisting on compulsion and centrality, the City asked the Court to look for guidance, in interpreting the applicability of the statute, to a religious authority above the level of the individual, an authority that mandated particular behavior, in order to determine the significance of a particular religious act. The lawyers for the plaintiffs responded that the individual choices of the plaintiffs were integral to their religious lives and consistent with their religious traditions such that their forced removal would "substantially burden" their "exercise of religion." The City argued that the statutory "burden" could only be proved by evidence that the plaintiffs were forced by the regulations to violate the prescriptions of the institutionalized authorities of their religious communities. The plaintiffs argued that the statutory "burden" could be shown by proof that the regulations substantially burdened practices that were consistent with a real compulsion felt by the individual plaintiffs with respect to the gravesites, a compulsion felt within the context of their religious communities and traditions.

The struggle in the court was, broadly speaking, between two understandings of what religion is. For the City, religion was something that had dogmas and rules and texts and authorities. Religion was something you obeyed, something about which you had little choice because of the imposition of an external authority. For the City, religious people were passive agents of their traditions. For the plaintiffs, religion was a field of activity, one in which an individual's beliefs and actions were the result of a mix of motivations and influences, familial, ecclesiological, aesthetic, and political. As the trial progressed, the plaintiffs seemed often truly (and understandably) at a loss to understand what exactly the City's lawyers were asking of them. The evidence of an inflexible religious authority demanded by the City was alien to them. It formed no ordinary part of their religious lives.

The case for the plaintiffs was dominated by the plaintiffs' own testimony. I will first summarize the plaintiffs' testimony about why they had chosen the cemetery and about how they had decorated the graves. This testimony constituted the plaintiffs' affirmative case concerning their actions and the religiousness of those actions, and how prohibition would substantially burden them. I will also occasionally supplement quotations from this testimony with quotations from the plaintiffs' pretrial deposition testimony, also a part of the record in the case.[12]

I will quote the testimony in the *Warner* trial at some length because I think that it is only through the witnesses' own words that one can understand the religious texture of this trial. The testimony of the plaintiffs at the trial was emotionally draining for the plaintiffs as well as for the others of us in the courtroom. Jim Green and his associates, Lynn Waxman and Charlotte Danciu (whose mother was one of the plaintiffs), led each plaintiff through her story. Collectively the plaintiffs' story was very consistent. Often repeated, it had gained a shape through the shared experience of their battle with the City and the encounter with the legal and religious languages around them.

The plaintiffs testified that they chose the Boca Raton Cemetery because they liked the look and feel of it. They liked what they saw when they visited the cemetery. It displayed "faith," "beauty," "love," and even "patriotism." They also chose the cemetery because of its convenient location near church and home. It was a familiar place. Individually, their stories gave a modest dignity and importance to the simple homemade shrines, particularly in contrast to the paltry standardized religious symbols offered by the City, those engraved on the flat plaques. The plaintiffs testified to the place the cemetery and the individual graves had in their own religious lives and to the pain caused by the threatened removal of the memorials. In addition, they liked the cemetary because it was nonsectarian. Many of the plaintiffs testified that they were attracted to the cemetery because, like their lives, it was not associated exclusively with a particular religious community. The cemetery embodied for them an ideal of American religious freedom, diverse and unconstrained.

Plaintiffs Caridad Monier and Barbara Cavedoni left Cuba in 1969 and immigrated to the United States, eventually settling in Boca Raton. They testified at the trial that they had purchased several plots in the Boca Raton Cemetery when their brother, Larry Dominguez, died in March 1996. The two sisters erected a small fence to define his grave and placed a twenty-inch statue of the Sacred Heart, and two planters, on the site. Theirs was an affecting story. Their brother had committed suicide and their pre–Vatican II theology had taught them that his soul was in mortal danger without their continual prayers.[13] Each sister also testified to the contrast between the political and religious freedom they observed and experienced in the United States and the political and religious prohibition they had witnessed and experienced in Cuba.

Ms. Monier was the first witness. Lynn Waxman asked her why they had chosen the cemetery. She answered:

> I am familiar with the cemetery. I drive by there all the time. It is very close to my home and my office. I've seen it thousands of times when I go to St. Joan's Church next door. I saw the expression of religion, the freedom, the love. I saw the statues, the crosses, the ground covers. All the religious articles. When my brother passed away I knew we wanted him in a cemetery where we could do that, express our faith and religion, and be close enough where we could visit him very often and pray.[14]

Ms. Monier went on to describe the grave: "We have a Sacred Heart of Jesus with his hands up in the air. Which it was placed for the salvation of my brother's soul. . . . And then we have some planters as offering with flowers there."[15]

Ms. Monier's brief description fits easily into a conventional Roman Catholic piety. What is known as the "Sacred Heart" in contemporary Roman Catholic religious practice is a painting or a statue of Jesus with his heart exposed and glowing, sometimes crowned with thorns, symbolizing the love of Christ. Devotion to the Sacred Heart of Jesus is derived from medieval monastic practice but was ecclesiologically officially blessed and established in the nineteenth and twentieth centuries by a series of papal encyclicals, beginning with *Haurietis aquas*, issued by Leo XIII in 1899. The *New Catholic Encyclopedia*, a publication of the Catholic University of America, summarizes the theology of devotion to the Sacred Heart: "Leo XIII called devotion to the Sacred Heart the most excellent form of religion; Pius XI, the synthesis of our whole religion and the norm of the perfect life; Pius XII, the most perfect expression of Christian religion and of strict obligation for all the faithful."[16]

Another article in the same *Encyclopedia*, however, bemoans certain forms of popular expression of this devotion: "Statues and paintings of disputable taste, often of vulgar sentiment repulsive to educated sensibilities, proliferated from the beginning of the 19th century. Occasional efforts have been made in reaction to these depictions of the Sacred Heart, but they have not affected a widespread and deeply meaningful image."[17] The Church's efforts to control popular piety, efforts interestingly parallel in some ways to those of the City, include official descriptions of appropriate images and of appropriate forms of devotion. Devotion to the Sacred Heart thus brings together popular forms of piety with the core of Catholic teaching about the love of Christ, but the devotional style of Sacred Heart piety also highlights the Church's occasional discomfort with and lack of control over, the way such images are used. Statues such as those of the Sacred Heart give material expression to core theological ideas but they also, sometimes extra-ecclesiologically, bridge the gap between orthodox Christianity and pre-Christian or heterodox forms of worship by providing a direct and unregulated connection with the divine.[18]

Ms. Monier described their regular practice at the grave. Asked how often she visited the cemetery, Ms. Monier said: "It depends, at least two or three times a week. . . . I go there to pray, to connect with him. To pray to God, Jesus, for him, for his soul, for his salvation. Just to pray." And further: "Out of respect and our belief and our faith, we don't walk on the grave site of the deceased. It's out of love and respect and our belief that it would be sacrilegious for us to do that." Removing the items from the grave would be "devastating," she said: "I cannot even imagine it, going there and just not having that."[19]

On cross-examination, Bruce Rogow asked Ms. Monier about her choices regarding the protection of her brother's grave, mentioning each item, and concluding with these questions:

Q. But you chose the method of denoting the perimeter of your brother's grave, did you not?

A. Yes.

Q. That was your choice?

A. (No verbal response; nodding head).

Q. There was nothing in your Catholic teachings that said to you this is the manner, the manner that you have used to denote the perimeter of your brother's grave?

A. No.[20]

During his cross-examination of each plaintiff, Rogow emphasized the personal nature of the particular choices that were made about the decoration of the graves, apparently seeking to prove that the plaintiffs were monadic creators of unsanctioned and idiosyncratic new religious forms.

After Rogow's cross-examination, on redirect examination, Lynn Waxman, one of Jim Green's associates, invited Ms. Monier to expand on her testimony:

Q. Is there anything in the history of the Catholic religion that allows protecting a grave with ropes or teaches you that that is important for you to do?

A. I don't know if there is anything that's written anywhere. And I don't know in particular about the rope. But I know that Jesus' grave was protected, was guarded, and it was not allowed to be walked on. And we were created in his image.[21]

Ms. Monier's testimony here reveals another theme at trial. Nowhere in the New Testament accounts of Jesus' death does it say that Jesus' grave was protected so that it would not be walked on. The plaintiffs often elaborated on biblical accounts, making such untutored and naive, sometimes plainly heterodox, efforts to articulate positions of biblical interpretation and theology, searching their personal repertoire of stories and images and teachings to explain what they had done and why.

Barbara Cavedoni, Ms. Monier's sister, also testified at trial. She began with a narrative about their immigration from Cuba and about religious persecution there:

I was originally born in Cuba and came over in '69 with my sister at the age of 14. . . . At the beginning we [could make our sacraments in Cuba].

Afterwards it got impossible to. It was a gradual deprivation of the right to practice. Slowly it was known that if you were seen going to a church or walking into a church, that was marked, it was held against you. Eventually the churches were stripped of all the saints and crosses. Ultimately the doors were locked and we were forced to practice our faith in our own homes. Which even at that case it was not safe. Because they reserve the right to barge into your house at any time they wanted to. And if they found any kind of religious statue or anything at all, whether it was something that the Catholic religion named or classified as a traditional religious item or not, if they deemed it to have anything at all with religious belief or practice your life could be in danger.[22]

She, too, explained why they had chosen the cemetery:

I drive through it all the time. And I used to long before my brother died. And there is a cross, I believe it is the gentleman's [referring to Plaintiff Souhail Karram] cross. It was beautiful. . . . And I used to see that cross because it's the one that stands out the most. And it always called my attention to how proud, how free, how beautiful it was that he could proclaim who he was, that they had the freedom to do that. And it was accepted. It was in the open and he didn't have to be hiding it from anybody. As well, I saw a lot of little statues, angels, different types of crosses, stars of David, little children playing. Just a variety of it. The freedom to be able to do it. Unless you have never felt what it feels like not to be able to, it's very difficult to understand the value of being able to. . . . To be free, to be able to say what you feel, to be able to be who you are. To be able to proclaim who you are.[23]

Asked why the cross must be displayed upright, Ms. Cavedoni, like her sister, reached for a biblical analogy, fusing religious and political ideologies: "Like when they crucified Jesus, they crucified him in an upright cross for the world to see as a witness, as a testimony. And *he died for us, for our right to be who we are and express who we are*" [emphasis supplied].[24] Jesus is here understood as dying for freedom of expression—which again is entirely extra-biblical.[25] Both sisters improvised creatively, elaborating on the biblical accounts—in part I think in an effort to oblige the lawyers and the judge.

Ms. Cavedoni also described her conversations with the cemetery manager:

Q. Did you discuss with him what you wanted to do with your brother's grave?

40

A. Well, when he took us over to the east side on the little golf cart I mentioned to him how beautiful it was and how many different things there were in there. All the different things that I saw. And I told him that we most likely, that we would be doing something most likely along the line of what was there. Then at that time he mentioned the regulations.

Q. What did he say?

A. He says, well, there are certain regulations that apply. And I said. Well, I'm sure there are, but we're not planning to do anything different than what is being done in here. And I can see it's being done everywhere. So it will be just along the same, you know, the same line. And then his comment was, well, as long as it's not something really outrageous, ten or fifteen feet tall. I said, Oh, no, no, it won't be anything like that. He goes, Oh, then absolutely no problem.[26]

Like Ms. Cavedoni, all of the plaintiffs expressed their willingness to conform their decorations within "reasonable" limits. While the cemetery apparently appeared disordered, even chaotic, to the judge and to the City, it appeared a highly ordered place to the plaintiffs.

Ms. Cavedoni, too, like her sister, was asked to describe the items on her brother's grave, and she explained their connection to her religious understanding: "There is a Sacred Heart of Jesus that is praying for his soul. That is praying for his salvation. The way I see it is I'm counting on the forgiveness and greatness of his heart to place him and welcome him into eternal life and not eternal damnation." Her brother's possible damnation was of enduring and critical concern:

I don't know if I'm supposed to say this or not. But my brother committed suicide. And in my religion that is like the ultimate sin. So it was very important for our family to do anything and everything that was available to us to, pray for the forgiveness and saving his soul. We had a mass at church and then we had some services at the grounds, at the burial site so that his grave could be deemed holy and sacred and so that God can forgive him for his sin and have mercy and compassion on his soul.[27]

There was a sense of urgency to her testimony and to that of her sister, a sense of urgency associated very directly and immediately with the grave itself, as if there were no time to be lost. The actions of the two sisters were *both* individually chosen *and* compelled by a higher authority.

Miriam Warner, the first named plaintiff, and her son Richard Warner testified concerning the burial of her husband and her other son, her husband in 1995 and her other son in 1994. Like the others, Ms. Warner explained the choice of the cemetery:

> It was very important that we bury him where our religion could be ob-
> served. And that was one of the reasons we selected the cemetery. My son
> died suddenly. My husband and I were devastated and we sent my other
> son who was here to investigate the possibility of plots there. We had
> driven past—when my son died we had lived in Boca for 15 years at that
> time, and had driven past many times. We saw crosses, Stars of David, et
> cetera. And it was close to where we lived. . . . We met with Mr. Jordan
> [one of the sextons]. And he assured us that it was totally non-sectarian
> and that everybody could practice his own religion. And we saw nothing
> there to tell us that this was not so.[28]

She also described the decorations on the graves of her husband and son:

> We have the double headstone in granite. That's engraved and it has Stars
> of David engraved into it. We have my son's single headstone also in gran-
> ite. It's also engraved with the Stars of David. We do have the individual
> graves outlined. There is a stone border that we have stones down and we
> have Mexican heather on those graves so that nobody can walk on them.[29]

Each of the Jewish plaintiffs described actions that were taken to accomplish a complete outlining of the grave, calling attention to the exact
placement of the body so that it would not be walked on.

To the lawyers, the Star of David apparently seemed to have an obvious
religious reference like the Sacred Heart, and the two were gathered together by them for that reason and excluded from skeptical questioning. As
in the book of acceptable symbols for the grave markers, religious symbols
are homogenized through secular regulation and interrogation. In this
case, of course, the analogy and association are both historically and philosophically dubious, as well as being offensive in terms of Jewish history and
practice. From the *Blackwell Dictionary of Judaica*:

> Magen David ("Shield of David"). The name given in Judaism to a sym-
> bol consisting of two superimposed triangles forming a star (it is also
> known as the Star of David). Although it was used in the synagogue at Ca-
> pernaum as early as the 3rd century, it was not commonly adopted as a
> Jewish symbol until much later. From the 13th century the name figures
> in practical kabbalah, and the symbol (believed to have magical proper-
> ties) is found in association with the pentagram (or Star of Solomon). The
> Magen David occurs in a Jewish context in Prague in the 17th century. In

the 19th century it was adopted by the First Zionist Congress as its symbol, and it appears on the flags of the Zionist Organization and the State of Israel. The Nazis employed a yellow six-pointed star as a Jewish badge.[30]

But none of this came up at trial. The Star of David was simply accepted as incontrovertibly religious.

At trial Ms. Warner was asked about the significance of the other objects on the grave, those objects delineating the perimeter of the grave, and about her activities at the grave, first by the plaintiffs' lawyer and then by the defense attorney:

Q. Can you please tell us what the religious significance to you is of not having anyone walk on your husband and son's graves?

A. This is what I've been taught always, is that it is a desecration to walk on a grave. In fact we selected these graves to make sure that we could get to them without walking on anybody else's grave, we feel so strongly about this as part of our religion. And my grandparents, my parents, everybody in the family. I make a trip up north once a year to go to my parents' graves, because we have ivy ground cover on them to make sure that the ground cover's properly maintained. So that nobody can walk on the graves. This is part of religion. This is not apropos of this. But I just cut a picture out of a 300-year old Jewish cemetery in Trinidad. Where there are practically no Jews. I don't know if there are any. But every grave is outlined.[31]

The plaintiffs seemed not to be entirely sure what would count for the judge as religious authority but obligingly offered the experiences of a lifetime.

In his cross examination of Ms. Warner, Rogow returned to his concern about the personal nature of the plaintiffs' choices:

Q. The marble chips that are there, do they have any independent religious significance to you?

A. Independently, no. They serve a religious purpose for me. They are not, marble chips in and of themselves are not holy in any way.

. . .

Q. Does the header have any independent religious significance?

A. No . . .

. . .

Q. And the edging stones have no independent religious significance?

A. Independently, no.[32]

Rogow asked each witness whether the items other than the statues of Jesus and the saints, crosses and Stars of David had "independent religious significance."

Concerning the City's threat to remove the items on the graves, Ms. Warner remarked, evoking Nazi desecration of Jewish graves:

> After this all started and the newspaper articles came out and we went to the council meetings, and somebody in authority said, well, if you don't take this off by a certain date we'll come in with a bulldozer and remove it. And all I could think in my mind was the beginning of the Holocaust. The first thing they did was desecrated, knocked down stones and desecrated the cemeteries. And I felt this was trodding [*sic*] on my religion and trodding [*sic*] on the religion of my loved one.[33]

A double headstone had been installed in the Boca Raton Cemetery so Ms. Warner could be buried next to her husband.

Miriam Warner's son Richard Warner also testified as to why they had chosen the cemetery: "I had seen the cemetery before. But I was very favorably impressed with it at that time, as there were many variety [*sic*] of expression of faith and love. It was just a very nice cemetery. Visually it wasn't grim. . . . I saw a variety of religious statues. I saw Stars of David standing. I saw a variety of crosses. Flowers . . ." Green asked him why they had put ground covering on his brother's grave, and why the marble chips: "So that others would not walk on it, would not disrespect it, desecrate it. My father, who was alive at the time, and his parents and parents before him had had very strong feelings about the religious belief that you do not walk on graves."[34] All of the Jewish plaintiffs testified that they were taught as children that it is wrong to walk on a grave, and each did what they could in the Boca Raton Cemetery to effect that teaching. (This teaching was later traced by the expert witnesses, in part, to Orthodox Jewish laws governing the behavior of descendants of the ancient Jewish priestly class, those known as *kohens*.)[35]

Richard Warner also talked about his own behavior at the grave:

> I visit my brother and father's grave probably five times a week in the early morning and pray there. . . . [I]t's part of the religion, part of Jewish religion and tradition to—when you visit a grave you pick up a stone from it and leave it on the headstone to state that you've been there, that someone has visited. If you go to any Jewish graves you will see stones where people have visited and left that stone behind to show that they have been there. It's not just my tradition.[36]

The common practice of leaving a stone at a Jewish grave to show that a person has visited a grave was later confirmed by Michael Broyde, the rabbi who testified as an expert for the plaintiffs.[37] Indeed, many peoples, not just Jews, leave stones to show they have visited graves.

Marie Riccobono, another of the plaintiffs and a parishioner at St. Joan of Arc Church, located next to the cemetery, buried her father in the cemetery in 1993. She placed a statue of the resurrected Jesus, a stone edging, an eternal light, and flowerpots on the grave. Asked at trial why she and other members of the family had chosen that cemetery, Ms. Riccobono answered:

> We had looked at so many and they looked like nobody cared about any-body there, they weren't taken care [of]. . . . On this one there was obvi-ous signs of faith. There was Jewish stars, there was crosses, there was flowers, there was, it just, you could see that there were people of faith there and the love people had for people that were there. . . . My father had a lot of friends that were of every culture and religion. It was impor-tant for us that they would feel, like if we put him in an only Catholic cemetery, that they would feel not a part of him. They were all a part of his life. We wanted something that would express everyone's love for him.

She was also asked about the "religious significance" of the statue:

> Q. Tell us about the religious significance to you. The meaning to you of the statue of Jesus on your father's grave?
>
> A. It signifies the resurrection, that's the reason it has to be up and with his hands up, and to say, welcome into the kingdom of heaven. It also happened to be, my father was real expressive and he always did that. It is also for that.[38]

In popular Catholic religious piety an image of Jesus in a variety of conven-tional poses symbolizes particular theological dogmas about his signifi-cance. In this case an image of Jesus with his arms extended symbolizes his resurrection. Ms. Riccobono, in not atypical fashion, collapsed the image into her memory of her father.[39] Ms. Riccobono also expressed an attitude toward the grave itself, as a whole: "It's a sacred place, just like a church would be."[40] Each time that one of the plaintiffs was given room by a lawyer's open-ended question, she would expand the religious framework, beyond the grave and the person there interred. It was as if their religious lives could not be contained in legal language or in the legal spaces assigned to them in the cemetery. These grave sites and their activities at them in-vited reflection on their entire religious experience and imagination.

Plaintiff Souhail Karram buried his wife of thirty-eight years in the cemetery in 1994. Born in Lebanon to an Orthodox Christian family, Mr. Karram
testified that he became a "born-again Christian," or, as he sometimes said, a
"believer," during a hospital stay in New York City in 1946. (Describing oneself as "born-again" or as a "believer" is a reference to the personal experience of conversion that defines one as a Christian for Evangelicals.)[41] He and
his wife had been active in church leadership in Boca Raton for many years.
Mr. Karram spoke first of his migration to the United States:

> Prior to my becoming a believer I was brought up in the Greek Orthodox
> faith. I came out as a child from Lebanon, came to the States, and then
> from here went on to live in Jamaica where our forefathers were. They
> had migrated there. . . . They left [Lebanon] because of persecution dur-
> ing the rule of the Ottoman when the Ottoman and the Turks were there,
> the Christians were persecuted. And so my grand uncles fled Lebanon,
> came to the Americas, ended up in Jamaica. And one by one they brought
> their nephews over and eventually my father ended up over there, and
> then we followed in 1938.[42]

Like the sisters from Cuba, Karram emphasized the contrast between the
"old" country and the new. He also closely associated his own religious
practice with his American citizenship, contrasting that association with
the religious persecution he had experienced in Lebanon:

> As a Christian in Lebanon in the early 1900s you couldn't walk on the
> street and pass a Muslim on his right-hand side. You had to pass him on
> his left because you were his inferior. And if you didn't, he would either
> push you back or shoot you or cut your throat. You were told to "get to
> my left you Christian swine." This is why most of the Christians fled
> Lebanon and came to America. . . . [I]n Lebanon during the reign of the
> Ottoman empire the converts who were converted to Christianity and
> those who were being persecuted were made to walk on crosses as a means
> of denouncing their Christian faith. Muslims made them walk on a cross
> to say . . . to prove then that they had denounced their faith. . . . I want to
> emphasize that I'm an American by choice. I was not born an American.
> Many of you don't have that privilege. It was a privilege for me to become
> an American and I'm proud of the flag. I'm also proud to be a Christian
> and I'm a Christian by choice.[43]

He spoke out of a conventional evangelical piety emphasizing the individualism and the voluntary nature of his Christian affiliation. The decorations on the grave represented both his citizenship and his faith.

46

Of all of the plaintiffs, Souhail Karram was the only convert and the only Protestant. He was also clearly the most accustomed to public witnessing about his religious beliefs. He and his wife had run a Bible study in their house:

[W]e started up with our kids plus maybe five other kids and eventually grew to where it was sometimes even a hundred kids, and my wife would prepare hot meals for the children who were attending, and they would come and they would have a meal on Friday night and worship together and sing and praise God.[44]

Mr. Karran described the objects on his wife's grave:

On my wife's grave, if I may read it, it says: Our Beloved Pamela Nadia Karekni Rani . . . Born August 23, 1938. Went home to be with her Savior September 11, 1994. And there is the Bible verse that says that, it is very comforting, I think: The resurrection and the life. He that believeth in me though he were dead yet shall he live. Her husband Souhail, her children and grandchildren rest in the assurance that because of Jesus Christ's death and resurrection they will be reunited in eternity. Her children rise up and call her blessed. Her husband also. And he praises her. And the names of her children in order . . . [There is a large white cross] which I made myself actually. . . . It's made of oak and covered with Easter Lilies.[45]

The large oak cross with white silk lilies that he had made and placed on his wife's grave also became something of an icon for many of the plaintiffs. It was one of the most readily visible of the plaintiffs' various installations, visible even to cars passing on the adjoining highway. Asked at trial to explain the significance of the cross, Karram explained:

The Bible says "absent from the body and present with the Lord." We have the assurance and the comfort, as we know it, although it is sad, death is a graduation to the Christian. He leaves earth, he goes to heaven. . . . To me [the silk cross] is a reminder that Christ was nailed to an upright cross, that he died for our sins, he died that we can have eternal life. He chose to come and died on the cross, and it means, it keeps reminding me whenever I visit there and I go there frequently, that it's comfort in the fact that although you have lost a loved one, you know the day will come when you will be reunited. It also means to me too that it is, it's preaching a gospel. . . . Christ says "go into the world and preach the gospel." It's a commandment that he has told all of us. And it is the

Great Commission, it's known as the Great Commission that we ought to preach God's word. The cross standing there is seen from 3rd Avenue, it's seen from 4th Avenue. People pass and they see the cross, and they also know what the meaning of the cross is. Those that know, knows it's a message that comes across. It's a form of witnessing.[46]

Like the Cuban sisters, Mr. Karram saw the Boca Raton Cemetery as a kind of synecdoche for the United States. It was a place where religious and national affiliation and enthusiasm came together.

Mr. Karram also testified at length about his conversations with cemetery personnel. He said, for example:

Kevin says as long as you're not going to do anything ridiculous, you know . . . go ahead and do it. And he also said to me, he says, there are rules and regulations. Nobody is enforcing them. And another comment that he made, and I hope I don't upset anybody with this, is that he says nobody on the City Council has the guts to come and tell any of the mourners here what they shouldn't do.[47]

He also told about installing the decorations:

Q. Did you put the permanent decorations on the grave yourself?

A. Yes, myself and my sons.

Q. And did you do that during the day?

A. Yes.

Q. And were there other cemetery personnel in the area?

A. Oh yes, they came and admired them.

Q. They came and admired the decorations?

A. Yes, as a matter of fact some came and looked and summoned some of the others and looked. Quite a few of them. They even helped me to water the plants.[48]

The City, through its representatives, both elected and otherwise, had acted in ways that indicate a mixed mind about the cemetery's increasing number of illicit shrines.

When their son died young in a car crash in 1983, Mr. and Mrs. Payne also chose the Boca Raton Cemetery. Mr. Payne testified at the trial about his reason for choosing this cemetery: "Firstly, it's close to home. For the first four years I went there every single day, sometimes twice a day. So we wanted something pretty close to home because I had to carry on working.

But more important than anything else was the way it was decorated, the beauty of it. I mean if a cemetery can be beautiful, this is it."[49] Mr. and Mrs. Payne had enclosed their son's plot with a fence and planted ground cover over the grave. English Jews, the Paynes explained that they had attempted to create a Jewish grave consistent with Jewish custom and practice in England where Jewish graves are conventionally entirely covered with a stone covering. Denied permission to install a stone covering, as was the practice in England, they had marked and protected the grave so that it would not be walked on, using plantings and marble chips purchased at a garden center. The Paynes created a little England, a little Jewish England, in the Boca Raton Cemetery.

In 1983 the Paynes had purchased three plots, making room for themselves, and placed a bench purchased by their son's friends, on one of the plots. The Paynes had also commissioned the carving of a stone Star of David from a mason recommended by the City. The Star of David is flanked by two stone flowerpots. At trial Mr. Payne explained the evolution of the design:

> We suggested to Kevin [one of the cemetery workers] when we saw him that to keep things simple and to keep it flush with the ground, we'd like to put a six foot marble slab in and a headstone as well. . . . And he said for some reason we couldn't cover it with a stone but we could cover it with some other form of covering so long as it was contained with some form of edging, which we did. . . . At one time when we were initially there he said to us, I'm dubious about having a standard [*sic*] star of David. We said to him, well, there are a number of crosses there that are standing upright which seem to be significantly higher than ours. And he said it is different if it's a star. I said, Are you suggesting you're anti-semitic? Oh, no, no, he said, just go ahead and put up the star.[50]

Mr. Payne, too, testified that no one objected to their activities when they were installing the various items on the grave site:

> *Q.* Did anyone from the cemetery stop [the stone mason] from erecting it even though it was unauthorized?
>
> *A.* Absolutely not. In fact, when we were putting the plants in they all came over and said how nice they were looking. . . . One in particular I remember he said to me, You must have loved him, you must have loved your son very much. He said, you spend so much time here and the grave looks so beautiful.[51]

A number of the plaintiffs, I think, felt betrayed by the City workers when they were asked to remove the items. Their earlier interactions with cemetery personnel, as with Mr. Payne, had often been positive and encouraging.

Mr. Payne is a frequent visitor at his son's grave. He testified at trial that twice over the course of the intervening years, the objects on his son's grave had been removed by the city:

> I went to the grave. I went there one day and everything had been removed and thrown into a hedge which is two graves away from my son's and they had taken all the flowers out, they had removed the stones, taken the edging out. . . . I immediately thought it was vandalism, called the police and made a report. . . . And I took everything and spent most of the night putting it all back in place again. . . . The next day I think we went back there and the same thing had been done. . . . I called the police immediately. . . . The police went in and . . . spoke to a couple of City employees. . . . The police said did you do it and they said yes. They said did you do it yesterday as well. They said yes. . . . They said we were told to get rid of them, to rid of [sic] these graves a bit at a time hoping that no one would object and no one would put these back again and gradually we would get rid of them without anybody noticing without too much of a turmoil.[52]

Mr. Payne was visibly distraught through much of the trial. He summarized their feelings about removal of the items from the grave: "My wife was just, it took her a long, long time to recover from it. You can imagine, you turn up at your son's grave and find it totally desecrated. . . . It was rather like the desecration the Nazis put upon the Jewish cemeteries."[53] In his wife's absence, Payne was comforted by several of the plaintiffs. (Mrs. Payne was not present at the trial but testified at a deposition before the trial.) It does seem odd that the City workers believed they could surreptitiously remove items without the plaintiffs noticing, given their intense involvement and intimate familiarity with these small plots of ground.

Also buried in the cemetery are the bodies of two-year-old Daniel Davis and his baby-sitter, Camille Hassan, both of whom were drowned at the beach in 1988, Ms. Hassan while trying to rescue Daniel. Joanne Davis, Daniel's mother, placed a group of statues of two children playing with a squirrel, a statue of the Virgin Mary, a statue of Jesus holding a child, and a cross on a grave adjacent to that of her child and of Ms. Hassan:

> I loved the whole cemetery there. The one thing that did stick out was the cross. [the Karram cross] . . . I saw a lot of expressions of love and religion.

50

It was really a warm place to go and visit. It was a place you could take children. . . . one of the things that I saw was a large Virgin Mary statue that we had been permitted to put up probably a year prior to that, on our aunt's cemetery site. . . . I saw a lot of religion expressed there through all types of religion, which was very important, because . . . Camille Hassan, our nanny, was born into the Muslim faith and had turned, living with us, she had decided she wanted to be Christian. So I felt like those grounds were perfect for her because it had a little bit of all kinds of religion there.[54]

For Ms. Davis the cemetery represented religious diversity as well as freedom.

Asked to describe the significance of the objects on the graves, Ms. Davis replied:

I have two children, bronze children that were purchased at my son's birth. They were placed there because I thought that it could express to my son that there was life hereafter with the children playing. . . . It's for my surviving children. It's more for my surviving children. . . . It shows life hereafter for me. . . . I have a small Virgin Mary, I have a Jesus holding a child, and I have a cross. I also have other little toys that have been donated or given. . . . I have lots of toys that children bring, children that I've never met before. . . . For me it is very important that my children know that there is life after death. When you're really born is when you die and you're born and you go to live with God, and that's what the children do there. . . . I felt like now he had the birth up in heaven. . . . I think that explains more to my young children, they look at it, it's young children, they are alive, they are playing. And I guess I also wanted my son to think that his brother was alive and his brother was up there and it was okay and it wasn't a scary thing; that you didn't die and get buried and it was all over. And it accomplished that, it really did. . . . It's a reminder that my son is up in heaven and he is alive.[55]

Whether or not the statues of the children on Daniel's grave had specific religious significance was an issue at trial. For Ms. Davis the statues of the children formed a part of a larger religious intention that drew a circle around the living and the dead:

I used to pray there all the time, almost everyday. My children would go there. They would run and they would play and they would get close with God and with their brother. Then all this happened and my children won't go back to the cemetery anymore. They are very very upset. . . . It is their sacred ground. It is my son's sacred ground. It's his little shrine. It's him. It is where we are. It's the place we go to be with him.[56]

Ms. Davis testified at trial that the statues of the children were greatly admired by the City workers who asked her to donate them to the city when the removal was requested, for placement in a common area of the cemetery.[57]

Eleanor Danciu was the final plaintiff to testify. Her daughter is a local attorney and was one of the attorneys representing the plaintiffs. Ms. Danciu's husband was mayor of Boca Raton from 1987 to 1993. It was clear at trial, from occasional references, that Ms. Danciu's husband was a public figure of some note. He was associated with various civic events and improvements, including a dispute over a civic holiday display in the town square. In February 1991, for example, then Mayor Danciu decided to put up a *hanukkiyah* (a traditional branched candelabra, used to celebrate the eight days of Hanukkah) in the town square next to the town's Christmas tree, to honor Boca Raton's Jewish citizens (more than a third of the population). After complaints from both Jews (some of whom objected to any religious symbols being erected in a public park) and Christians (some of whom wanted to erect a crèche as well) the hanukkiyah was taken down. A lawsuit was subsequently filed by Rabbi Moshe Denburg, a Habad–Lubavitcher rabbi in Boca Raton, to put the hanukkiyah back.[58] The Boca Raton city council then reversed itself and permitted both the hanukkiyah *and* the crèche. Four signs were erected by the display, one in front of each object, reading: "This display is provided by a private organization at no public expense and does not constitute an endorsement by the City of Boca Raton of any religion or religious doctrine."[59]

Ms. Danciu had buried her mother in the Boca Raton Cemetery in 1984. Like the other Catholic plaintiffs, Ms. Danciu is a parishioner at St. Joan of Arc Church, next to the cemetery. At the time of her mother's death, a mass was celebrated for her there and a graveside ceremony was performed by the priest. Some weeks later, Ms. Danciu installed a small statue of the Virgin Mary on the grave:

> The Blessed Virgin is my heavenly mother, and my mother taught me to love and to try and to live and emulate the life of the blessed mother. She was the mother of Jesus, and she was, my mother was dedicated to her. I'm Polish, and Polish people love the Blessed Virgin. If you know anything about Polish people, that's one thing they do.[60]

Again, the statue of the Virgin is a statue of a saint in the Catholic Church, the saint who is understood to be the premier example of a faithful Christian, but the statue also embodies religious doctrine about the nature of the deceased person and of her relationship to Christ. Catholics pray to the saints, who are understood to have influence in heaven, asking that they intercede with God on behalf of them and of the deceased. The Virgin is traditionally a particularly important intercessory figure in Polish devotional practice, as Ms. Danciu mentioned during the trial.

Ten years after her mother died, Ms. Danciu's father was also buried in the cemetery. She placed a statue of St. Francis on his grave. "My father was . . . a very, very loving and gentle man, like St. Francis. St. Francis was very—he was a hermit and he took care of animals and birds with broken wings. Well, that was just my father, and so that's the reason that I do have St. Francis on the grave."[61] The saints offer a huge array of religious personalities that can be correlated with the religious styles and personalities of the living. They enlarge the family and connect it to the church's faithful, past and present.[62]

A daily mass-goer, Ms. Danciu walks through and prays at the graves in the Boca Raton Cemetery every day. On Sundays, "whoever is with me in church on Sunday, the family, we go there and we pray and we hold hands and pray the Our Father and the Hail Mary and the Glory Be, and we ask eternal rest onto my parents and onto the souls in the cemetery." Asked why she chose the cemetery, Ms. Danciu responded: "Well, my father, who survived my mother, my brothers and my father and I went to Boca Raton Cemetery because that's local. I see the cemetery, I see it every day. . . . I see it when I go and pick up my grandchildren from school. So we wanted a local place where we could visit and take care of the grave." She, too, testified that no one had ever told her that she could not have the statues on the graves.[63]

The courtroom was hushed and sober during the plaintiffs' testimony. While one could hear echoes of a shared language that had developed among the plaintiffs over the course of their association and in response to the language of the law, the particular sadness of each story remained powerful. No one present doubted the sincerity and the grief there displayed. But what to do with this testimony? What legal significance did it have? Within the small spaces above the bodies of their relatives, spaces carefully calculated by the cemetery designers to maximize profit, homely little shrines had grown up, displaying the layered religious landscape of the city, and of the globe. Were these shrines the kind of religious activity intended for legal protection by the Florida RFRA?

The Trial: The Other Witnesses

THE OTHER WITNESSES for the plaintiffs included two city employees, Donna Driscoll, the city manager of Boca Raton, and Joseph Cogley, the deputy director for the Recreation Services Department; two experts in fields other than religion, John Metzler, the superintendent of Arlington National Cemetery, and Andrew Verzilli, a financial analyst; and the three experts on religion: Michael Broyde, John McGuckin, and myself.

The two city witnesses were called as "adverse" witnesses for the plaintiff, that is, although they were employees of the City, the plaintiffs called them to testify as a part of the plaintiffs' case in order to establish certain necessary elements of proof about the lines of municipal authority concerning enforcement of the regulations in order to establish the City's responsibility. Ms. Driscoll, the city manager, did not appear in person. (It is not unusual for minor and uncontroversial witnesses to appear only by way of written testimony, particularly in a trial without a jury.) Portions of Ms. Driscoll's deposition were read into the record by the plaintiffs' lawyers. She described the Boca Raton city government (a "weak mayor, strong council") and the chain of command in the management of the cemetery. She also established the city's position with respect to the interpretation of the regulations. She testified that the City's motivation in insisting on removal of the grave decorations was entirely one of safety, access, and ease of maintenance.[1] She denied any concern with aesthetics. Mr. Cogley, the deputy director of Recreation Services department, the City department charged with managing the cemetery, and the second City witness called as an adverse witness on the plaintiffs' behalf, was asked about the history of enforcement of the regulations and about the details of the interactions that the City had with individual plaintiffs.[2]

John Metzler was the first expert to testify for the plaintiffs. He is the superintendent at Arlington National Cemetery. Mr. Metzler was also not present at the trial, but portions of his deposition were read into the record at the trial by the plaintiffs' lawyer. Mr. Metzler testified concerning the regulations of Arlington National Cemetery, where vertical monuments are permitted. To rebut the City's claim that flat memorials are easier to maintain, Metzler described the ease and relatively low cost of maintenance of the vertical monuments in Arlington Cemetery.[3]

Andrew Verzili, a consultant with a firm providing financial and statistical analysis for litigation, testified for the plaintiffs concerning the cost of maintaining the vertical and the horizontal markers in the Boca Raton Cemetery in particular. Based on an analysis of the City's budget for the cemetery, Mr. Verzili's testimony was offered as evidence to show that the City lacked the statute's required "compelling interest" in insisting on flat memorials:

> [I]t's my opinion that the maintenance costs for the Boca Raton Cemetery are fixed with respect to the type of marker, either horizontal or vertical marker. . . . [T]here is nothing that I see that would indicate that maintenance costs have been higher as a result of having vertical markers and other coverings in the cemetery as opposed to if there was just the horizontal markers. . . . The maintenance costs that the cemetery will experience, these are such things as salaries for the caretaker and administrative salaries for the cemetery, disposal fees, equipment rental, water they pay, cemetery maintenance, fertilizer, chemicals, those costs are going to incur regardless of if they have vertical markers or just horizontal markers.[4]

On cross-examination, Rogow asked Verzili to admit, which he did, that he had never been to the Boca Raton Cemetery and asked him to admit that costs might increase if new equipment were needed or if personnel were asked to work overtime. On redirect examination, Mr. Green elicited the response from Mr. Verzili that the City's cemetery budget showed a surplus sufficient to absorb any increased costs due to the acquisition of new equipment or the use of overtime.[5]

The final witnesses for the plaintiffs were the experts in religion. The three of us were there to testify to the religiousness of the plaintiffs' activities at the cemetery, and to give expert credibility to the claim that the prohibition of these practices might "substantially burden" a person's "exercise of religion." Each of the three of us submitted a written report in advance of the trial that was used in the pretrial motions but none of us was deposed.[6] (Copies of the written reports of all five of the religion experts in the *Warner* case are reprinted as Appendix B.) The three religion experts were hired individually by the plaintiffs' lawyers.[7] We had no contact with one another before the trial. Indeed, we had little contact during the trial, as I was the only expert who was present for the whole trial. The other two of the plaintiffs' experts on religion appeared only for their own testimony. Each of us relied on the plaintiffs' depositions and the written reports of the other experts, rather than the testimony at trial, in preparing our opinions.

Michael Broyde testified on the first day of the trial. He testified for the plaintiffs as an expert on Jewish law. His testimony was intended to confirm and explain the testimony of the Jewish plaintiffs concerning the requirements of Jewish law and custom on the marking of graves. Michael Broyde is a graduate of Yeshiva University (B.A.) and New York University (J.D.). He is an Orthodox rabbi and a member of the Beth Din of America, a national council of Orthodox legal experts. (It is not the only such council. Different Jewish groups have different legal councils.) Broyde is also associate professor of law at Emory University. He is the author of *The Pursuit of Justice and Jewish Law: Halakhic Perspectives on the Legal Profession* and an editor of *Human Rights in Judaism: Cultural, Religious, and Political Perspectives*,[8] as well as many articles on Jewish law.

The expert report filed by Professor Broyde takes the form of a Jewish legal opinion, one formally approved, as it says, by the Beth Din of America.[9] The Report begins with these questions:

> Does the Jewish faith permit the removal of grave markers, tombstones, foot markers and other stone items from a grave to be replaced with a different marker that is less visible?
> Does the Jewish faith permit one to be buried without a full tombstone? What exactly constitutes a "full" headstone?[10]

The Report concludes with this opinion:

> The removal of tombstones and their replacement with a marker of lesser status would constitute a violation of Jewish law . . . [but] . . . [a] governmental regulation which prospectively requires small markers, rather than tombstones or any other type of marker, might not violate Jewish law, so long as such a regulation is confined to new cemeteries.[11]

Broyde drew a strong line in his report and at the trial between prospective and retrospective regulation of Jewish cemetery markers. Like the Jewish plaintiffs, he seemed less focused on how the Boca Raton regulations were drawn than with what was going to happen to the existing memorials. Local law might be variable, and, indeed, flat memorials might be consistent with Jewish law, even customary in some places, but the respect one should accord an existing burial site was constant. Broyde spoke for a religious community long accustomed, for better or worse, to strategic negotiation with local, non-Jewish, law.[12]

In arriving at his opinion, Broyde was careful first to explain the multiple sources for Jewish religious practice in both "law" and "custom":

Many areas of Judaism are fundamentally regulated by the legal aspects of the Jewish tradition, commonly referred to as *halacha*, Jewish law; the role custom plays in those technical areas of Jewish law is relatively small. . . . However, Judaism is as much a faith, a system of practices and religion as a legal system, and there are any number of areas of Jewish practice that are intensely governed by tradition—the ancient customs and practices of the Jewish people—as much as law. In some of these areas, law plays a very small role, in that classic Talmudic law codes say very little about how to engage in certain rites and rituals. Burial and funeral rites and practices are such an area. . . . However, this in no way shape or form diminishes the strength of the Jewish tradition in this area. To parse the Jewish faith into "law" and "tradition," and then to assert that "traditions" are not really part of the corpus of Jewish practices that faithful adherents need to live their lives observing, fundamentally misunderstands what practicing Judaism is.[13]

At the trial, too, Broyde began by carefully explaining to the judge the distinction he had made in his report concerning formal law and custom in Jewish tradition.[14]

It is important to note that the distinctions Broyde drew between law and custom are drawn more strongly than some Jewish legal experts would draw them and less strongly than others. How to think about the relative authority of law and custom has been a subject of extensive and subtle debate in the Jewish community for thousands of years.[15] Notwithstanding this diversity, however, Broyde's testimony, as a whole, still takes a rather unusual form in the context of Jewish legal practice. As a rule, a Jewish legal opinion would be given in response to a particular person about a particular situation, not, as here, as an advisory opinion to a secular court as to how Jewish law might rule in a particular situation. Broyde also did not speak as the plaintiffs' own rabbi, as would be customary in the Jewish context. He did not, therefore, enact traditional Jewish religious authority so much as advise the court. He undertook to translate Jewish religio-legal practice for an American secular context. He also spoke in silent reference to unidentified other Jewish legal experts, past and present, thereby participating by implication, as all of the experts did, in academic conversations and longstanding debates external to the courtroom.[16]

Turning to the issues in the *Warner* case, the obligation to mark a Jewish grave can be traced first, Broyde said both in his report and at the trial, to the biblical account of Jacob's setting up of a pillar to mark the grave of

Rachel, his wife, as recounted in Genesis 35:20.[17] That obligation is also attested to by the ongoing dispute in the Talmud[18] concerning the obligation of the Jewish community to bear the cost of burying and erecting tombstones for indigent Jews.[19] In what appeared "classic" fashion, both in his report and at the trial, Broyde engaged with rabbinic authority, ancient and modern, displaying his references and making his arguments, emphasizing, again both in his report and at the trial, his concern with the removal, or diminution, of existing memorials.

Broyde's report was fairly tightly focused on whether Jewish memorials *must* be vertical and whether they could be removed after installation. At the trial Broyde set these questions in a larger context. He gave three reasons at the trial as to why a grave marker is required in Jewish law:

> The first is that without a grave marker people will unintentionally disinter a person who is buried there. So it is important that a grave be marked in some way so as to prevent people from using this area for agricultural purposes. The second reason that a grave marker is placed is a grave marker is a way of preventing people from walking on a grave.... The third reason for a marker is to memorialize and honor the dead by putting things on the marker that tell us something about the person.... The reason we put what we call English tombstones rather than merely a grave marker is to inform the community around us of who was buried there, why that person is buried there, why that person is a person of merit in their life, and things that this person has accomplished.[20]

The prohibition against removal of existing gravestones is founded in a concern that there be no lessening of the respect given to the dead person:

> There is a very famous Jewish law opinion voiced by a contemporary American authority saying not only does the [replacement] marker have to be of the same height and size, it has to say the same words on the marker, because while a person has nine words of praise on their gravestone, and the gravestone breaks, do you then substitute three words of praise for the person? That's a diminution in the honor due the deceased.[21]

Broyde emphasized that an existing gravesite always commands respect in Jewish law:

> In the Jewish tradition grave markers become sacred, and when a grave marker is used it bears an intrinsic holiness in the Jewish tradition that requires that it be treated with a certain amount of sacredness. Thus, for example, grave markers when they break can't be disposed of in a normal

way. The classical custom when a gravestone broke is one buried it with another deceased person who had been buried, because gravestones themselves become sacred.[22]

The grave is consecrated, in part, by ongoing religious practices at the gravesite:

> The Jewish tradition wants people to note when they visited the cemetery and to mark it in some more permanent way than by placing flowers. Thus the custom was that one puts a stone on the tombstone, a small stone on the tombstone so as to indicate that one has been there. That small stone, when added to the tombstone, becomes some part of the memorialization process [see photograph]. . . . [T]he second reason that a grave marker is placed is a grave marker is a way of preventing people from walking on the grave. The Jewish tradition viewed walking on the grave as profoundly irreverent to the deceased.[23]

The practices testified to by the Jewish plaintiffs, the Warners and the Paynes, were thus contextualized and given authority: the need to demarcate the grave so it would not be stepped on, the practice of leaving a stone to show that a visit to the grave has been made, and the concern for the dishonor that subsequent alteration or removal would cause. Broyde also confirmed Mr. Payne's testimony concerning Jewish graves outside the United States: "Typically cemeteries in all places but America have a tombstone and a full covering of the tombstone so as to cover the body fully and completely. This will be a vertical tombstone and a horizontal covering."[24]

Bruce Rogow, the lawyer for the City, had several points to make when he cross-examined Broyde (points presumably refined in discussion with the City's experts on religion). Rogow began by asking whether Jewish law requires Jews to obey the law of the land. Broyde answered yes, but only as that law is enforced. He gave the example of traffic laws. Disobeying traffic laws might be condoned by Jewish law if they were not regularly enforced. Rogow also took Broyde back through the portions of his opinion that said that flat markers could be legal under Jewish law and custom, but only if prospective in application. He asked Broyde to concede that the key prescription for Jewish religious practice was visibility, and that visibility could be achieved through the use of a flat stone. Broyde agreed with Rogow that, if prospectively applied, it would not necessarily be a violation of Jewish law to limit memorials to flat plaques.[25]

Rogow also asked Broyde on cross-examination about the rule asserted by some of the Jewish plaintiffs as to the prohibition of walking on a grave.

In a careful shift of emphasis away from textual or institutional mandates, Broyde, in response, tried to explain the psychological structure of religious compulsion:

Q. [by Rogow] So the only purpose then is to delineate and denote the perimeter of the grave site?

A. Yes.

Q. So that people would be deterred from walking on it?

A. Deterred is too strong a word in a sense that there is no guard that prevents this. It's that people understand that one doesn't walk on a grave site. People consciously seek to adhere to that, and this provides them with the guidance that says this is an area that you can walk on and this is an area that you cannot walk on.[26]

Broyde also resisted a hard division of people into Jewish or non-Jewish, religious or not:

Q. Would an atheist or an agnostic have the same ability to claim this need to delineate a grave as would a Jew?

A. In the Jewish tradition the person who generally doesn't live their life in fidelity with Jewish law but at the time of burial says I wish to bury my loved one in a Jewish cemetery consistent with Jewish rites, we would respect that and grant them that wish rather than turn to them and say how come now you have a newfound observance of the religious faith. . . . The Jewish tradition believes that stepping on the graves . . . is errant, whether the person be a Jew or a non-Jew, and is uncomfortable with cemeteries that don't mark the perimeters of the graves.[27]

Broyde speaks of a religious adherent informed and eager to conform to God's law, rather than a religious adherent compelled only by an external religious authority. He speaks of a tradition of broad humanity rather than one narrowly focused on its own orthodoxy. Broyde's testimony was learned, lucid, and convincing. He brought Jewish law into the courtroom. He was also patient and obliging. He made, however, little impression on Judge Ryskamp, as will be discussed in the next chapter.

The second expert witness for the plaintiffs was John McGuckin. Educated at the University of London (B.A., M.A., Ph.D.), McGuckin is a priest of the Romanian Orthodox Church[28] and professor of early church history at Union Theological Seminary in New York. He is also a fellow of both the Royal Society of Arts and the Royal Historical Society in the

United Kingdom. McGuckin is the author of many books and articles, including *Standing in God's Holy Fire: The Spiritual Tradition of Byzantium* and *St. Gregory of Nazianzus: An Intellectual Autobiography.*[29]

McGuckin testified at the trial that he was "Irish English" and was brought up Roman Catholic. He had entered the Catholic religious order of the Society of Jesus, known as the Jesuits, at the age of seventeen, and had attended Heathrow College, a Jesuit seminary in London, where his studies focused on "early Greek theology." McGuckin further testified that he had found himself "moving increasingly eastwards in Christianity and became Orthodox ten years ago":

> I was visiting Romania in 1989 in the aftermath of the communist over-throw as a visiting professor to try and institute departments of religious studies which had been suppressed in that country, and Kiev in the Ukraine. And after I did my time as a professor in Romania, the patriarch of Romania asked me to serve as a priest for Romanians in the European diaspora, which I did for two years.[30]

Eileen McGuckin, Rev. McGuckin's wife, is a painter of icons.[31] Rev. McGuckin's long hair, clerical garb, and large pectoral cross, caused quite a stir in the South Florida courtroom. One of the plaintiffs, visibly im-pressed, leaned over to me and said, "It's like having Jesus in the court."

There was something surreal, and I think entirely accidental on the part of the plaintiffs' lawyers, who knew little of the differences among Christian churches, about having a Romanian Orthodox priest, particularly a British Irish Catholic Romanian Orthodox priest, represent Christian teaching in an American court. Approximately 2½ percent of American Christians are Orthodox Christians.[32] Most American Christians today are, like Judge Ryskamp, Protestant, and most American Christians throughout American history have been Protestant.[33]

The dominant form of Christian religiosity in the United States is evan-gelical Protestant, small "e," large "P." Evangelical Protestant churches are descendants of those Reformation churches emphasizing individual piety and the work of the spirit in the world. The evangelical Protestant tradition has tended to be iconoclastic in its religious orientation, in contrast to the central role that images, including icons, have played in Roman Catholic and Eastern Orthodox spiritual practice. Furthermore, while approximately 25 percent of Americans today are Roman Catholic, American culture and law have been permeated with anti-Catholicism for much of their history and Roman Catholicism has arguably been somewhat protestantized over that time. Indeed a persuasive case has been made that the doctrine of the separation of church and state, itself the central "doctrine" of American church/state politics today, developed popularly as an anti-Catholic tool in the nineteenth century.[34]

For the judge, I think, McGuckin's testimony came from another place and time, perhaps another religion. McGuckin spoke of an early Christianity divided within itself and continuous with forms of Judaism. He also spoke of an extra-textual Christianity, one attested to in stone monuments and epigraphy, a Christianity prior to and in addition to the New Testament writings. Finally, he spoke out of the high liturgical tradition, a tradition in which the sacramentality of the incarnation of God and Christ in the world is a central reality, one mediated through a hierarchical priesthood and set forms of worship.[35]

McGuckin took his task to be somewhat different from that of Broyde's, in part, of course, because he did not speak as an expert in law, as Broyde did, but also because Christianity is not legal in the same way as Judaism.[36] McGuckin's report states that its purpose will be to "formulate an opinion on [the rules and regulations of Boca Raton Cemetery] in relation to the expression of basic Christian religious belief in burial practice."[37] His report and his testimony partook of a mixed historical and theological discursive mode. He not only offered his expert opinion as an academic church historian on the historical practices of Christians, but he "performed" a high liturgical Christian religious sensibility.

McGuckin's account of the burial practices of Christians, both in his report and at the trial, was colored by the fact that his testimony was designed to refute the assertion by Daniel Pals, one of the City's expert witnesses (discussed in detail below), that burial practices are not, and never have been, central to Christian religious practice; Daniel Pals had offered the opinion in his report that the apostle Paul's teaching "directs Christian attention away from the state or circumstances of the physical body after death, and turns it decisively toward something beyond this earth."[38] Such a sweeping generalization on the part of one of the City's experts concerning the minimal significance of burial for Christians, generally, invited and permitted expansive testimony from the plaintiffs and their experts concerning two thousand years of Christian theology of death and burial. Much of McGuckin's extensive testimony concerning the burial practices of early Christian communities was thus offered to counter Pals's rather protestant reading of Christian history and practice, an iconoclastic reading that discounted the religious practice of almost all European Christians between the reign of Constantine and the Protestant Reformation, and of almost all

Catholic, Orthodox, and liturgical Protestant Christians (such as "high church" Lutherans and Episcopalians) since the Reformation.

In his expert report, McGuckin contrasted both early Christian and contemporary Christian burial practices with what he termed a "secularized consciousness." He first detailed Christian concern, generally, with the sanctity of graves:

> In the burial rituals of the Catholic and Orthodox churches, the emphasis turns on the committal of the dead person to sanctified ground. The Eastern liturgy uses a recurring phrase in the burial services and in memorials for the dead, a phrase that is a verse from the psalms and used with explicit reference to the dead body: "The Earth is the Lord's, and all those who *dwell within* it." Much of the Catholic burial service turns around the notions of honouring the dead body as a sacred thing, and of consecrating the gravesite as a hallowed place. . . . In earlier Christian civilizations the entire cemetery (a word that Christians invented—koimeteria—meaning a place of sleeping under the eye of God until the last Day) would have been consecrated in a formal rite as holy ground, in order the keep safe the holy bodies of the "images of God" who were destined to rest there until the time of God's Judgment on human history. . . .
>
> [T]he extremely close connection of the Christian religion with this principle of the reverence for the burial site, and for the sanctity of the dead body which rests in anticipation of the resurrection, is something that can be witnessed from the earliest origins of the Christian religion as a distinctive aspect of that religion. The Catacombs in Rome are among the most important of all archaeological sites for giving evidence on fundamental matters of Christianity in the immediate post New Testament period. The inscriptions of Crosses, and the listing of names and synopsis histories (epitaphs) are clearly developed by Christians in their own special ways from the normal burial practices of neighbours around them. Soon, with increasing affluence among the Christian communities, inscribed grave stones became more apparent. These are the first forays into Christian Art and Iconography which soon became a major element of the expression of Christian Faith—and still is within Catholicism and Orthodoxy (although Protestantism generally takes a more iconoclastic position on this—tending to reject imagery, statuary, and iconography from the fundamentals of Christian faith).[39]

And, at the trial McGuckin added: "[T]he body of the ordinary Christian who has, which has in its past received the Eucharist and the sacraments, in itself is a holy thing which awaits the resurrection of Christ. There's a very deep theological commitment to the idea that the Christian is absorbed into the mystery of Christ. It's what St. Paul talked about in the phrase *enchristo*."[40]

While Ryskamp and Pals took a Protestant religious sensibility as the norm, McGuckin (and the *Warner* plaintiffs who were Christians, even including Souhail Karram, because of his background in the Orthodox church), took a Catholic or Orthodox religious sensibility as the norm. There was little bridging of the two worlds. Protestants and Catholics have, in McGuckin's words, different "religious syntaxes." As questions came up at the trial concerning the significance of the plaintiffs' prayers at the cemetery, McGuckin commented at trial: "This is a kind of a fault line in some way with Reformed church spiritual consciousness. One of the factors of the Reformation was to deny the validity of prayer for the deceased."[41] Protestants reject the practice of praying for the dead as nonbiblical.[42]

McGuckin's report concluded:

> If we consider to what extent it is reasonable, or "mainstream," for a Christian to have a desire to mark the grave of a member of their natural, and Christian, family (for the relative is not just a "natural" relation, but bonded to them by religious ties and obligations too) then I would say that it is a fundamental part of Christian religious practice. Regulations that forbid a Christian family to erect a standing Cross, or even a standing stone Epitaphios contradict an ancient Christian practice, and do an objective violence to fundamental religious attitudes to those Christians who retain the classical "catholic" sense of this theology of death and grieving observance.[43]

Like many of the plaintiffs, McGuckin was intensely concerned that the cross be permitted to be displayed upright, "over" the grave. He returned frequently to that concern, commenting at the same time about the Orthodox prohibition against three-dimensional representational art, in contrast to Roman Catholic tradition.[44]

While the cross is today the most ubiquitous of Christian symbols, its use has varied over Christian history and among Christian communities. The cross is understood conventionally among Christians to refer most specifically to the Roman form of execution by which Jesus was crucified and the theology that developed in response to that event,[45] but it is also understood as a wider religious reference in which the cross is seen to symbolize the fundamental structure of the cosmos.[46] Its common use as the central identifying symbol for Christians does not begin until the fourth-century reign of Constantine, the Roman emperor who ended persecution of Christians and established Christianity as the religion of the Empire. Constantine reportedly attributed his success in battle to a vision of a cross in the sky.[47]

At the trial, Jim Green asked McGuckin to comment on Daniel Pals's assertion in his report that he had seen the cross displayed flat in the Church of the Holy Sepulchre in Jerusalem:

Q. I believe you testified that you visited the Holy Sepulchre in Jerusalem.

A. I've celebrated the liturgy as a priest in the Holy Sepulchre in Jerusalem.

Q. The City has an expert named Daniel Pals. Have you read his report?

A. I have.

Q. And I believe that he indicates that in the Holy Sepulchre there is a cross that you say [is] flush to the ground?

A. There are many crosses in the Holy Sepulchre. It would be unheard of in a church to put a cross flush on the ground. *It's against the Canons of the Catholic Church and the Orthodox Church to have a cross laid horizontally. Or to have a cross in a carpet or such thing is regarded as sacrilegious. Anything where the cross could be walked on is forbidden by the canons* [emphasis supplied].[48]

It is an index of the confusion about authority in the courtroom that this sole assertion (see above in italics) of a direct violation of religious law resulting from the Boca Raton Cemetery Regulations passed without notice.

Green continued:

Q. Have you ever seen a horizontal cross on the ground or the floor of any church, any Christian church?

A. I've never seen such a thing.

Q. And you've been to how many churches in Turkey and Israel and areas of ancient Christianity?

A. I've been in innumerable ancient churches and surviving contemporary churches. I've never seen any such a thing.

Q. Would you ever intentionally walk on a cross?

A. It would have a horrific resonance with Orthodox, any Orthodox Christian. It would be a serious disrespect to the Christian religion.[49]

The repeated assertion by the plaintiffs and by McGuckin that a cross *ought* to be displayed upright had no evidentiary weight, notwithstanding the City's lawyers' apparent concern about what Christianity "required." The religious etiquette of the liturgical churches with respect to sacramentals, that is religious practices by which grace is conveyed, such as the use of the sign of the cross,[50] had no place in an American courtroom, in a very real sense.

The importance of grave memorials being vertical in orientation, rather than horizontal, also had political significance for McGuckin, as for the plaintiffs. McGuckin commented in his report:

> If I was to consider: would it be a useful compromise to have a flat stone embedded in the cemetery grass, as opposed to a standing stone, I would respond that the Orthodox Christian church, at least, would regard this as sacrilegious: for the Cross ought to be over the grave—and the sacred sign of the Cross must never be placed in a position where it could be walked over. The canons of the eastern church have forbidden this since the time when Islam made walking on the Cross a way in which Greeks under the Ottoman domination were led to renounce their faith.[51]

Here McGuckin confirmed Mr. Karram's testimony concerning Ottoman persecution of Christians. Religious freedom meant, in a sense, both for the immigrant Cubans and the immigrant Lebanese in the *Warner* trial, a freedom for the church to realize herself in historic practices, practices that express not just devotion, but also a religious community free from hostile political control.

The difference in religious orientation between Pals and McGuckin was also evident in McGuckin's disagreement with Pals's reading of the Bible and the church fathers. McGuckin was asked at trial concerning his assessment of Pals's report with respect to the importance of tombstones:

> *Q.* Well, did you have occasion to read his, his comment that in none of the literature is the issue of burial monuments or tombstones ever directly addressed?
>
> *A.* He talks about the place of the tomb of Jesus in the New Testament, and the significance of tombs and burial practices for early Christians. I think— I don't know where he gets his historical analysis from. I think it's gravely flawed. Most interpreters of the New Testament would conclude quite the opposite of Dr. Pals's conclusion, that the Christians didn't find the empty tomb of any great significance in itself. Most commentators regard the physical fact of the empty tomb as being of profound importance for the Jerusalem church for many generations after the crucifixion of Jesus. And there are many comparable examples, in charismatic Judaism to the second and third century.[52]

There was little, in fact, about which McGuckin and Pals agreed concerning Christian theology and practice. They spoke of profoundly different religious cultures.

Like Broyde, McGuckin was also asked to comment on the plaintiffs' claim that they were taught that it was wrong to walk on graves:

Q. Without going into exactly what your grandmother said, what did you learn at an early age in your Irish Catholic tradition about walking on graves?

A. If you walked on a grave you should say a prayer for the person who was buried there.[53]

The judge interrupted:

The Court: Would the people who cut the grass at the cemetery have to be saying a prayer for each time they ran the mower over the graveyard?

The Witness: That's an interesting question of how far secularized attitudes go. But certainly in the early church the office of the caretaker in the crematoria was an important office in the structure of the early church. Some of the grave keepers in the catacombs in Rome actually immediately passed on to become the Popes.[54]

McGuckin was stopped by Green from testifying as to his grandmother's actual words because they constituted hearsay evidence, but his reference reinforces the tendency of the plaintiffs to cite relatives for authority as to their religious practice. At the level of folk practice, McGuckin's testimony concerning his grandmother's teaching also reveals an interesting overlap between Christian and Jewish practice.

McGuckin and I had together visited the cemetery that morning (Thursday of the week of the trial), I for the second time. McGuckin was asked about his visit, and focused not on the historical evidence but on contemporary piety:

Q. I believe you testified earlier that you have been to the Boca Raton cemetery; is that correct?

A. This morning.

Q. Did that change your understanding of this case in any way?

A. It surprised me to the extent that this was, the existence of statues, Roman Catholic statues, was far more prevalent than I thought before from seeing the few photographs that I had had before that. The extent of the practice was quite striking. . . .

In terms of the statues and the crosses, I think one's touching there some-thing very close to the heart of a mainstream Christian expression of reli-gion, understood from a popular aspect.[55]

He had earlier commented:

I was struck by the cemetery, both from the photographs and when I saw it this morning, that it seems to express a very clear idea of Roman Catholic spirituality of death. And by that I mean predominantly the stat-ues of Mary, Jesus and the saints. And there was one case which I saw from the photograph, and I immediately thought this is resonant for the Orthodox approach, where three-dimensional art is forbidden in the Or-thodox religion. The raising of the cross in the coherent Orthodox ex-pression. And it turned out that that was a Lebanese family which came from an Orthodox background. So both the raised cross and the larger majority of statues struck me as a very clear example of catholic, with a small "c," religious sentiment. . . . [T]his is actually not just Orthodox, it's very fundamental to Catholicism, too. The cross was raised over the grave to mark the fact that this piece of ground had actually been consecrated. And it also theologically symbolized the raising of the cross. It's called in the church's liturgy, the Catholic and the Orthodox, the elevation of the cross. It has a special feast day. The physical act of elevating or raising the cross symbolizes the victory of Christ's resurrection over death. So it marks a holy place, as well as being a symbol of hope.[56]

And, broadly summarizing diverse catholic practices:

Christianity isn't that kind of narrow religion where there is one quite clear definition of what would be religiously acceptable to one person. . . . [T]he popular piety of, say, Hispanic or Mediterranean Roman Catholics might differ from the Archbishop of Chicago but they are still in the same church. They are equally Roman Catholic.[57]

Finally, with respect to the decorations in the Boca Raton Cemetery, McGuckin said: "The religious art we're talking about is popular art, it's not high religious art."[58]

Like Broyde, McGuckin focused at the trial on the importance of the graves themselves, the particular graves at issue in the case, the existing graves, and the cultural logic impelling the plaintiffs' activities there. While he spoke at times from within a specific religious community, giving pride of place to a high liturgical sensibility characteristic of Orthodox and Catholic Christianity, he also carefully placed the plaintiffs' actions within a larger geographical and historical context, a context that permitted a variety of practices. Like Broyde, the compulsion to which he testified was not legal, in a positivist sense, but arose from the desire of religiously motivated people to conform their lives to a pattern set by God.

I was the third expert witness on religion who testified for the plaintiffs. My own testimony was offered as rebuttal testimony, after the defendant's case was presented. It was my role to comment on the City's expert testimony and to put all of the expert testimony in the context of American religious practice. Because I was the last witness at the trial, I will describe my report and my oral testimony below, following a description of the evidence for the City.

The witnesses for the City of Boca Raton were Joseph Cogley, the deputy director of the Boca Raton Recreation Services Department; Curtis Harris, the mausoleum manager of the Boca Raton Cemetery; Kevin Jordan, the cemetery sexton between 1991 and 1995; Lawrence Sloane, a consultant in cemetery management; and two experts in religion: Nathan Katz and Daniel Pals. The City's task at the trial was to prove that the activities of the plaintiffs at the grave sites were not significantly religious but were instead the result of what the City chose to call "purely personal preference." The City also aimed to show that the Boca Raton Cemetery Regulations were consistent with industry practice and that they were, moreover, necessary to the safe and efficient management of the cemetery. The City further claimed that the regulations themselves sufficiently accommodated religious expression.

Mr. Cogley set the stage by describing in some detail the procedures for a burial at the Boca Raton Cemetery:

> Once it's measured, then it's flagged off the four corners. Then the staff will come in with a sod cutter and remove the sod and stack it. . . . After the sod is removed, the backhoe with the front end loader will bring down what we call a cofferdam and that is placed over top of the outline where the sod was taken out. . . . [A cofferdam is] a metal box that's about eight feet by, I think around three-and-a-half feet wide and long . . . made of steel. . . . Once that's placed over the grave, then the backhoe is situated so that the backhoe can reach inside the box. . . . The tractor with the backhoe scoops the sand out of the box, dumps it into the back of the dump truck, then takes the backhoe arm and pushes the box down as it continues to dig, and the box goes all the way down until it's about an inch above ground level. . . . Then the monument company will come and drive their truck with what's called a vault down the graves, and it has a long arm with a chain on it, and they move the vault over and put it down inside the

cofferdam. . . . A vault can be concrete or steel. Mostly what we have is concrete. The casket is placed inside that after the funeral service. . . . [The vault] does protect the casket and it keeps the ground from settling in, because if you don't have a vault, the casket will eventually deteriorate and the ground will sink. So it does protect the casket and the body. . . . Then that truck goes away and the staff come back and put a green carpet and bolt leveling boards around the edge of the cofferdam, and put a green carpeting out which extends down over the walls of the cofferdam. And then on top of that they put the board, or casket lowering device, which is an item which the casket is put on during the graveside service. The staff then also puts a carpet out over the plots and graves, erects a tent for the family, and then we'll put chairs up for the family so that they can use that for their graveside service.[59]

Cogley also testified at length concerning the difficulties caused by vertical grave decorations for the management of the cemetery.[60]

Curtis Harris and Kevin Jordan testified concerning the size of the Boca Raton Cemetery and as to how graves were dug and burials managed. They also testified concerning the cemetery's experience with each of the plaintiffs and responded to the claim that the plaintiffs were never explicitly told that they could violate the regulations. There were minor discrepancies with the plaintiffs' testimony. That enforcement had been irregular was admitted, but that explicit permission was given to disregard the rules was denied. As with all of the cemetery personnel, Cogley, Harris, and Jordan were sympathetic but matter-of-fact about the business of burials.

Lawrence Sloane, president of L. F. Sloane Consulting Group, testified for the City as an expert on cemeteries. Mr. Sloane serves as a consultant to, in his words, "the cemetery and funeral industry."[61] Bruce Rogow asked him to give a brief history of American cemeteries:

Cemeteries in the United States typically were all municipal or religious for a period until the 1830s, 1840s. Due to primarily public health concerns . . . leading citizens in the communities formed what were called rural cemeteries under an Act of Congress. These were very large grand Victorian cemeteries. The first was in Mt. Auburn in Cambridge, Massachusetts, and city after city, all the way through to San Francisco, formed these cemeteries, partly from boosterism and partly public health. The church yards were consolidated into a large rural cemetery, generally established at the time at the edge of the city.[62]

Sloane was then asked to describe the "memorial garden" style of cemetery:

The memorial gardens date to the 1920s. . . . The memorial park is intended to create an atmosphere, a park-like atmosphere. It's diminishing the starkness of death. It's a different approach to marketing, to serving the customer, as to what they are looking for emotionally. It was established in part so that there was no competition between the Smiths and the Joneses having the largest monument and everyone was equal in the cemetery, so it appealed to a broad middle class that has emerged in the United States. The operation of the memorial park is in many ways easier. It's certainly easier from a marketing and sales perspective because memorials are standardized and products and services can be packaged into a combination sale and it's much easier to manage.[63]

A standardized consumer-oriented approach to memorialization of the dead contrasted at trial with the highly specific nature of the plaintiffs' mourning and their popular religious attitudes toward the cemetery and what occurred there.

The plaintiffs were looking for a place characterized by what one Palm Beach reporter called "devout diversity" rather than a place characterized by mass-market landscaping and generalized sentimentality. The plaintiffs liked the religious pluralism of the cemetery, a place where parallel religious practices occurred. The religious practices of the plaintiffs were, in each case, as they told it, an attempt to step out of time, an attempt to connect the graves with an eternal present, not an attempt to connect with current fashion.[64] All the plaintiffs were also, however, very practical about acknowledging the commonsense needs of the cemetery workers, offering to help move things if notified, in order to accommodate new burials. The plaintiffs did not claim a right to build anything at all on the graves, as Rogow implied from time to time, in his cross-examination.[65] For Rogow, on the other hand, it seemed that there was no room to be personal or practical with true religious obligations.

Mr. Sloane's testimony was intended to put the City in the center of current cemetery design, while the plaintiffs were made to appear out of step, unfashionable. Ironically, fashion seems to be changing. After lengthy testimony concerning the ease of management of memorial-garden-type cemeteries, on cross-examination, Mr. Green asked Mr. Sloane about the current practices at new national cemeteries. Sloane testified concerning a new law requiring upright memorials at those cemeteries:

[T]he marble and granite industry were very good at lobbying Congress, and Senator Leahy was instrumental in having that enacted. And there is a trend towards returning to the upright memorials in new veteran cemeteries. . . . I think it's a response to the customer. . . . There has been a return to more upright monumentation in the industry generally on a national basis as we move toward servicing the new generation. . . . [T]he baby boomers tend to have different memorialization desires than their parents.[66]

Nathan Katz and Daniel Pals testified for the City as experts on religion. Each spoke not as an expert on a specific religious tradition, as Broyde and McGuckin had, but as an expert on religion in general. Each was asked to come up with guidelines by which the Court could separate religion from the "idiosyncratic" and the "personal," for purposes of applying the Florida RFRA. In each case the defendants' experts responded by designing tests for that express purpose. Both tests suggest that legally protect-able religion is a highly bounded ideological and institutionalized regime, one to which adherents only assent, or not. (In contrast, religion for the plaintiffs was an event negotiated between the individual and the tradition, one that was to some extent improvised.)

Both Katz and Pals are well known in the field of religious studies. Each offered a structural scheme that would provide the Court with a test for determining whether the plaintiffs' activities in the cemetery were protected by the statute, a test for determining when a religious practice was important enough such that its prohibition would inflict a substantial burden on the "exercise of religion." Whereas the plaintiffs' experts spoke of entire grave sites and of the culturally and religiously specific details of the practices surrounding them, the City's experts spoke only of the monuments themselves, of the necessity, or not, for "vertical" memorialization, specifically.

The question Katz and Pals was asked was whether "Judaism" and "Christianity" demand that deaths be "vertically" memorialized. Each answered no, answering in each case for the traditions in their entirety. It is a curious notion, "vertical memorialization." I am not aware of religious laws that demand adherence to that kind of abstract spatial standard. Muslims orient themselves to Mecca, church buildings may be oriented with reference to cardinal points, and certainly there are vertical references in such structures as cathedrals, the placement of crosses, and in bodily practices in prayer, but in each case these are very specific cultural references. By asking about "verticality" *tout court*, is there not a sense in which the religious is necessarily excluded?

Nathan Katz, Temple University (B.A., M.A., Ph.D.), is professor and chair of religious studies at Florida International University in South Dade.

Professor Katz describes himself in his report as "expert in the history of religions, comparative religions, the religions of South Asia, and Judaism" (see Appendix B).[67] His many publications include a substantial number about Buddhism and Asian Judaism. He is the author most recently of *Who Are the Jews of India?* and *A Jewish King at Shingly: The Story of the Jews of Cochin.*[68] Katz's written report addresses the following questions: "What are the requirements of the major religions of this area—Catholicism, Protestantism, Judaism, and Islam—as regards markers or monuments at gravesites; and, Do the rules governing the Boca Raton Municipal Cemetery contravene these religious requirements?" After announcing these questions, the Katz Report then proceeds to consider, one by one, whether "Catholicism," "Protestantism," "Judaism," and "Islam" "require" their adherents to place upright memorials on graves. This task was a bit like shooting fish in a barrel, and that was how Katz treated the assignment. His conclusion: "My findings are that the rules of the Boca Raton Cemetery do not conflict with the religious requirements of Catholics, Protestants, Jews or Muslims."[69] Katz made no qualifications of this opinion.

Katz's Report first takes each of the listed "religions" in turn. Relying on the Code of Canon Law,[70] as interpreted for him by Mr. Frank Villaronga of the Archdiocese of Miami, who is not otherwise identified,[71] and a trade publication by the National Catholic Cemetery Association as to "recommendations" for memorials,[72] Katz concluded that "The Roman Catholic Church has very minimal requirements regarding markers or memorials."[73] The reason for the minimal nature of Catholic cemetery regulation, internationally, is because, Katz explains, regulation occurs at the local level. The trade publication of the National Catholic Cemetery Association, *The Catholic Cemetery: A Vision for the Millennium,*[74] cited by Katz, lists principles for their members, including the principle to avoid anti-Christian symbols. The fourth listed principle notes this local or community-based dimension:

> 4. Memorials must not offend religious proprieties, Church discipline or good taste. Because different cultural and ethnic groups in our society have various styles of faith expression, one cannot demand adherence to any universal form of memorialization that may serve to limit this expression, including recognition of an individual's life work, avocation or pursuit.[75]

Katz acknowledges in his report that principle 4 might present an issue for the Court because of its reference to the need to accommodate different styles of "faith expression," but refers the reader to the concluding section of his Report in which he purports to distinguish between what he refers to as "High Traditions and Little Traditions," which will be discussed below.

As to Protestants, Katz concludes in his Report: "Protestant requirements for markers and monuments are essentially the same as those for Catholics, although less formalized or codified. . . . The three basic principles of (1) respect for the dead, (2) testimony to the deceased's commitment to a Christian life, and (3) good taste govern the Protestant view."[76] It is not clear in the Report what the source is for this opinion. No authorities are cited on Protestantism.[77] The reference to "good taste" is interesting. Katz mentions "good taste" as a requirement for all three of the traditions. Some have argued that "good taste" is a peculiarly Protestant invention.[78] If so, the mention of "good taste" in Catholic and Jewish publications might be seen as the result of Protestant cultural influence. Certainly the concern echoes the alleged comments of Boca Raton residents about the appearance of the cemetery—that the grave decorations were "not Boca."

Finally, relying on a book summarizing Jewish death practices by Rabbi Maurice Lamm,[79] Katz concluded that the rules did not contradict Jewish law. Katz lists three purposes served by a marker in the Jewish tradition. The third states that the purpose of a marker is: "To serve as a symbol of honor for the deceased buried beneath it. For this purpose one should erect as respectable a monument as the heirs can afford, avoiding unnecessary ostentation." Concerning this purpose and its possible conflict with the Boca Raton Cemetery Rules, Katz again refers the reader to his discussion of "High Traditions and Little Traditions." Katz also added in his Report, after the section on Judaism, that on the basis of a conversation with a local Muslim leader in Pompano Beach, he had concluded that "Muslim traditions regarding markers and monuments are also rather minimal."[80]

The final section in Katz's Report is entitled "High Traditions and Little Traditions." He begins by defining the two kinds of traditions:

By "high tradition" is meant the textual-legal side of a religion, usually male dominated and church or synagogue-centered. By "little tradition" is meant the folkways and home-centered observances, usually orally rather than textually transmitted, often the domain of women in a traditional culture. Another way of making this distinction would be by using the concepts of "by law" and "by custom." In contemporary America, the "little traditions" are often based in ethnicity, and one can make a distinction between practices which are "religious" and customs which are "ethnic," the "high" and "low" traditions.[81]

During his testimony at the trial, he amplified, gesturing with his hand to emphasize for the judge the relative importance of a hierarchy of religious practices:

> To determine . . . what constitutes religious requirements or behaviors or norms or codes, the starting point would be with the system of divine law that the religion has. But that's just one of the moorings of a hierarchy of demands, of requirements, of customs. And somewhere below what's clear in the law would be long-held traditions, ethnic practices, things of that nature. Somewhere below that might be something like folkways, which may be fairly commonly practiced but very often folkways are at variance with the laws. Somewhere below folkways might be something like superstitious practices. And somewhere below that might be idiosyncratic behavior.[82]

In his Report, after introducing the concepts of "high" and "little" traditions, he analyzed the significance of these distinctions for the legal regulation of religion:

> "Little tradition" customs are nowhere codified; indeed, by their nature they are oral rather than textual, and as such run the risk of being idiosyncratic. No one could judge the "authenticity" of a little tradition practice; whatever an individual happens to feel could be argued to be a "little tradition." Very often, sincerely and passionately held religious beliefs turn out to be held only on an individual basis, with no source in the religious high tradition itself. If we accept all "little tradition" customs as valid and binding in the same way that "high tradition" laws and doctrines are, then we run the danger of falling into a relativism bordering on anarchy. . . . [T]here is nothing in the Rules and Regulations of the Boca Raton Municipal Cemetery and Mausoleum which interferes with the exercise of these religions as defined by their high traditions.[83]

No academic authority is given in Katz's Report for the categories he uses, that is, "high" and "little" traditions.

The terms "high" and "little" traditions are anthropological. "Little" was an appellation used by Robert Redfield, professor of anthropology at the University of Chicago in the 1950s, to describe the values and the way of life of small-scale peasant communities in Guatemala.[84] "High" and "little" describe a cultural dichotomy in what might be called "traditional" society, that is, they describe the relationship between elite and popular culture in traditional societies. (Although Katz's equation of little or popular religion with idiosyncratic or individual is problamatic. Just because a practice is not an elite practice does not mean that it lacks community-sanctioned form.) Whether "high" and "little" are useful (and, indeed, whether they are constitutional) in defining the legally protect-able religious practices of members of a secular pluralistic society at the beginning of the twenty-first century will be discussed in the next chapter.

Like Rogow, Katz was concerned about what is called in legal slang, the "slippery slope." In other words, he was worried about the result that a broad reading of religion would have on the law: "[R]elativism," Katz said, might lead to "anarchy."[85] At the trial, Katz was asked by Rogow to explain his opinion. He responded: "I don't think that it was the intent, if I may, of the Florida statute, to protect everything in that spectrum [from high to little] from any, what's the word, burden at all. . . . Just because someone believes something doesn't mean that's part of the religion. And just because someone believes it is part of the religion, I think, doesn't make that quite so."[86] So what does make it so? That was the question for Judge Ryskamp.

On cross-examination, Jim Green asked Katz:

Q. Have you ever stepped on a grave?

A. Probably, yes.

Q. Have you ever intentionally stepped on a grave?

A. Probably not.

Q. Why not?

A. I'm a hereditary priest in my religion and that's forbidden to me.[87]

Katz here entirely changes roles. He speaks not as a social scientist but as an insider—as a Jew—and when he does so he speaks with an entirely different authority, albeit one that reinforces the dogmatic nature of his report. In his report, Katz elaborated on the limitations on hereditary priests: "The hereditary priests of Judaism (*kohanim* [pl.]; sing. *kohen*) must avoid becoming defiled by close proximity to a corpse. In particular, the *kohen* must avoid walking upon a Jew's grave."[88]

On cross-examination, Jim Green pressed Katz concerning the plaintiffs' claim that protecting a grave from being walked on was a traditional Jewish practice:

Q. Would you consider protecting a grave to be idiosyncratic behavior?

A. Protecting a grave? From what?

Q. Other people walking on it?

A. Yes.[89]

It is apparently "idiosyncratic" for Katz if you are not a kohen. Yet, how can an American court take cognizance of this traditional Jewish category and the identifying of particular Jews as genealogical descendants of an ancient priestly class? Even to suggest such a practice is to evoke the racialization of law in Nazi Germany or South Africa. Particularly when both the Jewish plaintiffs and Rabbi Broyde saw this custom as more broadly binding.

Mr. Green continued:

Q. If it is idiosyncratic behavior, then, according to your definition, a person who attempts to protect that grave from being walked on because of personal religious beliefs would be entitled to no protection?

A. Personal religious beliefs is, according to the way I'm trying to use the word religion, I'm suggesting, the most accurate usage is something of an oxymoron. If it is purely personal, I'm suggesting it is not religious. It may be strongly felt, it may be sincere, it may be emotional, it may be aesthetic, it might have great psychological meaning. But I would hesitate to say that it has religious meaning.[90]

Consistent with his "High Tradition and Little Traditions" classification, Katz divided the religious practices of Jews, and others, according to a hierarchy of religious authority. At the lower end of the hierarchy what falls off the spectrum of "religious" is what he terms "personal."

Green also pressed Katz regarding his terminology and his sources:

Q. Now sir, I believe that on direct examination you testified about Protestant, or Catholic and Protestant law; is that correct?

A. I don't believe I used that word, Protestant law. I might have said custom.[91]

Q. [A]re you sure you wouldn't find anything in the Torah . . . [a]bout the Judaic laws regarding monuments and burial practices?

A. No, you wouldn't. The only thing you would find there is a reference. But it has nothing, the stone that was placed on the grave of Rachel . . . But that certainly has no legal status. You don't get law from Torah. You get it from rabbinic writings.[92]

At the conclusion of his cross-examination of Katz, Green asked:

Q. The concepts of high and low traditions, are an academic theory, isn't that true?

A. Yes.

Q. Is there any reason why the United States Constitution should make these distinctions?

Mr. Rogow: Objection; calls for legal conclusion.

The Court: High and low what?

Mr. Green: High and low traditions.

The Court: Overruled. I'm not sure I understand the answer. Maybe he can.

The Witness: Yes, I can imagine times where it would be very important for the courts of this country to make just those distinctions.[93]

Green tried again:

Q. Does the First Amendment, based on your understanding recognize a hierarchy between high tradition and low tradition?

Mr. Rogow: Your Honor, I object.

The Court: Sustained.[94]

(Judge Ryskamp was inconsistent in sustaining objections to questions that asked the experts to draw legal conclusions. All of the experts were asked such questions. When there were objections by counsel, sometimes he permitted us to answer, sometimes he did not. I was unable to discern a pattern in these rulings.)

Daniel Pals served as the second expert witness for the City. Professor Pals is, like Judge Ryskamp, a graduate of Calvin College (B.A.). He also holds degrees from the University of Chicago (M.A., Ph.D.). Pals is professor of the Department of Religious Studies and the Department of History at the University of Miami. He is the author of many articles on religion and of a well-known and well-regarded introductory religious studies text, *Seven Theories of Religion*.[95]

Professor Pals's report in this case was intended, he said, "to offer an instructive commentary on religious traditions and practices that underlie the dispute," and "to enter an informed professional judgment on the application of these traditions to the issues that will need resolution under the law."[96] Like Katz, Pals provided the judge with a way to distinguish between legally protect-able religion and legally un-protect-able religion, although he used slightly different terminology to draw a line between elite and popular religion. In contrast to the Katz Report, the Pals Report was quite detailed, with frequent reference to authorities. He also provided a lengthy bibliography.

Pals begins his report by quoting the text of the Florida RFRA, and by making a few general observations about his interpretation of the statute.

Pals comments that "[a]ll can agree that the state has the right to place some burdens on the exercise of religion." He then gives examples of "substantial" and unsubstantial burdens: "For example, if a city or state were to disregard completely both Biblical precedent and unbroken orthodox tradition and move to the closure of Christian Churches on Sundays, clearly that action would impose directly on free religious exercise. The same would apply in the case of Judaism if all synagogues and temples were ordered closed." He concludes these preliminary observations with a comment on the effect of enforcement of the Cemetery regulations on the plaintiffs' actions: "That they are 'burdens' of a sort is undeniable, as is the fact that they are perceived by certain religious persons as *inconvenient or personally disconcerting*. That they rise to the level of a 'substantial' burden upon any Jew or Christian is a much stronger claim." Pals further concludes that the claimed burden on the plaintiffs' practices "fall[s] into a category nearer to that of modest and natural burdens, such as traffic laws and zoning ordinances." Pals was sanguine that the Boca Raton Cemetery Regulations did not substantially burden Jewish or Christian religious exercise—that it did not forbid what is, in his words, "integral and essential to religious tradition."[97] There is a clear hierarchy to his distinctions. Churches and synagogues are substantial—they are integral and essential—while plaintiffs' religious practices are insubstantial.

Pals's report, like Katz's, establishes criteria for determining what is, and what is not, in his words, "integral and essential to *a religious tradition*." While RFRA focuses on the burden on the individual, Pals shifts the focus to the "tradition." It was his judgment that in order to meet the burden of the statute the prohibited religious practice must be "integral and essential to the tradition." He proposed a series of four questions to determine the importance of a particular practice:

[I]n the case of any given practice or custom, we can make a reasonable determination by posing four main questions: 1) Is it asserted or implied in relatively unambiguous terms by an authoritative *sacred text*? 2) Is it clearly and consistently affirmed in *classic* formulations of doctrine and practice? 3) Has it been observed *continuously*, or nearly so, throughout the history of the tradition? 4) Is it consistently practiced *everywhere*, or almost such, in the tradition as we meet it in most recent times?[98]

Answers to these questions would, Pals continued in his Report, place a particular practice on a continuum from "essential and integral" to "marginal and tangential." "Essential and integral" practices are those that are textual, classic, ancient, and ubiquitous. These four criteria establish a dichotomy similar to that proposed by Katz to distinguish "high" and "little" traditions, without the explicit gender bias. (Pals denied, however, on cross-examination, when presented with the Katz classification, that his model set up the same kind of hierarchy as a "high" tradition/"little" tradition distinction would.)[99]

In his report, Pals asked each of his four questions with respect first to Judaism and then to Christianity. As to Judaism:

> What we find, then, both in the Hebrew Bible and the Biblical era is rather little on the subject beyond a single incident from the patriarchal era, with no prescriptive inference drawn. . . . Thus the clearest and most prominent voices in the tradition of Jewish theology insist that at best tombstones of any kind (let alone vertical pillars or hills of stone piles) ought not to be mandatory and need not be permanent in nature. They have neither theological nor ceremonial justification, and have in certain instances actually been discouraged or prohibited, rather than tolerated. . . . It is among . . . Ashkenazic European Jews that there developed in more recent times a broad tradition of customarily marking the graves of the dead with a tombstone. Since most American Jews are of Ashkenazic background, it is this rather recent tradition that has come to be a fairly common practice in America. Jewish tombstones thus represent a tradition that, while currently practiced in America, is by no means part of an ancient or continuous Jewish heritage.[100]

"Ashkenazic" describes Jews whose medieval cultural heritage is northern European and whose liturgical rites are derived from the Palestinian Talmud. "Sephardic" refers to Jews of Mediterranean heritage whose rites are traced to the Babylonian Talmud. On the eve of World War II, 90 percent of the world Jewish population was Ashkenazic.[101] Most American Jews are of Ashkenazic origin. Citing Rabbi Maurice Lamm on Jewish burial practice and the acceptability of small markers, as Katz did, Pals concluded with respect to Judaism that "[s]urely, it is significant that this contemporary authority on Jewish mourning, despite a contrary preference of his own, clearly recognizes that at [sic] no substantial burden to religious exercise, current Jewish custom on this matter can be readily adapted to pertinent cemetery regulations."[102]

As to Christianity, Pals begins in his Report by announcing that the sacred text is the Bible. Pals insisted throughout his Report and his testimony that, based on his reading of the Bible, Christians are interested in spiritual, not material things: "For the gospel writers, this startling and crucial event [the crucifixion] signals victory over death, and by natural implication, marks a turn away from the *pagan*, and even certain earlier Jewish, types of concern with burial or the gravesite [emphasis supplied]."[103] In typical Protestant fashion, Pals contrasts pagan, and, by implication Catholic,[104] practice from authoritative biblical practice:

> [Paul's teaching] directs Christian attention away from the state or cir-cumstances of the physical body after death, and turns it decisively toward something beyond this earth—the great day of resurrection and final judgment. What will happen to the body on the day of resurrection is mo-mentously important; how it is cared for or memorialized between the present moment is not a serious or enduring concern.

The church fathers, he said, "left no mandate that graves must be univer-sally marked in any one particular fashion, let alone with a vertical marker or monument."[105]

Dismissing medieval burial practices as the result of "the growing wealth of the church mingled with the piety and vanity of the aristocracy," Pals concluded:

> The tradition of Christian burial practice cannot provide a warrant for monuments as integral and essential to individual gravesites when for most of its long history, most Christians have had no such thing as a per-sonal grave even to mark. . . . To the degree that Christians and Jews ever embraced this tradition [the rural cemetery movement], it is clear that they did so not as in any way a religious obligation, but as *a matter of per-sonal taste*—and a preference rather strangely at odds with their own reli-gious traditions [emphasis supplied].[106]

What McGuckin saw as ancient, Pals sees as recent—or late—that is, as be-yond the authoritative practice of the first generations of Christians. The rural cemetery movement he sees as "a matter of personal taste."

At the trial, Pals amplified concerning his test:

> I was interested in getting a set of more or less abstract criteria in hand by which you could make reasonable judgments as to, let's call it the profile or the pattern of a religion. And from that you could then address the legal question of the burdens placed upon religion. . . . I find the metaphor of a circle or the image of a circle with, let us say, concentric rings or radii going out from the center to the edge the most useful one for me to understand the nature of religious traditions.[107]

Asked about Katz' high/low distinction, Pals responded:

> *A.* I would much rather work from language of center and periphery than from high and low. Because the natural inference people make from that language is, well, we're talking about clergy and theologians and well established traditions on the one hand, which have protection, and the minor practices of lay folk, which do not. . . . If you simply stay with the language of center and periphery, you're not inclined to say that one thing is better than another. You're simply saying that it is more central. . . .
>
> *Q.* But you're aware that Florida RFRA says that exercise of religion is protected regardless of whether it is central to or mandated by a particular religion. . . .
>
> *A.* Yes, it's interesting; that is a puzzling feature.[108]

At the end of a very lengthy cross-examination in which Mr. Green asked Pals to categorize a wide range of religious practices, Green asked Pals:

> *Q.* In your opinion would it be constitutional to give legal protection only to textually based, classic, continuously and everywhere practiced religion?
>
> *A.* No, I don't think that would be constitutional.[109]

No objection was made by the City lawyer to this question asking Pals to give a legal opinion.

After the conclusion of the City's case, I testified as a rebuttal witness for the plaintiffs. I hold both a J.D. and a Ph.D. from the University of Chicago. I have practiced law and I have taught religion at the undergraduate and graduate levels. At the time of the trial I was assistant professor of religion at Washington and Lee University. My expertise for the trial was based on my work concerning the phenomenology of religion in American legal contexts, including a book on the varying models of religion employed by justices of the Supreme Court in a case concerning the constitutionality of displaying a crèche in a civic Christmas display.[110]

My Report was short and conclusory. I strove to summarize only the most unexceptional of scholarly opinions concerning both the religious significance of practices regarding dead bodies and the shaping effect on religion of the legal regulation of religion in the United States. I did not attempt to construct a test for distinguishing legal religion from outlaw religion. I regarded that as the province of the judge. As with the other expert reports, my report was not entirely successful in deflecting controversy, and I was cross-examined with respect to the opinions there offered.

At the time of preparing my report, I had not seen the reports of the other experts and I was concerned, given the fact that I am a licensed attorney, to avoid appearing to testify as a legal expert. I had insisted to the plaintiffs' attorneys that I could not and would not testify either as to the proper interpretation of the Florida RFRA or, as I had never met or talked to them, as to whether these particular plaintiffs were substantially burdened in their exercise of religion. I felt I had no evidence on which to base an opinion as to the plaintiffs' burdens, but that, moreover, that conclusion, too, was a legal conclusion properly made by the judge. In the event, I was overscrupulous. The judge permitted Mr. Rogow, on cross, to ask me and the other experts our opinions as to both those questions.

My report, filed in December 1998 (and reproduced in Appendix B), addressed the question of "the religious importance of practices surrounding burial and memorializing the dead."[111] Unlike McGuckin and Broyde, I did not speak as an authority on either Judaism or Christianity. My Report, like those of Katz and Pals, attempted to speak out of the larger field of religious studies or comparative religions. I first summarized the generally accepted views of religion scholars with respect to a broad field of religious burial practice and the importance of practices surrounding death:

> Religion scholars would largely agree, however, that practices surrounding human death, while of enormous variety, are close to the heart of religion and of the religious imagination, however it is defined. In all human societies human death is marked, ritualized and memorialized, and those practices form a central and important part of religion. Funeral rites, through gestures, behavior, words, songs, material objects, meals, and treatment of the corpse, function
>
> - to serve the future life of the dead person,
> - to console the surviving relatives and friends;
> - and, to contribute to the reconstruction of and preservation of the community.[112]

I also discussed the dangers of collective descriptions such as "Christianity," "Judaism," "Catholicism," "Protestantism." I offered a short discussion of religious authority, ending with the following:

> While for the external observer religious beliefs and practices may be radically indeterminate, however, for the individual believer they may have tremendous authority and power. The practices described in the deposi-

tions in this action: the design, orientation and placing of markers and statues, whether explicitly religious or not, the covering of the grave, the planting of shrubs, ground cover and flowers, the concern for the overall appearance and convenience of a cemetery, and the visiting, praying, and attention to the needs of the deceased, may all be considered important religious practices in the context of a particular individual's religious life.[113]

I further attempted to place these questions in an American political and legal context, arguing that the legal disestablishment of religion means that no authority outside the individual can be legally recognized in the United States.[114] I concluded:

> On the basis of my reading and research in the study of religion generally and relying in particular on the works cited below, it is my opinion that practices associated with a burial site could be so important to the exercise of a particular person's religion that prohibition of such practices could substantially burden that person's exercise of his or her religion.[115]

My role at trial was different from that of the other experts, in part because I had witnessed the entire trial and my testimony fell at the end of the trial. By the last day of testimony, we had had a wide array of often conflicting testimony about Jewish and Christian burial practices. I had also worked with Jim Green in the evenings in preparing cross-examination questions for Professors Katz and Pals, a point brought out by Bruce Rogow in my cross-examination.[116] I believe that Jim Green hoped that I could somehow provide a synthesis of the expert testimony that would allow the judge to see the plaintiffs' practices as significant, but that would also give the judge some comfort in recognizing the plaintiffs' claims, comfort that he was not throwing open the doors to anyone with a colorable and sincere religious belief who wanted an exemption from any Florida statute. Along with Broyde and McGuckin, I was clearly unsuccessful both at bringing the judge to a real appreciation of the context and value of the plaintiffs' religious actions or at assuaging his concern that a decision for the plaintiffs would be a victory for anarchy.

I am afraid that the larger effect of my testimony, and of its placement at the end of the trial, may have been to confirm Judge Ryscamp in the view that the Florida RFRA, and other statutes of its genre, are unworkable and probably unconstitutional because they favor religiously motivated persons over nonreligiously motivated persons. In his oral opinion at the end of the trial Judge Ryskamp said:

It might be argued, and I think that one of the experts, Winnifred Sullivan, makes the argument that to even undergo such a test as Dr. Pals has done is a test of orthodoxy and, therefore prohibited by the constitution. It might be argued that to the extent that this statute, the Florida statute requires the Court to do such a thing [accept such a broad reading], if she's indeed correct, the statute might be unconstitutional.[117]

Judge Ryskamp's concern about the constitutionality of the statute is also reflected in a footnote to his written opinion in the case.[118] But the constitutionality of the Florida RFRA was not an issue at trial. The City had not challenged the constitutionality of the statute.

The first question I was asked at the trial by the plaintiffs' attorney, Jim Green, was: "Could you tell the Court, give the Court a very brief history of the history of Christianity as it relates to Orthodox and Catholic and the Reformation and development of modern religion in America?" In response to this daunting invitation to summarize all of Christian history and all of religion in America, I answered quickly, speaking to the judge: "I'll make this short." He replied: "Well, I think I've got some background on that, but it's got to be in the record. So go ahead."[119] This was a clue to a fact that I did not entirely appreciate at the time, namely, that Judge Ryskamp regarded himself as an expert on the history of Christianity. In a very real sense, although he said he enjoyed hearing from the experts, he acted at times as if he did not really need us. He himself was expert enough.

The following are excerpts from my instant and conventional thumbnail history of Christianity in the West:

My own interest, as I said, has been in church state matters. So when I give this history I'm going to do it from the point of view of someone who is interested in the role of religion and the state. Early Christianity, as I think you know, your Honor, it was, in effect, a persecuted sect within the Roman Empire, and it had no legal status. Beginning with the Emperor Constantine, Christianity became an imperial religion. And gradually from the time of Constantine spread throughout western Europe, developing into what is known ... as Medieval Christianity.... [W]estern Christianity was almost completely congruent with the culture of Western Europe. So it was both legally established as the church of everybody in Europe, and it was also what provided the main, imaginative symbols and stories that people, as a basis for people understanding their lives. Beginning with Luther and the Protestant and Catholic reformations, western Christianity then splits up.... With the move across the Atlantic to the United States, you might even describe this move as a sort of further disestablishment.[120]

I also attempted to describe the effect of the Reformation and the Enlightenment on modern Christian religious practice and belief, particularly in the United States. Jim Green asked me finally to explain what made American religion distinctive. (I do, naturally, wish that I could nuance some of this testimony on re-reading. I am sure that is true also of the other expert witnesses.)

In his direct examination of me Mr. Green asked me also to comment on the opinions of the City's expert witnesses. I argued that in the American context it was inappropriate to set up a hierarchy of religious practices because there are no established or even well-recognized religious authorities in the United States for the court to look to for criteria in determining where to place certain religious practices in such a hierarchy. I was, as a result, reluctant to come up with a rival test. I, like Broyde and McGuckin, emphasized the need for context. I was also asked to describe my impressions in my visits to the cemetery:

> [A]s I think some of the other expert witnesses have said, visiting the cemetery makes quite a difference, it's quite a different experience from simply looking at the photographs of individual graves. Because in looking at the whole one sees both the modesty of these religious expressions but also the extent of it. And as you go from grave to grave, you see the creation of small sacred spaces, small shrines, if you like, in some cases, which attempt in a way, I think, the way I would understand it, to express religion, free exercise of religion in a context which has become increasingly dominated by commercialization of American funeral and burial practices. So that the model of the memorial garden, the pressure to conform and everything look uniform, it seems to me, is being resisted by these plaintiffs through their expression of their religion; and their creation, through the use of both objects that would conventionally be thought of as religion such as religious statues, but also through the use of more universal symbols, such as flowers and protective fencing, to both create a memorial to the individual who's died, but also it's a sacred space which links each of them to their own religious tradition.[121]

On cross-examination, Mr. Rogow asked me repeatedly in different ways to draw the line between religion and not-religion. Quoting from my report and remarking on its emphasis on the individual as the center of au-

thority, Rogow asked me to characterize plaintiffs' practices as "personal."
I answered:

> They're personal in the sense that they are constructed on the occasion of
> the death of a particular individual and in the context of that individual's
> family. They are not personal in the sense that there is something that is
> just totally idiosyncratic and invented like a little private religion by the
> people who do this. And in terms of their relationship to the institutional
> church, individual shrines or local shrines gain their religious meaning
> and their importance because of their replication of shrines at other
> places. . . . All of these plaintiffs are working . . . within an idiom and a
> culture that suggests to them and gives them an array of symbols and sto-
> ries to work with. That's how individuals operate as religious individu-
> als. . . . Religious people use the materials at hand to create religious
> meaning.[122]

Again he returned to the limits:

> *Q.* In your report you say a person could be substantially burdened in the
> practice of his or her religion if his or her beliefs and practices surrounding
> human death were interfered with, correct; is that your statement?
>
> *A.* Yes.
>
> *Q.* Is there no limit—that's what troubled me about this sentence.
>
> *A.* This is the same question again.
>
> *Q.* And the same answer?
>
> *A.* Yes.
>
> *Q.* You simply don't know?
>
> *A.* That's right.
>
> *Q.* And you also say each individual is, in effect, the expert on his or her own
> religious belief, a life which may be an idiosyncratic assembly of beliefs, in-
> terpretations and practices?
>
> *A.* Yes.
>
> *Q.* And so does that mean that every person is the keeper of his or her own
> religious beliefs and traditions?
>
> *A.* I think that within the American constitutional scheme, constitutionally
> it's impossible for courts to recognize religious authority as defining ortho-
> dox practice and that, therefore, constitutionally courts have to look to the
> individual. But it doesn't mean that the individual is not seen in the context
> of the community.[123]

The point I hoped to make was that, on the one hand, answering the questions about "requirements" demanded a kind of deference to institutionalized religious authority that was fundamentally un-American, while, on the other, such a lack of formal authority did not sever all ties between the individual and the norms and practices of religious communities. The *Warner* plaintiffs, like all persons who are religiously motivated, were profoundly connected to a wider community, dead and alive.

CHAPTER 4

Legal Religion

THE FOLLOWING DAY, Friday, the attorneys gave their closing arguments and Judge Ryskamp announced his decision. (I was not present for this last day, and so rely entirely on the transcript for this.) Jim Green's closing began with a summary of the testimony of the various witnesses, emphasizing, as he did in his opening, the religiousness of the plaintiffs' actions within the context of their various religious traditions:

> It may well be difficult to draw a bright line around what is religious and what isn't. This case, as I think your Honor must realize by now, does not involve a fringe or marginal religious practice. Death is a religious event close to the heart of most religious traditions. It's been demonstrated, I think it is pretty un-rebutted, that it's close to the heart of the religious belief and practices of these individual plaintiffs. The death of important religious figures such as Jesus Christ is a defining event in the Christian tradition.[1]

Green also argued that the City had failed to show that conformity to the cemetery rules was compelled by financial or safety interests of the City's, or that the City had used the least restrictive means in furthering those interests. The plaintiffs' argument on this point was that maintenance and safety considerations were not without importance, but that they could be otherwise safely and economically accommodated:

Bruce Rogow began his closing for the City by quoting my testimony:

> At the end of the trial the last question that I asked of Winnifred Sullivan, I think, takes us to a very helpful point. I asked her what would the Boca Raton cemetery be like if we adopted your approach, which is that any religious shrine or any shrine that is put on these graves by people, and they say that they are motivated by their religious beliefs, what would the Boca Raton cemetery look like? And she said it would celebrate, maybe these are not the exact words, but it would celebrate the diversity of the religious beliefs in Boca Raton. And really what that told me was that the position that the plaintiffs are taking, and their experts are taking, is to create a situation where basically you would have cemetery anarchy.[2]

Rogow also argued that the plaintiffs could not be understood to have been burdened by the City's actions because they had, in effect, brought the burden on themselves when they violated the rules of the cemetery.

Paradoxically, considering the fact that RFRA was intended to reverse the Supreme Court's decision in *Smith* (the "peyote case," discussed earlier), Rogow argued in his closing that the majority opinion in *Smith* was the key to interpreting RFRA. And, notwithstanding the fact that the Florida RFRA was explicitly intended to go beyond both federal constitutional protection and the federal RFRA, he implied that the *Smith* rule, namely that neutral laws of general application are not a violation of the First Amendment, even if they burden religious practice, determines the meaning of the Florida statute. Rogow argued: "The bottom line of this case, it seems to me, is the first question the Court has to answer is whether or not a neutral rule that does not target religion . . . poses a substantial burden on the free of exercise of religion."[3] In other words, Rogow argued that no religious practice, however "high" or "compulsory" or "central," could trump a neutral law of general application. That was the holding of Justice Scalia's opinion in *Smith*, and that was the very rule intended to be reversed by both the federal and the Florida RFRA.

In his rebuttal closing, Green took a conciliatory tack, emphasizing the reasonableness of the plaintiffs in contrast to the intransigence of the City:

> [I]f the City had . . . placed some reasonable restrictions on the size and scope, we would say fine, we probably wouldn't be here. If the City had passed the grandfather clause, which was presented to your honor, which was defeated on a 3-2 vote by the City of Boca Raton, which would have allowed existing decorations and memorials and ground coverings to stay, we wouldn't be here. . . . But the City did, we contend, it went to the fringe, it prohibited all vertical expression. In fact, by the wording of its own regulations it prohibits any religious symbols anywhere. It limits the expression on the flat markers to name, rank and other identifying lettering. . . . In essence the City seems to be arguing that plaintiffs cannot be substantially burdened if they violate the very rule that substantially burdens them. It's a Catch 22. In essence, the City is asking plaintiffs to take responsibility for the City's burdening of their religion.[4]

The plaintiffs, Green insisted, were not extremists. They were certainly not anarchists in any conventional understanding of that term. It was the City, he implied, that had taken an extreme and unreasonable position.

Immediately following the closing arguments, Judge Ryskamp issued an oral opinion from the bench finding against the plaintiffs. (Six months later he filed a written opinion in the case which is reproduced in Appendix C.) The City agreed immediately not to remove anything until the final written order was published by the judge. That agreement has continued through the appeals process so that nothing has been removed from the cemetery by the City as of this date. (See photographs showing the cemetery in March 2004, five years after the trial.)

In his oral opinion Judge Ryskamp was cautious. He went on for some time, reviewing the evidence, and ruminating about the applicable law, beginning with the following caveat to himself:

> We . . . know that the enforcement and application of the First Amendment, especially as it involves free exercise or establishment, is one of the most difficult tasks that the courts face. The Supreme Court is often divided on it. . . . And it's rather awesome that one judge at the District Court level is going to resolve this issue for all time. But it's got to start somewhere, so we'll take our best shot at it.[5]

Turning to the case at hand, Ryskamp emphasized the public nature of the property:

> Put aside religion, put aside anything else. What you have is some public property. And the City, well within the scope of its municipal functions, decides to say we're going to provide a cemetery here for people of this municipality. . . . When I went down there on Friday I walked all through the cemetery. I had no business there—well, I guess indirectly I did. But if I were anyone else, you could walk through that cemetery at will and nobody would stop you because it's public property. I think that is one of the first issues that we have to confront and one of the issues that the plaintiffs have trouble with is I think some of them think they own that little piece of land. And they don't. They don't own that piece of land. They're not paying taxes on it.[6]

Paying taxes gives you rights. And government property is special. The judge came back to the Supreme Court's decision in the *Lyng*[7] case several times. He reiterated the Supreme Court's holding in *Lyng* that the government can do pretty much what it wants with its land, even if the effect of what it does is to virtually destroy a historic religious practice, in that case the use of the high country for Native American vision quests, as long as the destruction of religion is not the explicit target of the government action.[8]

Ryskamp was also expansive in his oral ruling in expressing his views about religion, both his own and those of the plaintiffs:

I would say at the outset, of all the plaintiffs who testified and the depositions that I've read, I believe that all of them have sincere religious beliefs. This does not require any testimony of orthodoxy, because orthodoxy is not any issue. . . . In listening to the testimony, the views expressed weren't necessarily my views but I recognize them all as valid religious beliefs that are entitled to protection under the law. I'm sure that if I express my religious views some people would say that's very weird and that's very strange, you know, I can't argue with that. That's unorthodox. And that's what makes up religion, is that we all have a right in this country to have whatever religious views we choose to have.[9]

Ryskamp's opinion is, apparently, that religion is a matter of "views." And rights are attached to "views," not to the actions that one takes. Again, one sees a typically protestant (small "p") focus on religious opinions rather than religious acts. It should be enough, from this perspective, that one's opinions are free.

Ryskamp was less impressed with the views of the experts, particularly the experts for the plaintiffs. While comfortable in giving his American imprimatur to the views of the plaintiffs, he found the views of the experts less entitled to respect. As to the testimony of Michael Broyde, he said:

I think that he overstated his argument regarding a monument or a pillar, and citing from Genesis 35:20 where Jacob put a pillar on the gravestone of his wife. And then he concludes or infers—in fact he says: "Thus one can state with a high degree of confidence that the obligation to place a marker of some sort is quite ancient. And that one who buries without any marker is severely in violation of Jewish law and tradition." Obviously the patriarchs played a very important role in the Torah, what the Christian religion would refer to as the Old Testament. However, even as the point I made with him, Jacob had two wives and two concubines. Certainly we would not say that this is a mandate that we have multiple wives and concubines on the side.[10]

After discussing Jacob's sins for a while, the judge went on to compare Broyde's views with Katz's, concluding that neither had proven that Jewish graves were governed by religious law. Neither Broyde's status as a rabbi and as a legal authority within the American Orthodox religious community nor Katz's status as a kohen and expert on Asian Judaism held much weight with Ryskamp, who seemed to regard his own reading of the Hebrew Bible as of equal value.

As for John McGuckin, Ryskamp seemed to have taken against him entirely. What had impressed the rest of us—McGuckin's skillful invoking of the practices of the early church and evident concern with representing the religious sensibility of the Catholic and Orthodox traditions—apparently left the judge unimpressed. Ryskamp, in his oral opinion, continued to exhibit a highly protestant religious sensibility:

> I don't know how much I would recognize Dr. McGuckin's expert opinion. Not that he isn't expert in religion, but he seems to more or less make pronouncements that are not—in other words, he feels like he's an end to himself. I don't need any authority to say that I'm the expert and I will give you the opinion. And it's hard to determine who's validating this opinion. Whether they are learned treatises that recognize this. But he's obviously a very scholarly man. . . . He said much of the Catholic burial service turns around the notions of honoring the dead body as a sacred thing and of consecrating the gravesite as a hallowed place. A dead body is a sacred thing. Well, I guess that could be a valid religious belief. A living body generally is not considered sacred. But it becomes sacred when it dies? That's an unusual attitude. I don't know where he gets that from Catholicism.[11]

And yet several of the plaintiffs had said the very same thing. As with Broyde, McGuckin received no points for being a cleric or for having a position of authority within the tradition. Ryskamp relied on his own, largely mistaken, "knowledge" of Catholic teaching, rather than McGuckin's. Arguably Broyde and McGuckin were the only people in the trial with any claim to conventional religious authority and their testimony was almost entirely discounted by the judge, perhaps *because* they were clerics. They represented an authority without legal recognition in the United States.[12]

The judge read part of my opinion from my report aloud and commented: "A rather broad definition allowing any personal view to be recognized. And in some respects I agree with that. As long as it does not affect anyone else, anybody can have any religious views they want, no matter how idiosyncratic they might be. The question is what happens when it involves public land, public regulations and other people." Again he focused on "views"; he dismissed my testimony as "rather broad" and "more like that of a lawyer."[13] I, too, lacked recognizable authority. Broyde and McGuckin were, arguably, too religious. I was not religious enough.

Ryskamp liked Pals and his approach: "Pals seemed to have done a more organized or structured analysis of this problem in light of the statutes."[14]

He liked the fact that Pals's scheme comprised a set of numbered questions that could together provide a reliable and clear standard for enforcement of the statute. And perhaps he liked the fact that he and Pals shared a personal religious orientation, both being from the reformed Protestant church. His approval of Pals showed in his conclusion about the nature of the plaintiffs' activities:

> And I would conclude from the expert witnesses that I heard . . . that if I were to apply the test as I understand it under the Florida RFRA, that this certainly, these views aren't central, they are not mandatory, and they are peripheral or marginal. . . . I would conclude on the basis of the facts based upon the testimony of all the witnesses and following the expert witnesses, that it does not provide a substantial burden. . . . So with regard to the FRFRA and with regard to the First Amendment Free Exercise Clause, I believe that the City regulations are acting in conformity to the First Amendment requirements.[15]

And finally: "[T]he bottom line of this is that I don't believe, certainly on the issues that I've talked about under RFRA and the First Amendment, that plaintiffs are entitled to relief. I believe that the City has the right to make these restrictions."[16] It is, in the end, the City, rather than the plaintiffs, that have rights, according to the judge.[17]

In his written Findings of Fact and Conclusions of Law (published five months later, and reprinted here as Appendix C),[18] Judge Ryskamp was more circumspect, apparently conforming his conclusions more carefully to the language of the Florida RFRA. After reviewing the legislative history of the Florida RFRA, he arrived at an interpretation of the statute and his own test for determining what was a legally qualifying exercise of religion:

> Thus, the Court concludes that in order to establish a cognizable claim under the Florida RFRA, a plaintiff must demonstrate a substantial burden on conduct that, while not necessarily compulsory or central to a larger system of religious beliefs, nevertheless *reflects some tenet, practice or custom of a larger system of religious beliefs.* Conduct that reflects a purely personal preference regarding religious exercise will not implicate the protections of the Florida RFRA [emphasis supplied].[19]

Plaintiffs, he said, were required to prove that their conduct "reflects some tenet, practice or custom of a larger system of religious belief." Excluded from Florida RFRA protection is what he called "conduct that reflects a purely personal preference."

The distinction Ryskamp drew is elusive. It is both difficult to establish with the available testimony, and symptomatic of the constraining nature of the available language. If the plaintiffs' activities fall into the second category, that is, that they are understood to reflect merely "a purely personal preference," then one could argue that the modern disestablishment and "privatization" of religion has created forms of religion that *cannot* be legally protected, because they are insufficiently institutionalized. Personal preference in religious matters is arguably exactly what the First Amendment religion clauses guarantee.

In discussing the meaning of the Florida RFRA in his published opinion, Judge Ryskamp began with the rather odd assertion that

> [T]he plain language of the Florida RFRA implies that a practice must be more than a matter of purely personal preference regarding religious exercise in order to fall within the statute's ambit. That is, the fact that the Florida RFRA explicitly states that a practice need not be "compulsory or central to a larger system of religious beliefs" in order to be subject to protection of the statute, suggests that the practice must have some basis in a larger system of religious beliefs.[20]

Judge Ryskamp here read the words of the Florida statute to have exactly the opposite meaning to that which the legislature seems to have clearly said.[21] He used the words of the definitions section of the Florida RFRA to contract rather than to expand the reach of the statute. Ryskamp's motivation for this plainly oxymoronic exercise is revealed at the end of that section of the opinion: "In the context of the Cemetery's Regulations, the plaintiffs' proposed construction of the Florida RFRA would lead to cemetery anarchy."[22] He, like Rogow, was afraid that a ruling for the plaintiffs would be a ruling for chaos, and this fear distorts the logic of his opinion.

Ryskamp moved then, in his opinion, to an inquiry into the possible intention of the framers of RFRA laws, federal and state, with respect to this problem of defining religion. (Ryskamp was careful to appear particularly attentive to the intentions of the Florida legislature because *Warner* was the first case in which the Florida law was being judicially interpreted. He had no Florida precedent on which to rely for guidance, and federal courts are usually deferential to state courts in interpreting state statutes.) The federal RFRA, like the Florida Act, had explicitly prohibited government action that "substantially burdened the exercise of religion." The federal RFRA, however, as discussed above, contained no definition of "exercise of religion" (see Appendix A).

During the short period that the federal RFRA was in force, federal courts around the country were split in their opinion as to how to limit the reach of the Act, which appeared, on its face, to give religiously motivated individuals an exemption from any law that they deemed burdensome to their exercise of religion. A substantial number of federal appellate jurisdictions had limited the federal RFRA's application to religious practices that were "compulsory or central to a larger system of religious belief."[23] Florida's law had addressed this set of decisions by adding a definitions section to the Act that explicitly denied that any such limitation was intended. The definition of "exercise of religion" given by the Florida RFRA was "an act or refusal to act that is substantially motivated by a religious belief, whether or not the religious exercise is compulsory or central to a larger system of religious belief" (as explained above). This disclaimer put the problem faced by the interpreters of the federal RFRA right back in Ryskamp's lap.

In reviewing the possible meaning of the federal RFRA, Ryskamp quoted Representative Stephen Solarz, the original sponsor of the federal bill, who said that he had tried to find a line between protect-able and non protect-able religious practices. On the one hand, he said:

> Were Congress to go beyond the phrasing chosen by the drafters of the First Amendment by specifically confining the scope of this legislation to those practices compelled or proscribed by a sincerely held religious belief in all circumstances, we would run the risk of excluding practices which are generally believed to be exercises of religion worthy of protection. For example, many religions do not require their adherents to pray at specific times of day, yet most members of Congress would consider prayer to be an unmistakable exercise of religion.[24]

On the other, Solarz continued:

> To say that the "exercise of religion" might include acts not necessarily compelled by a sincerely held religious belief is not to say that any act merely consistent with, or not proscribed by one's religion would be an exercise of religion. As I pointed out in my testimony, it would not be reasonable to argue, for example, that a person whose religion did not proscribe the possession of a machine gun had a free exercise right to own one notwithstanding applicable federal laws.[25]

While explicitly rejecting an interpretation that would protect only acts "compelled or proscribed by a sincerely held religious belief," Solarz opens a wide field between what he would term "an unmistakable exercise of religion," such as prayer, whether or not religiously regulated and compelled, and what he terms acts "merely consistent with, or not proscribed by one's religion," such as "possession of a machine gun."

Groping for a way to place boundaries on protect-able religion under the Florida Act, Judge Ryskamp's conclusion in the *Warner* case was that Solarz's testimony showed that "conduct merely consistent with or not proscribed by one's religious tradition does not amount to an 'exercise of religion' under the Federal RFRA. In other words, the federal RFRA was not intended to protect conduct that amounts to a matter of purely personal preference regarding religious exercise."[26] Ryskamp, in effect, seemed to equate plaintiffs' actions with that category of actions that Solarz illustrates with the example of a person whose possession of a machine gun was not prescribed by his religion.

Ryskamp went on to conclude that:

> [T]he fact that Florida RFRA explicitly states that a practice need not be "compulsory or central to a larger system of religious beliefs," in order to be subject to the protection of the statute, suggests that the practice must have some basis in a larger system of religious beliefs. . . . If any act motivated by a sincerely held religious belief were protected under the Florida RFRA, then it adds nothing to the meaning of the statute to say that the act need not be compulsory or central to a larger system of religious beliefs. It is only where the act is presumed to have some basis in a larger system of religious beliefs that the qualification that the act need not be compulsory or central to such a system has any meaning. In short, in order to give effect to all the statutory language, the "exercise of religion" must mean conduct that, while not necessarily compulsory or central to a larger system of religious beliefs, nevertheless reflects some tenet, practice or custom of a larger system of religious beliefs.[27]

Reaching for some limiting language, Ryskamp here placed the emphasis on "a larger system of religious beliefs," rather than on "not necessarily compulsory or central," as the Florida legislative history would suggest was their intent. In doing so, Ryskamp added a new layer of language to the already murky definitional field: He added that protect-able religion is only that which "reflects some tenet, practice or custom of a larger system of religious beliefs." This language is also rather slippery, though. It is hard to imagine any even remotely religious practice that could not arguably be understood to "reflect some tenet, practice or custom of a larger system of religious beliefs." Certainly the practices of the plaintiffs in the *Warner* case would seem to reflect just that. Indeed it is hard to take seriously

Ryskamp's claim that he is actually applying any of these definitions to the evidence in the case, rather than simply going through the motions of doing so in order to rationalize what he has already concluded about the plaintiffs' activities and the necessary limitations on the reach of the Florida RFRA.

Whether one adopts Solarz's language or Ryskamp's, there would seem to be a good deal of room to maneuver between prayer and carrying machine guns—between actions that are "not necessarily compulsory or central" and those that are a matter of "purely personal preference." Yet that was the field in which this trial took place. The Florida federal court had treated the demand for a statutory definition of religion as a brand new one, requiring the crafting of a new test determining the substantiality of protected religion under Florida law. But there remains a strange disjunction between the tests and the evidence at trial.

Having determined the test that he would use to measure the plaintiffs' actions against the language of the statute, Ryskamp then proposed to use Pals's four criteria to determine whether the plaintiffs' actions met his test: "If a practice meets all four of these criteria, it can be considered central to the religious tradition. If the practice meets one or more of these criteria, it can be considered a tenet, custom or practice of the religious tradition. If the practice meets none of these criteria, it can be considered a matter of personal preference regarding religious exercise."[28] After reviewing the testimony at trial using the framework of the Pals test, he concluded that none of the plaintiffs' actions met the test. None reflected, in Ryscamp's words "some tenet, practice or custom of a larger system of religious belief." He achieved this rather incredible point by focusing, as did the lawyers for the City, on "verticality":

> In sum, nowhere in the sacred texts, doctrines, traditions or customs of either the Jewish or Christian faiths can the principle be found that grave markers or religious symbols should be displayed *vertically* rather than horizontally. The primary objective of grave markers in the Jewish tradition—to demarcate and prevent the grave from being walked upon—can be achieved with either horizontal or *vertical* grave markers. Similarly, the primary objectives of decorating graves with religious symbols in the Christian tradition—to foster the community's awareness of the deceased and to give witness to the deceased's Christian life—can be achieved with either horizontal or *vertical* religious symbols. Therefore, the Court concludes that while marking graves and decorating them with religious symbols constitute customs or practices of the plaintiffs' religious traditions, the plaintiffs' desire to maintain *vertical* grave markers and religious

symbols reflects their personal preference with regard to decorating graves [emphasis supplied].[29]

In spite of all his protests about the freedom Americans have with respect to their beliefs, by reducing plaintiffs' religious activities to "verticality," and thereby excluding the cultural forms by which such "verticality" is achieved, Judge Ryskamp was able to offer an expert opinion as to what "Christianity" and "Judaism" in general "require" with respect to their adherents. Furthermore, he did so in such a way as to exclude the plaintiffs' expressed objectives from the inner circle of "*primary* objectives" of their religious traditions.

Judge Ryskamp's decision was appealed by the plaintiffs to the Court of Appeals for the Eleventh Circuit. The plaintiffs were represented on appeal by H. Douglas Laycock, a distinguished First Amendment lawyer and professor of law at the University of Texas.[30] The City was represented on appeal by Bruce Rogow, as at trial. A three-judge panel of the Eleventh Circuit heard oral argument in the case. In its October 1, 2001, decision, because Judge Ryskamp's opinion presented the first time that the Florida RFRA had been interpreted in a published opinion, the federal appeals court deferred to the Florida Supreme Court for guidance in interpreting the statute, in a legal procedure known as "certification." Announcing that "[a]s the circumstances of this case demonstrate, the breadth of protection afforded by the state of Florida under state law can determine the outcome of this case as well as having wide ranging and profound implications for Florida," the Eleventh Circuit certified the following questions regarding interpretation of the Florida RFRA to the Florida Supreme Court:

1. Does the Florida Religious Freedom Restoration Act broaden, and to what extent does it broaden, the definition of what constitutes religiously motivated conduct protected by law beyond the conduct considered protected by the decisions of the United States Supreme Court?

2. If the Act does broaden the parameters of protected religiously motivated conduct, will a city's neutral, generally-applicable ordinance be subjected to strict scrutiny by the courts when the ordinance prevents persons from acting in conformity with their sincerely held religious beliefs, but the acts the persons wish to take are not 1) asserted or implied in relatively unambiguous terms by an authoritative sacred text, or 2) clearly and consistently affirmed in classic formulations of doctrine and practice, or 3) observed continuously, or nearly so, throughout the history of that religion, or 4) consistently observed in the tradition in recent times?[31]

The *Warner* case has now presented to a succession of three courts the question of how religion ought to be defined for the purposes of the Florida RFRA. Surprisingly, perhaps, these courts have very little precedent on which to rely.[32] One has the sense in reading the opinions of these courts that for each the problem of definition is presented as a brand new question. While the Florida RFRA, in particular, is recent, of course, and therefore naturally presents new problems of interpretation, what may be surprising to some is that the more general question—how religion ought to be understood for purposes of U.S. laws concerning religion (and there are many)[33]— also seems new to these courts. There is no accepted legal way of talking in the United States about the vast array of religious beliefs and practices that are represented. There is no accepted legal way of navigating the definitional ground that lies between the *Warner* plaintiffs' inclusive and expansive focus on individual motivation and context, on the one hand, and the City's restrictive attention to the mandates of institution and text, on the other.

American courts have always been shy about entering this arena, and with good reason. There are dozens of instances in which judges have expressed concern about being asked to pass judgment on religion. One sees expressed in these disclaimers both a feeling of incompetence and a feeling of impropriety. Take, for example, these quotations from leading cases:

> [I]t is not within the judicial ken to question the centrality of particular beliefs or practices to a faith, or the validity of particular litigants' interpretations of those creeds.[34]

> Particularly in this sensitive area, it is not within the judicial function and judicial competence to inquire whether the petitioner or his fellow worker more correctly perceived the commands of their common faith. Courts are not arbiters of scriptural interpretation.[35]

> Courts will find themselves taking sides in religious schisms if they must opine on matters of religious obligation.[36]

> Heresy trials are foreign to our Constitution. Men may believe what they cannot prove. They may not be put to the proof of their religious doctrines or beliefs. Religious experiences which are as real as life to some may be incomprehensible to others.[37]

These examples could be multiplied many times over.

Who is to say what legally counts as religion in the United States? Should courts and legislatures be doing so at all? One reading of the First

Amendment would suggest that when the government gets into the business of defining religion, it gets into the business of establishing religion. The result is necessarily discriminatory. To define is to exclude, and to exclude is to discriminate. Affirmative discrimination demands a powerful defense in American constitutional jurisprudence, as recent cases show, even when the category is race, where arguably the best U.S. case can be made for affirmative discrimination.

One of the most interesting lines of cases in the Supreme Court addressing the definitional question relates to the exemption from military service for conscientious objectors. Over the years the wording of the Selective Service Act was modified and reinterpreted to expand exemption from an initial restriction to members of the historically pacifist churches—Mennonite, Amish, and so on—to anyone who has a conscientious objection to war, whether religiously based in any conventional sense or not.[38] But, even in its expansive mode, conscientious exemption, a relatively unexceptional privilege historically given to religiously motivated persons by statute (that is, not a constitutionally mandated one), raises issues of discrimination. The Supreme Court held in 1971 that exemption did not extend to one who objected to a particular war, rather than to all war.[39]

The role of scholarship in formally assisting courts in arriving at these decisions has, as in the *Warner* case, not always been illuminating. There are many judicial opinions that consider the religiousness of a particular activity or opinion. In *U.S. v. Seeger*, a conscientious objection case, Justice Tom Clark, speaking for a unanimous Court, expanding the reach of the Selective Service Act exemption, wrote, "We believe this construction embraces the ever-broadening understanding of the modern religious community."[40] He then proceeded to quote from the writings of liberal Protestant theologians Paul Tillich and John A. T. Robinson, the documents of Vatican II, and David Muzzey, then the leader of the Ethical Culture Movement.[41] Langdon Gilkey, a leading liberal theologian, testified in one of the creationism cases.[42] But *Africa v. Pennsylvania*, a 1981 Third Circuit opinion considering the religiousness of a prisoner's dietary requests motivated by his membership in MOVE, is more typical in citing only other court opinions, and law review articles for the most part. The court, citing the need to move beyond theistic approaches, announced that it favored a definition by analogy, and then concluded that MOVE was not a religion, "having concluded that MOVE does not deal with 'ultimate ideas.'"[43] Neither approach seems helpful. Justice Clark's approach would suggest the need for an endless and ever-expanding list of "experts," while the Third Circuit's approach simply avoids the opinions of experts altogether.

The experts in the *Warner* case were asked to do two things. We were asked whether the plaintiffs' practices were what they claimed to be—that is, whether they were authentic Christian and Jewish religious practices. We were also asked how courts should generally distinguish which practices are sufficiently important to count in a scheme for the legal protection of the free exercise of religion. This chapter will return to the testimony at trial with a view to considering the various models of religion that were in use, first reconsidering the adduced evidence and the models implicit in that process, then turning to the models offered by the experts and the court. (The next chapter will consider the implications of the difficulties inherent in these models for laws protecting religious freedom.) The multiplicity and mutual incompatibility of the understandings of religion displayed in the *Warner* trial only underline the difficulties presented to the American legal system by RFRA, and by other laws that purport to use religion as a category for discrimination among persons. For the most part, legal academics, lawyers, legislators, judges, and theorists of religious freedom have simply used "religion" as a placeholder in a sentence, finessing the awkwardness and messiness of what lurks there.

All the *Warner* experts found themselves in the situation of being asked to offer opinions at a level of certainty and specificity they were not comfortable with—in a field in which it is notoriously difficult to find agreement. The scholarly study of religion is famously split between those who favor a scientific, and those who favor a humanistic, approach. At its most polarized, the scientists accuse the humanists of being crypto-theologians with apologetic agendas, while the humanists accuse the scientists of being reductionist wannabe sociologists, political scientists, neuroscientists, or economists.[44] All the religion experts in the *Warner* case on both sides would probably be considered on the humanistic end of the spectrum. In other words, our previous work, for the most part, had been work "interpreting" religion, not work using "scientific" methods of investigation. It could be argued that the humanistic approach is the only possible approach in such a context because a scientific approach would have as its object the reducing of religious motivation to naturalistic explanations, thereby defining out of existence the very phenomenon intended for protection by statutes such as the Florida RFRA. Not even the City was trying to do that. Indeed one might also argue that limiting our explanations to humanistic ones made our task impossible. Humanistic explanations are by their very nature historically bound, while laws about religion demand a trans-historical field, one that could only be defined by an established religious authority.

All the religion experts had written about religion in various contexts. The contrast between Daniel Pals's trial testimony in the *Warner* case and his published work is most striking. His 1996 *Seven Theories of Religion*, a widely used undergraduate textbook on religion, summarizes and compares the classic theories of E. B. Tylor, J. G. Frazer, Sigmund Freud, Émile Durkheim, Karl Marx, Mircea Eliade, E. E. Evans-Pritchard, and Clifford Geertz.[45] In the comments he makes on the work of these theorists in the book, Daniel Pals is expansive in considering the possible range of human religious behavior. He finds scholars divided as to how to "explain" religion but to have a remarkable consensus as to a definition of religion. They seem to agree, he thinks, that religion is "belief and behavior associated in some way with a supernatural realm, a sphere of divine or spiritual beings." Pals concludes his book surveying these great theorists of religion with this observation: "[R]eligion in the end seems to be a matter not of impersonal processes that can be known with certainty because they have been scripted by the laws of nature, but of personal beliefs and behaviors that can only be plausibly explained because they have arisen from complex, partly free and partly conditioned choices of human agents."[46] This description of human religious behavior is similar to those Pals has given in other contexts and very close to those of the plaintiffs' religion experts. It is at odds with Pals's insistence at trial that objects have "independent religious significance" "instinctively" understood by all observers and that religious events could be mapped using a center and periphery model. His book is also more in line with contemporary theories of religious motivation.[47]

The City worked from several theories about religion in its cross-examination of the plaintiffs and in the presentation of expert testimony. The City wanted to show that the plaintiffs' behavior was "personal" or "idiosyncratic," even heterodox. Rogow also, in an unconscious play to the decline theory of American religious history,[48] seemed at times to be trying to show that the plaintiffs were not as religious as they asserted; that they did not attend church or synagogue with sufficient frequency; or, that they did not consult the proper religious authorities. The City's strategy was to show that the plaintiffs' practices were simply choices, consumer choices, decorating choices, if you like, not religiously mandated behavior. The City offered tests by which the judge could rationalize a conclusion that what plaintiffs were doing was not really religious or was not really religious in an important way.

"There's *no genuine religious reason* for insisting on displaying a religious symbol upright rather than lying flat [emphasis supplied]. There is absolutely *no religious significance* to most of the vertical decorations, even though the appellants have attempted to clothe their decorations with personal religious significance [emphasis supplied]." Thus did Bruce Rogow, echoing his cross-examination of the plaintiffs at the trial, dismiss the plaintiffs' claims to the local press after the most recent round of appeals.[49] What would count as a "genuine" religious reason or as "religious significance" for him? A threat of martyrdom or of instant excommunication for disobedience?

The City's position at the trial implies that only language in a sacred text somewhere that says that God himself demands that Jews, Protestants, and Catholics all be buried with vertical monuments over their graves would constitute sufficient evidence of the religious significance of the plaintiffs' practices and the consequent burden to them if they were to be prohibited. Even had the plaintiffs been able to produce such evidence, however, such religious authority has often been insufficient in past free exercise cases. The plaintiffs in the *Smith* case were unsuccessful although they asserted that peyote was *the* sacrament of the Native American Church, attested to by tradition and text.[50] Mr. Reynolds was unsuccessful although he asserted that Mormon written revelation declared that he would be damned if he were prohibited from practicing polygamy.[51] The Supreme Court itself agreed in its decision in the *Lyng* case that defacing of the high country in California through the construction of a logging road could entirely destroy the religion of the indigenous peoples of that area—and yet that was insufficient.[52] Yet the implication persisted during the *Warner* trial that there was theoretically somewhere evidence that would suffice. The implication was that the *Warner* plaintiffs' faithful obedience to a nonnegotiable institutionalized textual authority would escape being labeled a "purely personal preference." The existence of such an authority would also, it was implied, prevent "cemetery anarchy." (The fear of anarchy is reinforced by an almost hysterical amicus brief filed in the Florida Supreme Court in the *Warner* case by the Florida League of Cities. The League's brief details a multitude of Florida laws that would be at risk under an expansive reading of the Florida RFRA and asserts that "the extreme construction of FRFRA offered by Plaintiffs will lead to unconstitutional and absurd results by effectively creating a separate system of laws for religiously motivated persons.")[53]

Bruce Rogow may have been the most dogmatic and consistent theorist of religion in the courtroom. Judge Ryskamp, in contrast, exhibited multiple personae with respect to religion. Sometimes religion was whatever anyone said it was and the only test was "sincerity." Sometimes religion was defined by the Bible, individually interpreted. Sometimes religion consisted of the very arguments being had before him, what he called "talking theology." At times, Ryskamp even appeared to be close to throwing up his hands at the magnitude of the task before him and to have accepted Pals's test as simply one way out of the morass. If religion was whatever anyone said it was, the statute was unworkable, and he did not feel it was his place to simply dismiss an act of the Florida legislature as nonsense. Religion therefore had to be measured and bounded by an expert test—and Pals's was as good as any, and better than most in terms of form. I think that for Ryskamp there was no middle ground. Perhaps had the plaintiffs' experts been able and willing to express their opinions in the form of tests with numbered criteria they might have been more useful to the judge and there-fore to the plaintiffs. But it was hard to believe, given his other comments, that Ryskamp really believed in this testing of orthodoxy.

The plaintiffs themselves spoke largely out of a family-based religious sensibility. The authorities to whom they most often referred were mem-bers of their families. Their concern was for the souls of their dead rela-tives, the comfort of the living, and fidelity to a larger religious community. The compulsion to do what they did came not from religious leaders, their own or those of more remote hierarchies, or from texts directly, but from the sometimes inchoate yet often culturally structured logic of their indi-vidual contexts and situations. They went about assembling statues, Stars of David, crosses, plantings, benches, and fences with determination and with a clear sense of what was necessary, of what ought to be done. The items were carefully selected with an effort to improvise within the reli-gious palette with which each was familiar, but the improvisation, contra Rogow, was not simply "personal preference," in the consumerist sense of the word. There was indeed a sense in which they had no "choice." They had to do what they did.

The testimony of the religion experts displayed the broad spectrum of humanistic religious studies. Together we had studied a variety of religions from a variety of perspectives. We were insiders and outsiders, structural-ists and post-structuralists, particularists and universalists. We taught at seminaries, state universities, and private colleges and universities. Had we been in a seminar together, we might have had much in common and much to learn from one another. Roughly speaking, though, the American ad-versary system magnified two starkly divergent views of religion, of law, and of how to talk about religion in a secular legal context. In both our re-ports and our trial testimony, expert witnesses for the plaintiffs strove to fold the plaintiffs' stories into an expansive, complex, compelling, and con-stantly changing religious history, one in which the sacred and profane are tightly related, not easily distinguished, and always dependent on the ambiguities of language and human motivation—one in which the individual riffs on a tradition rather than one in which the individual obeys authorities. Expert witnesses for the defendant, on the other hand, accepting a hard-edged separationist ideology, obligingly attempted to devise bright line tests for the judge. They attempted to exclude the plaintiffs' activities from a trans-historical religious core by sharply dichotomizing the sacred and the profane in order to identify and limit protected religious exercise under the Florida RFRA.

The plaintiffs' religious imaginations and the memorials themselves are less determined than the expert academic polarization would suggest. Although disruptive in a sense to the clean modernist aesthetic of the new part of the cemetery, the nonconforming memorials in the Boca Raton cemetery evince a religious sensibility that is at once modern and postmodern. They are of a piece both with the undifferentiated and the separationist model. They participate both in a neo-Jeffersonian restraint about public religion and a late modern florescence of the religious into the public sphere. There is in that place a tension between reason and desire, between certainty and the terror of the unknown, between order and chaos. The Boca Raton memorials are both specific to the religious traditions of the various plaintiffs—Jewish, Catholic, and Protestant—and yet strangely alike. Statues of the Sacred Heart, Stars of David, plastic flowers, crosses, all flourish in an egalitarian and democratic brotherhood, free in a sense and yet ordered and bounded by modern secular law.

By the time the trial started, the key issue in the *Warner* case was how legally to characterize the plaintiffs' actions. There were few factual disputes. To be sure, the plaintiffs said that the City let them do it and the City said that they did not give such permission. But the resolution of that question was of little legal significance because the resolution did not affect the legality of the regulations under the Florida RFRA and their constitutionality under the religion clauses of the First Amendment. In any event, most of the people in the courtroom believed that the City workers had in some sense tolerated, if they did not outright encourage the rule breaking. Further, what the workers did could only affect enforcement with respect to the existing grave decorations. The larger issue concerned future enforcement of the rule. Only the legality of the rule itself and of its prospective application remained in question. Was the rule limiting memorialization actually burdening the exercise of legitimate religion? Were the plaintiffs' actions "religion"? Were they religion of sufficient stature to demand exemption from laws that applied to everyone else? (A larger question, and one that will be treated in the next chapter, was whether such laws protecting religion should exist at all.)

The Florida statute (reproduced in Appendix A) seems to call for a two-step legal inquiry. First, a court must determine whether a particular claimant's action was an "exercise of religion." (If it was not, presumably no further inquiry would be required.) An "exercise of religion" is defined by the Florida statute as "an act or refusal to act that is *substantially motivated* by a religious belief, *whether or not* the religious exercise is compulsory or central to a larger system of religious belief [emphasis added]."[54] The definition is expansive and seems deliberately to shift the focus of the trier-of-fact toward the motivation of the religious actor and away from the location of a particular activity within "a larger system of religious belief." The definitions section requires only that an action, in order to qualify as an "exercise of religion," must be "substantially motivated by a religious belief." Having established that the activity in question is an "exercise of religion," within the meaning of the statute, a court must then determine whether the government "substantially burdened" that exercise of religion. There are, thus, two layers of substantiality imposed by the statute. The religious actor must be *substantially* motivated in his exercise of religion, and that exercise of religion must itself also be *substantially* burdened—an odd, almost Aristotelian, insistence on *substance*, as if the legislators feared that there was something here that could get away from them.[55]

At trial, the two steps, proof of an actual exercise of religion and proof that the plaintiffs were substantially burdened, seemed to collapse into one step, perhaps as a result of the statute's repetition of the word "substantial," although the repetition was not noted. Almost all seemed to concede that what the plaintiffs were doing was, in some sense, a sincerely motivated exercise of religion and even that that religious exercise was, in some sense, burdened. The question thus became: Was this religious activity, and that which motivated it, substantial enough itself, in the larger scheme of things, however that might be defined, such that its prohibition, in the abstract, not with respect to the particular plaintiffs, could constitute a substantial burden? The plaintiffs were asked not simply to prove that their own actions were substantially motivated by religious belief and that those actions were substantially burdened by the City, but they were also asked to prove that their actions were a substantial exercise of religion—that the particular exercise of religion was important in some sense to the religious tradition as a whole. What was apparently intentionally excluded by the modifying language of the definition, that is, "whether or not compulsory or central to a larger system of belief," was reintroduced through the curiously doubling language of substantiality.

The City initially took the position that persons could only be "substantially burdened" in the exercise of their "substantially motivated religious exercise" if the actions that were so burdened were "required" by their religion. Attorneys for the City insisted at the depositions, at trial, and in their briefs, that what the plaintiffs had done had insufficient status within their respective religious traditions to support a claim of substantiality. The plaintiffs' actions were not "required" by their religions but were merely the result of what came to be called "purely personal preference."

This additional layer of proof, beyond substantiality in the context of the individual, as apparently required by the statute, attributed *legal* agency to the religious traditions. It brought the religions themselves into the courtroom as actors, actors who were incarnated—or not—in the various objects in the cemetery. The City asked the judge to decide whether the religions themselves demanded certain actions on the part of the plaintiffs. And then, if they did, were the religions themselves "burdened" by the City's actions? In an early brief in the *Warner* case,[56] the attorneys for the City argued that:

> The disputed facts here are whether the no vertical decoration rule substantially impedes religious observance. The City's expert witness reports establish that the rule does not substantially burden *religion*. . . . That the Plaintiffs may be sincerely motivated to want vertical symbols begs the question of whether the preclusion of all vertical decorations substantially burdens their free exercise of religion. . . . The City respects the Plaintiffs' beliefs. But beliefs that a grave should be covered; that the symbolism of Christ being crucified on an upright cross should be transposed to a grave; that offerings "to the soul and spirit, the afterlife of the person buried" must be vertical; that the "marble railings and guards" at the grave of St. Peter must be replicated; that absent "a statue of Jesus" and "edging blocks and stone" religious freedom is abridged; that grave statues are a "channel of prayer to God" and that "St. Francis was a gentle man to animals," and therefore the Plaintiffs can transform the nature and appearance of a municipal secular cemetery and establish *their own standardless cemetery rules*, underscores the need for trial on the disputed issues of fact [emphasis supplied].[57]

The opinions of the City's experts as to the lack of a burden on "religion" itself is here contrasted to the plaintiffs' "own standardless cemetery rules," apparently implying their anarchist sympathies.

In promoting the position that the plaintiffs' activities were merely the result of "purely personal preference," the City and its experts slipped into the habit of discussing whether the religion itself was burdened, rather than whether each plaintiff's "exercise of religion" was substantially burdened by the state, as apparently required by the statute. The plaintiffs were asked to take on the burden of proving that religion itself, or a particular religion, was substantially burdened. Indeed the language of most at trial, not just that of the City's lawyers and experts, slipped uneasily between the religious lives of the plaintiffs themselves and large reified constructions: religion, Christianity, Judaism, Orthodoxy, Islam. The language of substantiality, and certainly the language of requirements, seemed to demand the specter of institutionalized religious authority, authority consecrated by the ages. Each object in the cemetery was asked to embody that authority through the having of what the City's lawyers called "independent religious significance."

What exactly is being protected by RFRA laws? Or, indeed, by the First Amendment? Is it religion itself that is being protected? Because RFRA laws were passed in response to the Supreme Court's decision in *Employment Division v. Smith*,[58] and because that decision was understood by many to be a general attack on religion, the statute's focus on the individual seems easily transposed into a battle between religion and the forces of secularization: Rather than the individual defending himself against the state, the usual posture of suits to protect civil liberties, religion defends itself against modernity. The state (the incarnation of the modern), in turn, defends itself against superstition and overbearing clerical authority and wealth. The City took advantage of this mood to belittle the plaintiffs' activities. The City seemed to be saying: How can anyone seriously believe that this is religion—that this is religion powerful enough and important enough to challenge state sovereignty?

The court in the *Warner* case was, in other words, asked by the City to arrive at a decision as to what demands particular religions make with respect to burial. The individual's motivation, substantial or not, was often lost. Or perhaps it would be more accurate to say that no one quite knew what to do with the actions of individuals that were quite evidently "substantially motivated by religious belief," in some sense, and as clearly "substantially burdened," but both in a very personal way. Could the legislators have really meant that all such relatively modest religious gestures should trump state sovereignty, in the absence of a showing that there was a real threat of an Antigone-like martyrdom—of a state-imposed choice between adherence to one's religion and adherence to the law?[59]

An amicus brief filed in the *Warner* case on behalf of Governor Jeb Bush, in the Florida Supreme Court, vigorously argues that Judge Ryskamp completely misread the statute, ignoring the clear intent of the Florida legislature to eliminate the need for any proof beyond proof that the plaintiff was sincerely religiously motivated. The only conduct that is excluded, according to the governor's brief, is conduct that is not sincere or is "motivated by a secular belief or philosophy."[60]

Even the Boca Raton sexton got involved in testifying with respect to the requirements of various religions—and his was a much broader religious palate than that of anyone else at the trial. Curtis Harris was manager of the cemetery at the time of the trial. He testified as follows:

> We have a nonsectarian cemetery. We bury everybody. We don't discriminate, whatever religious ideas or customs they have is kind of irrelevant. My job is to bury people, maintain good order. . . . I'm familiar with certain customs when it comes to burying people. I'm familiar with certain things that people may or may not want present at the funeral for various types of religious things. For example, when I have a Catholic funeral, I keep an extra bottle of holy water in my office just in case they forget. If it's a Jewish funeral, I will provide them with a golden container with sand in it and a small shovel for ceremonial shoveling of sand onto the casket. If it's a Greek Orthodox funeral I allow them to light incense burners at the grave and perform their services in their manner. If it's an Oriental funeral, sometimes I will remove the chairs at the grave site so they can get on their knees and by rights pray to whoever they pray for. . . . People like to be facing east when they die . . . it's been done that way for hundreds of years. . . . [T]he study of death is a hobby of mine, and I have pursued information about it all my life. I have traveled around the world and one of my hobbies anywhere I went, and I have traveled to Africa and Europe and South America and the Pacific Islands, people have one thing in common. They all die. And everywhere I go I go to the cemetery. It is a fascination I have. I'm not a professional. I'm an amateur. And over the last thirty years I've learned a lot about burial traditions throughout the world, and one of the burial traditions that goes back almost to the beginning of time is people are buried with their feet to the east so on resurrection day if you're Christian or Mayan holidays or whatever, when a person comes out of the grave, as the sun comes up they'll be facing it.[61]

Harris has an appealingly tolerant typology not much cruder than those offered by the rest of us.

For the most part, the City's position was that religious identity is fixed and identifiable and that religious actions and religious objects also have fixed religious identities and meanings. One ought to be able to hold up a picture of the ideal religiously faithful mourner of a particular tradition and then see if the relevant plaintiff matched the picture. The City's lawyers sought a fixed and stable relationship between signified and signifier, and between individual and community. The religious identity of individuals was to be determined by whether they prayed and attended services at a synagogue or church regularly and whether they were knowledgeable about and deferential to religious authority. The religious identity of objects was to be determined by asking whether they had "independent religious significance." Were they sacred, or holy, in themselves? As established by religio-legal textual authority? The City's lawyers successfully increased the burden of proof on the plaintiffs by asking them to show that their activities were of some significance within their respective religious traditions—that their acts were in themselves "substantial" in some objective sense.

Proving such substantiality requires a model of religion that arguably cannot be constitutionally sustained in the American context. Proving such substantiality leads to a view of religion as including recognized authority structures that would determine for a court the importance of the plaintiffs' activities. Both the plaintiffs and the experts were being asked to locate the plaintiffs' activities with respect to such an authoritative religious structure. The City wanted a hard line between the religious and the secular and between the religiously important and the religiously insignificant. The fixity of the religious symbolism was to be determined by evidence of coercion, coercion by an external authority. The question at trial was: Did an external authority regard the plaintiffs' actions as "central to" or "necessary to" their religious traditions? Were the plaintiffs "required" to do what they did? As if the law could take cognizance only of what could be construed as a competing set of norms, norms finding their authority in an alternative but recognizable religio-legal structure. Religion, and particular religions, were granted intentionality and importance. They became shadow players in the trial.

In the previous chapter, the plaintiffs' testimony was described in the rough order it was presented at trial, deemphasizing their religious differences. The words below from the plaintiffs' testimony will illustrate the religious sensibility of the plaintiffs, here grouped by religious tradition. Two recurrent sets of questions were asked of the plaintiffs in order to establish the religiousness—or not—of the objects on the graves. One set of questions attempted to establish how religiously observant the plaintiffs themselves were; the other asked about the "independent religious significance" of the objects. An orthodox practitioner, it was implied, would be placing only what was unambiguously religious on her grave.

The Catholic plaintiffs, Caridad Monier, her sister Barbara Cavedoni, Maria Riccobono, and Joanne Davis, all women, evinced what McGuckin called a "Latin" religious sensibility, although what is termed "Latin" here ranges from Poland to Cuba. The Catholic plaintiffs' display of religious statuary, their incarnational theology, and the way in which they understood the value of their intercessory prayer on behalf of the deceased, all might be understood as "Latin."[62] Their religion was incarnated in their relationship to the individual grave sites. Their relationship to God was mediated not by priests but by sacramental objects.[63]

In the depositions and at the trial, lawyers for both sides asked each plaintiff a similar set of questions about religious identity. Caridad Monier responded, for example, on direct examination:

Q. What is your religion?

A. Catholic.

Q. Do you identify yourself through your religion?

A. Absolutely, yes.

Q. How long have you practiced Catholicism?

A. Since I can remember. Since I was born. It's my family's religion. I was baptized. Went to Sunday school. Catechism. Celebrate the holidays. It's my everyday life.[64]

These responses could be given by most "practicing" Catholics in this country. But it was how to get from that confident self-identification to the way each manifested that identity in their actions at the cemetery that troubled the lawyer for the City. His theory was that there must be some way in which the Church with which each plaintiff identified herself made her do it. It could not be that such a self-identification gave her license to call whatever she did "religion."

On cross examination at the trial, Bruce Rogow pressed Ms. Monier concerning the decorations on her brother's grave:

Q. Now, on your brother's grave, Miss Monier, there are four posts with ropes attached—

A. Uh-huh.

Q. —correct? Do those posts and ropes have any religious significance to you?

A. The posts and the ropes don't. It's just an article to make sure the grave is protected.

. . .

Q. Now, also on your brother's grave, Miss Monier, are two planters, correct?

A. Uh-huh.

. . .

Q. Is there any religious significance to those planters in your mind?

A. No, they were just placed there in order for the flowers to stay in place.

. . .

Q. Does that gardenia bush have any religious significance to you?

A. No, that was just for the shade and the flower and the smell. And he liked that.

. . .

Q. Do those wood chips have any religious significance to you?

A. No, the rope, the posts and the wood chip is just for protection of the grave.

. . .

Q. Now, of course, there is a statue also at the head of your brother's grave?

A. Yes, Sacred Heart of Jesus.

Q. And that statue has religious significance to you, of course?

A. Yes, it does.

. . .

Q. . . Miss Monier, the idea that people shouldn't walk on your brother's grave, what is that derived from in your mind?

A. That derives from my religious belief, my practice, my faith, that a grave should be respected. And they are to a point sacred, they are not to be walked on.[65]

At Ms. Monier's deposition Rogow had also pursued this line of questioning, seeking the authority for her actions:

Q. When you say your faith and your belief, the Catholic faith and belief?

A. I don't know if it is part of the Catholic faith. It was the way I was raised and my mother's belief.

Q. I understand, but I am trying to find out if when you say your faith and belief, in terms of faith, is that a religious faith that you are speaking of?
A. Yes.

. . .

Q. Can you tell me of any time you have heard in church services or your Catholic teachings anything about protecting a grave site so that—
A. Only when they refer to Jesus Christ's grave site.

. . .

Q. And what's the religious significance of the flowers?
A. It's an offering to the soul and the spirit. The afterlife of the person.
Q. And what is the source of that?
A. Through my belief through my church and through what I see when I go, candles and flowers, and offerings to the altar, a symbol.[66]

Ms. Monier, like the other plaintiffs, struggled to make the connection for the court, the connection between her Catholic identity and what she had done with the objects on the graves. She deflected and decentered the City's quest for the direct link between official church authority and her practices, while the City continued to make an effort to segregate religious and not-religious objects and practices on the basis of official church action.

At her deposition, Barabara Cavedoni, Ms. Monier's sister, had also been questioned by Rogow concerning Catholic teaching:

Q. Now, the things that you have described, tell me which of those things have any religious significance to you and your family?
A. What do you mean like religious significance?
Q. In your lawsuit you are alleging that this restriction upon vertical decorations somehow or other has an adverse effect upon your religious beliefs. So I'm trying to find out what on that grave site is related to your religious beliefs?
A. For my own personal practice, my own personal belief, everything is related.

. . .

Q. Let me ask you this: If you simply had something that marked the grave in a flat way that was flush to the ground so that it was clear that that's a grave site, would that be consistent with your religious beliefs?
A. Just something flat, I would not be able to like put a statue of Jesus Christ or a cross or something like that . . . ?

Q. It would be flat.

A. I feel personally that it would.

Q. Tell me how.

A. Because all through my life and handed down for generations, we have learned to respect and honor and worship a cross that is standing up, a statue that is standing up, things that are just accepted, that that's the way things are. It's a tradition, it's something that has always been respected. It has always been honored.[67]

She was also asked at trial to explain the religious significance of the various decorations on the grave:

Q. [W]hat religious significance does the covering on your brother's grave have to you in your religious beliefs?

A The belief to us is that the ground where he is buried is sacred, to me it is a sacred, holy place. It's the place that holds and safekeeps the body that the soul occupied, the vessel that it occupied while it was on earth.

Q. Barbara, who taught you your religious beliefs?

A. It was a combination of family, like I say, my family has been Catholic for generations, church, priests, catechism. It's just books, tradition, TV. There is a lot of things that play into it.[68]

Ms. Monier's beliefs and those of the other Catholic plaintiffs about the doctrines of the church respecting her brother's suicide, the iconography of the cross, interpretation of the biblical account of Jesus' death, and appropriate forms of worship, are not necessarily those of the Vatican today. Indeed some would be considered plainly unorthodox. The official teaching of the Roman Catholic Church today would display a more complex understanding of the causes of suicide, be more nuanced and historical in its biblical interpretation and less welcoming of certain popular forms of religious devotion. Should that matter in an American court?

Marie Riccobono, another Catholic plaintiff whose father is buried in the cemetery, was asked by Danciu on direct examination:

Q. What is your religious belief?

A. I'm Catholic.

Q. Is that the religion of your father?

A. Yes, my whole family is Catholic, all generations, everybody is Catholic.

Q. Do you practice your Catholic faith?

A. We do. You know, as a family we practice it together. We practice on a daily basis. It's part of everything we do.

Q. Did you receive the sacraments growing up?

A. Yes.

Q. And who taught you your faith, who was primarily responsible for teaching you your faith?

A. Well, we always went, if we went to public school we went to catechism and then to Catholic school. It was always a part of our house. It's part of everything that we do. So it is your family, your church, it's part of everything.[69]

During redirect examination Ms. Riccobono was asked to explain the significance of the statue of the resurrected Jesus on her father's grave: "That's very significant. Jesus is there as a monument and a respect and a reminder that God is protecting my father's soul and he is there and always will be there with him."[70]

Rogow asked Ms. Riccobono also, during his cross-examination, about each item on her father's grave:

Q. Is there any religious significance to the edging blocks?

A. No, there isn't.

Q. Is there any religious significance to the stones that are there?

A. No, there isn't.

Q. Is there any religious significance to the flowers that are there?

A. The flowers show life going on and the life that my father made and the grandchildren and everything, it signifies to me that that is the life he gave us going on.[71]

Ms. Riccobono, like the other Catholic plaintiffs, closely identifies her deceased relative with Jesus and the Christian saints. The two are mapped onto one another through a homology with the statues and their gestures. The plaintiffs also repeatedly use "he" interchangeably referring to Jesus and their deceased father or brother or son. The sacrificial death of Jesus, through word and gesture, is fused with the sacrificial death of their relatives.

Joanne Davis, also Catholic, the mother of the small child who was drowned, was asked on direct to describe her religious affiliation:

Q. Had your little boy been baptized?

A. Yes, he was baptized in St. Joan's.

116

Q. What faith was he baptized in?

A. He was baptized in the Catholic faith, with everybody else in my family, the rest of my children.

    . . .

Q. How often do you pray?

A. I just finished praying. I pray all the time, that's what gets me through the day. It's what makes me who I am. . . .

Q. Then where do you pray?

A. Everywhere. I was just praying in the chair over there. I pray at home and I pray at the cemetery. I prayed at the beach when my son passed away, along with Camille in '88.[72]

Asked to describe the significance of the objects she put on her child's grave:

It shows life hereafter for me. It does for my son. . . . For me it is very important that my children know that there is life after death. When you're really born is when you die and you're born and you go to live with God, and that's what the [statues of the] children do there. . . . It's a reminder that my son is up in heaven and he is alive . . . and every year we have a religious memorial service at the cemetery site. . . . It is my son's sacred ground. It's his little shrine. It's him. It is where we are. It's the place we go to be with him.[73]

Again, Ms. Davis identifies very closely, almost merges, her deceased son with the person of Jesus. The language of these plaintiffs exemplifies the theological project of sacralization and identification described by McGuckin in his testimony concerning Catholic religious practice with respect to burial.

Eleanor Danciu was the final Catholic plaintiff to testify. In her deposition she had been asked a series of questions about her religious motivation:

Q. The decision that was made by you to put these statues up so that you could pray through the two saints, did you talk to anyone about putting those statues up? Did you discuss it with anyone?

A. No.

Q. A decision you made on your own because of your mother's feelings about the Virgin Mary and your father about Saint Francis?

A. They were devoted to them.

Q. Okay. You said you attend church regularly and you mentioned the church. The name of the church is?

A. Saint Joan of Arc.

Q. A Catholic church?

A. Yes.

Q. Do you know whether or not in the Catholic religion there's any requirement that you have standing decorations on a grave site?

A. I don't believe there's any requirement.

Q. So the decision that you had to place these statues was a personal decision made by you so you could accomplish religiously what you wanted to accomplish?

A. What I wanted from my heart, yes.

Q. From your heart?

A. From my heart, because my religion and my faith are like the core of an apple that's inside of me. Everything I do is based on that.

Q. Okay. Mrs. Danciu, have you talked with any priests or other people knowledgeable in the area of religious symbolism regarding your placing the statues?

A. No.

Q. Did you seek advice from anyone?

A. No.[74]

Rogow asked her, as he had asked the others, to acknowledge that her choices with respect to the decoration of the graves of her parents were private decisions—that no one had told her to do it.

McGuckin's testimony at the trial was designed to provide the religio-cultural context in which the Catholic plaintiffs worked—the larger frame of their creations, a frame that for McGuckin is embodied in a transnational two-thousand-year church history. But this effort backfired, I think. One might think that McGuckin was exactly the kind of priestly authority that the City, through its experts, was demanding, and yet in the courtroom McGuckin had no authority. In the United States each person has to create his or her own religious context. She or he does not work in a larger legitimating religious culture that is understood and taken for granted. There is something foreign and threatening to most Americans about the closed and internally coherent nature of the religious communities described by McGuckin and Broyde.

Mary, St. Francis, the Sacred Heart, and the Immaculate Conception do not come out of nowhere, of course. Neither did the practice of using statues of the saints for personal devotion. They are part of a long and complex

118

tradition—but that tradition has no authoritative representation in the American context. Each person must supply their own context and each does so also within a particular American political commitment with respect to religion. In theory it seemed that text and institutionalized mandates were needed. In practice they carried little weight.

The Jewish plaintiffs were asked a parallel set of questions about their attendance at services and the connection between any religious teaching they had received and their activities at the Boca Raton Cemetery. Miriam Warner, for example, was asked concerning her religious upbringing:

Q. What is your religious belief or faith?

A. I'm Jewish.

Q. What was the religion of your husband and your son?

A. Jewish.

Q. How long have you had this faith?

A. I was born into this faith. And I'm currently in this faith and this is my faith until I die.

Q. Do you attend temple or synagogue?

A. I do.

Q. Do you pray?

A. I pray but not necessarily in the synagogue. I pray at the cemetery. I pray at home. I pray.[75]

Asked by the plaintiffs' lawyer why "you believe you have to have this public expression of your faith?" Ms. Warner replied: "It's not a matter of public expression of my faith. My faith is within me. But to us this is desecration if you walk on a grave."[76] She distinguishes carefully between her personal religious faith and the customs of her community, seeing the latter not as a mere "expression" of the former, but as having its own logic and importance. Not walking on a grave is independent of "faith." It is a question of religious "etiquette," as McGuckin would put it.[77]

At her deposition, Miriam Warner was also questioned by Rogow concerning her Jewishness:

Q. And I see the marker has Jewish stars inscribed on it?

A. Yes, it does.

Q. And those were important to you to be able to have those Jewish stars, correct?

A. Yes.

Q. And why is that?

A. Because I'm a practicing Jew.

Q. And the Jewish stars signify?

A. Signify Judaism. To identify the grave as a grave of a Jewish-thinking, believing person.[78]

For the Jewish plaintiffs, the primary concern was with identity, with identifying the grave as a Jewish grave, in order to prevent disrespect.

Ms. Warner's son, Richard Warner, was the most successful among the plaintiffs at retaining control of the terms on which he was speaking. Although all of the plaintiffs were articulate and insistent about their motivations and religious identities, Richard Warner was most self-conscious about the effect of his words and most successful at resisting the fragmentation of personality that the defendant's lawyers seemed to want to impose on the plaintiffs at their depositions. When Rogow asked Mr. Warner at his deposition the purpose of the grave covering, Mr. Warner answered:

To maintain the dignity and the—we believe that graves should not be walked upon. By doing this we were able to ensure that they wouldn't be; that it would remain a place where the things we wanted to—the grave to stand for, so to speak, in our hearts and minds would be represented, and that people would not walk on the graves and defile them by doing so. . . . It's a religious tradition. The first time I heard it was from my grandparents including my father and my mother, both. That's where I learned it. My father, in particular, was very conscious of it. . . . I didn't know the specific person who taught it to them. I would assume that it came down from generation to generation. The first time I ever heard it was from my grandparents. . . . In our religion you don't walk on graves.[79]

"In our religion you don't walk on graves." There is no need to cite chapter and verse. Pressed by Rogow as to the "*religious* significance of the edging stones and ground cover," Mr. Warner responded:

To me this is a religious place. This is a shrine. I loved these people. You know, if you break it down to building materials it is a little bit more difficult to explain, perhaps, but this is somewhere I can bring my four-year-old daughter or, for that matter, my son, other members of my family. . . . This is a religiously significant place to us. This is my father and my brother. It's not just rocks and the like that's symbolized by . . . [T]his was thought out.[80]

But Rogow insisted:

Q. Let's break it down. . . . [W]ould you agree that the edging stones in and of themselves independently have no religious significance?

A. No.

Q. You would not agree?

A. Are you speaking for yourself?

Q. No, I'm asking—I'm speaking edging stones. Did you buy these, by the way, at a garden shop?

A. Yeah.

Q. And so at the garden shop where you saw the edging stones in and of themselves they have no religious significance?

A. To you, perhaps, but to me they do.

Q. Purchased at a garden shop?

A. They have religious significance on my father's and my brother's graves.

Q. Well, you've got a Jewish star on the marker. There is a religious significance of the Jewish star, is there not?

A. Yes.

Q. What is the significance of the Jewish star?

A. Just a symbol of faith.

Q. By the way, does that star have to be upright or can it be engraved and equally a symbol?

A. I think you're trying to put—this is my personal feeling. You're trying to put value judgments, so to speak, on upright, lying flat. I think it is—to call it religious to me, what it is to me it may not be to you. To me it's all a religious symbol. No, I didn't buy this ground cover in a religious store, but that doesn't make it any less a religious symbol to me. . . . To me the ground cover meant more to me than the Jewish star.[81]

To the lawyers the star seemed obviously religious while the rest were dangerously ambiguous and unstable. At the deposition, Ms. Danciu, a lawyer for the plaintiffs, asked Richard Warner: "Can you imagine that some non-believers would attach no more religious significance with respect to the Jewish star that they would to a rock or a stone?" He responded: "[I]f nothing is sacred then the cross or the Jewish star or anything else is no more significant than anything you find in the field."[82] Such a position made the court very uneasy.

Ian and Bobbie Payne had had the most contentious relationship with the City and the managers of the cemetery. Mr. Payne was visibly distraught throughout the trial and testified that his son's death and his wife's subsequent diagnosis with breast cancer had caused him to seek counseling and be medicated for stress. Rogow questioned both Paynes extensively about the extent of their religious observance. At her deposition, Mrs. Payne, who was not present at the trial, was asked by Rogow to describe her religious upbringing:

Q. What is it in your religious beliefs that requires or suggests or encourages you to have a standing star of David on the grave site—on the marker?

A. My religion and my beliefs and my desires request that the grave be easily identifiable.

Q. And what is the source of those religious beliefs? What can you point to?

A. My religious upbringing and teachings.[83]

Asked why she felt so strongly that the grave ought to be covered, Ms. Payne answered:

A. Because we feel that it is a dishonor to the dead to walk across the grave, and that is why we keep the perimeter of the grave marked off.

Q. And what's the basis of that feeling?

A. It's not a feeling. It is also part of my heritage, part of my upbringing, part of my religious belief what I've been brought up to believe and I believe that strongly.[84]

But that was not enough. Rogow also required her to testify, in effect, as to whether she was a good Jew:

Q. Do you belong to a synagogue or a temple here in Boca Raton?

A. I do not.

Q. Tell me about your religious upbringing.

A. I don't understand what part you wish to be told about. . . . I was brought up as a Jew.

Q. And where was that?

A. In England.

Q. Did you attend temple or shul?

A. Yes, I did.

Q. Were you bat mitzvahed?

A. I was not.

Q. Were you confirmed?

A. I was not.

—

Q. Do you belong to or attend a temple or synagogue anywhere in Florida?

A. Is that relevant sir?

Mr. Green: You can answer.

Ms. Waxman: You have to answer.

A. No, I don't.

Q. And when was the last time that you attended any Jewish religious services?

A. I don't recall.[85]

Laws protecting religious freedom invite such intrusive and offensive questions. How else are the lawyers to establish a connection between the individuals asserting rights to religious freedom and the tradition with which they associate themselves? The questions also reveal Rogow's apparent ignorance about Jewish religious practice, a practice that, for the most part, does not consider synagogue attendance a measure of adherence in the same way as church attendance might for some Christians.

Rogow also asked Ms. Payne the religious significance of each item on her son's grave, referring as he did so to a photograph of the grave:

Q. Does this bench have any religious significance?

A. No.

Q. Do the cement flower pots have any religious significance?

A. No.

Q. Do the edgings, edging stones and marble chips have any religious significance?

A. Yes. . . . Their significance is that of ground cover for the grave so that nobody walks across the grave.

Q. So independently do edging stones have any religious significance?

A. They mark the area of the grave site.

Q. Maybe I'm not being clear. I understand that a star of David has religious significance. Isn't that true?

A. Yes.

Q. And no matter where that star of David is it has religious significance. Isn't that true?

A. It serves also as a marker, as a standing marker to show where the grave is.

. . .

Q. When one sees a star of David, it has religious symbolism, does it not?

A. Yes.

Q. No matter where you see that star of David?

A. Some people wear a star of David as talismans rather than religious symbols.[86]

You can hear Ms. Payne backing away from Rogow's insistence on "religious significance," unsure as to whether she and he are meaning the same thing. They went around and around with this. Finally, Rogow asked:

Q. Where it is written or said in the Jewish religion or tradition that the grave site had to be fully demarked?

A. I am not a religious scholar. I really don't know. It's part of my upbringing and belief.[87]

It is difficult to understand what Rogow expected. He seemed to want to prove by her testimony that her religious life was not orthodox, that, without a capacity to cite chapter and verse, she was unconnected with the thousands of years of Jewish history.

At trial, her husband, Ian Payne, was also asked on direct examination about his Jewish upbringing:

Q. Mr. Payne, what is your religion?

A. My religion is Jewish. I was born Jewish, my parents are both Jewish, my wife is Jewish, her parents are Jewish and all grandparents and ancestors that go back as far as we can recall, were always Jewish.

Q. Could you describe your Jewish education?

A. Yes. I was educated in London. My grammar school, as they call it in England, was a very Orthodox Jewish school, which is where I actually graduated from. And I used to go regularly to Jewish studies on a Sunday. I was barmitzvahed as was my son, and my daughter was not because we come from the old school where for some reason only the man gets barmitzvahed and not the woman. I don't know why but that's the way our teachings were and I do abide by the old teachings.[88]

He, too, was asked to testify to his regular religious practice:

Q. Do you presently attend a synagogue?

A. No, I don't.

Q. Why is that?

A. They are just too expensive and I really can't afford it. It's just as good to pray at home as it is in a temple, and basically we just can't afford it.

Q. How often do you pray at home?

A. Everyday. Several times a day.

Q. Do you observe religious holidays at your house?

A. Yes, in our own way.

Q. With your family?

A. Approximately. That's depleted somewhat. My daughter is off at Boston in college. And there is only me and my wife. Before the accident and before this aggravation started we used to have a large number of friends around for the holidays such as Passover and Hanukkah, etc. But now there's just the two of us, we just celebrate quietly the two of us.

. . .

Q. Mr. Payne, how important is your Jewish faith or identity to Judaism been to you?

A. This is all I have been brought up to recognize, that we are Jewish. Maybe there are certain things that we don't keep up with that we should do, but we've only known Judaism. . . . I think religion is important to every-body, the belief in God, your own God, whatever that might be, is very im-portant and it is what keeps, I think, mankind going.[89]

On cross examination by Rogow, Mr. Payne further explained his rela-tionship to the Jewish community in Boca Raton, revealing his tension with the orthodox tradition:

Q. Was there a graveside ceremony for your son?

A. Yes, Rabbi Senior (phonetic) from the temple.

Q. What temple is that?

A. Temple Beth El.

Q. Are you familiar with the Temple Beth El area [in the cemetery] the tem-ple has purchased?

A. Yes, I knew they purchased a number of lots.

Q. And are any of those Jewish graves, graves that have an upright marble or granite star like yours?

A. No. Because that particular temple, they don't even have to wear head coverings. It's an extremely conservative temple. We in the Jewish religion don't look upon them really being Jewish to the true sense of the word. I've even seen the Rabbi go without wearing a head covering. Although I don't wear a head covering, I don't go to temple without a head covering, it's sac-rilegious. So what they do there is not strictly in line with the Jewish religion as such.

Q. You say they are conservative?

A. I believe they are. They certainly don't follow anywhere near the true teachings of the Bible.

Q. And who in the Jewish religion does? Which group does?

A. The Orthodox and also the Reform. But that is a branch in England which we use which is, I don't know the equivalent of it here.

Q. How long have you lived in the United States, Mr. Payne?

A. Just under 20 years.

Q. Let's go back to Orthodox, Conservative and Reform. Do you have some idea in the United States where those three groups are within the Jewish religion?

A. No, but basically I was only concerned with Orthodox. My family, although they would be pretty upset with me not going to temple more. I can't afford to. Not having a head covering all the time.[90]

Rogow leapt on this confession:

Q. I don't understand, you can't afford to have a head covering on?

A. No, no, no, no, no. I can't afford to go to temple, because it's extremely expensive to become a member. And other times you are not allowed to go to high holidays unless you have a ticket. For that you have to be a member.

Q. Stop there for one second. Are you saying you have to be a member of a temple or a synagogue in order to go?

A. No, but the only way to go on the high holidays you have to be a member or purchase an extremely expensive ticket. There is very few of those available.

Q. So you are saying if a Jew is too poor to afford a ticket . . . then you would not be able to go to Yom Kippur and Rosh Hashannah service?[91]

The sneer is palpable. The questions continued:

Q. What are the requirements for joining a temple or a synagogue?

A. You join, you fill out an application form. Some of them even ask how much you earn and they judge membership according to salary, which I don't agree with but that's what they do.

Q. How much does it cost to join a temple or a synagogue?

A. I don't know at the moment.

Q. Is there a difference between a temple and synagogue?

A. We call it a synagogue in England. . . . In England it's rarely referred to as temple. That could construe a number of religions. There are other religions that pray in temples . . . although it's not necessary, of course, this thing about going to temple is overdone. You don't have to go to temple to pray, it's really not necessary. We all use religion as we see appropriate. And I say use religion. We all use religion for our own benefit at time of needs, at time of comfort, at times just generally praying and being thankful for what you've got. You don't have to be a minister to do that. . . . Besides you can do it in your own way and own time. You can do it in Hebrew, in English. You don't have to use the words in the Bible, you can use your own words.[92]

Again, it is a little difficult to see what Rogow was trying to achieve here. It comes pretty close to harassment. Was he trying to show that Mr. Payne was a bad Jew? Was he trying to show the greed of religious congregations? Particularly Jewish ones? Or that Mr. Payne had a negative view of Jewish congregations? Or that he was confused as to where he belonged among Jewish groups? Mr. Payne tried to explain the nature of his religious practice but Rogow did not seem to have a framework within which to hear his testimony as being "religious." Does RFRA demand that you be an orthodox member of your religious community and a regular practitioner in order to have its protection? Can that be constitutional in the United States?

At Mr. Payne's deposition, Rogow had also pressed him with respect to the decorations on his son's grave. Mr. Payne struggled to describe the importance to him of the stone Star of David that he had placed on the grave:

Q. Now talk to me about the vertical star of David.

A. Well, vertically we are supposed to have, and they wouldn't permit this, we are supposed to have a stone with engraving on the stone so it's immediately recognizable. . . . The City would not allow a stone that big there so as a compromise we just put the star as recognition standing up and the writing on the horizontal, although we would have wanted it on the upright as we had in England.

Q. Do you know anything or what the source is if there is in religious tradition or teaching that a star of David must be vertical?

A. It's a tradition, as I say, it's a tradition, it's how it is done in the Jewish religion in England. . . . It's not necessarily a religious belief. It's a tradition which in turn is my belief.[93]

Mr. Payne here explains the genealogy of authority for him. What he wanted to do on his son's grave was not necessarily prescribed in Jewish law, but it was how things were done in his Orthodox Jewish family in England, and that, in turn, became a part of his own religious belief structure, a structure that linked him to a Jewish community that was local, English, and transnational.

Although Broyde was generous and careful in extending the mantle of his authority to local Florida Jewish practice, his own authority was bounded within the tight circumference of orthodox Jewish law, a world, in a sense, unto its own and remote from the lives of both the Jewish plaintiffs and the judge. The Warners and the Paynes did not directly acknowledge his authority in their testimony, although they knew he would testify and they were all present in the courtroom when he testified. (He testified after the Warners but before Mr. Payne.) The Warners and the Paynes said that they did what they did because that is what their families had taught them. They did not need to ask anyone's advice or permission. Rogow sought institutional authority. The Jewish plaintiffs practiced what they had been taught by their families, what was customary.[94]

The experts for the plaintiffs were also directly questioned concerning the relationship of the individual to the tradition and concerning the "independent religious significance" of the objects on the graves. McGuckin, for example, was asked in his direct examination about "idiosyncratic" religious behavior:

Q. Who was the first Christian?

A. Well, people would give different answers. But Catholic and Orthodox tradition would say . . . the Virgin Mary.

. . .

Q. Were the Virgin Mary's beliefs and understanding about Jesus Christ idiosyncratic?

A. In a way all belief is idiosyncratic. . . . Christianity starts off from its earliest origins, of course, as a communal religion. The approach to Christianity as a very personalized experience, is a late modern conception of Christianity.

Q. Well, get back to your visit to the Boca Raton Cemetery. Are the grave decorations that you saw there, the above-the-ground decorations that you saw there, idiosyncratic?

A. If I take your sense of idiosyncratic, I would say no. I would think archetypal of a Catholic religious piety. It may not be high art or high intellectual tradition, but—I'm thinking primarily in terms of the size of the statues and so forth—but it is very, very typical of Mediterranean Catholicism.[95]

On cross-examination, McGuckin returned to the question of individuality, in response to Rogow's questions about the use of horizontal markers:

Q. So are you saying that there is historical evidence that would support the notion of flat horizontal markers in settings in which there may be a single cross in the center of the consecrated graveyard ground or perhaps a church there . . . ?

A. In times that was a form of burial.

Q. And so this notion of horizontal markers only then is not atypical or inconsistent with historical Christian religious practice?

A. If you ally the history, the, in fact in times past there wouldn't be any marker of an individual grave at all, say in the Middle Ages. But the difference, I would sort of think, would be apparent—

[nonverbal interruption by Rogow]

Mr. Green: Let him finish his answer.

Mr. Rogow: He hasn't answered my question yet, If I could get a yes or no and then he can explain.

Mr. Green: If he can finish his answer, your honor.

The Court: He can answer.

The Witness: I find it very difficult to answer yes or no. Because the Christian practice that we're talking about here, if there was no raised marker, would presume a consecrated church burial ground with central cross. And if you have those things you would have no individual markers. If you have, if you don't have the consecrated graveyard, say in the case of a municipal cemetery, individual Christians tended to mark the grave site more individually.[96]

McGuckin here identifies one of the central issues in this case. Context is everything. In a secular pluralist society, it is the individual who has rights. RFRA asks whether the individual is burdened in her or his exercise of religion. But everyone would agree that religion is not just an individual matter. Individual religious practitioners are asked, in a sense, then, to justify their own practices with reference to only vaguely defined larger religious contexts. It is those larger religious contexts that posed a problem for this trial. What contexts mattered?

Katz's high/low typology purported to offer a solution to this problem: The relationship of the individual to the tradition is defined authoritatively by the institutionalized carriers of the tradition. McGuckin argued that the typology did not solve the problem, for both historical and ethical reasons. Asked about Katz's high/low typology, he responded:

I found [a high/low typology] in Dr. Katz' report and also implied in Dr. Pals' report. It's one that's used in modern sociology of religion. And the high tradition designates intellectual but predominantly Protestant northern hemisphere. And the low tradition is crudely used to designate folk religion. I think it's an inappropriate context and certainly one that can't be sustained when you go back to the study of ancient Christianity. Which is the Jesus movement in its fundamental origins is not a high tradition and doesn't become anything like a high tradition until the fifth and sixth century when it connects with the Roman imperial system and becomes established. To this day there are obviously high aspects of the Christian tradition. My own school, Union, is taken to be a typical high liberal Protestant ethos. But it's based in northern Manhattan, adjacent to Harlem. And the local population around that are certainly not high intellectual liberals and their religious sentiment is quite clearly of a different order. I'm thinking of Hispanics and African Americans in Harlem. And I think that the distinction of their kind of religion or their kind of Christianity as low and popular and mine as high and intellectual, is not only inaccurate but I think it verges on the offensive.[97]

McGuckin sees high and low religion as being an inappropriate division in Christianity, but in any event, as making equal claims on the individual.

Each of the plaintiffs' experts was also asked, as the plaintiffs had been, to comment on whether the objects in the cemetery had "independent religious significance." Rogow asked Broyde, as he had asked each of the plaintiffs, about each item on the graves—the benches, plants, vases, marble chips—whether each had religious significance:

Q. Do you consider a glass pot or a cement vase to be an expression of religious significance in the Jewish law or tradition?
A. As a general proposition things that hold flowers aren't part of the Jewish ritual, but when one puts something on a grave to mark the grave, even if it's untraditional, it becomes in some level consecrated so that I wouldn't be prepared to go to a cemetery, attach the vase on a tombstone, put flowers in it and bring it home to my wife.[98]

And also to McGuckin:

Q. Did you find there to be any, or do you think there is any religious significance in those edging stones?

A. I think there is some significance in those boundary markers.

Q. And what would that significance be?

A. It's the twofold issue of marking off the site of the grave, which in the religious consciousness has been sanctified by the ritual but also contains the
body of the loved one. And secondly, a vague, hopeful aspiration that people
wouldn't walk on that and desecrate the psychology of the place.

Q. That is only aspirational, it obviously cannot prevent the walking of the
grave?

A. Certainly.

. . .

Q. Did you also see out there any of these little plastic windmills . . . and
toys. . . . Any religious significance to those?

A. I wouldn't like to say anything at all about windmills because I just won-
dered what they meant. . . . If you were to ask me is that a religious thing, the
child's toy . . . I would agree that it certainly isn't in the classical canon of
Christian symbols . . . I would take a wider view that that grief is clustering
the children's kind of vestigial remains around the religious icon and to a
certain real degree you could regard that as a religious spiritual action.[99]

I was asked similar questions and made similar replies. On cross-examination
Rogow pushed me to limit the nature of objects that might be placed on
the grave:

Q. So you're saying that some symbols would be outside this context that
you're just talking about?

A. Yes.

Q. For example, wood chips—inside or outside?

A. I don't think you can talk about these objects individually like that.

Q. Because they have all been placed there as a part of some religious expression as expressed by the plaintiffs?

A. Because it's not the wood chips—the wood chips serve to mark out and
protect sacred space. People who are practicing their religion reach out for
the materials that are at hand to create religious expression.[100]

After a long interchange with McGuckin concerning religious symbolism,
Rogow asked:

Q. And so the only people who could claim this, quote, right, end quote, to erect the religious symbolism would be those that are setting forth that these symbols are part of their religious belief system?

A. Well, again, insofar as I understand the structure of your question, it would seem to me that what you're saying is only those that have a religious syntax can actually claim to erect a religious language structure. And I think that would be logically self-evident.[101]

On cross-examination, the plaintiffs' lawyers challenged Pals and Katz on the possibility of identifying objects as having "independent" religious significance. Green asked Pals, for example:

Q. What does it mean to say that an object has, quote, independent religious significance?

A. I would take it to mean that it's an object which has been recognized by a tradition over time and through a wide variety of places to be an object which has religious significance. I can do this best by way of example. I would say St. Peter's Cathedral in Rome has independent religious significance because instinctively people know that is a religious site.[102]

Instinctively? That seems inconsistent with Pals's insistence on tradition and text.

With respect to the testimony of Joanne Davis which he had just heard, Katz was asked by Rogow:

Q. In your opinion as an expert on religion, is there any religious significance to these things, [the statues on the grave] not just to her, because we know they have them to her, but in terms of something under customs or traditions?

A. [M]y understanding of religion is that it essentially and necessarily has a corporate social dimension to it.[103]

We all agreed with Katz on that—that religion has a corporate dimension. The question was the nature of that corporate dimension and the way in which that corporate dimension might lend context and authenticity to plaintiffs' individual actions and to the objects on the graves.

The Court was left with a serious problem of authority and very little guidance from previous cases. What did the five experts in religion contribute, if anything, to the resolution of the defining of legally recognized religious exercise? Because there was no jury, there was no reason to draw a strong line between law and fact in the courtroom. (Juries can only decide facts, leaving the law to the judge, but judges decide both. Jury trials make a careful distinction between the two while trials before judges tend to mix them.) At the trial, the experts seemed to be speaking at times as academics and at times as consultants on the possible meanings of the statute. The relationship of their testimony to that of the plaintiffs with respect to the plaintiffs' religious activities was often tangential. The plaintiffs were engaged in mourning, using a complex religious symbolic vocabulary. The experts were talking about religion as academics would. It is unclear which way was called for by the statute.

Judge Ryskamp, for his part, in his opinions and in his questions, was not deferential to religious authority, whether clerical or academic. He appeared both fascinated with the issues presented to him and intensely aware of what he was being asked to do, more aware perhaps than anyone else in the courtroom. What significance was he to give to the plaintiffs' testimony? Was he to rely on the experts? If so, how to choose among them? He accepted the plaintiffs' testimony for what it was, I think, rarely interrupting them. On the other hand, he constantly questioned the experts at trial. You could hear him thinking out loud as he developed his own theory of religion. At one point he mused, "[T]he Supreme Court of the United States has said secular humanism is a religion. Atheism may be a religion also. Non-belief may be in the same category. I don't know that you can find anybody who has no religious belief. Maybe religion in the concept we usually think of it . . ."[104]

With each expert Ryskamp tried to work out his own view of what religion is and what particular religious traditions demand of their adherents with respect to burial. You could also see him working, however, from within what is a basically Protestant understanding of authority. It is the individual who decides. And he does so by reading the Bible. Neither Broyde nor McGuckin was acknowledged as a religious authority, academic or clerical, by the judge. With Broyde, for example, Ryskamp jumped right in to discuss biblical teaching, giving primacy to his own reading of the biblical authors. When Jim Green concluded his direct examination of Michael Broyde, the judge said immediately, "I have a few questions."[105] He went on then to question Broyde at length:

The Court: I believe that you said that there's nothing in the law that prohibits it but you're referring to tradition, right? . . . About walking on a grave . . .

The Witness: Walking on a grave is a violation of Jewish law.

The Court: Jewish law. What Jewish law?

The Witness: The classic law code recounts that it is improper to walk on a grave site.

The Court: Well, let's start with the Torah, there is nothing in the Torah—

The Witness: There is nothing in the Torah. The Torah does make mention of the fact that Jacob put up a monument for Rachel.

The Court: Does that create a precedent?

The Witness: It creates a custom.

The Court: He also had two wives, so you don't recommend that as a custom?

The Witness: Absolutely not, your Honor, this is, of course—the gristmill of Jewish law is determining does the conduct of the patriarch rise to the level of something that we should imitate and when it does not.

. . .

The Court: The ceremonial law is found primarily in the book of Leviticus, right?

The Witness: No. You see, Jewish law isn't grounded in the Old Testament in the same sense that you are using it.

The Court: Are you using the Talmud and the Mishnah?

The Witness: That's right.

The Court: Do they say anything about graves or burial ceremonies?

The Witness: The Talmud recounts that it is improper to walk on graves.

The Court: The tradition, is that constantly changing or once a tradition is there does it never change?

The Witness: It's somewhere in between those two assertions.[106]

The judge also had his own ideas about what "holy" means. To Broyde:

The Court: You said that the grave was sacred and I think the counsel used the word sanctified. Do you use those interchangeably?

The Witness: Yes. Both of them are a translation of the Hebrew term Kodesh [*sic*], which literally means holy.

The Court: That means set aside for a special purpose?

The Witness: Set aside for a special purpose, yes.

The Court: Obviously a grave is set aside for a special purpose.

The Witness: Yes.

The Court: That doesn't make it holy. In fact, immediately upon death isn't the body unclean and isn't anyone who touches the body unclean ?

The Witness: The Jewish tradition doesn't observe the impurity rituals found in the book of Leviticus at all.

The Court: Maybe I ought to ask you, are you Orthodox or are you Hasidic or—

The Witness: I'm Orthodox. None of the Orthodox community observes the ritual prohibitions on purity and impurity found in the book of Leviticus, other than our practice that priests don't defile themselves for a dead person. The reason why this is so is because we treat ourselves like we're always impure. And since there is no prohibition of impurity in and of itself, it's only, impurity is only relevant if one is going up to the temple. Which we don't do because the temple has been destroyed. . . . [I]n the Jewish tradition when the person is buried the body doesn't become holy in the sense of, that you would use the term. It becomes sacred in the sense that I would use the term. It can't be used for anything other than its designated purpose. That's a classic measure in the Jewish tradition of holiness. Because it is set aside for a purpose to the exclusion of every other purpose. That makes something holy.[107]

These lengthy interchanges led nowhere, in the end. Are "holy" things legally protected while "sacred" things are not?

The judge also freely challenged McGuckin's authority and expertise. McGuckin was asked during his direct examination about the suicides buried in the cemetery, as to whether their graves were also "sacred":

The Witness: [I]t's actually the love, the Christian love and the Christian prayers of the surviving family that keep such a soul in the concept of the grace and mercy of Christ. It is a very, very important spiritual and pastoral concern from the family and also from the clergy who ought to support them.

The Court: When you say keeps the soul, are you talking about the soul of the deceased or the soul of the survivor?

The Witness: Both, in a sense, your honor. . . .

The Court: Are you suggesting that the prayers after the death of an individual, you pray for the soul of the deceased and that changes something?

The Witness: In Catholic and Orthodox theology it is believed that the survivors have a duty to offer the Eucharist for the soul of the individual. In Orthodox theology the Eucharist is offered as an intercession for the deceased person. And every Sunday, for example, when I celebrate Eucharist, it's Orthodox liturgical custom for Orthodox people to bring names—Catholics also do this—that the priests will particularly pray for over the consecrated Eucharist. In the Orthodox Church for each name we mention, a piece of the bread, which isn't Eucharist, is cut out in memory of them and the names—in other words, the pieces of bread is dropped into the Eucharistic chalice after the people have communicated this. It's an ancient and very profound theology that the prayers of the living Christians and the prayers of the communion in heaven will affect the judgment of other souls. It's what I would refer to as the Doctrine of the Communion of the Saints. . . . It's one of those doctrines that the Reformation took issue with, and the Reformed Christian tradition, by and large, doesn't share that religious approach.[108]

The reformed Protestant Ryskamp and the orthodox McGuckin had here reached an unbridgeable divide. I think Ryskamp really did not credit what McGuckin was saying.

With Katz the judge returned again to the respective meanings of holy and sacred, interrupting the direct examination of the defendant's lawyer. Bruce Rogow asked:

Q. So would you agree that even municipal cemeteries comprised of Catholics and other Christians and non-Christians are sacred and holy places?

A. Again, I have problems with the word sacred.

The Court: Well, would you have the same problem with holy?

The Witness: No. I don't have the same problem with the word holy.

The Court: Well, holy is set aside?

The Witness: Yes. Set aside.

The Court: Not inherently divine but sacred—

The Witness: That's the kind of distinction I need to make, yeah.[109]

Ryskamp seized opportunities to confirm his own religious worldview, one in which the graves had a very limited and restrained religious field, in his words "holy" but not "sacred." A certain respect was due but very little in the way of ongoing religion happened there. Nothing more was to be done, in a very real sense, within his religious worldview, for those buried there.

In spite of his expressed pleasure and confidence, I think that Ryskamp became convinced over the course of the trial that his pleasure was in some sense illicit, that "talking theology all day" was perhaps not what federal judges ought to be doing when they are on the bench. Indeed, he began to suspect, I think, that what he had been doing was constitutionally dubious.

Ryskamp hinted at this concern in a footnote to his published opinion in the case (also discussed above):

> n11 Because the Court finds that the plaintiffs have not established a cognizable claim under the Florida RFRA, the Court need not address the statute's constitutionality. The Court does note, however, that the statute, which operates to exempt religious but not secular conduct from compliance with neutral laws of general applicability, evidences a preference for religion which arguably runs afoul of the Establishment Clause of the First Amendment. *Cf.*, *City of Boerne*, 521 U.S. at 536 (Stevens, J. concurring) ("In my opinion, the [Federal RFRA] is a 'law respecting an establishment of religion' that violates the First Amendment to the Constitution.")[110]

Ryskamp here expresses a concern about the constitutionality of the Florida RFRA. But one might go further. Perhaps, by "talking theology," he himself, like the statute, had been evincing an unconstitutional "preference for religion," or a particular kind of religion. One might even say that, by "talking theology," as a federal judge, he violated his own often expressed confidence in the unboundedness of American religion.

Free Religion

E VEN IF THE JUDGE, the lawyers, and the expert witnesses in the *Warner* case had gotten it right, in some sense, even if they had understood and proved faithful to what they were hearing from the plaintiffs, would that have made religious freedom possible in this case? The argument of this book is, finally, that the law probably cannot get it right—today, at the beginning of the twenty-first century. It depends, in part, on how *law* is imagined, of course, as well as religion and religious freedom. But if, by *law*, we mean statutes and constitutions—the positivist secular law of states and of the international community—then legally encompassing the religious ways of people in an intensely pluralist society is most likely impossible. With all the good will in the world and unlimited expertise, the religious life of the *Warner* plaintiffs (and, indeed, perhaps of most people at most times, but certainly today) resists legal definition in a fundamental way.

Ordinary religion, that is, the disestablished religion of ordinary people, fits uneasily into the spaces allowed for religion in the public square and in the courtroom. Should that make a difference to the promoters of freedom and the defenders of civil liberties? This chapter steps back from the particulars of the *Warner* case: first, to set that case in the wider religio-legal context of the United States and its history; and, then second, to explore the alternatives to laws protecting religion. I will, in the end, suggest that freedom and equality are better realized, and liberty better defended, if religion, *qua* religion, is not made an object of specific legal protection. The legal defense of human dignity and of life beyond the state must be honored in other ways.

One of the peculiar ironies of the *Warner* case is that, while the plaintiffs were in many ways typically American in their individualistic and democratic religious ideas and practices, the City of Boca Raton promoted, and Judge Ryskamp at times seemed to adopt, an understanding of religion profoundly at odds with both the dominant American Christian theology and that of Ryscamp's church, in particular. The City promoted, and Ryscamp sometimes approved, a "high" deference to centralized institutionalized authority, a religious authority that for Christians was fundamentally challenged in the Protestant critique of the Roman Catholic

Church during the Reformation, and for Jews was arguably lost in 70 C.E., when the Romans destroyed Jerusalem and the Temple. The Reformation was complicated and resulted in the short term in a wide range of church-state arrangements, most of them "establishments," in the modern sense. But the Protestant reformers stressed the capacity of individuals to make their own religious decisions without mediation by priests, and that capacity has been progressively more and more realized in the cultures of those churches. Rabbinic Judaism, too, has a highly dispersed form of religious authority.

Like Anne Hutchison and other early American religious iconoclasts, American Protestants today, and increasingly persons of other religious traditions, locate religious authority in their own religious experience and judgment. The New England colonies, for all of their apparent rigidity, produced a steady stream of religious visionaries who resisted the discipline of the Puritan church/state. The importance of experience as a source of authority in religion is not new but has taken a particular form in modern secular states. Danièle Hervieu-Léger, for example, notes a similar phenomenon in contemporary French Catholicism. She comments that secularization should be understood not as "the process of the eradication of religion ... but one of the re-composition of the religious within a broader redistribution of beliefs in a society within which no institution can lay claim to a monopoly of meaning."[1] Governor Jeb Bush, in his amicus brief filed in the *Warner* appeal, agreed, defending the Florida RFRA in the Florida Supreme Court: "[S]imply because some individuals may not hold institutional beliefs of ancient origin does not mean that these beliefs are not religious."[2]

The religious lives of the *Warner* plaintiffs, as revealed in the trial, are, notwithstanding the religious diversity of the United States, characteristically American, both in regard to U.S. religious history as a whole, and with a view to the peculiarities of the late twentieth century. There are some interesting and important exceptions,[3] but American religion has largely been dominated by antiauthoritarian ideologies and practices that have resulted in a multiplying fragmentation of communities. The conditions of late modernity, that is, increased migration, rapid communication, a more visual culture, and a more complex and extensive religious diaspora, have extended and magnified that tendency in new ways. Americans confront a dizzying array of religious alternatives. And the expectation is that they will make their choices as individuals.[4]

Another way to say this is that the *Warner* plaintiffs testified to religious lives that are integrated only at the local level. Significantly, given the iconoclastic bias evident at times in the *Warner* trial, "local" means for them not simply a distancing of translocal and institutional religious authority; "local" means a more embodied religion, one less intellectual and doctrinal than that often expressed by religious elites. The *Warner* plaintiffs repeatedly said that their understanding of their religious lives was not limited to formally endorsed and explicitly denominated religious activities. Religion flowed into everyday activities and objects. This kind of religion is what David Hall, Robert Orsi, and others have recently described as "lived religion."[5] "Lived" religion could also be called "popular" or "folk" religion, although these terms may imply a hierarchy of religious practices in ways that "lived" does not. Lived religion is not conceived in opposition to elite religion. "Lived" religion shifts the focus to the local, a local that is increasingly also transient. Integration happens temporarily and at the instigation of individuals and families, and even occasionally local congregations, but is spectacularly resistant to hierarchical control.

Robert Orsi begins an essay on lived religion with this description of popular Catholicism in New York City:

> The Roman Catholic Church of St. Lucy at the corner of Bronxwood and Mace Avenue in the North Bronx boasts a huge outdoor construction of rocks and plants that "replicates," according to a brochure available at the parish, the topography of the countryside in Lourdes, France, where in 1858 a woman in white appeared to a girl named Bernadette and announced herself to be the "Immaculate Conception."[6] St. Lucy's is famous throughout New York City for this reproduction. The site, which is in a working-class Italian American neighborhood, is popularly known as the Bronx Lourdes. The grotto was built in 1939 at the peak of the vogue among American Catholics for copying European locations of Mary's appearances. "It looked like someone's patio had exploded," a woman recalled of the days of the grotto's construction. "People brought in stone and cement. . . . Everyone helped. Some of the women who knew handicrafts helped in decorating and painting the statues; the men did the heavy work."
>
> A stream of cold, clear New York water pours down the face of the grotto from a pipe hidden (but only just) in the rocks. . . . Lourdes water is the most powerful of modern Catholic devotional media. . . . An endless procession of cars pulls up to the grotto on warm spring and summer afternoons (the water is shut off in cold weather). . . . Visitors were holding white plastic gallon jugs, paper cups, and glass tumblers beneath the

stream. . . . They drank water there and took the water home with them; they made the Sign of the Cross with dripping hands and ladled scoops of water onto their heads for a "blessing."

I was standing one afternoon at the foot of the rocks watching the family of a very old woman who could not walk lift her out of her wheelchair so she could hold a cup to the grotto water herself. . . . "Where does the water come from?" I asked her. At the time the grotto was constructed. . . . a rumor [had gone] around . . . that builders had—miraculously—discovered a spring of fresh water. . . . "What do you mean, where does the water come from?" She looked at me sharply, apprehensively, as if she were suddenly afraid that I was the sort of excessively, perhaps dangerously, pious man who believed in such crazy rumors and discussed them with women at shrines. "It's city water—it comes from the reservoir, I guess [footnotes in original omitted]."[7]

Orsi contrasts this scene with the ideas about religion held by his Midwestern students:

Students in my class on U.S. urban religions are offended by the practices that take place at St. Lucy's. They are especially outraged that the people involved consider these practices "religious." . . . [N]ot one student in all the years I have taught . . . has ever been willing to say that the practices at St. Lucy's are of obvious importance to the people who do them and therefore worthy of our serious attention. The image of holy water being poured into car engines is especially disturbing to students, an instance of the general blurring of categories they want to keep distinct (sacred/profane; spirit/matter; transcendent/immanent; nature/machine) which occurs at St. Lucy's. *What happens at the Bronx grotto is literally inadmissible, because it is not "religion"* [emphasis supplied].[8]

"What happens" is not "admissible" to some U.S. college students and it is not "admissible" in a U.S. court of law. Nor is it apparently protected by laws protecting religious freedom. Judge Ryskamp and Bruce Rogow, like Orsi's students, saw the practices of the *Warner* plaintiffs, practices arguably analogous to the activities of Italian Catholics at the Bronx Lourdes, as not really religion. Only for Ryscamp and Rogow, it was not simply a question of ignorance or unfamiliarity. It was a question of law.

Colleen McDannell, another historian of American religion, has written powerfully about the role that objects have played in American piety, Protestant and Catholic. In *Material Christianity*,[9] McDannell shows us the

material life of everyday home-based American Christianity, arguing per-
suasively that it is in part through objects that Americans sacralize their
materialistic culture:

> Artifacts become particularly important in the lives of average Christians
> because objects can be exchanged, gifted, reinterpreted, and manipulated.
> People need objects to help establish and maintain relationships with su-
> pernatural characters, family and friends. Christians use goods and create
> religious landscapes to tell themselves and the world around them who
> they are.[10]

She suggests that her analysis could be extended to immigrants from other
religious traditions, including Jewish ones.[11] Such a use of objects and
landscape to sacralize and personalize the death of their relatives, the space
of the Boca Raton Cemetery, and their own ongoing relationship to the
graves is evident throughout the *Warner* plaintiffs' testimony.

At the *Warner* plaintiffs' depositions, which were held in October 1998,
the plaintiffs were asked repeatedly by Bruce Rogow whether and in what
ways their religion "required" them to do what they did. They were cate-
chized as to their religious training, their religious beliefs, and the frequency of their attendance at religious services. They were asked to
document the sources of customs, and they were asked whether each object
on the grave had what Rogow rather mysteriously referred to as "independent religious significance." Independent of what? The plaintiffs struggled
to describe a complex process of identity formation and motivation. All of
the plaintiffs combined references to religious institutional affiliation with
references to family tradition, personal piety, and the immediate religious
context of the deaths to support the description of what compelled their religious exercise. The plaintiffs tried to explain why they did what they did.
The lawyers wanted them to say who and what made them do it. Rogow's
aim was crystallized in a question he asked McGuckin at the trial, "My
question, though, relates to placing that cross or that statuary on the grave
site—that's a personal matter, not a religious, traditional, compelled or
suggested or needed matter?"[12]

Two parallel conversations seemed to be taking place at the trial. Plaintiffs, it could be said, epitomized a subaltern religious sensibility. No one
made them do it and yet they were compelled by the logic of their own religious, cultural, and psychological location. Like Orsi's Bronx pilgrims,
who knew both that the water was New York City water and that it was a
conductor of God's favor,[13] the *Warner* plaintiffs knew that the objects they
assembled were ordinary rocks and plants and cement statues, but they also

knew that these things represented all that was holy. Also like Orsi's Bronx pilgrims, they did not need ministers, priests, or rabbis to tell them either of those things.

"Lived religion" has a political as well a religious dimension. There is a peculiar shape to the relationship of an individual to one or more religious traditions and communities in a country with a fiercely disestablished religious sensibility. Thomas Curry, in a wonderful and provocative book, *Farewell to Christendom*,[14] argues that the difficulty today in the United States is not that the rights of religion are incompletely implemented in the courts, as many would argue, but that the radical promise of religious freedom in America has been betrayed by most of its most energetic self-appointed promoters. Curry vehemently disagrees both with the so-called separationists, those dedicated to a high wall being vigilantly maintained between church and state, and with the so-called accommodationists, the sponsors of laws such as RFRA. In his view, the neo-Jeffersonians and the liberal Baptists, on the one hand, and the "new religionists"[15] and evangelicals, on the other, both misunderstand, the nature and significance of the U.S. commitment to religious freedom. The separationists do so, he says, because the very effort to separate implicates government in delineating the boundaries of religion, making separation inherently discriminatory. Accommodationists do so because they succumb to the trap of promoting a functionalist definition of religion: Religion is allowed no authority of its own but should be accommodated because it is good for the country. Religion, the accommodationists say, promotes civic responsibility. Both positions, in Curry's view, betray the radical nature of the American experiment with respect to religion. Both positions also, in his view, undermine religious belief and practice by giving government authority over religious authenticity.

Curry notes what is apparent in the *Warner* case: that, because of what he sees as the arrested development of the religion clauses, courts have been put into a position in which they are asked to decide the right and wrong of religious practice. Curry quotes the Supreme Court's decision in the *Lyng* case (discussed above). "In [*Lyng*]," he says, "the Court correctly pointed out that judging what was 'central' and, by implication, what was 'peripheral' to religion did not fall within its purview and that to attempt to decide these issues would 'require us to rule that some religious adherents misunderstand their own religious beliefs.'"[16] Ryskamp did exactly that. In his effort to decide what was central and what was peripheral, what was compelled and what was personally preferred, the judge, as well as the lawyers and the experts in the *Warner* case, frequently implied that the plaintiffs did not understand their own religion or were not faithful adherents of that religion. Curry calls the churches to abandon the culture wars of the First Amendment religion-clauses debate and take up the utopian challenge of radical freedom, a freedom that depends in no way on government.

Christian Smith, a sociologist of American religion, makes a related point about American churches when he describes the churches' often distorted reading of history. Smith points to what he calls the "conventional mentality" in the telling of U.S. evangelical protestant church history. Christian churches in the United States, he says, bemoan constantly the decline (or, in other words, the accommodation to modernity) of religious life in the United States. Smith comments: "The first problem is the tendency to read religion ahistorically: reifying the religious group's past into a sort of golden age of orthodoxy and ethics, one that never really existed. Set against such a mythical past, it is easy to read the contemporary religious reality as in decline." He adds: "Part of the problem here lies in the tendency of accommodation-stories to compare normative views of historical religious elites . . . with empirical descriptions of religious believers."[17] One sees the decline story at various points through the *Warner* trial, probably most acutely in McGuckin's testimony. But one also sees at various points the tendency to compare religious elites with contemporary laypersons, a comparison that lends a normativity to the former and a thinness to the latter. The plaintiffs were often compared disfavorably to a religious ideal. Whether one considers such judgments theologically mistaken, as Curry does, or descriptively mistaken, as Smith does, asking courts to distinguish between true and false religion raises serious political and constitutional concerns.

Is the religious life of the United States today, as described by Hall, Orsi, McDannell, Curry, and Smith, new? Has "lived religion" ever been in sync with the law? American religion has arguably been anarchic from the beginning. Forty years ago, in the preface to his enduring and unmatched set of essays about American religion, *The Lively Experiment: The Shape of Christianity in America*, Sidney Mead described what happened to religion when it was transplanted to the United States. In his introductory tribute in that volume to Philip Schaff, a great German historian of American religion, Mead tells of Schaff's comments to German scholars upon his return to Germany from the United States in 1854:

> Uncommonly aware of the continuity of history, Schaff told them that America was "destined to be the Phenix grave . . . of all European churches and sects, of Protestantism and Romanism." For there, under religious

freedom and separation of church and state, these groups contend as equals and no one is strong enough to dominate. He urged them to see the religious situation in America as a "motley sampler of all church history." There "all powers of Europe, good and bad, are . . . fermenting together under new and peculiar conditions." And while to be sure everything "is yet in chaotic transition state," yet "organizing energies are already present, and the spirit of God broods over them, to speak in time the almighty word: 'Let there be light!' and to call forth from the chaos a beautiful creation."[18]

Schaff's expectation that order would emerge out of chaos may sound like a failure of nerve to some today, but the conditions of American religion that Schaff observed a century and a half ago remain much the same.

Mead went on:

I have quoted Schaff not merely to enlist the defenseless dead in support of my views—which, like most historians, I am constantly tempted to do—but because in my opinion he correctly sensed the uniqueness of the American religious scene and suggested the motifs to be followed in interpreting its significance. The motifs are that the history of the Christian Church is an unbroken continuum, that the fragmentation in America is due primarily to the transplantation of all the churches and sects of Europe, that the religious freedom there practiced and the "frontier" situation placed the church under new and peculiar conditions, and that out of the ferment and conflict which give the appearance of chaos, "something wholly new will gradually arise."[19]

Again, while their faith in religious order and progress sounds dated to our jaded ears, Schaff and Mead presciently described the "chaos" of American religion, and the cause of that chaos: radical disestablishment and religious freedom, present in the United States from the beginning.

In the first chapter of the same book, a chapter entitled "The American People: Their Space, Time and Religion," Mead wrote:

[F]rom the beginning, the subtle magic of space began to work upon the tight little islands of the transplanted authoritarians themselves, eroding their most ingeniously contrived and zealously guarded barriers of creed and logic and doctrine, until by the time of Crèvecoeur, it was no more than repetition of a platitude to say that "zeal in Europe is confined; here it evaporates in the great distance it has to travel; there it is a grain of powder inclosed, here it burns away in the open air, and consumes without effect."[20]

Law, in the form of disestablishment, and open available space, made orthodoxy impossible to enforce. Dissenters could, and did, simply move down the road and set up shop elsewhere. Mead describes Americans as having had, in contrast to Europeans, plenty of space but little time. Americans can still seem to be in a hurry and the zeal may seem mostly to burn away in the open air, "without effect."

The religion experts in the *Warner* case offered opinions that were for the most part tangential to the story delineated by American religious historians from Schaff to Orsi. Significantly, four of the five experts chosen by the lawyers in the *Warner* case were not experts on American religion—and the religion they described was not very American, in the sense just described. There were, as a result, important and repeated disjunctures between the world of the experts and the world of the plaintiffs. The two groups spoke of different religious realities. In his Report, as already discussed, Katz divides religion into two kinds:

> By "high tradition" is meant the textual-legal side of a religion, usually male dominated and church or synagogue-centered. By "little tradition" is meant the folkways and home-centered observances, usually orally rather than textually transmitted, often the domain of women in a traditional culture. Another way of making this distinction would be by using the concepts of "by law" and "by custom." In contemporary America, the "little traditions" are often based in ethnicity, and one can make a distinction between practices which are "religious" and customs which are "ethnic," the "high" and "low" traditions.[21]

The two kinds of religion, according to Katz, are: first, hierarchical male religion, that is, religion established in *law*, religious *law* and secular *law*; second, there is ethnic religion and folkways, folkways that are often "at variance with the laws"—that is, at variance with what Katz calls "divine law." What Katz terms "little" or "low" is thus doubly un*law*ful on his telling. It is un*law*ful as a religious matter and it should also be un*law*ful as a secular matter. Secular law thus is understood by Katz simply to replicate religious law in its own dealings with religion. In Katz's world there is no legal place for religion that is not legally legitimated in a religious sense.

Nearly everything that the *Warner* plaintiffs did falls into a category Katz calls "folkways." There is almost a complete absence in the plaintiffs' testimony of what Katz calls the "textual-legal side of a religion, usually male dominated and church or synagogue-centered." The church and the synagogue and the texts are almost entirely absent as authoritative voices about individual practice. The plaintiffs did not look to divine law, as expressed in texts, or to the opinions of clerics. They did what they were brought up to do and what they were brought up to do was sometimes at variance with the law, divine and secular. It was lawless, in a formal sense. While textual and institutionalized religion does exist in the United States, both within particular religious communities and in the national "civil" religion, the authority of their texts and institutions is continuously subverted by disestablishment so that one might say that much American religion is "low" or "little" or "female."[22] It is often formless and chaotic and "feminine," being only tangentially and episodically related to established institutions and authoritative texts.

Pals's scheme also contrasts with the picture of "lived" religion offered by American religious historians today. Pals's four questions were recapitulated and then employed by Judge Ryscamp to determine what religion is on the periphery and what religion is in the center:

> [I]n the case of any given practice or custom, we can make a reasonable determination by posing four main questions: 1) Is it asserted or implied in relatively unambiguous terms by an *authoritative sacred text*? 2) Is it clearly and consistently affirmed in *classic* formulations of doctrine and practice? 3) Has it been observed *continuously*, or nearly so, throughout the history of the tradition? 4) Is it consistently practiced *everywhere*, or almost such, in the tradition as we meet it in most recent times [emphasis supplied]?[23]

The difficulty with this appealingly formalized test is that there is no religious center in the United States defined by authoritative texts, classic formulations of doctrine and practice, continuous tradition, and ubiquitous practice. There are only occasional and unevenly distributed voluntary associations with texts, classic formulations, and traditions, combined with oral tradition, recent innovation, and local variation. One might even say that much of American religion is on the "periphery," in Pals's terms, of normative religion.

Judge Ryskamp's own formula, as expressed in his written opinion, that the religion that counts *legally* is religion that "reflects some tenet, practice or custom of a larger system of religious beliefs," appears more open and inclusive in formulation than either Pals's or Katz's. In Ryscamp's actual application of that formula, however, he betrays that openness in his use of Pals's four questions to delimit the field, putting himself at odds with the mainstream of American religion as well.[24] Indeed, if what the plaintiffs in the *Warner* case did is not real religion, legally, then perhaps there is very little real religion in this country.[25] What the plaintiffs did, and how they explained what they did, *is* American religion, if anything is. It may be the best that there is.

There is religion that *looks* institutional and authoritarian in the United States. There are what look like traditional forms of traditional religions, such as the Roman Catholic hierarchy, on the one hand, and aspects of the sacralized state, on the other. The power of the first kind derives from its persuasive ability. The second tends to be invisible although powerful. The first looks plenty religious but increasingly lacks state backing to enforce its norms and practices. The second is religiously invisible, having been assimiliated into "secular" culture, though it may have enforcement power through legislation. But both of these are subject to the corrosive power of memberships with highly developed understandings of their rights, as is evident from the economic vengeance being exacted by Catholics unhappy with the bishops' handling of clerical sex abuse and the willingness of many to flout state marriage-licensing laws. In the end, the forms of institutionalized religious authority that would fit the tests designed by Katz, Pals, and Ryskamp are subject to the desires of their masters, the individuals who make up their congregations.

The second form, a kind of nationalism, has produced in the United States and elsewhere something that looks a lot like an established religion, what Robert Bellah called "civil religion."[26] Indeed American civil religion may be textual-legal in a way that many American religions are not. American civil religion has sacred texts: the Declaration of Independence, the Constitution, Lincoln's Second Inaugural, among others. It also has institutions to give authoritative interpretations of those texts, and laws mandating observance of its rituals and protecting its holy shrines and objects. This national religion would be religion "by law," in Katz's terms, as opposed to religion "by custom." It would be the religion of the "center," rather than of the "periphery," in Pals's terms. The religion clauses are a part of that religion—if one wants to call it religion. But what is it they are protecting?

How should an acknowledgment of the anarchic and materialistic folkways of U.S. religion affect interpretation of the U.S. Constitution? And the religion clauses of the First Amendment in particular? When law claims authority over religion, even for the purpose of ensuring its freedom, lines must be drawn. Problems of definition arise when decisions are made by prisons as to the regulation of inmate religious observance; by zoning commissions when decisions are made as to the placement of places of worship; by taxing authorities when decisions are made as to exemptions from taxa-

tion; by schools when children claim a right to be excused from requirements on the grounds of religious conscience; by cities when they celebrate
ethno-religious holidays; by legislatures that are asked to regulate religious
butchering; by military authorities administering a chaplaincy program; by
judges who are asked to substitute religious ex-offender programs for other
kinds of rehabilitation efforts. These definitional decisions are rendered
more difficult by the diffuseness of American religion. They also form part
of a larger issue for a pluralistic society, whether that pluralism is religiously or otherwise understood. Decisions about legal accommodation
can be an appropriate acknowledgment of difference but they can also be
discriminatory, giving legal muscle to only some among competing anti-
egalitarian normative regulatory schemes.[27]

Fair legal accommodation of differences among humans is a major problem for law. Other kinds of difference have been affirmatively accommodated by American law from time to time—differences, for example, in
gender, race, ethnic origin, and culture. If religion deserves to be on this list,
even given pride of place, as some would argue,[28] then courts and legislatures
will be required to decide when a particular practice is religious and when a
practice is "cultural." Courts would have to decide whether and when Muslim veiling is religious, political, or cultural, for example, in considering
whether Muslim women have the right to wear the hijab in their passport
photos. And whether circumcisions, male or female, are religious or cultural,
in considering whether they are legal. Each time a decision is made to tailor
law to account for difference, a question of equal treatment is presented.

What would be lost if law focused not on the special case of religion but
on the accommodation of difference generally, and what compromises any
such accommodations imply for commitments to equality? Without an explicit protection for religion, guarantees of freedom of speech, of the press,
and of association would continue to protect most of those institutions, including religious ones, usually thought necessary for a free democratic society. With respect to some religious practice, though, religious persons
and communities would, like other groups asserting difference, have to
make arguments for the special legal accommodation of difference to legislative bodies, as they do today under the *Smith* doctrine. Government fa-
voritism (or endorsement) could be prevented by vigorous insistence on
principles of equality, as is happening now in the case of gay marriage.
Groups making a case for differential treatment would be required to make
a very strong showing, as in race cases, of past discrimination or present
need, to justify special legal treatment.

Such a focus on equality and difference, rather than on religion, would also acknowledge the fact that equality has arguably been and continues to be *the* dominant political value of American politics and of constitutional jurisprudence, and that a drive for equality has already succeeded in significantly undermining any protectionist promise of the religion clauses.[29] Issues of equality, and attendant concerns about discrimination, arguably became a more and more important influence on the interpretation of the religion clauses in the second half of the twentieth century. Legal historian Mark deWolfe Howe argued almost forty years ago that the Supreme Court's new mid–twentieth century insistence on neutrality and equality between religion and non-religion, modifying the eighteenth-century's primary concern with equality among religions, could be traced to delayed enforcement of the Civil War Amendments, a delay that intensified the Court's concern for legal enforcement of nondiscrimination. The mutual reinforcement of a mood in the Court that anticipated the decision in *Brown v. Board of Education* and assertions of federal power in the religion cases of the 1940s meant, in Howe's words, that "[t]his century's theory of religious freedom was a by-product, as it were, of its theory of political liberty."[30] But it was also the result of changes in religion.

Without a plausible political consensus about why and how religion *qua* religion, and religiously motivated persons, should be privileged in law, and a corresponding capacity to define what is meant by religion, the principle of equality would suggest that for purposes of the "free exercise" clause, simply including "other" religions is not enough. Persons not explicitly motivated by religion should have the same rights to "free exercise."[31] Likewise, for the "establishment" clause, entirely excluding religion from government places and government benefits solely because such benefits are religious is increasingly understood as discriminatory to persons identifying themselves as religious.[32] If the religion clauses continue to be understood to guarantee equal rights to those who do not claim explicitly religious motivation and to permit religiously motivated persons to receive government benefits on the same ground as those who are not so motivated, the religion clauses will lose their exclusive purpose—although perhaps not their rhetorical value.[33]

This book is intended, at the simplest level, to show that "religion" can no longer be coherently defined for purposes of American law. It is impossible to make sense of the religion clauses of the First Amendment without a coherent sense of what is at stake. But it is not just a question of coherence. It is also a question of justice. The Fourteenth Amendment guarantees "equal protection of the law."[34] If the definition of religion is expanded for purposes of the free exercise clause to include all self-described "religiously motivated" behavior, are not the fear mongers right? To do this would be to give every American the power to determine whether a particular law comports with their religion, as they define it. And it privileges these persons over those who would not so describe their motivation. To expand the definition of religion for the purposes of the establishment clause is to imitate an almost French-style secularism and a corresponding sacralization of the state, limiting the access of religiously motivated persons to public goods. It is to give law the power to determine what counts as religion, the power to divide citizens into believers and nonbelievers.[35]

While the legal protection of religious freedom as a political idea was arguably once a force for tolerance, it has now arguably become a force for intolerance. My case study is drawn from the United States, but I mean to suggest a larger point, one not confined to the narrow dogmatisms of the debate over interpretation of the First Amendment to the U.S. Constitution. Parallel situations exist in all pluralistic democracies today, notwithstanding different histories, different religious minorities, and different structures of government. The effort to assimilate Muslim citizens and their religious practice in Europe, for example, reveals quite different legal and cultural assumptions and formations[36]—different as among European countries, and different from the United States. But, legal protection for "religion" anywhere demands a definition of religion. While definitions of various kinds, or at least workable local practices with respect to line-drawing, were arguably available in some sense when political rights to religious freedom were first invented, such consensus definitions or practices are rapidly becoming unworkable.

Religion, consciously separated from society and culture by the Protestant and Catholic Reformations, the wars of religion in Europe, and the various Enlightenments, is being reincorporated, intellectually, and in practice, into other cultural and social realities, in myriad ways—through art, tourism, music, international political movements, a rediscovery of so-called spirituality, and the internet. This may be because society in general is becoming less differentiated, in a sociological sense.[37] It may also be so because religion, in particular, is understood in a more inclusive way. The power of the established churches of Europe is fading in memory. Religion is seen to be fragmentary and diffuse and egalitarian. It is there in private and in public, in acts of charity as well as in acts of terror, on the internet as well as in churches.

We live in a new moment, a time of undifferentiation—in which a postmodern consciousness is reluctant to see sharp divisions such as those historically described as the sacred and the profane. The events and social changes that marked the advent of modernity are destabilized: The nation-state is challenged by transnationalism of various sorts, including the growth of diaspora communities and international institutions and instruments;[38] the monopoly of military and police power by the sovereign is threatened by the spread of entrepreneurial violence; the importance of printing and literacy is giving way to a visual culture; capitalism and the money economy is being changed by globalization; reason and science have in places produced fear rather than progress; the promise of the "rule of law" is undermined by the specters of Nazi and Soviet law and by the assaults of legal realism and critical legal studies; and finally, religion has proved to be not an irrational, private, and authoritarian premodern relic destined to fade away, but has proved remarkably vital and ubiquitous, refusing the place assigned it by the modern consciousness. The study of religion has changed, too. No longer an extension of theology, religious studies is an interdisciplinary branch of the humanities and the social sciences, now better understood as focusing on an enormously important, complex, and fascinating cultural reality—religion—a reality that may be necessary for human survival but the truth and goodness and definition of which is not taken for granted, and therefore cannot claim special legal protection.

Explaining these changes in court can be challenging. Legal instruments guaranteeing religious freedom may not be able to protect "little" religion anywhere. Customary religion has arguably had a certain protection in homogenous societies in which it has filled out a field defined in part by the hierarchical power of "high" religion. There it is often invisible, being continuous with culture and custom. In a state that is radically disestablished and pluralistic in its religious life, however, "little" religion needs legal rights, too, if any religion is to have rights.

There is a sense in which religion moved from "norm" to "fact" in modernity. Laws guaranteeing religious freedom meant that religion no longer would provide norms for society, but that religion must prove itself as a social fact in court. The defining of religion and the subordination of religion to a secular legal authority are projects, both political and academic, of the modern West. They are the products of the early modern disestablishment and differentiation of religion and of a growing positivistic and scientist understanding of the world. Sociologists of religion from Max Weber to José Casanova have described the disenchantment of the medieval world and the resulting secularization and privatization of religion. Much of Western scholarship about religion—and law—is defined by this understanding. And modern laws protecting religious freedom are built on it. But that differentiation was being subverted from the beginning, and perhaps that is something that law should now take account of.[39]

Almost all countries now contain a proliferating pluralism and spiritual individualism that defies any one establishment. There is a growing disjunction between the expectation of both these fissiparous communities and their members with respect to their rights to self-determination as *religious* communities, and the realities of legal regulation. These conditions are true for world organizations like the Catholic Church and the Episcopal Communion as well as for local home-grown religion. All countries also now contain religious diasporas of many of the world's religious traditions. Religions in most places lack the legal and epistemological muscle that once gave them shape. And secular positivist law, the rule of law, is king.[40]

If one difficulty with enforcing laws guaranteeing religious freedom—the one given most attention in this book—is the impossibility of fairly delimiting the contours of contemporary religious life, the other is the incapacity of law. Proponents of laws guaranteeing religious freedom tend to work with a definition of law as problematic as that of religion. There is a tendency to accept modern law's representation of itself as autonomous, universal, and transparent. Such a representation makes religion, not law, the problem. There is a history here too. Modern secular law emerged in the modern West as the product of a deliberate effort to rid law of ecclesiastical authority and of religious ideas, language, and goals.[41] Modern secular law is not, however, indifferent to religion. Religion was seen as the problem. So, as a whole host of contemporary legal historians have explained, secular law only *appears* secular. In fact, it is replete with ideas and structures that find their origin in, and are parallel to, ideas and structures in religious traditions: crime, sin, and so forth—ideas and structures that in many instances cannot be coherently defended using simply utilitarian forms of argument. Secular law implies a subordination and submersion of religion.

Law cases concerning religion, whether in the United States or elsewhere, reveal the peculiar relationship between law and religion in late modernity. They also reveal the extraordinary staying power of religion. It is by now stale news that religion has "returned." The eventual and inevitable secularization of society predicted by some seems at least delayed.[42] But the "return" of religion, or, perhaps more accurately, the returned attention to religion, highlights the conditions of religion's persistence, and the changes that have occurred in those conditions. The "return" of religion takes place in a space structured and conditioned by law—secular law, the "rule of law," a law that enjoys an unprecedented hegemony.[43] The vaunted "freedom" of religion is bounded, and in a very particular way. Religious communities, like other private associations, are extensively regulated, as they always have been.[44] In the rare cases when religion is able to claim a privileged legal status, that is, to claim a privileged status as "religious," as over against associations that are not-religious, the exception is closely monitored by law.

Religion has a curiously Janus-faced quality in the late modern period—in relation to law. Religion's one face is associated with the irrational, the savage, and the "other" in a profoundly constitutive way. That face is to be feared and kept separate. That religion is the religion of Jefferson's "impious clerks"[45] and of religiously inspired terrorists. At the same time, however, religion's other face is regarded as a primary source of ethical reflection and behavior and thought by some as the only such source. This latter face of religion is sometimes explicit, in the writing of some ethicists and public theologians,[46] but it is more often invisible, in the "golden rule" religion, or "overlapping consensus" religion, that most Americans hold in common.[47] This face of religion is considered desirable, even indispensable, as a foundation for a country ruled by law, not by men.

Legally enforced religious freedom as a political goal denies and conceals the profound ambivalence toward religion revealed in this split personality. Furthermore, the denial is arguably accomplished, in part, through the use of the Delphic utopian language of human rights, whether in national constitutions or in international instruments. The denial may certainly be necessary to the political consensus underlying the promotion and protection of religious freedom. But the denial also conceals the fact that religion is not always, in fact, absolutely free, legally speaking. The right kind of religion, the approved religion, is always that which is protected, while the wrong kind, whether popular or unpopular, is always restricted or even prohibited. While this schizophrenia about religion is often noted, it is less often noted that it is in everyday legal contexts that the betrayal at the heart of laws guaranteeing religious freedom is most apparent. It is in the words and acts of courts and legislatures making specific the promises of rights that the balancing act fails and the impossibility of realizing religious freedom reveals itself. The impossibility is as much about law as it is about religion.

Neither religion nor law today can be understood apart from an understanding of the cluster of ideas and practices around the modern invention of religious freedom, disestablishment, and the rule of law. The instability of religion as a category is a product of the history of the legal regulation of religion, a history that, in turn, radically undermines the liberal political commitments that have underlain that history. The instability of religion as a category also limits the capacity of law to enforce rights to religious freedom. Modern law wants an essentialized religion.

Religious freedom is one of a set of rights or freedoms that are today understood together as forming the foundation of free democratic societies. They are enumerated in the U.S. Constitution, in the UN Declaration of Human Rights, and in many other legal and political documents around the world. Constitutional protection for religious freedom is considered a sine qua non of modern industrial society. Does it make sense for religion to be on that list? To be sure, all political freedoms are bounded. Freedom of speech, a free press, freedom of association, the right to vote, and so forth, are all circumscribed. They are only "free" in a manner of speaking, free within a particular political system and given the limitations of that system, whether understood cynically as the limitations imposed by an arbitrary police power or ideally as limitations built into life in community. One may not say anything anywhere. One may not print anything. One may not associate with others for any purpose. Not everyone can vote. The state controls all of these human activities, and does so for its own purposes. So too, with religion. Religion is not limitlessly free in any human society, even in the United States.

With respect to religion in particular, however, the legal limits to religious freedom are often expressed by rhetorically set boundaries that are strangely unhelpful when it comes to actual cases. Everyone understands, it is said, that religious freedom is not absolute. Religious communities are naturally bound by local fire and police regulations at one end of the spectrum and by the boundaries of civilized behavior, on the other end, that is, by the horror of human sacrifice. Yet there is a great deal of religious activity that falls between parking lots and the shedding of blood. And most of it intersects with legal regulation of some sort.

Religion is also arguably different from speech, movement, association, and the like. The limits come not only from the state or even from the nature of human society. It is the peculiar nature of religion itself to restrict freedom. Those fiercely religious persons whom we admire, or despise, are those with an unbending devotion to the rules of their religion, as they understand them, whatever their source. They seem to live in a world that makes sense, a world in which one has a place and in which certain non-negotiable things are demanded of one. At a very profound level, religion competes with law—and also, perhaps more importantly, with science and a scientistic reading of law—for comprehensive explanation and control.[48] Religion challenges the rule of law. To be religious is, in some sense, to be obedient to a rule outside of oneself and one's government, whether that rule is understood to be established by God, or otherwise. It is to do what *must* be done. To be religious is, for most people, to live *without* a certain amount of freedom. To be religious is not to be free, but to be faithful.

To be free, on the other hand, is today understood to mean to have the ability to choose for oneself in all areas of life, without restraint. To be free is to be faithful only to oneself or to such ideologies and communities outside of oneself that one freely chooses. Freedom can, as many have observed, be profoundly unnerving. Religion seems to answer a profoundly important human need. It organizes things and creates imperatives. One implication of the refrain at this trial, that the plaintiffs' actions were the result of "purely personal preference," can be understood to contain a moral judgment. The implication is that the plaintiffs acted out of "desire," out of what they individually wanted to do, as opposed to what ought to be done—the ethical. Sadly, I think, this implication resulted from a profound misunderstanding of the plaintiffs' motives and actions. They *were* doing what must be done, and doing so at some personal cost.

What can the "free exercise of religion" mean, then, if it is not the freedom to do what we desire? Religious freedom, affirmatively understood, must mean something like the freedom not to be free, in ways not already constrained by biology, culture, government, or economic circumstance—the freedom to be bound by claims beyond "this world" and beyond the state. Understood within the context of American history, however, and that of some other countries, particularly France, religious freedom can be understood to have a negative meaning as well, a rejection both of religious foundations for government and of governmental support for religion. At the time of the founding, Americans of all sorts arguably committed themselves to a secular national government that claimed, perhaps for the first time in human history, no authority in matters religious. This commitment is an austere and demanding vision, probably a utopian one, the full realization of which has been a bumpy process. Thomas Curry, as noted above, has called the United States to task for failing to realize the radical nature of this commitment.

Religion is also different in that, as usually understood today, it divides rather than brings together the human community. When religion was historically differentiated from politics, science, and so forth, it also became optional. Modern humanity, unlike medieval humanity, was rhetorically divided between those with faith and those without. In an effort to end violence, in deference to the supposed virtue promoted by religious education, and from a failure to imagine a society without religion, religion was given legal privileges. Increasingly, however, those privileges are seen to violate the higher American principle of equality. Unless "religion" is to be broadened to include everyone, to give legal protection to religion is to privilege those who understand themselves to be religiously motivated over those who understand themselves to be motivated by equally deeply held secular values. (Such secular values might be regarded as "religious," in some sense, by some scholars and theologians, but it would likely be politically unacceptable to so denominate them.)

Among the components of the coming world order, as conceived by the many proponents of the "rule of law," is the cultural extension and legal enforcement of human rights. Among these rights, rights that conceive a world order respectful of human dignity, is a guarantee of, in the words of the United Nations, "freedom of religion and belief." Written at a time of hope in the capacity of nations to work progressively toward the establishment of laws protecting human rights for all human beings, religious freedom is now vigorously promoted by a new generation of internationalists. Curiously, this enthusiasm for religious freedom coexists with a revival of exclusivist religious movements that understand themselves to be the singular path to salvation, that regard religious "freedom" as the work of the devil, or perhaps of a pernicious and soulless consumerist secularism. The right demanded is often the right to proselytize.

The tension here described with respect to religion between the promise of universal claims and the actual realization of those guarantees in national law schemes has, with respect to all human rights, been extensively critiqued by scholars and activists.[49] This critique takes several forms. Anthropologists, postcolonial theorists, and other cultural relativists question the possibility of effectively guaranteeing rights in a language that is culturally and historically bound to the West.[50] Others have questioned the possibility of enforcing justice through law, at all, given its dependence on the violence of the state. Whether it is possible to find any ground for the critique of law outside of legal regimes controlled by nations and therefore subject to political manipulation is a pressing political question today. How should we solve the problem that "the legal system of rights recognizes only what is predetermined as acceptable on the basis of evaluating the different through questions such as 'does it meet our definition of what we share in common, of our common-being, that is our definition of the human?'"[51] In other words, do human rights regimes do what they purport to do? Can they be an effective tool for the reform of law and society globally?

Guarantees to religious freedom are only one subset of the range of guarantees made by constitutions and international legal instruments around the world, guarantees that envision a future free from oppression and want. All these guarantees are undermined by the limitations of language and of human will as well as the inherent violence of state law. One alternative to the statist monopoly of law common in the modern nations of the West is a formal acknowledgment of normative pluralism, a normative pluralism that exists at many levels, from the international to the local. John Bowen's fascinating new study of the recent history of the interaction among customary law (*adat*), Islamic law, and state law in Indonesia, inserts anthropology into the debate.[52] Bowen insists on understanding these three legal traditions as equally valid voices in the Indonesian context, thereby delineating the conditions of legal pluralism. Each legal tradition is also internally diverse. Each is institutionalized in complex ways at the local and national levels, and all interact in a situation of serious discursive instability. Naming Islamic law religious does not necessarily either privilege it or exclude it, except rhetorically for some people in some situations. All three are seen by Bowen to contribute to an effort to reimagine law in Indonesia. All three struggle with changing economic conditions, with the changing roles of women, and with the challenge of a nonexclusive claim to defining what is to be normative.

The right to freedom of religion claims a right to transcendent fidelity to a life outside the state and outside oneself. For some, the right to religious freedom is therefore to be enthroned as the first right in an absolute sense, the right without which the others are meaningless. Much is made, for example, by some American theorists, about the fact that the religion clauses are listed first in the Bill of Rights, although there is little evidence that the placement was intended by the drafters to have any significance.[53] While the question might be asked as to whether all human "rights" demand a transcendent reference,[54] the guarantee of a right to religious freedom is almost perversely insistent on the necessity of transcendence. While the argument can be made that all rights depend on a religious understanding of the person, the right to religious freedom makes that argument a necessary part of law. Only then can the resulting discrimination against those who claim to have no religion be justified. That is the best argument for legal guarantees of religious freedom. But as with other rights against the state, such rights are paradoxically dependent on state enforcement. The evidence in the *Warner* case could be understood to suggest that what is sought by the plaintiffs is not the right of "religion" to reproduce itself but the right of the individual, every individual, to life outside the state—the right to live as a self on which many given, as well as chosen, demands are made.[55] Such a right may not be best realized through laws guaranteeing religious freedom but by laws guaranteeing equality.

Appendix A
Relevant Law:
Excerpts from U.S. and Florida Constitutions, RFRA, FRFRA, and Rules and Regulations of Boca Raton Cemetery

U.S. CONSTITUTION, AMEND. I.

Congress shall make no law respecting an establishment of religion, or prohibiting the free exercise thereof; or abridging the freedom of speech, or of the press; or the right of the people peaceably to assemble, and to petition the Government for a redress of grievances.

U.S. CONSTITUTION, AMEND. XIV, SEC.1.

All persons born or naturalized in the United States, and subject to the jurisdiction thereof, are citizens of the United States and of the State wherein they reside. No State shall make or enforce any law which shall abridge the privileges or immunities of citizens of the United States; nor shall any State deprive any person of life, liberty, or property, without due process of law; nor deny to any person within its jurisdiction the equal protection of the laws.

FLORIDA CONSTITUTION, ART. I, § 3.

RELIGIOUS FREEDOM.

There shall be no law respecting the establishment of religion or prohibiting or penalizing the free exercise thereof. Religious freedom shall not justify practices inconsistent with public morals, peace or safety. No revenue of the state or any political subdivision or agency thereof shall ever be taken from the public treasury directly or indirectly in aid of any church, sect, or religious denomination or in aid of any sectarian institution.

RELIGIOUS FREEDOM RESTORATION ACT (2003)

42 USCS § 2000BB (2003).

Congressional findings and declaration of purposes

(a) Findings. The Congress finds that—
  (1) the framers of the Constitution, recognizing free exercise of religion as an unalienable right, secured its protection in the First Amendment to the Constitution;
  (2) laws "neutral" toward religion may burden religious exercise as surely as laws intended to interfere with religious exercise;
  (3) governments should not substantially burden religious exercise without compelling justification;
  (4) in *Employment Division v. Smith, 494 U.S. 872 (1990)* the Supreme Court virtually eliminated the requirement that the government justify burdens on religious exercise imposed by laws neutral toward religion; and
  (5) the compelling interest test as set forth in prior Federal court rulings is a workable test for striking sensible balances between religious liberty and competing prior governmental interests.

(b) Purposes. The purposes of this Act are—
  (1) to restore the compelling interest test as set forth in *Sherbert v. Verner, 374 U.S. 398 (1963)* and *Wisconsin v. Yoder, 406 U.S. 205 (1972)* and to guarantee its application in all cases where free exercise of religion is substantially burdened; and
  (2) to provide a claim or defense to persons whose religious exercise is substantially burdened by government.

§ 2000BB-1 (2003).

Free exercise of religion protected

(a) In general. Government shall not substantially burden a person's exercise of religion even if the burden results from a rule of general applicability, except as provided in subsection (b).
(b) Exception. Government may substantially burden a person's exercise of religion only if it demonstrates that application of the burden to the person—
  (1) is in furtherance of a compelling governmental interest; and
  (2) is the least restrictive means of furthering that compelling governmental interest.
(c) Judicial relief. A person whose religious exercise has been burdened in violation of this section may assert that violation as a claim or defense in a judicial proceeding and obtain appropriate relief against a government. Standing to assert a claim or defense under this section shall be governed by the general rules of standing under article III of the Constitution.

§ 2000BB-2

Definitions

As used in this Act—

(1) the term "government" includes a branch, department, agency, instrumentality, and official (or other person acting under color of law) of the United States, or of a covered entity;

(2) the term "covered entity" means the District of Columbia, the Commonwealth of Puerto Rico, and each territory and possession of the United States;

(3) the term "demonstrates" means meets the burdens of going forward with the evidence and of persuasion; and

(4) the term "exercise of religion" means religious exercise, as defined in section 8 of the Religious Land Use and Institutionalized Persons Act of 2000 [*42 USCS § 2000cc-5*].

§ 2000BB-3

Applicability

(a) In general. This Act applies to all Federal law, and the implementation of that law, whether statutory or otherwise, and whether adopted before or after the enactment of this Act [enacted Nov. 16, 1993].

(b) Rule of construction. Federal statutory law adopted after the date of the enactment of this Act [enacted Nov. 16, 1993] is subject to this Act unless such law explicitly excludes such application by reference to this Act.

(c) Religious belief unaffected. Nothing in this Act shall be construed to authorize any government to burden any religious belief.

§ 2000BB-4 (2003).

Establishment Clause unaffected

Nothing in this Act shall be construed to affect, interpret, or in any way address that portion of the First Amendment prohibiting laws respecting the establishment of religion (referred to in this section as the "Establishment Clause"). Granting government funding, benefits, or exemptions, to the extent permissible under the Establishment Clause, shall not constitute a violation of this Act. As used in this section, the term "granting," used with respect to government funding, benefits, or exemptions, does not include the denial of government funding, benefits, or exemptions.

FLORIDA RELIGIOUS FREEDOM RESTORATION ACT.
FLORIDA STATUTE § 761.01.

Short title

This act may be cited as the "Religious Freedom Restoration Act of 1998.

§ 761.02.

Definitions

As used in this act:

(1) "Government" or "state" includes any branch, department, agency, instrumentality, or official or other person acting under color of law of the state, a county, special district, municipality, or any other subdivision of the state.

(2) "Demonstrates" means to meet the burden of going forward with the evidence and of persuasion

(3) "Exercise of religion" means an act or refusal to act that is substantially motivated by a religious belief, whether or not the religious exercise is compulsory or central to a larger system of religious belief.

§ 761.03.

Free exercise of religion protected

(1) The government shall not substantially burden a person's exercise of religion, even if the burden results from a rule of general applicability, except that government may substantially burden a person's exercise of religion only if it demonstrates that application of the burden to the person:

(a) Is in furtherance of a compelling governmental interest; and

(b) Is the least restrictive means of furthering that compelling governmental interest.

(2) A person whose religious exercise has been burdened in violation of this section may assert that violation as a claim or defense in a judicial proceeding and obtain appropriate relief.

§ 761.04.

Attorney's fees and costs

The prevailing plaintiff in any action or proceeding to enforce a provision of this act is entitled to reasonable attorney's fees and costs to be paid by the government.

§ 761.05.

Applicability; construction

(1) This act applies to all state law, and the implementation of that law, whether statutory or otherwise, and whether adopted before or after the enactment of this act.

(2) State law adopted after the date of the enactment of this act is subject to this act unless such law explicitly excludes such application by reference to this act.

(3) Nothing in this act shall be construed to authorize the government to burden any religious belief.

(4) Nothing in this act shall be construed to circumvent the provisions of chapter 893.

(5) Nothing in this act shall be construed to affect, interpret, or in any way address that portion of s. 3, Art. I of the State Constitution prohibiting laws respecting the establishment of religion.

(6) Nothing in this act shall create any rights by an employee against an employer if the employer is not a governmental agency.

(7) Nothing in this act shall be construed to affect, interpret, or in any way address that portion of s. 3, art. I of the State Constitution and the First Amendment to the Constitution of the United States respecting the establishment of religion. This act shall not be construed to permit any practice prohibited by those provisions.

RULES AND REGULATIONS OF THE BOCA RATON MUNICIPAL CEMETERY AND MAUSOLEUM (1996)

INTRODUCTION

For the mutual protection of all purchasers, and for the preservation of all lots, plots, crypts and niches in the Boca Raton Municipal Cemetery and Mausoleum, these Rules and Regulations shall govern the ownership, use and control of all said lots, plots, crypts and niches. Reference to these Rules and Regulations in the Certificate of Ownership or Deed, or in the recorded plot shall have the same force and effect as if these rules and amendments were set out therein in full.

SECTION I

Definitions

(1) Articles—Including, but not limited to, boxes, shells, toys, ornaments, chairs, settees, crosses, statues, benches, vases, rocks, fencing, borders, windchimes, candles, candle holders, plants, shrubs, trees or herbage of any kind.

(2) Cemetery—The Boca Raton Municipal Cemetery and Mausoleum.

(3) Certificate of Ownership—The original conveyance given by the City of Boca Raton or the Boca Raton Mausoleum, Inc., to the original purchaser with burial rights to the spaces listed.

(4) Crypt—A space of sufficient size to accommodate at least one casket holding remains entombed above ground.

(5) Entombment—The permanent disposition of a deceased person in a crypt, columbarium, sarcophagus, or niche within a mausoleum.

(6) Disentombment—The removal of a deceased person in a crypt, columbarium, sarcophagus, or niche within a mausoleum.

(7) Grave—A plot containing an in earth burial.

(8) Interment—The permanent disposition of the remains or cremains of a deceased person in earth burial.

(9) Disinterment—The removal of the remains or cremains of a deceased person in earth burial.

(10) Legal Holidays—Those annual holidays which are given by the City of Boca Raton to its employees.

(11) Lot—A numbered division as shown on the Cemetery map, which consists of more than one plot.

(12) Lot Marker—A concrete or suitable material used by the City to locate corners of the lot or plot.

(13) Marker—A memorial which does not extend vertically above the ground and is constructed of approved metal or stone containing names, dates, or other engraved lettering used in identification of one or more persons and placed at the head of a lot or plot.

(14) Mausoleum—A building or structure above ground for entombments in vaults, crypts, niches, columbariums, sarcophagus or a combination of any one or more than one thereof.

(15) Memorial—A monument, marker, tablet, headstone, private mausoleum or tomb for family or individual use, tombstone, coping, lot enclosure, and surface burial vault, urn, crypt and niche plates or bronze lettering on crypts or niches.

(16) Monument—A tombstone or memorial of granite or other approved materials, which shall extend vertically above the surface of the ground.

(17) Niche—A space of sufficient size to accommodate at least one urn holding cremated remains above ground.

(18) Plot—A space of sufficient size to accommodate a single depth in earth burial.

166

(19) Plot, Double Depth—A space of equal surface area as a single plot with the depth capacity to accommodate two in earth interments, one atop the other.

(20) Resident—A natural person having his or her place of residence within the City of Boca Raton, and having the intention to continue residing in Boca Raton for an indefinite period of time.

(21) Scatter Garden—A specially designated and maintained area set aside for the exclusive purpose of disseminating cremated human remains.

(22) Vault—Also termed as an "outer box," is an encasement or container constructed of concrete, concrete and steel, stone or other suitable material used to encapsulate the casket, cremains or other burial containers in order to maintain the shape and integrity of the plot.

SECTION II

General Supervision

(1) Admission to Cemetery and Mausoleum—The City of Boca Raton, a municipal corporation of Florida, reserves the right to compel all persons driving motor vehicles into Boca Raton Municipal Cemetery to bring their vehicles to a full stop at the entrance and further reserves the right to refuse admission to the Cemetery grounds, and to refuse the use of any of the Cemetery or Mausoleum facilities at any time to any person or persons whom the Cemetery Manager determines is unwilling or incapable of abiding by these rules or the rules of general decorum.

(2) Cemetery Manager in Charge of Funeral—All funeral processions, on entering the Cemetery grounds, shall be under the direct control and supervision of the Cemetery Manager, provided that the funeral director for the funeral shall be present to conduct the burial services in accordance with the applicable Florida Statutes and these rules and regulations.

(3) Casket Not to Be Disturbed—Once a casket containing human remains is transported into the Cemetery, a funeral director, or his embalmer, assistant, employee or agent, is prohibited from opening the casket with the following exceptions:

(a) The legal representatives of the deceased at the time of interment or entombment, pursuant to a court order or a valid disinterment or disentombment permit, may cause the casket to be opened in the event that an item(s) was not removed or placed with the deceased.

(b) The casket may be opened if an examination of the deceased is required by the medical examiner's office or other law enforcement agency. Cemetery or Mausoleum staff shall not open any casket. Viewing of the deceased is prohibited at the Cemetery or Mausoleum.

(4) Funeral Directors Responsible for Transporting Deceased's Remains—All funeral directors, their representatives, and aides shall be responsible

for transporting the remains of a deceased person from the funeral coach containing the deceased's remains to the grave or crypt. At least one person from the funeral director's staff shall be in attendance as a witness during interment or entombment of the deceased's remains.

(5) Supervision of Disinterment or Disentombment—Upon receiving an order from the owner of record to disinter or disentomb human remains from a cemetery plot or Mausoleum crypt or niche, the Cemetery Manager will direct the removal and final disposition of said human remains in the presence of a licensed funeral director. The Cemetery Manager or Cemetery staff shall not perform removal or transfer of human remains in the absence of a licensed funeral director unless under order of court.

SECTION III

Entombments or Interments and Disinterments or Removals Generally

1. Subject to Law—In addition to these rules and regulations, all interments, entombments, disinterments and removals are made subject to the orders and laws of the applicable governmental authority.
2. Holidays—No interments, entombments, disinterments, disentombments, removals or interments services shall be permitted on Thanksgiving, Christmas Day or Easter Sunday. Services for Saturday, Sunday, or on any legal holidays may be permitted by the Cemetery Manager upon the payment of applicable charges, provided those services do not interfere with a scheduled holiday event such as Veteran's or Memorial Day services hosted by the Cemetery.
3. Notice for Interment or Entombment—The Cemetery Manager shall be notified at least twenty-four (24) hours prior to any interment or entombment and at least one (1) week prior to any disinterment or disentombment or removal, or except in case of emergency or court order. The Cemetery Manager may refuse to make an interment or entombment until a more expedient time if the remains arrive at the Cemetery gate after 3:00 P.M., or if more than one funeral arrives at the same hour. No service may continue after 4:00 P.M. unless granted by the Cemetery Manager under extenuating circumstances and applicable fees are paid.
4. Application for Interment or Entombment—The Cemetery Manager reserves the right to refuse interment or entombment in any plot, niche or crypt and to refuse to open any burial or entombment space for any purpose if a written application by a qualified plot, crypt or niche owner of record is not submitted to the office of the Cemetery Manager prior to the close of normal business hours defined as Monday through Friday, 8:00 A.M. to 4:30 P.M., excluding holidays.

5. Vault or Outer Box—Every earth interment, including cremated remains, shall be enclosed in an encasement or container constructed of concrete, concrete and steel, stone or other suitable material used to encapsulate the casket, cremains or other burial container in order to maintain the shape and integrity of the plot. An outer vault or outer box provided by the funeral director shall be of a type approved by the Cemetery Manager and be installed by the Cemetery staff or a designated vault manufacturer under the supervision of the Cemetery Manager.

6. Location of Interment Spaces—When instructions regarding the location of an interment space in a lot cannot be obtained, or are indefinite, or when the interment space cannot be opened where specified, the Cemetery Manager may at his discretion, open it in such location of the lot as he deems best and proper, so as not to delay the funeral.

7. Orders Given by Telephone—The Cemetery Manager shall not be held responsible for any order given by telephone, or for any error resulting from imprecise or improper instructions regarding the particular space, size, location and memorialization in a lot, crypt or niche where interment or entombment is desired.

8. Errors May be Corrected—The City of Boca Raton may correct any error made by it in making interment, disinterment, or removal, or in the description, transfer or conveyance of any interment property, by cancelling such conveyance and substituting and conveying in lieu thereof other interment property of equal value and similar location as selected by the Cemetery Manager, or by refunding the amount of money paid on account of said purchase. If the error involves the interment of the remains of any person in a different location, the Cemetery Manager shall have the right to remove or transfer such remains so interred to such other property of equal value and similar location as may be substituted and conveyed in lieu thereof. The Cemetery Manager shall also have the right to correct any errors made by placing an improper inscription, including an incorrect name or date, either on the memorial, marker, crypt, niche or on the container for cremated remains.

9. Delays in Interments or Entombments Caused by Protests—The City of Boca Raton shall not be liable for any delay in the interment of a body resulting from a protest against the interment or from noncompliance with these rules and regulations. Under such circumstances, the Cemetery Manager has the right to place the body in a receiving vault until full rights have been determined. The Cemetery Manager shall be under no duty to recognize any protests of interments or entombments unless accompanied by supporting documentation, including, where applicable, a court order.

10. Cemetery Manager Not Responsible for Permits, Embalming or Identity—The Cemetery Manager shall not be responsible for obtain-

ing interment or entombment permits or for the identity of the person sought to be interred, or the embalming of the body.

11. No Interment Permitted Unless Property or Space has been Paid For in Full—No interment shall be permitted on, or memorial placed in or on, any lot or plot in Boca Raton Municipal Cemetery where the purchase price thereof has not been paid in full.

12. Interment of More than One Body or Cremated Remains in a Standard Single Depth Plot—Not more than one body, or the remains of more than one body, shall be interred in any one plot or single crypt, except in the case of a mother and her infant, unless the plot has been purchased with the written agreement that more than one body or the remains of more than one body shall be interred therein; provided that proper identification is made of such interment or interments on one regulation marker. The space required for the interment of cremated remains shall be standard plot size, established by the Cemetery Manager; however the remains of two (2) of such cremated decedents may be interred in one standard single depth plot.

13. Interment of Two Human Remains in a Standard Double Depth Plot—Not more than two (2) human remains shall be interred in any one double depth plot. The plot shall be purchased with the written agreement that more than one (1) human remains or the cremains of more than one (1) body shall be interred therein, but not more than (2) remains in any combination may be placed, provided that proper identification is made of such interment or interments on one regulation sized marker. The agreement shall also provide the name of the person authorized to designate the identity of the person other than the purchaser of the plot whose remains may be interred in the double depth plot.

14. Interment in Church or Lodge Plot—In instances in which the burial rights are owned by a church, lodge, or other society, interments shall be limited to residents who are members of the organization, husbands and wives, and to immediate members of the families.

15. Interment in a Section Reserved for Cremated Remains—The Cemetery Manager shall designate an appropriate section of the Cemetery for interment of cremated remains. Plots within this section shall be of appropriate size, and the cremated remains of only one (1) deceased person may be interred in each plot.

16. Interment in a Section Reserved for Infants—The Cemetery Manager shall designate an appropriate section of the Cemetery for interment of infant remains. Plots within the reserved section shall be of appropriate size to permit the interment of one (1) infant less than one year of age.

SECTION IV

Disinterments and Removals

1. Larger Plot May Be Obtained—A body or cremated remains may be removed from its original lot or plot to a larger or better lot or plot, crypt or niche in the Cemetery or Mausoleum, where there has been an exchange or purchase for that purpose and where all fees and additional charges have been paid in full.
2. Care in Removal—The Cemetery Manager shall exercise reasonable care in making a removal, but assumes no liability for damage to any casket, burial case, vault or outer box or urn incurred in making the removal.

SECTION V

Services Charges

Payment of Services Charges—The charges for services in connection with an interment must be paid by the funeral director prior to the closing of the grave. Charges for disinterments or removal must be paid at the time of issuance of the order for same.

SECTION VI

Interments and/or Burial Rights of Owners—Cemetery Only

1. Right of Interment under Owner's Certificate of Ownership or Deed—At the time of purchase of a lot or plot, an owner shall, and at any time thereafter during the purchaser's lifetime, an owner may execute a Declaration of Reservation specifically designating the persons entitled to be buried in the plot or in any or all of the plots in a lot, or vesting the right of designation for unreserved plots in a named peson.

    Upon application by any person for interment of a body in a given burial space, the burden of proof as to the identity of the person to be interred rests upon the applicant. The Cemetery Manager is authorized to rely on the representations as provided in the application.
2. Right of Interment in Absence of Owner's Declaration of Reservation—In the absence of a Declaration of Reservation by the registered owner of a burial space, the order of interment shall be:
    (a) One burial space shall be forever reserved for the owner and for the owner's surviving spouse, if any.
    (b) Lineal descendants of the owner, or owners, and their respective spouses.
    (c) Parents of the owner, or owners.

3. Vested Rights of Owners—The burial rights of an owner shall be presumed to be the sole and separate property of the person named as grantee in the Certificate of Ownership or Deed, provided, however, that the spouse of an owner shall have a vested right of interment of his or her body in any burial space conveyed to the other spouse, provided that such person shall remain the spouse of the owner or shall be the spouse at the time of the owner's demise. No conveyance or transfer of a lot or plot shall be made by a married owner without the joinder of the spouse.

4. Inalienability of Cemetery Plots—All lots, the use of which has been conveyed in a Certificate of Ownership or Deed, are indivisible. Whenever an interment of the remains of the record owner, or of a member or a relative of a member of the family of the record owner, is made in a lot, the lot thereby becomes inalienable, and shall be held as set forth in the Declaration of Reservation.

SECTION VII

Transfers of Assignments—Cemetery Only

1. Cemetery Lots or Plots May Be Transferred and Assigned—Provided that, upon such transfer, the City of Boca Raton shall be paid a transfer fee and the difference between the original charge for the lot or plots and the current charge for such lots or plots. No cost differential shall be charged by the city upon a transfer to a resident of Boca Raton who is a lineal descendant or ascendant of the transferor. No Cemetery lot or plot may be transferred or assigned to any person who is not a resident of Boca Raton.

2. Consent of the City of Boca Raton—No transfer or assignment of any lot or plot or interest therein shall be valid without the consent in writing of the City Manager. Transfer or assignment must be made upon forms provided by the City of Boca Raton for this purpose. The original Certificate or Deed must be presented at the time application for transfer is made.

3. Transfer Charges—The approved transfer fee shall be charged for a transfer of ownership in lots or plots which shall be paid when the transfer is recorded.

4. City May Repurchase—In the event the original lot owner moves his residence from Boca Raton permanently, and is not able to find a suitable buyer for his lot, the city may repurchase the lot at the original price.

SECTION VIII

Control of Work by City

1. Work to Be Done by City of Boca Raton—All grading, landscape
    work and improvements of any kind, the care of plots, lots, crypts and
    niches, all planting, trimming, cutting and removal of trees, shrubs
    and herbage, all openings and closing of plots, lots, crypts and niches,
    and all interments, entombments, disinterments and removals shall be
    performed by the City of Boca Raton or a designated contractor under
    the supervision of the Cemetery Manager.
2. The City of Boca Raton Must Direct and May Remove
    Improvements—All improvements or alterations of lots, plots, crypts
    and niches in the Cemetery or Mausoleum shall be performed under
    the supervision of the Cemetery Manager; if any improvements, in-
    cluding landscape materials such as trees, shrubs, flowers or herbage,
    and alterations are made without his written consent, he may remove,
    alter or change the improvements or alterations at the expense of the
    owner. The Cemetery Manager may also remove or change any im-
    provements or alterations, at the owner's expense, if at any time, in the
    Cemetery Manager's judgment, they become unsightly.
3. Benches—Public convenience benches shall not be placed on any lot,
    plot, grave or any other location not approved by the Cemetery Man-
    ager. Plot owners or persons desiring to donate to the City for the
    purpose of purchasing benches for Cemetery use, must contact the
    Cemetery Manager for approval of a standard bench to be purchased
    by the City at the donor's expense. The Cemetery Manager shall de-
    termine the location of placement, and upon installation, the bench
    shall become the sole property of the City and may be relocated or re-
    moved at the City's discretion. The City reserves the right to limit the
    number of benches installed.

SECTION IX

Decoration of Cemetery Plots and Mausoleum Crypt or Niches

1. Floral Regulations—No flower receptacles may be placed on any plot
    unless of approved material, size and design. Flower receptacles which
    are not an inclusive part of the marker design shall not be permitted.
    Flower receptacles placed in grass areas on the plot or surrounding
    the marker, are subject to damage by maintenance equipment and are
    therefore considered to be the sole responsibility of the plot owner.
    The planting of flowers, shrubs, trees, plants or herbage of any kind
    shall not be permitted without the expressed written consent of the
    Cemetery Manager. The Cemetery Manager shall have the authority
    to remove all floral designs, flowers, weeds, trees, shrubs, plants or

herbage of any kind, from the Cemetery or Mausoleum as soon as, in the judgment of the Cemetery Manager, they become unsightly, dangerous, detrimental or diseased, or when they do not conform to the standard maintained. The City of Boca Raton shall not be liable for floral pieces, baskets or frames in which, or to which, such floral pieces are attached, beyond the acceptance of such floral pieces for funeral services held in the Cemetery or Mausoleum. The Cemetery Manager shall not be responsible for frozen plants, or herbage of any kind, or for plantings, damages by the elements, thieves, vandals, maintenance operations or by other causes beyond his control. The Cemetery Manager reserves the right to regulate the method of decorating plots so that a uniform beauty may be maintained. The Cemetery Manager reserves the right to prevent the removal of any flowers, floral designs, trees, shrubs, plants, or herbage of any kind, unless consent is given.

2.   Certain Articles Prohibited—The placing of any articles of any kind upon plots or upon or in front of crypts and niches that are not specifically authorized under these rules and regulations shall not be permitted. The Cemetery Manager reserves the right to remove same. The placing of small articles on a headstone memorial after a sixty (60) day period from the date of burial shall be prohibited. The placing of small articles on a headstone memorial on the deceased's birthday, Mother's Day, Father's Day, the anniversary date of the deceased's death, and on national holidays may be permitted. The small articles may be permitted for a period commencing one (1) day before and ending five (5) days after such birthday, anniversary or holiday. The Cemetery Manager reserves the right to remove all articles which interfere with the maintenance of the Cemetery or Mausoleum, or interfere with the accessibility to another plot, crypt or niche in the preparation of an interment, disinterment, entombment or disentombment.

3.   Certain Flowers Prohibited in Mausoleum—No artificial flowers, except silk flowers, are permitted in or around Mausoleum buildings. Anything contained herein to the contrary notwithstanding, no flowers of any kind whatsoever, including, but not limited to, fresh flowers, artificial flowers and silk flowers, shall be permitted in the Rotunda Building and the Remembrance Chapel of the Mausoleum. No flowers can appear on front of crypts or niches unless the holder is installed by the City of Boca Raton. All remembrances (flowers) must be placed in front of or near a particular crypt or niche and fresh flowers can remain for a maximum period of three (3) days. After the third day, or in the case of silk flowers, when the Cemetery Manager determines that the flowers have become unsightly, said flowers and holder shall be removed and disposed of in a manner acceptable to the Cemetery Manager.

4.   Potted Plants Regulated in Mausoleum—No potted plants containing soil, perlite, or other loose materials are permitted in chapels or walkways in the Mausoleum except for the holidays of Easter, Mother's

Day, Father's Day and Christmas; in those instances, the potted plants shall be removed within 48 hours after the holiday or the posted holiday time frames.

5. City Shall Not Be Liable for Damage to Articles Placed on Grave Plots, Markers, Memorials or Monuments—Articles placed on grave plots, markers, memorials or monuments which protrude or extend above ground level, except for approved floral containers, constitute interference to proper maintenance of plots and the City shall not be liable for damage to such articles.

SECTION X

Conduct of Persons within the Cemetery and Mausoleum Grounds

1. Must Use Walks—Persons within the Cemetery and Mausoleum grounds shall use only the avenues, walks, alleys and roads.
2. Persons in the Cemetery and Mausoleum—Only authorized personnel, and visitors, owners and relatives shall be permitted on the Cemetery and Mausoleum grounds.
3. Children—Children under fifteen (15) years shall not be permitted within the Cemetery or its buildings unless accompanied by an adult.
4. Flowers, Etc.—All persons are prohibited from gathering flowers, either wild or cultivated, or disturbing trees, shrubbery or plants, or feeding or disturbing the wildlife, within the Cemetery or Mausoleum grounds.
5. Refreshments—No person shall be permitted to bring food or refreshments within the Cemetery or Mausoleum grounds.
6. Lounging on Grounds—No one shall be permitted to sit or lounge on any of the grounds, graves or monuments in the Cemetery or Mausoleum.
7. Littering—Littering is expressly prohibited anywhere within the Cemetery and its buildings.
8. Vehicular Traffic Requirements—No persons shall drive any motor vehicle within the Cemetery grounds at a speed greater than is reasonable in light of any activity then occurring within the Cemetery, provided that no motor vehicle shall be operated at a speed greater than ten (10) miles per hour. All motor vehicles shall be driven on the right side of the Cemetery roadway, and shall at all times remain on the paved portions of such roadways which are specifically provided for motor vehicle usage. No motor vehicles shall be parked or driven on or upon any pedestrian paths, walkways, or unpaved areas, nor parked or stopped adjacent to any open grave except in attendance for the services in connection therewith.
9. Bicycles and Motorcycles—No bicycles or motorcycles shall be admitted to the Cemetery except such as may be in attendance at funerals or on official business.

10. Skates and Skateboards—No roller skates, inline skates or skateboards shall be admitted to the Cemetery.
11. Peddling or Soliciting—Peddling of flowers or plants or soliciting the sale of any item is prohibited within the boundaries of the Cemetery.
12. Firearms—Possession of firearms is prohibited within the Cemetery except by duly authorized law enforcement agencies.
13. Notices and Advertisements—No signs, notices or advertisements of any kind shall be allowed in the Cemetery unless placed by the City of Boca Raton.
14. Pets—Pets shall not be allowed on the Cemetery grounds except in the case of service animals used to assist disabled patrons or visitors.
15. Time Grounds Open—The Cemetery grounds shall be open during normal daylight hours.
16. Decorum—Strict decorum shall be observed at all times within the Cemetery grounds, whether set forth in these rules or not.
17. Cemetery Manager to Enforce Rules—The Cemetery Manager shall enforce these rules and regulations, and may exclude from the Boca Raton Cemetery and Mausoleum any person whose actions are not in compliance with the rules and regulations. The Cemetery Manager shall be in charge of the grounds and buildings, including the conduct of funerals, traffic, employees, plot owners and visitors, and shall supervise and control all operations of the Cemetery or Mausoleum.

SECTION XI

Fees, Gratuities and Commissions

Gratuities Not to Be Accepted by Employees—No person, while employed by the City of Boca Raton shall receive any fee, gratuity or commission, except from the City of Boca Raton, either directly or indirectly.

SECTION XII

Protection against Loss

The City shall take reasonable precaution to protect owners and the burial rights of owners within the Cemetery or Mausoleum from loss or damage; but it expressly disclaims all liability for any loss or damage from causes beyond its control, damages caused by the weather, an act of God, common enemy, thieves, vandals, strikers, intentional malicious action, explosions, invasions, insurrections, riots, civil disturbances, or order of any military, civil or judicial authority.

SECTION XIII

Change in Address of Plot Owners

It shall be the duty of the lot or plot owner to notify the Cemetery Manager of any change in his post office or current mailing address. Notice sent to a lot or plot owner at the last known address on file in the office of the Cemetery Manager shall be deemed sufficient legal notice.

SECTION XIV

Memorials, Monuments and Markers

1. Approval by Cemetery Manager Required—The placement, location, erection and construction of all memorials, monuments, and markers within the cemetery grounds shall be done subject to the approval and under the supervision of the Cemetery Manager. The Cemetery Manager shall approve the format for mausoleum crypt plates or face inscriptions and limit the number and style of designs allowed and their dimensions in order to maintain the established standard. No variations or alterations will be permitted without written permission from the Cemetery Manager. Whenever possible, all new memorials shall be located in line with those previously established, and all placements shall conform to the size of the plot or lot for which it is intended.
2. Restrictions on Above Ground Memorials and Monuments—No memorials, monuments, or enclosures shall be permitted above ground in any section of the Cemetery grounds except in Section "A." Stone or bronze markers are allowed in all other sections provided that they are level with the ground surface.
3. Foundations Required—A foundation of suitable size and material must be placed, when necessary, for a memorial or markers at the time of installation by the company furnishing the memorial or marker.
4. Limited Liability on Markers and Memorials—Due to the necessity of continuous maintenance and control of the Cemetery grounds, it is understood that unavoidable damage may occur to the borders and edges of memorials and markers. The City shall not be held liable for such damages except for the defacing or obliteration of names, dates, or engraved emblems on the face of the markers or memorials.
5. Sales and Service Charges Must Be Paid—All installation charges, inspection and placement fees, marker sales charges and other fees or charges applied by the City to memorials, monuments, or markers must be paid in full prior installation.

SECTION XV

Purchase of Plot Sites

1. Reservation unto City Residents—The existing plot sites in the Boca Raton Municipal Cemetery remaining unsold are hereby reserved for purchase only by the residents of the City of Boca Raton, Florida.
2. Plot Site Charges—The charge for plot sites in the Boca Raton Municipal Cemetery shall be set by ordinance of the City of Boca Raton and included in the Code of Ordinances.
3. Veterans Plot Sites—In a reserved area of the Cemetery designated for such purpose, and to the extent that such space is available, all honorably discharged service men and women of the armed forces of the United States of America who were residents of the City of Boca Raton at the time of their death, shall be permitted to be interred in the Boca Raton Municipal Cemetery at a reduced plot site charge as set forth by ordinance of the City of Boca Raton and included in the Code of Ordinances. This fee may be paid to the City of Boca Raton by the funeral director or the family of the deceased. In each case, the plot site to be used for interment shall be selected by the Cemetery Manager and the specific location of a veteran's plot site cannot be reserved. Any veterans preferring burial in a family lot outside the reserved area will be charged the standard plot price.
4. Indigence—Any resident of the City of Boca Raton who is declared indigent at the time of his or her death shall be interred in a burial plot to be designated by the Cemetery Manager.

Appendix B
Expert Reports of
Broyde, Katz, McGuckin, Pals, and Sullivan

IN RE: WARNER, ET AL V. CITY OF BOCA RATON
CASE NO 98-80554-CIV-RYSKAMP
EXPERT REPORT OF MICHAEL J. BROYDE

This report will address the following issues:

> Does the Jewish faith permit the removal of grave markers, tombstones, foot markers and other stone items from a grave to be replaced with a different form of a marker that is less visible?

> Does the Jewish faith permit one to be buried without a full tombstone? What exactly constitutes a "full" headstone?

In order to answer both of these two questions, a brief background to the Jewish faith, Jewish law and its methodology generally needs to be provided. Many areas of Judaism are fundamentally regulated by the legal aspects of the Jewish tradition, commonly referred to as *halacha*, Jewish law; the role custom plays in those technical areas of Jewish law is relatively small. Thus, for example, there is an intricate analytical discussion of when is abortion permissible, prohibited or mandatory in Jewish law. This discussion contains nearly no mention of "custom"[1] as determinative of normative Jewish law. Jewish law in that context refers to the legal codes that govern Jews.

However, Judaism is as much a faith, a system of practices and religion as a legal system, and there are any number of areas of Jewish practice that are intensely governed by tradition—the ancient customs and practices of the Jewish people—as much as law. In some of these areas, law plays a very small role, in that the classical Talmudic law codes say very little about how to engage in certain rites and rituals. Burial and funeral rites and practices are such an area. The Talmud and its related codes do not treat this area of Jewish practice as governed by the same type of legal norms as other areas of Jewish practice. However, this in no way shape or form diminishes the strength of the Jewish tradition in this area. One is frequently dealing with customs that are more than 2,000 years old, and an intrinsic part of the Jewish faith. To examine Judaism in a way that is limited to its legal traditions and only protect those faith-grounded rituals and rites that the Jewish faith labels "law," rather than "tradition," would be a vast misunderstanding of the Jewish faith, and improper. As a simple example of that, consider that the right of men to keep their head covered, as a sign of their faithfulness in God, is "merely" a matter

---

[1] Hebrew, *minhag*, which literally refers to the practices of the people.

of ancient tradition according to the Jewish tradition, and not formally a matter of Jewish law. That distinction is fundamentally irrelevant, particularly when the Jewish faith is examined to determine whether any particular activity is permissible (or prohibited) to adherents of Judaism. Jews sincerely view—and the Jewish law and tradition accept—that there is a religious duty placed upon Jews to adhere not only to the technical obligations of Jewish law, but even on the duties imposed by ancient custom and tradition. To parse the Jewish faith into "law" and "tradition," and then to assert that "traditions" are not really part of the corpus of Jewish practices that faithful adherents need to live their lives observing, fundamentally misunderstands what practicing Judaism is.[2]

Jewish funeral practices focus on two concepts: (1) that which honors the deceased, and that (2) which honors the living. Except for the duty to bury speedily, tradition—rather than law—govern nearly every aspect of this rite. Thus, for example, as noted by Rabbi Moses Feinstein (*Iggrot Moshe, Yoreh Deah* 4:57), the obligation to place a marker of some type on a grave is derived from the fact that the bible notes that the patriarch Jacob marked the grave of his wife, Rachel, with a gravestone or marker, so that people will know where she is buried (See Genesis 35:20).[3] Thus, one can state with a high degree of confidence that the obligation to place a marker of some sort is quite ancient, and that one who buries without any marker is severely in violation of Jewish law and tradition.

One can see that the Jewish faith viewed the placing of a marker as mandatory, and not merely a matter of discretion from the fact that there is an intricate dispute within Jewish law as to who bears the financial burden of fulfilling the custom of erecting a tombstone. Thus, the Pitchai Teshuva (*Shulchan Aruch Yoreh Deah* 356:1), cites a response of Rabbi David Ibn Zimra (15th century, Egypt) that one must use public charity funds not only to bury a poor person, who has no money but even to build a tombstone for him as that is a form of activity which honors the deceased, and thus must be done, even at public expense.[4] So, too, Rabbi Ibn Zimra rules that a Jewish court may require that the heirs of this individual spend their money to not only build a tombstone, but to

---

[2] Of course, that does not stand for the proposition that all matters of "tradition" or even all matters of "law" are on the same level. Some traditions are less sacred than others are, and some laws require less pressing circumstances than others to be relieved of the obligation to observe them. Suffice it to note that the obligation to mark a grave is a very ancient one (as noted on page 2 of this report), and that the Jewish tradition is prepared to discuss who must pay to observe this custom, an indication that the custom must be kept.

[3] Indeed, there is quite a dispute within Jewish law as to how one is supposed to build a tombstone; should it be made from a single stone or from a collection of stones? If it is to be a collection, how many stones should be collected? For more on this dispute, and how one contemporary American decisor resolved this issue, see Rabbi Moses Feinstein, *Iggrot Moshe Yoreh Deah* 4:57.

[4] Indeed, the Jewish tradition seems to favor the custom of erecting a tombstone to honor a deceased person even when the body of the person cannot be found, as such conduct minimally honors a dead person even when their body cannot be found; see *Iggrot Moshe Yore Deah* 4:57(6).

build a proper tombstone, similar in type to other tombstones found in that cemetery. Jewish law will enforce a duty not to deviate from the customs and norms of the community.[5]

The Jewish tradition does not regulate exactly of what type and manner should the deceased be memorialized. However, the custom and practice provides some guidelines.

A deceased should not be marked with a tombstone that is less than the normal proper tombstone used in any given Jewish society; to provide a deceased person with less of a marker than those given to his peers is irreverent to that deceased person. (*Shulchan Aruch, Yoreh Deah* 364:2, and Comments of Rabbi Shabtai ben Meir Hacohen (*Shach*), 3&12.)

One should note that the Jewish tradition treated tombstones with a form of sacredness; once a tombstone was used to mark a person's grave it could not be reused for any other person or other purpose; tombstones belongs to the person who was buried near it. See *Bet Yosef,* commenting on *Tur, Yoreh Deah* 364(1) and *Rama Shulchan Aruch, Yoreh Deah* 364:1, who notes that even sitting on a tombstone while visiting the dead was wrong. Indeed, one who was working on writing a tombstone for a deceased person has the same status of one who was working to actually bury the person, as the burial is not complete until the proper tombstone is erected; See *Tur, Yoreh Deah* 365, and Rabbi Yecheil Mecheil Tukachensky, *Gersher Hachaim* 25:1.

What exactly constitutes a "proper" tombstone differs from location to location. At least three different customs can be found in the Jewish tradition:

One custom was that a tombstone was placed actually on the grave itself, instead of some of the earth, and this tombstone marked the gravesite itself, in that under this stone was the corpse.

One custom was that the full length of the corpse was covered with stones (typically 12), so that one could tell not only that there was a body at rest here, but where exactly the beginning and end of the body was.

One custom placed the tombstone before the head of the body, such that the tombstone did not rest on the same location as the body itself.[6]

Each of these customs has a valid place in the Jewish tradition, and is a reasonable expression of the normative Jewish practice.[7]

---

[5] This responsa ("responsa" is the term used to denote a question and answer of the type presented to Ibn Zimra) is important, as it shows that the Jewish tradition clearly views the obligation to build a tombstone as more than a mere custom of the type that one can choose to fulfill or not, but a duty that the law—Jewish law—will enforce.

[6] All three of these customs are explained and commented on by Rabbi Yecheil Mecheil Epstein, *Aruch Hashulchan Yoreh Deah* 364. He argues there that the removal of tombstone markers in customs 1 and 2 entails a greater violation of Jewish law than in custom 3, as in custom 3 the tombstone is not directly on the grave. I am uncertain if that argument is correct.

[7] Indeed, the issue of which type of marker is viewed as "better" according to Jewish law depends on what purpose a tombstone is supposed to serve. Some think that the minimal purpose of a tombstone is to prevent people from walking on the grave, in which case a marker to the side is less than ideal. Others think that the primary purpose of the tombstone is to

Once a tombstone is provided for a deceased, that deceased person has a property type right in that tombstone, and diminishing it is improper.

Thus, *Shulchan Aruch Yoreh Deah* 364:1 (and commentaries *ad locum*), the classical code of Jewish law, mandates that tombstones may not be removed, and when broken they have to be replaced by similar tombstones—similar in height, status, beauty and other measures. For an example of how far this concept is carried, Rabbi Moses Feinstein rules that when the letters on an old tombstone are washed away by age, and one wishes to place a new tombstone in its place, one may not write fewer words of praise for the deceased on that new tombstone than was on the original one, as such a diminution of worth of praise violates the rule prohibiting one from diminishing the honor to the deceased; see *Iggrot Moshe Yoreh Deah* 1:228.

With these two rules in mind, we can now return to our initial questions and examine whether Jewish law would view the removal of existing tombstones from a cemetery and to have them replaced with a mere marker. The answer to that question is quite clear: The removal of tombstones and their replacement with a marker of lesser status would constitute a violation of Jewish law.

Such an activity would infringe on the rights of the deceased, and would be improper according to Jewish law. It is my view that the relatives of the deceased would have a "right of action" in Jewish law to compel such activity to stop, as it violates Jewish law.

The second question—can such a regulation be promulgated prospectively, and restrict what type of tombstone can be used from now on—is more complex, and requires a more complex answer. As a matter of theory, Jewish law would see no problem with a Jewish society deciding to mark its graves with markers, rather than tombstones or full covers. In such a society, all the graves would be marked in that way, and no one would view such a marker as irreverent to the deceased individual. Many cemeteries in Israel (particularly for Jews from Arab lands) adhere to this view even currently (even though such is not the normal practice in America). However, in my view, Jewish law and tradition would not permit such to be done in a cemetery already in existence with classical tombstones and coverings already in place, as the new—and less visible markets—that would be put in place for those who are recently buried are denigrating to those who are buried next to those who have classical tombstones. People will think that those who have smaller markers were lesser people.

With that concept in mind, one can understand why the Jewish tradition did not allow for a pauper's cemetery, and instead mandated that all Jews be buried in the same type of cemetery; see *Shulchan Aruch Yoreh Deah* 356:1 and commentaries there.

In sum, a regulation which changes the type of markers used in Jewish cemeteries, and does so by actually removing tombstones and markers currently in place clearly violates Jewish law, and infringes on the free exercise rights of adherence to Judaism when this is done to graves owned by Jews. A governmental regulation which prospectively requires small markers, rather than

---

memorialize the deceased, in which case a visible tombstone is most proper. For a long essay on this topic, see *Gesher HaChaim* in chapter 25:1.

tombstones or any other type of marker, might not violate Jewish law, so long as such a regulation is confined to new cemeteries (or maybe new sections in old cemeteries), and thus prevents the comparison of the relative merits of different deceased people.[8]

I have agreed to a wage rate of $100 per hour for my work as an expert in this case. As with all fees that I earn for explaining Jewish law, I hereby assign any income I earn from this matter to the "Charity Fund of the Congregation," Young Israel of Toco Hills, Atlanta, located at 2074 Lavista Road, Atlanta, Georgia, 30329.

I have been deposed a number of times about matters of Jewish law, both in the courts of the State of Georgia and in the courts of the State of New York. So too, the Beth Din of America is occasionally called on to provide advice to various courts about matters of Jewish law. This is the first time I have actually written an "expert witness report" as governed by the Federal Rules of Evidence, Rule 702.

Michael Broyde is the senior lecturer at Emory Law School and the Acting Director of the Law and Religion Program at Emory University. His primary areas of interest are Jewish law and ethics, Law and Religion, and comparative religious law. Besides Jewish law, Michael Broyde has taught Federal Courts, Alternative Dispute Resolution, Secured Credit and other courses. He received a *juris doctor* from New York University and published a note on the *Law Review*. He clerked for Judge Leonard I. Garth of the United States Court of Appeals, Third Circuit. He is ordained as a rabbi by Yeshiva University (*yoreh yoreh ve-yadin yadin*), and serves as the Rabbi of the Young Israel of Toco Hills, Atlanta. In addition, he is a member (*dayan*) of the Beth Din of America, a Jewish law court in the United States, where he was the Director during the 1997–1998 academic year while on leave from Emory.

Michael Broyde published more than 50 articles in various aspects of Jewish law. His first book, *The Pursuit of Justice and Jewish* Law was published by Yeshiva University Press and his second, *Human Rights and Judaism* by Aronson Publishing House. He is the author of a recent article in the Connecticut Law Review entitled "Cloning People: A Jewish View," and a forthcoming book tentatively entitled *Marriage, Divorce and the Abandoned Wife in Jewish Law: A Conceptual Understanding of the Agunah Problems in America*.

This expert opinion is written both in the capacity of a professor of Jewish law and as a member of a Jewish law court. This expert opinion represents the formal view of the Beth Din of America on this matter.

---

[8] The expert report submitted in support of the defendants, which maintains that Jewish tradition allows for the removal of tombstones and their replacement with simple markers, seems profoundly flawed in that it does not distinguish between removing markers already in place and prospectively prohibiting new tombstones.

More generally, the expert report seems defective in its understanding of Jewish tradition and Jewish law; the distinctions between "law" and "custom" are not generally supportable in this context. Indeed, it is unclear if the expert who wrote the report can read Hebrew, the lingua franca of Jewish law—there are essentially no references to classical Jewish law sources at all.

EXPERT REPORT OF NATHAN KATZ

The question I investigated is as follows: What are the requirements of the major religions of this area—Catholicism, Protestantism, Judaism, and Islam—as regards markers or monuments at gravesites?; and, Do the rules governing the Boca Raton Municipal Cemetery contravene these religious requirements?

In order to answer this question, I (1) investigated burial and funerary practices of Catholics, Protestants and Jews; (2) interviewed a number of clergy who are familiar with this issue; (3) consulted standard sacred lawbooks, such as *The Code of Canon Law* (Catholic) and the *Shulchan 'Arukh* (Jewish); (4) visited the Boca Raton Municipal Cemetery on October 23, 1998, and interviewed the manager, Mr. Curtis L. Harris; and (5) I studied the *Rules and Regulations of the Boca Raton Municipal Cemetery and* Mausoleum.[1] I commissioned a student to assist with parts of this research.

My findings are that the rules of the Boca Raton Cemetery do not conflict with the religious requirements of Catholics, Protestants, Jews, or Muslims.

CATHOLICISM

The Roman Catholic Church has very minimal requirements regarding markers or memorials. In fact, in reading Canon Law on the subject of funerals and related topics, no specific mention of markers or memorials is found.[2]

In part at least, the Canons silence on the topic of markers and memorials is due to its delegation of the implementation of its principles to local religious authorities. As Canon 1243 teaches: "Particular law is to determine appropriate norms on the discipline to be observed in cemeteries, especially regarding the protecting and fostering of their sacred character."[3] Catholic tradition understands this law as follows: "This canon is another example of the Code's emphasis on subsidiarity, leaving details of the legislation to local churches."[4] In other words, beyond a few basic principles, local dioceses may set and enforce appropriate standards.[5]

The Church is clear that specifically Catholic cemeteries are to be established, and that burial there is preferred: "The Church is to have its own cemeteries wherever this can be done, or at least spaces in civil cemeteries destined

---

[1] Rules and Regulations of the Boca Raton Municipal Cemetery and Mausoleum (photocopied document, no date, made available by Curtis L. Harris, October 23, 1998).

[2] In reading through *The Code of Canon Law: A Text and Commentary* (The Office of Sanctifying in the Church), pp. 837–42, with Mr. Frank Villaronga of the Archdiocese of Miami, I found absolutely no mention of markers or memorials, although many other topics—rites, cemeteries, offerings, death registers, ecclesiastical/lay rites, etc.—are discussed in detail.

[3] *The Code of Canon Law: A Text and Commentary* (The Office of Sanctifying in the Church), Canon 1243.

[4] Ibid.

[5] The emphasis on local autonomy was affirmed by Mr. Frank Villaronga, of the Archdiocese of Miami, with whom I read relevant Canon Law on October 15, 1998. In response to an

for the faithful departed and properly blessed. If, however, this cannot be achieved, individual graves are to be properly blessed as often as possible."[6] These Catholic cemeteries may be established by a local authority (diocese or archdiocese), by an individual parish, or even by an individual family.[7]

The Associated Catholic Cemeteries' rules governing designs and inscriptions on markers and monuments are intended for a Catholic cemetery, but are applicable for all Catholics. Designs must "perpetuate Catholic ideals" and "No anti-Christian symbols, and particularly, no anti-Catholic symbols will be allowed."[8]

The Church's recommendations for memorials in specifically Catholic cemeteries as found in The Catholic Cemetery—*A Vision for the Millennium* include the following principles:[9]

1. "Every person buried in a Catholic cemetery is entitled to some type of memorialization."
2. "Every Catholic cemetery needs clearly defined rules and regulations relative to the type of material, size, design, inscription and installations of memorials."
3. "Memorials are an important part of fostering the community's awareness of the sacred. A memorial keeps remembrance alive. It commemorates. In a Catholic cemetery, it is lasting evidence and a reminder of a Christian life lived."
4. "Memorials must not offend religious proprieties, Church discipline or good taste. Because different cultural and ethnic groups in our society have various styles of faith expression, one cannot demand adherence to any universal form of memorialization that may serve to limit this expression, including recognition of an individual's life work, avocation or pursuit."
5. "Memorialization has great significance for the survivors of the deceased. For the Catholic, this significance is enhanced by the prescription that each Catholic memorial bear a Christian Cross in its design."

---

e-mail query, Mr. Richard Peterson, Director of Cemeteries of the Archdiocese of Seattle, wrote on September 23, 1998, in confirmation of Mr. Villaronga's assertion: "[E]ach diocese is independent of the others all united with the pope. Obviously, there are matters of faith and morals which are universal as well as Church laws, but practical implementation at the local level for items like operations of the Catholic cemeteries rests with the local bishop."

[6] Canon 1240.

[7] Canon 1241.

[8] *Associated Catholic Cemeteries Memorial Policy* (revised January 1, 1998); cited by Richard Peterson, Director of Cemeteries of the Archdiocese of Seattle, in an e-mail dated September 23, 1998.

[9] *The Catholic Cemetery—A Vision for the Millennium* (National Catholic Cemetery Conference, 1997). These citations were provided by Mr. Peterson, with the very important stipulation that "This book sets forth a vision but does not establish policy, directives, or mandates" (Peterson, September 23, 1998).

The manager of Miami's Our Lady of Mercy Catholic Cemetery, Mr. Jack Averell, confirmed these principles, succinctly stating that the only requirement is that at least one Christian emblem be incorporated into a marker or monument, and that the only prohibition is the avoidance of symbols or sayings "contrary to Church teachings."[10]

When viewing these recommendations (not formal requirements) alongside the City of Boca Raton's Municipal Cemetery's regulations, it is obvious that standards #1, #2, #3, and #5 are fulfilled. Only #4 might be an issue; however, these recommendations were intended for specifically Catholic cemeteries, where faithful Catholics are recommended for burial, and not to public or municipal cemeteries. I shall address some of the implications of this point below, in a section titled "High Traditions and Little Traditions."

PROTESTANTS

Protestant requirements for markers and monuments are essentially the same as those for Catholics, although less formalized or codified. Like the Catholics, the Protestant's grave may be honored with Christian symbols and must avoid pagan or anti-Christian symbols. As is the case with Catholicism, we could find no directive or regulation preferring a monument over a marker. The three basic principles (1) respect for the dead (2) testimony to the deceased's commitment to a Christian life, and (3) good taste govern the Protestant view.

JUDAISM

The first requirement for Judaic burial is that it take place in an area consecrated for this purpose. This may be either a Jewish cemetery or a Jewish section of a larger, often municipal, cemetery. In the latter case, the Jewish section of the cemetery should be fenced off from the larger areas for gentile use.[11] At the Boca Raton Municipal Cemetery there was one area of 150 graves which had been purchased by Temple Beth-El, but it was not marked off by a fence. Curiously, the grave of the Jewish litigants' deceased family member was outside of the Jewish (Temple Beth-El) section.[12]

According to Judaic tradition, a marker or monument serves three purposes:

"To mark the place of burial, so that priests may avoid defilement from the dead—a ritual impurity that the Bible prohibits. For this purpose only a simple marker would be required."

"To designate the grave properly, so that friends and relatives may visit it. For this, what is required is only the name of the individual on a modest stone."

---

[10] Jack Averell, cemetery manager, our Lady of Mercy Catholic Cemetery, Miami, telephone interview, October 7, 1998.

[11] Rabbi Maurice Lamm, *The Jewish Way in Death and Mourning*, p. 68.

[12] Visit to Boca Raton Municipal Cemetery, October 23, 1998.

"To serve as a symbol of honor for the deceased buried beneath it. For this purpose one should erect as respectable a monument as the heirs can afford, avoiding unnecessary ostentation."[13]

Point #1 above may be unfamiliar to many people. The hereditary priests of Judaism (*kohanim* [pl.]; sing. *kohen*) must avoid becoming defiled by close proximity to a corpse. In particular, the *kohen* must avoid walking upon a Jew's grave. For this purpose, some rabbinic authorities recommend that both the "top" (i.e. the head) and the "bottom" (i.e. the foot) of the grave be marked. While not specifically stated in the *Rule and Regulations of the Boca Raton Municipal Cemetery and Mausoleum*,[14] I was told by Mr. Harris that foot markers in addition to head markers are permitted.[15] Given this information, even the stricter Judaic interpretation of point #1 is permitted by the cemetery's rules and regulations, although simply a head marker is sufficient according to most authorities.

As for whether a marker or monument is required, "Good taste, quiet dignity, and the avoidance of ostentation are the only guidelines for selecting the monument."[16] And "Styles of monuments vary. The particular shape is of no consequence to the tradition."[17] The marker or monument should contain such information as: the Hebrew name of the deceased, his/her father's name (and for some, mother's name), the English name of the deceased, and the Hebrew and English dates of birth and death. It is also customary to include a symbol to indicate the deceased's Judaic status: a pair of hands for a *kohen*, a water pitcher for a *levi*, and some other Judaic symbol, such as a menorah or the two tablets, for *yisrael*.[18]

Double monuments, usually for husband and wife, are a fairly common Jewish funeral practice,[19] and as the Boca Raton Municipal Cemetery allows for double markers,[20] there is no conflict. However this Jewish custom does not have the force of law; it is not a requirement but a custom.

Point #3 above might raise some questions regarding the Boca Raton Municipal Cemetery's rules, as might the requirement that the marker "be a clear, visible demarcation of the gravesite."[21] Our discussion of "High Traditions and Little Traditions" (below) will address some of the ramifications of point #3.

Rabbi Lamm, an eminent authority on all matters pertaining to Judaic laws governing death, bereavement, mourning, and burial, has addressed the question of markers specifically: "While the form of the marker is of little religious signif-

---

[13] Rabbi Maurice Lamm, *The Jewish Way in Death and Mourning*, p. 188.

[14] Rules and Regulations of the Boca Raton Municipal Cemetery and Mausoleum, Section XIV, "Memorials, Monuments and Markers," page 13.

[15] Curtis L. Harris, interview, October 23, 1998.

[16] Rabbi Maurice Lamm, *The Jewish Way in Death and Mourning*, p. 191.

[17] Ibid.

[18] Ibid., pp. 191–192.

[19] Ibid., p. 189.

[20] Curtis L. Harris, interview, October 23, 1998.

[21] Rabbi Maurice Lamm, *The Jewish Way in Death and Mourning*, p. 189.

icance, what is important is that there be a clear, visible demarcation of the gravesite. For example, there are cemeteries that utilize small, flat stones that are flush with the earth, and it is difficult to determine whether they are footstones or headstones. These are not generally desirable, unless the whole outline of the grave is clearly evident. If only footstones are permitted by the cemetery, they may be used and the small size is not considered a belittling of the deceased."[22]

MUSLIM

Muslim traditions regarding markers and monuments are also rather minimal. According to Imam Nitham H. Hasan,[23] Islamic markers should be inscribed only with the name of the deceased and his/her dates of birth and death. In particular, verses from al-Qur'an are not to be inscribed because the markers are walked and sat upon, and this would be disrespectful and unbefitting religious symbols or holy verses, according to the Imam.

"HIGH TRADITIONS AND LITTLE TRADITIONS"

Scholars of religious studies often make a distinction between "high traditions" and "little traditions," a distinction which might prove useful for the current discussion.

By "high tradition" is meant to [sic] textual-legal side of a religion, usually male dominated and church or synagogue-centered. By "little tradition" is meant the folkways and home-centered observances, usually orally rather than textually transmitted, often the domain of women in a traditional culture.

Another way of making this distinction would be by using the concepts of "by law" and "by custom."

In contemporary America, the "little traditions": are often based in ethnicity, and one can make a distinction between practices which are "religious" and customs which are "ethnic," the "high" and "low" traditions.

For example, point #4 in our discussion in our discussion of Catholicism above held that "Because different cultural and ethnic groups in our society have various styles of faith expression, one cannot demand adherence to any universal form of memorialization that may serve to limit this expression, including recognition of an individual's life work, avocation or pursuit."

Indeed, the ethnicity of the deceased often plays a role in decoration of the Christian monument. Ukrainian markers often depict the domed churches of the Orthodox Church. Depictions of Christ and Mary are also common.[24] Ital-

---

[22] Ibid.

[23] Nitham H. Hasan, spiritual leader of the Islamic Center of South Florida, Pompano Beach, telephone interview, October 3, 1998.

[24] Thomas E. Graves, "Keeping Ukraine Alove though Death: Ukranian-American Gravestones As Cultural Markers," *Ethnicity and the American Cemetery*, ed. by Richard E. Meyer (Bowling Green, OH: Bowling Green State University Press, 1993), p. 67–69.

ian and Mexican Catholic markers often portray images of Mary or Christ or local patron saints. Small shrines or reliquaries on Mexican monuments may include "An effigy of the Virgin, a tiny crucifix, a candle, or some icon." A distinctive feature of the Mexican headstone is the bright a [*sic*] festive colors of the markers. Colorful objects such as marbles, charms, and plastic crucifixes, are often pressed into the wet cement of a marker. Individuality and conviviality are favored. "Death, with its Germanic blacks and purples, finds no suggestion in the gaily painted Mexican memorials and abundant flowers."[25]

Similarly among Jews, the style of the marker or monument is dictated by ethnic custom rather than by religious requirement. For example, Sephardim prefer a monument placed horizontally over the grave, while the Ashkenazi custom is a vertical monument.[26]

"Little tradition" customs are no where codified; indeed, by their nature they are oral rather than textual, and as such run the risk of being idiosyncratic. No one could judge the "authenticity" of a little tradition practice; whatever an individual happens to feel could be argued to be a "little tradition." Very often, sincerely and passionately held religious beliefs turn out to be held only on an individual basis, with no source in the religious high tradition itself. If we accept all "little tradition" customs as valid and binding in the same way that "high tradition" laws and doctrines are, then we run the danger of falling into a relativism bordering on anarchy.

As we are considering religions with vigorous high traditions—Catholicism, Protestantism, Judaism and Islam—we have clear guidelines as to what are and what are not acceptable ways of marking the graves of the deceased. And there is nothing in the *Rules and Regulations of the Boca Raton Municipal Cemetery and Mausoleum* which interferes with the exercise of these religions as defined by their high traditions.

CONCLUSIONS

This research about grave markers and memorial leads to several observations and generalizations. The modern trend in grave monuments for all religions is the in-ground plaque or marker, which requires minimal care and maintenance. Bronze is the typical metal used for these markers, and a granite or marble base may be used to add height and definition to the marker. The symbols which adorn traditional monuments are available for decoration of the markers.

According to some scholars, these markers represent a changing attitude among Americans towards death. The new ideal is "reconciliation with the natural environment." Traditional monuments, on the other hand, stressed the individuality of the deceased and tended to "elicit the very sense of the continued presence of the dead that the landscaped cemetery by design is meant to

---

[25] Terry G. Jordan, *Texas Graveyards: A Cultural Legacy* (Austin, University of Texas Press, 1982), p. 53.
[26] *The Encyclopaedia of Judaism* (1989 edition), p. 154, s.v. "Cemetery."

suppress."[27] As death is relegated to the further reaches of American consciousness, the individuality of monuments is being discouraged. Uniformity is becoming the norm. Scholars view the emphasis on public or municipal, or in some cases privately-owned, commercial cemeteries, as shifting the responsibility of caring for the dead away from the community, its churches and synagogues, and thereby away from public awareness. What Roberta Halporn wrote about Jewish cemeteries holds true in general: "[I]n more contemporary Jewish cemeteries one can now view acres of stones, bearing little more design that [sic] the name of the deceased and the death date."[28]

THE AUTHOR OF THIS REPORT

This report was prepared by Nathan Katz, Ph.D., professor and chair of the Department of Religious Studies at Florida International University. Dr. Katz is an expert in the history of religions, comparative religions, the religions of South Asia, and Judaism. He has published a dozen books and more than one hundred scholarly and popular articles, has lectured at leading universities across North America as well as in Europe and Asia. Among his awards are four Fullbright grants. He was named the scholar-of-the-year in 1990 when he was on the faculty of the University of South Florida, and for six consecutive years has been selected by the Florida Humanities Council to lead seminars for teachers. He has submitted a copy of his complete curriculum vita.

Dr. Katz was compensated at the rate of $200/hour. This is the first time he has served as an expert witness.

Curriculum Vitae: [original c.v. was forty pages; Professor Katz has published over forty books and written over fifty articles; original has been edited by author for this appendix]

Nathan Katz

EDUCATION

Ph.D.	1978	Temple University	Religion
M.A.	1975	Temple University	Religion
A.B.	1970	Temple University	English

[27] John Matturi, "Windows in the Garden: Italian-American Memorialization and the American Cemetery," *Ethnicity and the American Cemetery*, ed. by Richard E. Meyer (Bowling Green, OH: Bowling Green State University Press, 1993), p. 23.

[28] Roberta Halporn, "American Jewish Cemeteries: A Mirror of History," *Ethnicity and the American Cemetery*, ed. by Richard E. Meyer (Bowling Green, OH: Bowling Green State University Press, 1993), p. 147.

ACADEMIC APPOINTMENTS
1994–   Florida International University, Professor of Religious Studies
1984–94 University of South Florida Professor of Religious Studies
1979–84 Williams College, Assistant Professor of Religion
1978–79 Naropa Institute, Core Faculty in Buddhist Studies

BIBLIOGRAPHY
Books (since 1990)
Reconnecting East and West: Judaism and Eastern Religions (planned).
Maharajas, Mystics and a Mahatma: The Religious Life of the Cochin Jews (Aurora, CO, Dorset Press, contracted).
A Jewish King at Shingly: The Story of the Jews of Cochin (Aurora, CO, Dorset Press, contracted).
Who Are the Jews of India? Identity Balanced, Identity Transformed, Identity Aloof (Berkeley, University of California Press, in press).
Studies of Indian-Jewish Identity, editor and contributor (New Delhi, Manohar, 1995).
The Last Jews of Cochin: Jewish Identity in Hindu India, with Ellen S. Goldberg (Columbia, University of South Carolina Press, 1993).

SCHOLARLY ARTICLES IN REFEREED JOURNALS (SINCE 1990)
"From Legend to History: India and Israel in the Ancient World," *Shofar: An Interdisciplinary Journal of Jewish Studies* 17, 3(1999): 1–15.
"A Bibliography on Indian Jewry, Part I" (with Frank Joseph Shulman). *Journal of Indo-Judaic Studies* 2 (1999): in press.
"Obituary: Ashin Das Gupta," *Journal of Indo-Judaic Studies* 2 (1999): in press.
"How the Hindu-Jewish Encounter Reconfigures Interreligious Dialogue," *Shofar: An Interdisciplinary Journal of Jewish Studies* 16, 1(1997): 28–42. Popular version: "The Hindu-Jewish Encounter and the Future." In *The Fifty-eighth Century: A Jewish Renewal Sourcebook* [Zalman Schachter Festschrift], ed. by Shohama Wiener (Northvale, NJ: Jason Aronson, 1996), 331–43.
"Understanding Religion in Diaspora: The Case of the Jews of Cochin," *Religion Studies and Theology* 15, 1(1996): 517.
"Leaving Mother India: Reasons for the Cochin Jews' Migration to Israel," with Ellen S. Goldberg, *Population Review* 39, 1 & 2 (1995): 35–53.
"The Judaisms of Kaifeng and Cochin: Parallel and Divergent Styles of Religious Acculturation." *Numen: International Review for the History of Religions* 42(1995): 118–40. Abridged in Jonathan Goldstein, ed., *The Jews of China* (2 vols., M. E. Sharpe, 1998, in press.)
"The Sephardi Diaspora in Cochin, India." *Jewish Political Studies Review* 3, 3–4(1993): 97–140
"Jewish 'Apartheid' and a Jewish Gandhi," with Ellen S. Goldberg. *Jewish Social Studies* 50, 3–4 (1988–1993):147–76. Reprinted: *Ethnic Studies Repot* 10, 2 (July 1992): 18–35.
"Perfection without God: A View from the Pali Canon," *Studies in Formative Spirituality* 14, 1(1993): 11–22.

"The Synagogues of South India." *Arts of Asia* 23, 1 (Jan.–Feb. 1993): 131–34.

"Contacts between Jewish and Indo-Tibetan Civilizations through the Ages: Some Explorations." *Tibet Journal* 16,4 (1991): 90–109. Reprinted: "Contacts between Jewish and Indo-Tibetan Civilizations through the Ages," *Judaism* 43, 1 (Winter 1994): 46–60. Reprinted: "Contacts Between Jewish and Indo-Tibetan Civilizations." *Points East* 8, 1(1994):1, 5–10.

"The Jewish Secret and the Dalai Lama–A Dharamsala Diary," *Conservative Judaism* 43, 4(1991): 33–46.

Revised: "A Meeting of Ancient Peoples: Western Jews and the Dalai Lama of Tibet," *Jerusalem Letter* 113 (1 March 1991): 1–8.

Union Theological Seminary
3041 Broadway @ 121st St. New York, NY 10027.
Revd. Dr. John A. McGuckin, FR Hist. Soc.
Professor of Early Church History.
Tel. 212 280 1391.
Fax 212 280 1416
Email jmcguckn@uts.columbia.edu
December 4th 1998.

REPORT OF REVD. PROF. JOHN ANTHONT MCGUCKIN CASE OF WARNER ET AL. VS. CITY OF BOCA RATON FLORIDA.

This report has been prepared by :
Rev. Dr. John Anthony McGuckin.
Professor of Early Church History,
Union Theological Seminary, New York.

Professor McGuckin is a Theologian-Priest of the Eastern Orthodox Church in addition to his role as academic teacher and scholar in a graduate school of higher research in the City of New York.
He is a Fellow of the British Royal Historical Society.

A list of his professional qualifications, and of his academic writings, is attached to this report in the form of a *Curriculum Vitae*, and a *Bibliography of Published Work*.

Prof. McGuckin has not previously appeared in any legal case in the United States to give expert testimony.

Report:

A. Introduction and Synopsis of Opinion.

I have studied the rules and regulations of Boca Raton Cemetery, with a view to the specific question that was posed to me: how would I formulate an opinion on these rules, and their implications in relation to the expression of basic Christian religious belief in burial practice. I will try to distinguish (a) what might be regarded as 'fundamental' Christian attitudes (such as arise from the ancient Christian tradition as can be witnessed in burial praxis over past centuries which continues in to the present century in many living forms of Christian religious traditions) and (b) what could legitimately be regarded as 'genuine religious sentiment' based within the spiritual traditions of Christian religion but which are more personal in character, related to the individual only.

From that point of consideration let me state my overall belief at the outset: The rules and regulations of Boca Raton cemetery, forbidding anything but a flat memorial stone, seem to me to represent a distinctly secularized and hyper-individualized consciousness that appears to presume a view of death, and the dead body, as spent commodity, and of the grave as a place where only temporary remembrance of immediate family members needs to be preserved. The widespread pervasiveness of such a view in modern American society should not be taken as a standard norm from which to assess how basic Christian tenets (that is Christian religious views of death, afterlife and burial practice) ought to be applied in the concrete, even though many Christian persons will, of course, be influenced by such a consciousness to the extent of adopting and conforming, without protest, to the generic forms of burial custom of the surrounding society. In this light I can foresee that many Christian religious persons might have no objection to the regulations of Boca Raton Cemetery, while others would have fundamental religious objections to them if they were to be enforced in their cases—to the point that, in my opinion, this enforcement would represent a definite invasion of such people's fundamental religious beliefs. Popular graveside practices, rising out of Christian belief-systems about death, burial and mourning rituals, which I think the Boca Raton Cemetery regulations seek to restrict, could be shown to be those of the majority of the mainstream of the Christian Church which has developed basic forms of religious praxis through its approach to central life-events (such as marriage, births, deaths) for long centuries, in the process creating a widespread Christian consciousness, and set of expectations, over such things. In relation to death practices, the patterns of Christian behaviour witnessed over centuries accumulate in the individual Christian's consciousness (even when, as is often the case, ordinary Christian people might not be able to articulate these beliefs theologically) and so become an encultured pattern of belief. This pattern in the form of historical 'catholic' Christianity (a term that embraces many varieties of the Christian religion such as the Roman Catholic, the Eastern Orthodox, the Episcopalian, the Methodist, and the Presbyterian, among others) is called the 'Tradition of the Faith'. It is not something that is primarily represented in ecclesiastical law books, though partially it can be witnessed there;

nor is it something that is represented only in Scriptural passages considered as 'proof texts,' or in formal decisions made by Church leaders. The Christian Tradition is something that the whole body of Christians represents[1] through its long continued practice through the centuries, but especially in regard to practices that are allied with, and meant to protect (even as they express them) the fundamental beliefs of the Religion. To interfere with the right of Christians to express their belief through the customary popular rituals (in this case I consider only the rituals of burial, and mourning) does, in my opinion, represent a genuine curtailment of fundamental religious freedoms.

The opinion is one that needs to be substantiated and explained by some reference to Christianity's theological attitude to the dead body and to the grave, and also to the expectation of the bereaved family members in regard to the dead person—the forms and rituals of mourning that are observed (both formal liturgies, and personal rituals of remembrance stemming from the sense of reverence towards the dead that is deeply encultured in the Christian religion). It is in regard to the last point that the issue of religious belief intersects with the particular matter of the form of gravestones and the manner in which mourning rituals are observed at the graveside—families expressing grief, intercessory prayer, and penitential supplication to God, at the actual site of the grave. In my opinion the restrictive rules of the Boca Raton Cemetery in regard to grave marking represent not a neutral or reasonable view about death and humankind, but one that could even be seen as inimical to the expression of Christian philosophy and the praxis that follows from it.

I would like to offer some background in support of this viewpoint, as to why the practice of erecting a standing Cross, or a religious statue (of Christ, the Virgin Mary, an Angel or a Saint) can be claimed, objectively, as a matter relating to fundamental religious expression of belief. I would like to do so by first of all discussing some doctrinal-theological attitudes of Christianity (Section B); secondly by giving a few selected examples from historical practice (in so far as they demonstrate a deep-seated Christian attitude to this issue which makes it irreducible to merely contemporary custom) (section C); and lastly by considering the particular issues of standing grave-markers and grave edgings raised by the Boca City regulations, in terms of the question: do they impinge upon an 'objective' Christian religious sensibility, or upon a 'subjective' religious sense of the families involved? (section D)

B. Christian-Theological Grounds for This Opinion

The de-sacralisation of the concepts of space (holy place) and person (sanctified presence) have been one of the results of late modern developments in many parts of the Western world, but the older, and mainstream, beliefs of Christian consciousness have maintained quite a different approach, and this is represented still in a lively way in the fundamental expressions of liturgy and prayer

---

[1] A point I have more fully elaborated, with historical examples in my article: *The Concept of Living Tradition in Orthodox Theology.* St. Vladimir's Theological Quarterly. Winter. 1998.

rituals in the churches. To this extent I take what the liturgical services and prayers represent to be a central part of religious belief and praxis, certainly for Catholic and Eastern Orthodox Christians, and also for those reformed traditions whose liturgies of burial I have witnessed: Episcopalian, Lutheran and Presbyterian. [Much of what I have to say about the sacredness of the grave as space, and the sanctity of the dead person awaiting the Judgement applies equally to Jewish religious belief—though I will not develop that here.[2]]

The classical Christian understanding of burial devolves from the central Christian doctrine that the human person is the Image and Likeness of the Divinity. It is closely related to the prior doctrine, which underpins it, of the revelation of Jesus Christ as the incarnation (appearance within embodied flesh) of the Godhead. The fundamental sanctification of the Church which results from the incarnation and saving acts of Jesus is a tenet which underlies all central forms of Christian faith.[3] The Christian is seen to be redeemed, sanctified, elected—whatever terms are used. In the burial rituals of the Catholic and Orthodox churches, the emphasis turns on the committal of the dead person to sanctified ground. The Eastern liturgy uses a recurring phrase in the burial services, and in memorials for the dead, a phrase that is a verse from the psalms and used with explicit reference to the dead body: 'The Earth is the Lord's, and all those who *dwell within it.*' Much of the Catholic burial service turns around the notions of honouring the dead body as a sacred thing, and of consecrating the gravesite as a hallowed place. The idea of 'consecration' of the Cemetery is far more, in the Christian consciousness, than the mere dedication or setting apart of land, by a secular agency, for the purposes of burial of bodies: rather, it connotes this fundamental sense of the hallowing or making-sacred of ground for the purpose of receiving the body, and for the purpose of serving as a place of sober reflection and grieving prayer for those who visit the place thereafter. The old Christian rituals of consecration (still used in Roman Catholic, Episcopalian and Orthodox practice wherever the land used belongs entirely to the respective churches) stress this element of the graveyard itself becoming a place of prayer to teach the living how to prepare for their own deaths, as well as a place where they can pray for their dead.

In earlier Christian civilisations the entire cemetery (a word that Christians invented: koimeteria—meaning a place of sleeping under the eye of God until the last Day) would have been consecrated in a formal rite as holy ground, in order to keep safe the holy bodies of the 'images of God' who were destined to rest there until the time of God's Judgement on human history.[4] Christian belief has never accepted the view that human persons were 'souls' trapped temporarily in a body, but has, rather, taught as a basic foundational doctrine, that human persons as 'embodied souls' are the image and likeness of God. The aspect of image, in other words, also involves the aspect of embodiment: be it as alive, or dead—waiting for the Word of God.[5] As such, the Resurrection of the

---

[2] For further elaboration of this point of a classic discussion of the theme in Bender (1893–4).

[3] cf. Burghardt (1957).

[4] Di Berardomp (1992); Grabar (1946).

[5] Cullmann (1958).

Body is a fundamental tenet of Christianity (reflected in all the early creeds of Christendom), and the need for sanctified ground in which to lay that body is a common and important part of Christian practice from earliest times. If the church cannot own and consecrate ground for the purpose, it is customary in Catholic and Orthodox practice, for the priest at the burial service to consecrate the actual grave that is being used. The ground itself, as well as the body which is blessed and incensed, in several forms of burial service, is regarded as something mysterious and deserving of reverence.

It is widely expected in many major forms of Christianity (less noted in modern protestant religious consciousness than in catholic forms of Christianity), that the families will pray for their dead, as well as grieve for them, at the site of the grave, as well as in their churches and homes. In the Eastern Orthodox Christian liturgy, as also in Catholic practice in many parts of the world, it is a regular part of church life for the parish to meet in the graveyards and conduct services there on a regular basis—not just at the time of burial. The place is felt to be important. The grave becomes a place of prayer. The sites of the graves of ancient (and modern) Christians who had an especial reputation for holiness have often become places of pilgrimage, and churches have been built over them in due course. This was the origin of so many ancient churches—which were built over the grave-sites of the earliest martyrs of Christianity (and was the original reason why many Christian churches to this day bear dedications of saints' names).

C. An Historical Background to Christian Burial Rituals

I will not make here a whole series of historical notes on what is a very large body of data, but I think it important to note that the extremely close connection of the Christian religion with this principle of the reverence for the burial site, and for the sanctity of the dead body which rests in anticipation of the resurrection, is something that can be witnessed from the earliest origins of Christian religion as a distinctive aspect of that religion.[6] The Catacombs in Rome are among the most important of all archaeological sites for giving evidence on fundamental matters of Christianity in the immediate post New Testament period.[7] The inscription of Crosses, and the listing of names and synopsis histories (epitaphs) are clearly developed by Christians in their own special ways from the normal burial practices of neighbours around them. Soon, with increasing affluence among the Christian communities, inscribed grave stones become more apparent. These are the first forays into Christian Art and Iconography which soon became a major element of the expression of Christian Faith—and still is within Catholicism and Orthodoxy[8] (although Protestantism generally takes a more iconoclastic[9] position on this—tending to reject imagery, statuary, and iconography from the fundamentals of Christian

---

[6] Snyder (1958). Toynbee (1971).

[7] Stevenson (1978).

[8] DT Rice (1957). Wulffe (1914). Morey (1942).

[9] Bryer & Herrin (1975).

faith). The Latin Christian poet Prudentius, in the 4thC, gives a whole account of the careful tending of Christian graves and the making of gravestones. His is one of the first recorded texts of a Christian burial service ritual in the Latin world and in it the erection of the stone and the laying of flowers constitute the fundamental symbolic forms of the ritual.[10] The Greek Christian Poet and theologian Gregory of Nazianzus shows in his writings (c. 387) how the account of the life of the believer ought to be inscribed on a tombstone and set over the place of burial to serve as a focus for the prayer of the believers for that person.[11] This is the specific Christian custom of the Epitaphios serving as an intercessory prayer as well as a grave marker. The earliest 'important' example of Christian Epitaphios is the stone of Bishop Abercius, from the late 2nd century, but the epigraphic remains from Rome and Asia Minor show that this engraving of the sacred sign of the Cross or other devices, was a custom that was almost as ancient as the Christian religion itself.

The more common custom, in later Christian centuries, was for the sacred Cross to be lifted up over the grave site to mark the place of the body and to signify that this was a holy place, the resting place of a Christian. The 'lifting up of the Cross' was a ritual form that paralleled liturgical services of the Cross, and which used the 'elevation' to symbolise, almost sacramentally, the victory over death won by the crucified Saviour. This remains the standard form of ritual Christian grave-practice in many parts of the world to this day, although the custom of inscribing an Epitaphios on the gravestone (a synopsis of life) often led to the preference for a standing gravestone as well as, or in place of, the Cross. Reformed Christianity began in later centuries to prefer the standing gravestone. Orthodox practice preferred the Cross (and now it is regarded as a part of the religious duty of the family to raise a Cross over the site of the grave). Roman Catholic practice often combined several variations on this theme: the Epitaphios is sometimes written on a Cross, and sometimes written on a stone, with a statue of the Christ-Lord, or an Angel, or the Virgin Mary, serving the same role as a Cross: to mark and bless the site of the grave.

The pagan emperor Julian, in the 4th Century, criticised the Christians for making churches into 'charnel houses', and many who approach the issue from a rationalist frame of reference may regard this reverential attitude to the dead as something bizarre, or fixated. However, I think that it is a fundamental expression of the communion of love which serves as the basic 'Constitution' of the Christian Church (what the creeds call the 'Communion of the Saints' and define as one of the fundamental characters of Christianity.[12])

The late modern period (18thC onwards) has seen a massive movement of desacralisation across western societies in general. The concept of sacred place and sacred thing (including the sacred ground of graveyards, and the sacred 'vessels' of the dead Christians' bodies) has become a notion that the late mod-

---

[10] Waddell. (1975).

[11] Paton (1919).

[12] The Nicene Creed expresses it by placing three fundamental 'attitudes' together as deeply related: 'I believe in . . . the communion of saints, the forgiveness of sins, the resurrection of the dead.'

ern mind does not much consider. The late modern existential attitude, as I said earlier, might be described as dominated by the idea of persons and bodies as dispensable commodities; as such it conflicts with Christianity on several fronts, which is, of course, in essence an eschatological religion with a central belief in the sacredness of the person and of the body as a sanctified image of the incarnate Godhead.

D. Objective or Subjective Elements

If we consider to what extent is it reasonable, or 'mainstream', for a Christian to have a desire to mark the grave of a member of their natural, and Christian, family (for the relative is not just a 'natural' relation, but bonded to them by religious ties and obligations too) then I would say that it is a fundamental part of Christian religious practice. Regulations that forbid a Christian family to erect a standing Cross, or even a standing stone Epitaphios contradict an ancient Christian practice, and do an objective violence to fundamental religious attitudes to those Christians who retain the classical 'catholic' sense of this theology of death and grieving observance.

If I was to consider: would it be a useful compromise to have a flat stone embedded in the cemetery grass, as opposed to a standing stone, I would respond that the Orthodox Christian church, at least, would regard this as sacrilegious: for the Cross ought to be over the grave—and the sacred sign of the Cross must never be placed in a position where it could be walked over. The canons of the eastern church have forbidden this since the time when Islam made walking on the Cross a way in which Greeks under the Ottoman domination were led to renounce their faith. In other forms of catholic practice the flat stone marked with a Cross is deemed not to be sacrilegious, and to many it has become a modern form of practice. Those who still find it objectionable have the historical precedent behind them: that this modern form cannot be regarded as fulfilling the religious task of 'raising the Cross' over the grave; in practical terms it is not sufficiently visible, and in religious terms it cannot represent the ritual of the 'raising of the Cross' (a liturgical aspect of catholic Christianity in the churches—which denotes the 'victory' of Christ over death) over the gravesite because of its very nature as a supine symbol. I regard the issue of religious statues of Christ, the Virgin, or a Saint as a modern form of western catholic practice paralleling the ritual of the elevation of a Cross. In this instance the statue is meant to stand over the head of the grave as a protective symbol: a religious statement which would also be wholly vitiated by a supine two-dimensional image.

I have also been made aware how some wish to construct little walls or ledges around the actual site of the grave. This is a custom in keeping with Christian sensibility, though in my opinion not a mainstream issue in the way the previous ritual of grave-marking is. The desire for the small grave edging reflects the same attitude of the sacredness of space, to which I have alluded to earlier, though it does not, of course, ensure the hoped-for result of separating off the 'sacred space' from people who might walk over it. In a more widely Christianised civilisation, as evidenced by common practice in earlier times, and even by the strict protocol in many Christian countries to this day, no-one would ever dream of walking over a grave, but many bereaved people today (and probably with good reason) fear this sense of de-sacralisation around them, and wish to express their reverence in this way. I would think, personally, that the forbidding of the grave edgings does not impinge 'objectively' on their fundamental Christian beliefs, or the expression of them, but does impinge on a reasonable religious attitude on their part that has been fostered by main-stream Christian traditions in many times past, and to this extent the forbidding of this custom of edging-markers could be said to conflict 'subjectively' with sincerely held religious views, by suppressing them.

Brief Bibliography

AP Bender	'Beliefs, Rites, and Customs of the Jews Connected with Death, Burial and Mourning.' Jewish Quarterly Review. 6. 1893–94. pp. 317–347.
A di Bererdino	'Cemetery'. Encyclopedia of the Early Church. (ed. Idem). vol. 1. Cambridge. 1992. Pp. 155–158.
A Bryer & J Herrin	Iconoclasm. Birmingham. 1975.
WJ Burghardt	Image of God in Man According to Cyril of Alexandria. Woodstock Md. 1957. (—Early Christian theology on the human person as divine image.)
O Cullman	Immortaility of the Soul or Resurrection of the Dead? London. 1958.
A Grabar	Martyrium: Recherches sur le culte des reliques et l'art chrétien antique. Paris. 1946.
CR Morey	Early Christian Art. Princeton. 1942.
WR Paton	The Greek Anthology. vol.2. (Loeb classical Library). London. 1919. (—for translations of Gregory Nazianzen's epitaphs.)
DT Rice	The Beginnings of Christian Art. London. 1957.

EXPERT REPORT OF DANIEL PALS
Warner vs. City of Boca Raton
Submitted by
Daniel L. Pals, Ph.D.

This report, requested by the defendant, addresses issues raised in the pending class-action complaint brought by Richard and Miriam Warner, et al. against the City of Boca Raton, Florida. Its purpose is to offer an instructive commentary on religious traditions and practices that underlie the dispute. The discussion opens with a brief introductory statement on the issues that are considered by the defendant to be central to this case, which turns in large measure on attitudes toward the dead and the role of burial markers or monuments in religious practice. It then offers a review primarily of Jewish and Christian traditions that bear on the matters of death, burial, and memorials for the dead. Finally, both in the course of the discussion and in concluding remarks, it attempts to enter an informed professional judgment on the application of these traditions to the issues that will need resolution under the law.

I. THE DEFENDANT'S POSITION ON THE LAW

It is clear from the Complaint that the plaintiffs allege violations of several state statutes and federal constitutional provisions that bear on such matters as the free exercise of religion, freedom of speech, and due process of law. In correspondence received prior to the preparation of this report, Counsel for the City has explained that while most of these allegations appear to be without merit, the one possibly significant claim is that which is brought under a Florida statute that has become effective in recent months: the State of Florida's Religious Freedom Restoration Act of 1998 (hereafter RFRA). Accordingly, the assessment presented here confines itself specifically to this statute, the relevant portion of which claims the following:

> The government shall not substantially burden a person's exercise of religion, even if the burden results from a rule of general applicability, except that the government may substantially burden a person's exercise of religion only if it demonstrates that application of the burden to the person: Is in furtherance of a compelling governmental interest; and Is the least restrictive means of furthering the compelling governmental interest.

With regard to this article of the RFRA, two initial observations would seem to be in order:

1.   It would appear that the City has plausible grounds to mount a first defense of its action under the provision for exception allowed by this statute. The City administration can reasonably claim a compelling interest in the efficient and economical administration of properties entrusted to its care, and a policy which allows a certain a kind of grave marker, but not those found to be obstructive, is as minimally restrictive a policy as one can imagine, given the need for continuous access and maintenance. Hence a burden on the religious exercise of some, even if substantial, might reasonably be borne by those who are directly affected in order to maintain in good order a property which as civic land belongs to all.

2.   Setting aside the clause of exception, and attending to the article itself, the central and obvious question is this: Do the City's restrictions on memorials or monuments constitute a substantial burden on the exercise of religion by those persons who choose to make use of its public cemetery? In answering, we should note that in the statute as written, the crucial term of decision is not "burden," but "substantial." All can agree that the state has the right to place some burdens on the exercise of religion. Churches, temples, and synagogues are no more free than any other organization, or individual citizen, to

flout traffic laws, ignore zoning ordinances, or disregard basic safety regulations merely because they might claim to be doing so in the name of religion. To the extent that they accede to such laws on occasions when mere convenience or optional religious preference would lead them to do otherwise, religious organizations and individuals plainly accept certain burdens of citizenship placed upon them by the state. Under the RFRA, it is only when these burdens become "substantial" that the issue of religious exercise becomes a relevant consideration. For example, if a city or state were to disregard completely both Biblical precedent and unbroken orthodox tradition and move to the closure of Christian Churches on Sundays, clearly that action would subject practicing Christians to a substantial burden. It would impose directly on free religious exercise. The same would apply in the case of Judaism if all synagogues and temples were ordered closed each week from Friday to the following Saturday evening. In both the Jewish and Christian instances, while certain modest burdens can be borne as reasonably within the rights of the state to impose, these substantial burdens could not be. Needless to say, then, appropriate application of the Florida law in this case will depend on what the court decides to be a truly substantial burden upon a person's exercise of religion. Do the City's restrictions on burial monuments fall into a category nearer to that of modest and natural burdens, such as traffic laws and zoning ordinances? Or do they take a place alongside a law (here hypothetical, of course) mandating the closure of houses of worship on their historic and traditional days of assembly? This report contends that the City's ordinances pertaining to its cemetery clearly belong to the former, not the latter category. That they are "burdens" of a sort is undeniable, as is the fact they are perceived by certain religious persons as inconvenient or personally disconcerting. That they rise to the level of a "substantial" burden upon any Jew or Christian is a much stronger claim. It is a proposition that, in my professional judgment, the relevant evidence from the religious traditions cannot be read to support. Before turning to this evidence, however, some comment needs to be made on the criteria for assessing it.

II. DETERMINING "SUBSTANTIAL BURDEN:" ESSENTIAL AND INTEGRAL VS. MARGINAL OR TANGENTIAL CUSTOM

In the extreme examples cited above, it is not hard to see which restrictive actions of the state impose substantial burdens and which do not. But not all cases are so clear cut. What is needed for a clear grasp of the issue is a general and guiding principle by which to distinguish "substantial" burdens from those that are insubstantial—what I have earlier called "modest and natural." The only way to deduce such a principle is, for any given practice or custom, to examine it in context, so as to determine where it stands in the religious tradition that houses it. To the degree that a given practice or custom is judged to be marginal or tangential—that is, a matter either of irrelevance, general indifference, or merely personal preference—within a religious community, it is hard to see how a restriction upon it can be construed as a burden that is in any meaningful way substantial. If a church prefers angle parking at Sunday worship, and a civic ordinance requires parallel, that ordinance is a burden, but it can hardly be construed as substantial. Parking practice is marginal at best to the concerns of religious practice. On the other hand, to the degree that a given practice or custom is integral and essential to a tradition, a restriction upon it is much more likely to constitute a substantial burden. A restriction on worship that permitted sermons and homilies while it prohibited rituals and sacraments would be regarded by churches, quite rightly, as an unlawful state imposition. Most every religion in the world regards a sacrament or ritual of some sort to be integral and essential to its practice. The applicable principle in the matter of "substantial burden" thus comes to be the role, or place, of a practice or custom in a religious tradition, is it essential? Or marginal? Is it integral? Or tangential—that is, largely a matter of indifference or optional preference within the tradition?

Given this general principle, we need to state some criteria for its application. How do we determine what is—and what is not—integral and essential to a religious tradition? Religions like Judaism and Christianity are notoriously large and complicated entities, which change through history and are known at given moments to exhibit remarkable diversity. The determination of what is essential and integral is not likely to be a simple task. Nonetheless, in the case of any given practice or custom, we can make a reasonable determination by posing four main questions: 1) Is it asserted or implied in relatively unambiguous terms by an authoritative sacred text? 2) Is it clearly and consistently affirmed in classic formulations of doctrine and practice? 3) Has it been observed continuously, or nearly so, throughout the history of the tradition? 4) Is it consistently practiced everywhere, or almost such, in the tradition as we meet it most recent times? To the degree that a custom or practice possesses all of the characteristics stipulated in these questions, it can be said to qualify decidedly as essential and integral. To the degree that it displays none, it clearly would have to be designated as marginal or tangential. To the degree that it meets some of the qualifications and not others, it will fall somewhere on a line between the one extreme and the other, its position being determined by the number of the four relevant areas in which it qualifies and the relative weight accorded to each.

III. DEATH, BURIAL, AND BURIAL MARKERS
IN JUDAISM AND CHRISTIANITY: A REVIEW

With the criteria above in mind, we can undertake a review of both the Jewish and Christian traditions pertaining to beliefs about death, grave sites, and vertical burial monuments or markers.

Judaism

Is the placement of vertical tombstones asserted or implied in reasonably un-ambiguous terms by an authoritative sacred text?

The Hebrew scripture (Torah) is virtually silent on the matter of tombstones and memorial monuments for the dead. There is no commandment or pre-scription on the subject in the moral principles of the decalogue (Exodus 20; Deuteronomy 5). Nor is there anything specific on the issue in the detailed legal material of the Book of Leviticus, where one would expect find to find such a regulation if it were of essential importance to the early Hebrews. In its narrative portions, the Torah records only two noteworthy specific incidents in which monuments or memorials were erected in ancient Israel. The Book of Genesis (35: 20) tells how the Patriarch Jacob placed a pillar (Hebrew: matse-vah) on the grave of his wife Rachel, and the Book of II Samuel (18:18) reports that Absalom, the rebellious son of King David, built a monument for himself because he had no son to carry on his name. It is not clear that Absalom's mon-ument, which he erected for himself while he was living; was ever intended to be a kind of tombstone, so its relevance as an example is in some doubt. Rachel's pillar, on the other hand, does reasonably qualify as the ancient equiv-alent of a tombstone but there is no injunctive material associated with it either in the immediate context elsewhere in the Hebrew Bible. Providing a stone is simply something that Jacob did, the text does not command or suggest that anyone else to do the same.

Archaeological evidence indicates that at some point in Biblical times, the custom of marking graves did make an appearance, and it may be that the story of Jacob's pillar for Rebecca offered a useful model for the practice. But about the particular form and character of the monuments we know next to nothing. Other sources from the Biblical era—and in one place the Biblical text itself—suggest that where graves were marked, the purpose was not theological prin-ciple, but either momentary expedience or practical necessity of a sort peculiar to the ancient world. For example, an oracle in the Book of Ezekiel (39:15) in-structs people who come across a human bone to "set up a sign" by it "till the buriers have buried it." The purpose here is not to place a monument on a grave, obviously, but to mark the location of an object so that it can be buried later. Again, in Judaism of the post-biblical Talmudic era, as in other religions of antiquity, there was commonly a fear of the places where the dead were buried, and graves were often marked out so people, especially priests, would not walk over them and thereby become ritually unclean (Wigoder, p. 708). It is impossible to deduce from the texts, however, that there was anything nec-essarily permanent or vertically prominent about such markers. On the contrary, at least one text (in the tractate Shekalim 1.1) of Mishnah (the in-structional material of the Talmud) assumes the opposite. Rather than raise a marker, the surface soil of the grave was simply to be painted white, with mark-ings that were purely seasonal, put in place once a year at Passover for the specifically temporary purpose of warning pilgrims as they passed (Wigoder,

p. 708). Practical considerations seem to have been the main rationale also for a related custom. Biblical and other texts do indicate that stones were sometimes piled at gravesites. But no theological or ceremonial reasons for the practice are indicated. Most likely their purpose was, again, simply to mark the space so passers-by could walk around it, and to keep roving animals from eating the unprotected bodies (Rabinowicz, p. 114). What we find, then, both in the Hebrew Bible and the Biblical era is rather little on the subject beyond a single incident from the patriarchal era, with no prescriptive inferences drawn. Archaeological and other sources suggest only markings that were practical and temporary in nature, with no prescribed, consistent shape or necessarily vertical form. Stone piles, where they appeared, obviously were heaped above the ground, but it is unlikely that more than a few graves enjoyed the luxury of this much protection. There is little to no evidence that markers of some other kind rose vertically above the soil; what evidence we do have beyond the occasional stone pile, suggests quite the opposite: temporary and horizontal markings made directly on the surface of the grave.

Is the placement of tombstones clearly and consistently affirmed in classic formulations of doctrine and practice?

The formulations that have guided Jewish life and thought from the end of the Biblical era to modem times are the classic commentaries of ancient rabbis found [in] the Talmud. In actuality, there are several such collections, the most prominent of which are the Babylonian and Jerusalem Talmuds, assembled roughly between 100 and 500 A.D. Talmudic commentary, though not always consistent, offers little support for the practice of marking a tomb with any permanent vertical monument. Where it can be read as accepting such displays, it understands them to be at best temporary and optional, as is clear in the passage from the Mishnaic tractate in Shekalim noted above. A later tractate (2.5) indicates that tombstones are purely optional entities, to be purchased only if there was a surplus remaining from the funds collected for a burial (Wigoder, p. 708). More significantly still, the Jerusalem Talmud (Shekalim 2.5), in a statement of pivotal significance to later Jewish thought, records a rabbinical verdict that explicitly forbids tombstones for the graves of the righteous, stating instead that "their deeds are their memorial" (Jacobs, p. 561). It was this important ruling that was codified in the Middle Ages by Judaism's greatest theologian, Moses Maimonides (1135–1204). Maimonides exercised a crucial shaping influence on the whole spectrum of Jewish learning after the 12th century A.D. Without exploring in detail the views of lesser thinkers, many of which simply do not address this subject, we can assume that most would have deferred to Maimonides' authority and example. In the great code of Jewish Law produced by Joseph ben Ephraim Caro (1488–1575), whose influence rivals that of Maimonides, there is a slightly more generous ruling, which nonetheless still concludes that tombstones are in no way obligatory on Jewish graves (Werblowsky, p. 696). Thus the clearest and most prominent voices in the tradition of Jewish theology insist that at best tombstones of any kind (let alone vertical pillars or hills of stone piles) ought not to be mandatory and need not be permanent in nature. They have neither theological nor ceremonial justification, and have in certain instances actually been discouraged or prohibited, rather than tolerated.

Has the practice of placing tombstones on graves been observed continuously, or nearly so, throughout the history of the tradition?

Comment on this question can be brief, since the residue of nearly 5000 years of history affords little material evidence from burial sites to draw upon, and relatively little extended discussion in texts. Few graves from either the ancient or medieval world remain intact. In the Biblical and Talmudic eras, as we have seen, there is some evidence, both literary and material, of grave sites marked with stone piles and of burials in caves, though whether caves were in any way marked is another point of uncertainty. Even so, as the Biblical New Testament story (John 19:38–42) of the burial of Jesus in a borrowed tomb belonging to Joseph of Arimathea suggests, such special graves and memorials were an option of luxury, available only to the rich or well-placed, and certainly could not pass for the norm. The minute regulations laid down in the Talmud and other Codes for the collection of bones into ossuaries for second burial (Rabinowicz, p. 115) when the original sites became too crowded, also suggests that through the long centuries prior to the modem era, Jewish practice did not differ greatly from Christian (which will be discussed below). The vast majority of those who died may well have been buried at common gravesites, with no enduring individualized marker of any kind.

The first notable departure from this mainstream tradition did not occur until the beginnings of the modem era. In the middle years of the sixteenth century an expatriate from Spain, Isaac Luria (1534–1572), established a community of unorthodox Jewish mystics in Palestine. Luria drew on the occult and unorthodox tradition of folklore, symbolism, numerology, and mystical teachings known well to Jews as cabala (also kabbalah) or mystical "tradition." Among his other dissenting views, Luria introduced the idea that a tombstone was not an option but a necessity. He went so far as to claim, in opposition to the Talmud and Maimonides, that the tombstone was actually important to the welfare of the deceased (Jacobs, p. 561; Wigoder, p. 708). Despite their unorthodox character, cabalist notions like these exercised a certain underground fascination in the Jewish communities, especially in times of severe oppression (Hopfe, p. 287). Eventually, they found adherents not only in the Sephardic Jewish cultures of Spain and the Middle East, but also in the Ashkenazic communities of Northern and Eastern Europe. It is among these Ashkenazic European Jews that there developed in more recent times a broad tradition of customarily marking the graves of the dead with a tombstone. Since most American Jews are of Ashkenazic background, it is this rather recent tradition that has come to be a fairly common practice in America. Jewish tombstones thus represent a tradition that, while currently practiced in America, is by no means part of an ancient or continuous Jewish heritage (Werblowsky, pp. 695–96).

Is the placement of vertical tombstones consistently practiced everywhere, or almost such, in the tradition as we meet it [in] most recent times?

Jewish custom today varies considerably on the matter of tombstones and gravesite memorials. Most Jews of Ashkenazic heritage do place a vertical marker of sorts on the grave of a family member at some interval—usually a month or a year—after the burial (Lutske, p. 83). This is not the case, however, with respect to either Sephardic Judaism or Jews in modem Israel. Interestingly, in Israel, the land to which contemporary Jews worldwide look as both inspiration and example, Ashkenazic and Sephardic communities both make almost exclusive use of a horizontal, rather than vertical, tombstone (Werblowsky, p. 696). Beyond this, in Reform Judaism, which has a widespread presence in America, burial itself has become a matter of choice. Cremation, with neither remains nor a public burial site to attend to, is now a not uncommon practice.

In connection with current practice and the rationale for tombstones as currently understood, it is worth citing an authoritative recent work of Jewish burial custom, Maurice Lamm's *The Jewish Way in Death and Mourning* (New York: Jonathan David Publishers, 1975). Lamm (p.188) offers three rationales for the placement of a marker or monument on a grave: Its purposes are: 1) "To mark the place of a burial, so that priest may avoid defilement." 2) "To designate the grave properly, so that friends and relatives may visit it." 3) "To serve as a symbol of honor to the deceased buried beneath it." The first of these principles reaches back to the ancient fear of pollution that threatens any person who treads on a grave, particularly a priest, who is specially consecrated to service of God. Its relevance to the modern cemetery, where those who enter know the location, where walking paths are obvious, and where gravesite[s] are visible, would seem to be marginal at best. The second is simply informative, and can be addressed with markers that are horizontal no less than those which are vertical. And the third is a matter of courtesy and memory, which also can be served by horizontal as well as vertical markers. It is important to notice, finally, that Lamm's entire discussion is placed in a framework not of theological necessity, but of largely optional preference—a matter of both practical convenience and personal courtesy. Lamm's main concern is that there be a "clear, visible, demarcation of the gravesite," and even though he personally does not consider markers that are flush with the earth desirable, he finds them nonetheless acceptable. Most significantly, Lamm clearly states that if only very small markers are permitted by the cemetery rules, then "they may be used and the small size is not considered a belittling of the deceased" (189). Surely, it is significant that this contemporary authority on Jewish mourning, despite a contrary preference of his own, clearly recognizes that at no substantial burden to religious exercise current Jewish custom on this matter can be readily adapted to pertinent cemetery regulations.

Christianity

Is the placement of tombstones asserted or implied in relatively unambiguous terms by an authoritative sacred text?

The authoritative sacred text of Christianity is the Christian Bible, which embraces both the Hebrew Bible (considered above, and called by Christians the Old Testament) and the New Testament. The New Testament consists of three kinds of literature: 1) the four Gospels and the Book of the Acts of the Apostles, the first of which recount primarily the life and teachings of Jesus and

206

the second of which reports deeds and teaching of his first followers; 2) the Epistles, which claim to offer in the form of letters to Christian communities advice and teachings from their apostolic founders, most notable of whom was the Apostle Paul, Christianity's first great theologian; and 3) the Book of Revelation, purportedly written by John the Apostle, which in the form of cryptic symbols and oracles claims to disclose what will happen at the end of days.

In none of this literature is the issue of burial monuments or tombstones ever directly addressed. There are occasional passing references to tombs, as when the Gospel of Mark mentions that a man possessed by demons, whom Jesus healed, had "lived among the tombs" (Mark 5: 3). And there are in the gospels three important stories of resurrection miracles which Jesus performs on the dead: the story of the daughter of a man named Jairus (Mark 5:21–43; also found in Luke and Matthew), the story of the son of the widow from the town of Nain (Luke 7:11–17) and the well-known story of the resurrection of Lazarus, the brother of Jesus' close friends Mary and Martha (John 11:1–57). In the first two of these, the daughter and son are recently deceased, so the issue of a grave or gravestone does not arise. In the third, it is stated that the tomb was a cave, with "a stone upon it." Undoubtedly this was simply a covering stone of the sort that was common when caves were used as places of burial. In any case, we know nothing more than these simple facts, which are consistent with the final incident of this kind, recorded in all four gospels—the death, burial, and resurrection of Jesus himself. According to these accounts (Matthew 27, 28; Mark 15,16; Luke 23, 24; and John 19–21) Jesus after his crucifixion was placed in a cave as yet unused for burials; his body was treated with spices and ointments; and a stone was rolled in front of the cave opening. Consistent with the account of Lazarus' tomb, there is no mention of a monument, memorial, or marker of any kind, and consequently no report of any address to the subject either by Jesus, his disciples, or others associated with the events. On the contrary, it is clear from the closing chapters of each gospel that all emphasis falls not on the burial of Jesus or the practices associated with it, but on the sudden and dramatic events of Easter Sunday morning. It is Jesus' own miraculous resurrection from the dead, and his reappearance, alive and recognizable to others, that forms the center of the stories and gives inspiration to his disciples. For the gospel writers, this startling and crucial event signals victory over death, and by natural implication, marks a turn away from pagan, and even certain earlier Jewish, types of concern with burial or the gravesite.

The Biblical Epistles are concerned mostly with theological discourse, rather than narratives of historical events, so in these writings there is even less occasion to recur to the subject of graves or grave markers than there was in the gospels. There are, of course, several important and substantive discussions of the subject of death and its aftermath. It is notable, however, that these discussions, which were probably produced before the accounts of Jesus' life found in the gospels, stress the same overriding theme. With Christians, as with Christ himself, the burial and disposition of the body of the deceased is a now a matter of small importance, because a truth of far greater importance— the final resurrection and transformation of the body—has overwhelmed it. The most notable discussions of the subject, penned quite probably by the

Apostle Paul, are found in the Books of Romans (chapter 8), I Corinthians (chapter 15), and I Thessalonians (chapter 4). (Scholars dispute the authenticity of certain New Testament epistles, arguing the [sic] some, or even most, were written by personages other than those that claim in the texts to be the authors; since Christian tradition has regarded the texts as sacred and inspired regardless of such contentions, this dispute does not bear on the present discussion.) The significant thing about all of these discussions is that they show no interest in the particulars or customs of Christian burial because their entire focus, like that of the gospels, is on the momentous Christian teaching of the resurrection of the body. Its classic formulation is given by Paul in the Book of I Corinthians 15:51–53: "Lo! I tell you a mystery. We shall not all sleep, but we shall all be changed, in a moment, in the twinkling of an eye, at the last trumpet. For the trumpet will sound, and the dead will be raised imperishable, and we shall be changed. For this perishable nature must put on the imperishable, and this mortal nature, must put on immortality."

This doctrine was not entirely new; the Jewish sect of the Pharisees, of which Paul may once have been a member, had taught it earlier. But like the gospel writers, Paul makes this teaching central and crucial to Christianity in a way that it was not to Judaism. And as in the gospels, the implications of this theological shift are of considerable significance for later Christian theology and tradition. It directs Christian attention away from the state or circumstances of the physical body after death, and turns it decisively toward something beyond this earth—the great day of resurrection and final judgment. What will happen to the body on the day of resurrection is momentously important; how it is cared for or memorialized between the present moment and that day is not a serious or enduring concern.

The Biblical Book of Revelation trades heavily in apocalyptic symbolism whose interpretation and application to present-day religious concerns is the subject of considerable dispute among scholars. Mainstream scholarship does not find it to represent religious views that are significantly inconsistent with those of the Gospels and Epistles. Hence discussion and interpretation of this text can yield to that which has be provided with respect to these other types of literature, which represent the bulk of both text and teaching in the New Testament.

Is the placement of tombstones clearly and consistently affirmed in classic formulations of doctrine and practice?

On the matter of death and burial, as on most other matters, the classic doctrinal statements are to be found of [sic] the writings of Christian theologians and bishops of the first four to five centuries. Their formulations have set the framework within which most all of subsequent Christian thinking has been carried on. Most important among these are three early theologians from about the year 200 A.D. who gave these subjects extended attention. They are Irenaeus of Lyons in his treatise *Adversus Haereses*, Tertullian of Carthage in *De resurrectione carnis* and *Minucius Felix* in Octavius (Bynum, p. 34). All three center their attention on the paradox of the resurrected human body, asking such questions as: How can the body be resurrected and made imperishable? After decay, are its pieces reassembled like a puzzle? Or is it transformed like a seed that dies and grows into a plant? Related to these questions, naturally, was also that of the state of the body after death. Should it perhaps receive special care and attention, being preserved safely in a tomb with a proper memorial, so as to facilitate resurrection? It is significant that whatever other differences they exhibit, the theologians engaged in these discussion agree unanimously that how the body is preserved, or cared for, or marked, ultimately has no effect on the power of God to resurrect and restore it on the final day. Writing in the midst of persecution, these church fathers were well aware of martyrs whose bodies had been eaten by animals or torn apart by persecutors, yet in their view, there was no doubt that the resurrection would bring complete restoration. As St. Augustine, the most influential of all early Christian fathers in the West and himself author of a treatise *De cura pro mortuis gerenda* would later write in *The City of God* in the case of a person who might have died of starvation, "His own flesh, however, which he lost by famine, shall be restored to him by Him who can recover even what has evaporated. And though it had been absolutely annihilated, so that no part of its substance remained in any secret spot of nature, the Almighty could restore it by such means as He saw fit" (Bynum, p. 104).

The effect of such teaching, accepted universally in both the Eastern and Western portions of the Church, was to be evident in all of subsequent Christian thought and practice. The church made no special investment of its authority in any particular form of preserving or protecting the bodies of the dead, still less in any specific form of individualized monument or memorial by which to remember them. Its focus was not on the life now past, but on the glorious new life to come. As it happened, most church fathers did prefer burial to cremation, but felt no need to insist on the matter (Douglas, p. 168). Even more clearly, they left no mandate that graves must be universally marked in any one particular fashion, let alone with a vertical marker or monument.

Has the practice of placing tombstones on graves been observed continuously, or nearly so, throughout the history of the tradition?

As we might expect, given the refusal of early theologians to offer any clear rule on the matter, Christian practice with respect to burial sites and monuments has varied enormously from the first centuries to the present. A number of early Christian burials took place in underground locations like the celebrated catacombs in and about the city of Rome. Because masses were said for the dead in these locations, the misconception has arisen that these were places of public worship. In fact, they were not. The catacombs, some of which existed prior to the Christian era, were visited mainly for burials and rituals associated with the dead (Ferguson, p. 163). At these sites bodies were deposited in chambers dug into the walls of narrow tunnels, a practice that discouraged the placement of monuments of any size, and by definition excluded markers visible above the surface of the ground. Archaeology shows no record of anything resembling a monument before the end of the second century. In the catacombs, Christians might simply carve the name of the deceased into the wall and perhaps add the symbol of the fish, the word for which, in Greek, served as an acronym for a simplified Christian creed: "Jesus Christ, Son of God and Savior" (Berardino, p. 155–56).

In subsequent Roman centuries, and especially after the end of persecution, specifically Christian cemeteries began to emerge both above and under ground. At these locations, writes one authority, practice was guided by the Christian attitude that normal dead bodies "should not be accorded special treatment. While the ancient Greeks and Romans often carved portraits on tombs or painted images of the dead on wooden markers, Christians turned away from the pretentious tomb as a symbol of worldly concern. Only the remains of holy men and women deserved special respect, and these might be in the church" (McDannell, p. 105). The general rule was modesty and restraint. As another authority notes, Christians even opposed the Roman practice of placing a crown on the head of the deceased; though fully hidden after burial, such an adornment was nonetheless regarded as idolatry; all honors were to be reserved to those saints who had won the crown of martyrdom (Paxton, p. 25).

Over time, and as Western culture moved into the early medieval era, this growing cult of the saints and martyrs had a profound effect of its own on burial customs. The hope of most ordinary Christians was not to be housed in a private tomb, with some enduring personal monument, but to be buried, nameless and with no abiding memorial, in a common grave ad sanctos—"near the saints" (Aries, Hour, p. 33). In the later centuries of antiquity, there developed throughout the Christian world the firm belief that both the presence and prayers of the saints, especially those martyred for the faith, offered the only real assistance available on the journey toward heaven that awaited all on the day of death. Saints often were buried with great honors in the churches themselves, and once they had been so placed, Christians of every succeeding generation strove to be buried as near as possible to these now immortal sources of spiritual power (Aries, Attitudes, p. 16). If possible, they hoped for burial in the church; if not, in the churchyard, for that was still near enough the saints to be sacred ground, offering the promise of easier access to heaven.

Of course, not all Christians were buried nameless in common graves. By about the 11th century, the midpoint of the medieval period, the growing wealth of the church mingled with the piety and vanity of the aristocracy to open the way toward burial effigies, memorials, and monuments on a grand scale. In the later Middle Ages and throughout the Age of the Renaissance, the trend toward such display was to give the churches of Europe some of its very finest art, architecture, and sculpture (Aries, Hour, pp. 202–93). The crucial point to notice here, however, is that these were always rare and optional enterprises reserved only for saintly heroes of the church and those very few others whose wealth or power enabled them to claim special attention from the ecclesiastical hierarchy. For the vast majority of Christians, a nameless common burial was all that was expected; and the theology of the church made it clear that nothing more was needed. Individualized monuments or markers were neither required nor, for most, realistic. It is important to note further that the custom of unmarked common graves was not confined to the limited medieval episode of hardship and privation often called the Dark Ages. The custom of unmarked communal burial for the masses persisted in Western culture up to the very edge of the modern era, often creating formidable problems of health and sanitation. As has been noted by Phillipe Aries, the French cultural historian whose *Hour of Our Death* remains the classic study of the subject, the customary procedure of communal burial made the churches and churchyards of Europe "veritable cities of the dead" (p. 49) from Christian antiquity up until barely two centuries before our own. The bearing of this evidence on the present case would seem now to be fairly clear. The tradition of Christian burial practice cannot provide a warrant for monuments as integral and essential to individual gravesites when for most of its long history, most Christians have had no such thing as a personal grave even to mark.

Is the placement of vertical tombstones consistently practiced everywhere, or almost such, in the tradition as we meet it most recent times?

If a case for vertical tombstones can be made at all, perhaps the nearest justification would have to come from modern, if not quite contemporary, practice. Aries and other authorities on Western attitudes toward death agree that approximately two centuries ago in middle-class Western communities, a shift of burials away from the churchyard and toward individual marked graves gradually did begin to take place. This development was driven in part by the problems of overcrowding and sanitation that appeared with the growth of large cities in Europe (McManners, pp. 303–67). In part as well, it was occasioned by a rise of individualism of the post-Reformation era and, more significantly, by the secularism of philosophers of the Enlightenment and the Romantic sentimentalism of poets and artists in the Napoleonic era and after (Stannard, pp. 171–88). Whatever the mix of underlying causes, Western Europe and America saw by the early 1800s the flowering of what historians have called the "rural cemetery movement"—the development in the areas surrounding major cities of large, mainly rural, public cemeteries designed to provide for burials in a peaceful, pastoral setting removed from the influence of the churches. The most noteworthy European case of this sort was the famous Pere Lachaise cemetery in Paris, while in America, Mount Auburn Cemetery in Boston, Laurel Hill in Philadelphia, and Greenwood in Brooklyn, all founded in the 1830s, represented the same cultural trend (McDannell, pp. 105–108; Stannard, pp. 171–88). Their purpose was to provide a place of serenity and beauty, away from ecclesiastical influences, where families and friends could gather to contemplate and to remember those they had loved in life. And it was is in these cemeteries especially that over the period from the 1830s up to about the 1960s that the option of erecting monuments for loved ones came to full expression.

The rural cemetery movement has always had its critics both esthetic and cultural, but it offers almost the only historical precedent that can be found to justify recourse to vertical monuments or markers in cemeteries. Unfortunately, however, there is a serious problem with an appeal even to this quite limited and recent development. The great difficulty—and indeed irony—in appealing to this precedent is that of all burial customs found in Western culture, this is among those least tied to the exercise of religiously inspired practices of burial and remembrance. In America, though Christians and Jews certainly participated, the rural cemetery movement was propelled not foremost by churches and synagogues, but by an effort to move away from traditional religious forms while embracing a new, more secular and purely sentimental artistic sensibility. Its purpose was actually to escape the interests, forms, and customs of conventionally religious burials. Thus, while an appeal can perhaps be made to the rural cemetery precedent, it is an exceedingly poor fit for legal arguments that claim to rest on principles of the free exercise of religion in either the Jewish or Christian traditions. To the degree that Christians and Jews ever embraced this tradition, it is clear that they did so as not as in any way a religious obligation, but as a matter of personal taste—and a preference rather strangely at odds with their own religious traditions.

A final point. The evidence of both Christian and Jewish burial practice in recent decades offers additional proof of just how much a matter of personal taste—that is, marginal or tangential to religious exercise—the rural cemetery custom of gravesite monuments has always been in American life. Recent years have brought a trend not only away from the monumental display of the past, but toward its very opposite. Religious individuals today readily turn to cremation, with ashes kept privately or scattered to a favorite locale. To the degree that cremation, with no recourse at all to a public memorial, is now found by many to be not only an acceptable but even preferred option, it remains fundamentally unpersuasive to claim even that burial, either in itself or accompanied by a monument of some specific form, is essential and integral to either Jewish or Christian religious traditions.

To summarize this report briefly: By the main criteria relevant to the issue, the erection of burial monuments in vertical or any other specific form cannot be shown to be essential and integral to either the Jewish or Christian religious traditions. There is no relatively unambiguous assertion or implication of such a practice in either set of sacred scriptures. There is no clear and consistent affirmation of such a custom to be found in the classic formulations of doctrine. There is no long-standing or nearly continuous history of such a practice in either tradition. And there is no evidence that such a custom is consistently and widely practiced in more recent times. If the practice of erecting vertical tombstones were to meet the criteria in just one or two of these categories, one might well have at least the beginning of a persuasive legal argument in this case. In fact, however, it seems to clear the threshold of qualification in none of them. Hence, there would seem to be no reasonable ground for the plantiff's contention that the defendant's restrictions on such monuments violate the legal standard enacted by the RFRA. In sum, the combined testimony of theology, history, and tradition indicates that such restrictions do not "substantially burden a person's exercise of religion."

BRIEF COMMENT ON PROFESSIONAL CREDENTIALS:

I currently serve as the Associate Dean of the College of Arts & Sciences in the University of Miami. For sixteen years prior to my appointment as a dean, I served as the Chair of the Department of Religious Studies in the College. I am the author of academic articles and books in the history of religions; my most recent book is Seven Theories of Religion published by Oxford University Press in 1996.

BIBLIOGRAPHY/SOURCES CITED

Aries, Philhipe. *Western Attitudes Toward Death From the Middle Ages to the Present.* Translated by Patrica Ranum. Baltimore, Maryland: The Johns Hopkins University Press, 1974.

———. *The Hour of Our Death* translated by Helen Weaver. New York Oxford University Press, 1981.

Berardino, Angelo Di. *Encyclopedia of the Early Church.* New York: Oxford University Press, 1992, s.v. "Cemetery."

Bible, The Holy. Oxford Annotated Edition. New York: Oxford University Press, 1973.

Bosse, T.S.R. *Death in the Middle Ages: Mortality, Judgment, and Remembrance.* New York: McGraw Hill Book Company, 1972.

Bynum, Carolyn Walker. *The Resurrection of the Body in Western Christianity,* 200–1336. New York: Columbia University Press, 1995.

Choron, Jacques. *Death and Western Thought.* New York: Corner Books, 1973.

Douglas, J. D., ed. *The New International Dictionary of the Christian Church.* Grand Rapids, Michigan: Zondervan Publishing House, 1978, s.v. "Burial Services."

Dunnigan, Pat. "Constitutional Rights Standing for Religion?" *Broward Daily Business Review* 43:5 2:A17.

Ferguson, Everett. *Encyclopedia of Early Christianity.* New York: Garland Publishing, Inc. 1990, s.v. "Burial."

Geary, Patrick J. *Living with the Dead in the Middle Ages.* Ithaca, New York: Cornell University Press, 1994.

Geddes, Gordon E. *Welcome Joy: Death in Puritan New England.* Ann Arbor, Michigan: UMI Research Press, 1981.

Hopfe, Lewis M. *Religions of the World,* 6th edition. New York: Macmillan & Co., 1994.

Jacobs, Louis, ed. *The Jewish Companion.* New York: Oxford University Press, 1995, s.v. "Tombstone."

Lamm, Maurice. *The Jewish Way in Death and Dying.* New York: Jonathan David Publishers, 1969.

Lutske, Harvey. *The Book of Jewish Customs.* Northvale, New Jersey: Jason Aronson, Inc., 1986.

McDannell, Colleen. *Material Christianity: Religion and Popular Culture in America.* New Haven: Yale University Press, 1995.

McManners, John. *Death and Enlightenment Changing Attitudes to Death among Christians and Unbelievers in Eighteenth-Century France.* Oxford: Clarendon Press, 1981.

Moller, David Wendell. *Confronting Death: Values, Institutions, and Human Mortality*. New York: Oxford University Press, 1996.

Paxton, Frederick S. Christianizing Death: *The Creation of a Ritual Process in Early Medieval Europe*. Ithaca, New York: Cornell University Press, 1990.

Pelikan, Jaroslav. *The Shape of Death: Life, Death, and Immortality in the Early Fathers*. London: Macmillan & Co., Ltd., 1962.

Rabinowicz, Harry M. *A Guide to the Life: Jewish Laws and Customs of Mourning*. London: Jewish Chronicle Publications, 1964.

Stannard, David E. *The Puritan Way of Death: A Study in Religion Culture and Social Change*. New York: Oxford University Press, 1977.

Thielicke, Helmut. *Living with Death*. Translated by Geoffrey W. Bromiley. Grand Rapids, Michigan: William B. Eerdmans Publishing Company, 1983.

Walker, D. P. *The Decline of Hell: Seventeenth-Century Discussions of Eternal Torment*. Chicago: The University of Chicago Press, 1964.

Werblowsky, R. J. Zwi, and Geoffrey Wigoder, eds. *The Oxford Dictionary of the Jewish Religion*. New York Oxford University Press, 1997, s.v. 'Tombs."

Wigoder, Geoffrey, ed. *The Encyclopaedia of Judaism*. New York: Macmillan & Co., 1989, s.v. 'Tombstone," pp. 708–09.

EXPERT REPORT OF WINNIFRED FALLERS SULLIVAN
DECEMBER 2, 1998

I have been asked to give expert testimony on the religious importance of practices surrounding burial and memorializing of the dead. I have read the depositions and documentary evidence in *Warner v. City of Boca Raton*, No. 98-8054-CIV-RYSKAMP, filed in the United States District Court for the Southern District of Florida. The rules and practices of Boca Raton Municipal Cemetery and Mausoleum, with respect to the decoration of graves are at issue in this action.

I am Assistant Professor of Religion at Washington & Lee University in Lexington, Virginia. I hold a Ph.D. in religious studies and a J.D., both from the University of Chicago. My expertise is in theory in the study of religion, in American religion and in how religion is defined and dealt with in a legal context.

Scholars of religion do not agree on a definition of religion. Religion is understood variously to be, for example, rituals, beliefs, actions, myths and symbolic structures:

- that are associated with supernatural beings;
- that are concerned with the ultimate meaning of life;
- that formalize and reinforce political and economic power;
- that are psychologically produced;
- that are the characteristic production of structures of the human brain;
- that express the self-understanding of a particular society;
- that construct and express individual and communal identity
- or, that are expressions of a universal human experience of the sacred; among others.

Religion scholars would largely agree, however, that practices surrounding human death, while of enormous variety, are close to the heart of religion and of the religious imagination, however it is defined. In all human societies human death is marked, ritualized and memorialized, and those practices form a central and important part of religion. Funeral rites, through gestures, behavior, words, songs, material objects, meals, and treatment of the corpse, function

- to serve the future life of the dead person,
- to console the surviving relatives and friends;
- and, to contribute to the reconstruction of and preservation of the community.

Religion scholars would also largely agree that authentic religious practices include both those founded in textually based doctrine taught by institutionalized hierarchies as well as in folk traditions and customs passed down through families and communities.

A cemetery is a place where remains are both preserved and concealed. It is a place of transformation, closely associated with the maternal symbolism of the earth. Important religious practices associated with cemeteries might include:

- identification of the deceased and the deceased's religious commitments and community;
- covering of the grave to emphasize its sacredness and to prevent people from walking on it;
- planting of flowers, symbolic of life or as an offering;
- placing of material objects symbolic of the dead person's life or of the mourner's religious devotion;
- placement of statues as a focus for religious devotion;
- erection of a cross, the quintessential Christian symbol;
- creation of a space conducive for prayer;
- lighting of candles;
- family visitation.

A person could be substantially burdened in the practice of his religion if his beliefs and practices surrounding human death were interfered with. The religious importance of such beliefs and practices might be determined by reference to the historic prescription or custom of a particular community, by consideration of its place in the larger religious life of the community or the individual and its relation to other religious actions or events, or by analogy to other beliefs and practices.

"Catholicism, Judaism, Protestantism" and other such catch-all descriptive terms are convenient abstractions of complex realities. Generalizing about "all" Catholics, or Protestants, or Jews in terms of belief or practice is very hazardous. In each case, there is enormous variety within the tradition, both across space and across time. For example, what is "Catholic" in one place and time may vary enormously from what is "Catholic" at another place and time. And it would depend on who you asked. There is no such thing, therefore, as "the church" as a constant entity, except in a highly philosophical or theological sense. One cannot accurately speak of Catholicism, or Judaism, or Protestantism "requiring" a particular practice or belief. One can only speak of Jewish or Protestant or Catholic authorities in a particular community at a particular time—and even then they are likely to disagree. It is in the nature of religion to be both local and to be a constantly changing reality.

In the American context, in particular, it is particularly difficult to speak of religious beliefs or practices being "required" by a particular religion. Because of disestablishment and of the religion clauses of the First Amendment and of state constitutions, no established religious authority is publicly acknowledged as having greater authenticity than another. In other words, the state has no way to determine the orthodoxy of a particular religious practice or even to determine which authority is the appropriate one to determine the orthodoxy of a particular practice. Each individual is, in effect, the expert on his or her own religious life, a life which may be an idiosyncratic assembly of beliefs, interpretations and practices. The state may not give preference to one sincerely motivated religious expression over another because of its supposed historicity, orthodoxy or pervasiveness. The state has no way to make such theological determinations without giving an unconstitutional preference to a particular religious world view. While for the external observer religious beliefs and practices may be radically indeterminate, for the individual believer they may have tremendous authority and power. The practices described in the depositions in this action: the design, orientation and placing of markers and statues, whether explicitly religious or not, the covering of the grave, the planting of shrubs, ground cover and flowers, the concern for the overall appearance and convenience of a cemetery, and the visiting, praying, and attention to the needs of the deceased may all be considered important religious practices in the context of a particular individuals religious life.

On the basis of my reading and research in the study of religion generally and relying in particular on the works cited below, it is my opinion that practices associated with a burial site could be so important to the exercise of a particular person's religion that prohibition of such practices could substantially burden that person's exercise of his or her religion.

SELECTED BIBLIOGRAPHY

Sydney Ahlstrom, *A Religious History of the American People*. New Haven: Yale University Press, 1972.

Catherine L. Albanese, *America Religion and Religions* 2d. Ed. Belmont: Wadsworth, 1992.

Pierre Bourdieu, *Outline of a Theory of Practice* Translated by Richard Nice. Cambridge: Cambridge University Press, 1977).

Carolyn Walker Bynum. *Fragmentation and Redemption: Essays on Gender and the Human Body in Medieval Religion*. New York: Zone Books, 1991.

Emile Durkheim, *The Elementary Forms of Religious Life*. Translated by Joseph Ward Swain. New York: The Free Press,1918.

Mircea Eliade, *Patterns in Comparative Religion*. Translated by Rosemary Sheed. New York: Sheed & Ward, 1958.

Clifford Geertz, *The Interpretation of Cultures*. New York: Basic Books, 1973.

Will Herberg, *Protestant Catholic Jew*. Chicago: University of Chicago Press, 1955.

Charles Long, *Significations, Signs, Symbols, and Image in the Interpretation of Religion*. Philadelphia: Fortress, 1986.

Bronislaw Malinowski, "The Role of Magic and Religion," in William A. Lessa and Evon Z. Vogt, *Reader in Comparative Religion: An Anthropological Approach* New York: Harper & Row, 1965.

Sidney Mead, *The Lively Experiment*. New York: Harper & Row, 1963.

Frank Reynolds and Earle Waugh, *Religious Encounters with Death: Insights from the History and Anthropology of Religions*. University Park: Pennsylvania State, 1977.

Jonathan Z. Smith, *Imagining Religion: From Babylon to Jonestown*. Chicago: University of Chicago Press, 1982.

———, *Map Is Not Territory*. Leiden: E. J. Brill, 1978.

Louis-Vincent Thomas, "Funeral Rites," in Mircea Eliade, *Encyclopedia of Religion*.

Arnold Van Gennep, *The Rites of Passage*. Translated by Monika B. Vizedom and Gabrielle L. Caffee. Chicago: University of Chicago Press, 1960.

Appendix C:
Ryskamp Opinion

[Note about page numbering: This reproduction of Judge Ryscamp's published opinion indicates in brackets the asterixed page numbering that refer to the pages of the official reporter.]

Richard and Miriam WARNER, Souhail Karram, Ian and Bobbie Payne, Carrie Monier, Marie and Louise Riccobono, Emil and Eleanor Danciu, and Joanne Davis, individually and on behalf of all others similarly situated, Plaintiffs, vs. THE CITY OF BOCA RATON, a Florida municipal corporation, Defendant.

No. 98-8054-CIV-RYSKAMP United States District Court, S.D. of Florida, Northern Division
August 31, 1999
64 F. Supp. 2d 1272

Charlotte Danciu, Boca Raton, FL, Lynn G. Waxman, James Kellogg Green, West Palm Beach, FL, for Plaintiffs.
John Orrin McKirchy, Boca Raton, FL, Bruce S. Rogow, Ft. Lauderdale, FL, Beverly A. Pohl, Boca Raton, FL, for Defendant.

[*1275] FINDINGS OF FACT AND CONCLUSIONS OF LAW
RYSKAMP, District Judge. THIS CAUSE came on for trial before the Court and the issues having been duly tried, the Court hereby renders its findings of fact and conclusions of law

I. FINDINGS OF FACT

In this action, it is alleged that certain Rules and Regulations (the "Regulations") promulgated by the City of Boca Raton (the "City") for the maintenance of its Municipal Cemetery (the "Cemetery") violate the plaintiffs' federal and state guarantees of freedom of religious exercise, freedom of speech and due process of law. A trial on the issues established the following material facts by a preponderance of the evidence.

A. The Cemetery

The City owns, operates and maintains a 21.5 acre Cemetery for its residents. Since 1944, the Cemetery has been located south of Palmetto Park Road, on Fourth Avenue, in Boca Raton, Florida. The Cemetery grounds extend east and west of Fourth Avenue which runs north and south.

The Cemetery is divided into several sections. The oldest section, known as Section A, is located west of Fourth Avenue and contains graves and monuments that were moved from a prior site. The newer sections of the Cemetery are located east of Fourth Avenue. Purchasers of Cemetery plots[1] (the "Plot Owners") receive a Certificate of Ownership which identifies the Plot Owner's interest in the "exclusive right of burial of the human dead in [the plot]." *See* Def.'s Ex. 7. This interest is subject to the following express limitations:

1. That the burial right herein granted will be used only in conformity with the Cemetery Rules and Regulations as they may be from time to time adopted or amended.
2. That the property herein described shall forever remain under the exclusive control of [the City] for the purposes of care and maintenance.

Id. The purchase and sale transaction does not convey property *via* a deed nor is the transaction recorded. Moreover, Plot Owners do not pay property taxes on the plots.

[*1276]

B. Management of the Cemetery

The Boca Raton City Council is charged with managing the affairs of the Cemetery. *See* Boca Raton Code of Ordinances, art. II, § 13–36 ("The city cemetery shall be known as the Boca Raton Municipal Cemetery and its affairs shall be administered and supervised by the city council"); § 13–43 ("The city council may establish policy from time to time regarding curbs, foundations, monuments and markers in the Boca Raton Municipal Cemetery"). Pursuant to this express authority, the City has promulgated Regulations for the Cemetery which have been incorporated into the City ordinances and which have the effect of law. *Id.* § 13–37.

1. The 1982 Prohibition on Vertical Grave Decorations
    In November 1982, the City adopted a Regulation which prohibits vertical grave markers[2], memorials[3], monuments[4] and other structures (collectively re-

---

[1] The cemetery is divided into lots and plots. A lot is a numbered division as shown on the cemetery map and consists of more than one plot. A plot is a space of sufficient size to accommodate a single-depth in-earth burial. See Cemetery Rules and Regulations (hereinafter "Regulations") §§ I(11) & I(18).

[2] The Regulations define a "marker" as a "memorial which does not extend vertically above the ground and is constructed of approved metal or stone containing names, dates, or other engraved lettering used in identification of one or more persons and placed at the head of a lot or plot." *Id.* § I(13).

[3] The Regulations define a "memorial" as a "monument, marker, tablet, headstone, private mausoleum or tomb for family or individual use, tombstone, coping, lot enclosure, and surface burial vault, urn, crypt and niche places or bronze lettering on crypts or niches." Regulations § I(15).

[4] The Regulations define a "monument" as a "tombstone or memorial of granite or other approved materials, which shall extend vertically above the surface of the ground." *Id.* § I(16).

ferred to hereafter as "grave decorations") on Cemetery plots. *See* Regulations § XIV(2). In particular, § XIV(2) of the Regulations provides:

> No memorials, monuments, or enclosures shall be permitted above ground in any section of the Cemetery grounds except in Section "A."[5] Stone or bronze markers are allowed in all other sections provided that they are level with the ground surface.

The horizontal grave marker style adopted by the City in 1982 is known as a "memorial garden" and has become the industry standard for modern cemeteries. The use of horizontal grave markers promotes the City's interests in: 1) making the most efficient use of Cemetery space; 2) ease of access of earth-moving equipment to plots for burial and disinterment purposes; 3) ease of grounds maintenance; 4) ensuring the safety of grounds keepers and visitors; and 5) maintaining a uniform appearance and aesthetically pleasing environment in the Cemetery. The City established that the use of vertical grave decorations would permit fewer grave sites in the Cemetery, impede access to the grave sites, make grounds maintenance more difficult and dangerous for grounds keepers and visitors, and create visual clutter. Most importantly, the use of vertical grave decorations would make it difficult to access and dig graves with the large machinery used by the City for this purpose. Although the City could avoid this problem by digging graves by hand, this practice would be more dangerous because of the risk that the ground would collapse on the grave diggers.

2. The 1988 Regulation Vesting Cemetery Manager With Discretion to Make Temporary Exceptions and Modifications to the Regulations

In 1988, the City adopted a Regulation which granted the Cemetery Manager the discretion to make temporary exceptions and modifications to the Regulations. *See* Regulations § XVI(1). In particular, Section XVI(1) of the Regulations provides:

> (1) Exceptions and Modifications—Special cases may arise for which the literal enforcement of any rule may impose [*1277] unnecessary hardship. The Cemetery Manager, after consultation with the Recreation Services Department Director, reserves the right to make temporary exceptions, suspensions and modification [*sic*] of any rule or regulation, when in the Cemetery Manager's discretion such modification seems advisable. Such temporary exceptions, suspensions and modifications shall in no way be construed as effecting [*sic*] the general enforcement of these rules and regulations nor as eliminating the authority of the City Council in approving or disapproving all permanent changes in rules or policies of the Cemetery/Mausoleum.

---

[5] Section A is exempt from the prohibition because it was already in existence at the time the Regulation was enacted, and because it contained vertical monuments that had been moved from a previous cemetery site.

C. The Plaintiffs' Use of the Cemetery

The named plaintiffs are all residents of the City who have purchased plots in the Cemetery. Between 1984 and 1996, the plaintiffs decorated the graves of family members and loved ones with standing statues, crosses, starts of David, ground covers and borders in violation of the Regulations.

It is undisputed that the plaintiffs placed vertical decorations on their Cemetery plots in observance of sincerely held religious beliefs.[6] Several of the plaintiffs erected vertical decorations in observance of their Jewish faith. For example, plaintiff Richard Warner and his mother plaintiff Miriam Warner placed ground cover and edging stones on their family members' graves in observance of a Jewish tradition that grave sites are to be protected and never walked upon. Plaintiffs Ian and Bobby Payne placed a standing star of David and grave coverings on their son's grave in order to identify their son as Jewish and to protect the grave from being walked upon.

Additionally, several of the plaintiffs erected vertical grave decorations in observance of their Christian faith. For example, plaintiff Souhail Karram placed a standing cross on his wife's grave because he believes that Jesus Christ was crucified on a standing cross and rose again, and, therefore, the standing cross symbolizes that his wife will also rise again. Plaintiff Carrie Monier placed a vertical statue of the Sacred Heart of Jesus as well as a rope around her brother's grave because she believes graves should be protected and never walked upon. Carrie Monier's sister, plaintiff Barbara Cavedoni placed a standing cross on her loved one's grave site because the crucifixion and death of Christ has for centuries been depicted on a standing cross and, therefore, in her view, it would be disrespectful to honor and pray to a horizontal cross. Plaintiff Marie Riccobono decorated her father's grave with a statue of Jesus to watch over him and surrounded the grave marker with edging blocks and stone. Plaintiff Joanne Davis memorialized the grave of her infant son with a two-foot high bronze statue of two children playing, with small crosses and with a statue of Jesus holding a child. Finally, plaintiff Eleanor Danciu believes the statues of the Blessed Mother and St. Francis which decorate her parents' graves are her channels of prayer to God.

D. The City's Response to the Plaintiffs' Conduct

In August 1991, the City sent notices to Plot Owners who had placed vertical decorations on their plots requesting that the plots be brought into compliance with the Regulations within thirty days. Plot Owners were informed that if they did not comply with the City's request, the City would remove the non-

---

[6] By Order filed August 17, 1998, this Court dismissed count I as to plaintiffs Richard and Miriam Warner, Carrie Monier, and Marie and Louise Riccobono because these plaintiffs had failed to allege that they placed standing decorations on their cemetery plots in observance of religious beliefs. At trial, however, these plaintiffs established that they had in fact placed standing decorations on their cemetery plots in observance of religious beliefs.

complying structures. This communication created some controversy, and a minority of Plot Owners failed to comply with the City's request.

[*1278] A second notice requesting compliance with the Regulations was sent in July 1992. Plot Owners were advised that after 15 days, any remaining vertical decorations would be removed and held for a 10-day period and then disposed of if not claimed. Again, not all Plot Owners complied with the City's request.

Those who objected to the enforcement of the Regulations voiced their views to the City Council which agreed to postpone removal of the vertical decorations pending further study. On August 17, 1992, the City Manager's office issued a memorandum which stated in pertinent part that:

> City staff will *not* be moving forward with the removal of memorial items from grave sites at this time. Instead, staff will be re-evaluating the existing ordinance to determine if any modifications should be made. A complete analysis of the ordinance and its impact will be accomplished prior to any such activity. [emphasis in original].

In July 1996, the City revised the Regulations to accommodate the needs of grieving families. *See* Regulations § IX(2). In particular, § IX(2) of the Regulations provides:

> The placing of any articles[7] of any kind upon plots or upon or in front of crypts and niches that are not specifically authorized under these rules and regulations shall not be permitted. The Cemetery Manager reserves the right to remove same. The placing of small articles on a headstone memorial after a sixty (60) day period from the date of the burial shall be prohibited. The placing of small articles on a headstone memorial on the deceased's birthday, Mother's Day, Father's Day, the anniversary date of the deceased's death, and on national holidays may be permitted. The small articles may be permitted for a period commencing one (1) day before and ending five (5) days after such birthday, anniversary or holiday. The Cemetery Manager reserves the right to remove all articles which interfere with the maintenance of the Cemetery or Mausoleum, or interfere with the accessibility to another plot crypt or niche in the preparation of an interment, disinterment, entombment or disentombment.

On August 27, 1996, while the Regulations were being studied and evaluated, the City Council directed the City Manager, as an interim measure, to refrain from removing any decorations on graves which were in place as of that date, and directed the Cemetery Manager to enforce the Regulations with respect to decorations placed on graves after that date.

Additionally, the City commissioned a survey of Plot Owners, designed and conducted by researchers at Florida Atlantic University ("FAU"), to identify

---

[7] The Regulations define "articles" as "including, but not limited to, boxes, shells, toys, ornaments, chairs, settees, crosses, statues, benches, vases, rocks, fencing, borders, windchimes, candles, candle holders, plants, shrubs, trees or herbage of any kind." Regulations § I(1).

the Plot Owners' desires with respect to vertical grave decorations in the Cemetery.

The FAU survey concluded that:

> The results of this survey have revealed that the majority of the plot owners, regardless of the time length of plot ownership, location (east or west) of plot, or frequency of visitation, believe that the July 23, 1996 Rules and Regulations should be followed by all plot owners as required by the City of Boca Raton. They believe that contributions to a Tree Legacy landscape beautification program is a much higher priority than allowing plot owners to decorate plots with no limitations. They believe that the regulations should apply to all current owners and to future owners.

The FAU study recommended, *inter alia*, that the Regulations be implemented and uniformly enforced by the City and that all plots be brought into compliance with the Regulations.

[*1279] On June 10, 1997, at the regular meeting of the City Council, the City took up the issue of grave decorations in the Cemetery. The City Council first considered and rejected, by a three to two margin, a resolution "to permit existing articles on plots to remain and to permit owners of plots, as of the effective date of this resolution, to place articles of the same character and nature as currently exist at the cemetery." Def.'s Mot. Dis. Compl. Ex. 19. Thereafter, the City Council adopted the following Staff Recommendations:

1. The Rules and Regulations adopted on July 23, 1996 for the Cemetery and Mausoleum should be implemented and enforced uniformly; and
2. All cemetery plot decorations should be brought into compliance with the July 23, 1996 adopted Rules and Regulations within 90 days.

Id. Ex. 20. Plot Owners were subsequently notified that if they did not comply with the Regulations by January 15, 1998, the City would remove all noncomplying articles.

E. The Plaintiffs' Lawsuit

Thereafter, the plaintiffs filed suit in the Circuit Court of the Fifteenth Judicial Circuit in and for Palm Beach County, Florida against the City of Boca Raton, Mayor Carol Hanson, Deputy Mayor William "Bill" Glass, and City Council members Steven L. Abrams, Wanda E. Thayer and Susan Welchel.[8] The defendants timely removed to this Court on January 30, 1998.

On June 12, 1998, the plaintiffs filed an amended class action complaint naming the City as the sole defendant, and alleging that the prohibition on vertical grave decorations violates their federal and state rights to freedom of religious

---

[8] The City agreed to stay enforcement of the challenged Regulations until the conclusion of this lawsuit.

expression, freedom of speech and due process of law. In particular, count I alleges that the prohibition substantially burdens the plaintiffs' exercise of religion in violation of the recently enacted Florida Religious Freedom Restoration Act of 1998 (the "Florida RFRA"), Fla. Stat. § 761.01 *et seq.* Count II alleges that the prohibition violates the plaintiffs' First Amendment rights to the free exercise of religion and freedom of speech. Count III alleges that enforcement of the prohibition would deprive the plaintiffs of a property interest in maintaining vertical grave decorations on their Cemetery plots in violation of the Due Process Clause of the Fourteenth Amendment. Finally, count IV alleges that the prohibition violates the plaintiffs' rights under the Florida Constitution to the free exercise of religion, freedom of speech and due process of law.

By Order filed August 17, 1998, this Court dismissed count I as to plaintiffs Richard and Miriam Warner, Carrie Monier, and Marie and Louise Riccobono. On the same date, this Court granted the plaintiffs' motion to maintain a class action and directed class members to be notified.

II. CONCLUSIONS OF LAW

This case evokes strong emotions and raises a host of complicated legal issues. In the end, however, the case presents a simple question: Does any federal or Florida law relieve an individual from the obligation to comply with Regulations which uniformly prohibit vertical grave decorations in the Boca Raton Municipal Cemetery? In this Court's view, the answer is no.

A. Count I—The Florida RFRA

In count I of their amended complaint, the plaintiffs allege that the City's prohibition on vertical grave decorations substantially burdens their exercise of religion in violation of the recently enacted Florida RFRA. The Court disagrees.

1. The Historical Background of the Florida RFRA

There are no reported decisions construing the Florida RFRA. However, the [*1280] Court does not write on a blank slate, because this statute is merely the latest attempt in a long struggle to define the scope of protection that should be afforded to religious practices burdened by neutral laws of general applicability.

Early Supreme Court decisions yielded the general principle that the Free Exercise Clause does not relieve an individual of the obligation to comply with a neutral law of general applicability. *See Reynolds v. United States,* 98 U.S. 145, 166-67, 25 L. Ed. 244 (1878) (rejecting claim that criminal laws against polygamy could not be constitutionally applied to those whose religion commanded the practice). The *Reynolds* Court explained:

Laws are made for the government of actions, and while they cannot interfere with mere religious belief and opinions, they may with practices . . .

Can a man excuse his practices to the contrary because of his religious belief? To permit this would be to make the professed doctrines of religious belief superior to the law of the land, and in effect to permit every citizen to become a law unto himself.

Id. Some years later, Justice Frankfurter reaffirmed this principle in *Minersville School Dist. Bd. of Ed. v. Gobitis,* 310 U.S. 586, 594, 84 L. Ed. 1375, 60 S. Ct. 1010 (1940), observing that "[c]onscientious scruples have not, in course of the long struggle for religious toleration, relieved the individual from obedience to a general law not aimed at the promotion or restriction of religious beliefs."

Beginning with the seminal decision in *Sherbert v. Verner,* 374 U.S. 398, 10 L. Ed. 2d 965, 83 S. Ct. 1790 (1963), the Supreme Court began to expand the scope of protection afforded to religious practices. Eventually, the Court adopted the rule that a neutral law of general applicability which substantially burdens an individual's religious practices will run afoul of the Free Exercise Clause if it is not narrowly tailored to achieve a compelling governmental interest. *See, e.g., Thomas v. Review Bd.,* 450 U.S. 707, 718, 67 L. Ed. 2d 624, 101 S. Ct. 1425 (1981) ("The state may justify an inroad on religious liberty by showing that it is the least restrictive means of achieving some compelling state interest.").

In 1990, while purporting not to do so, the Supreme Court again reversed course in *Employment Div., Dept. of Human Resources v. Smith,* 494 U.S. 872, 108 L. Ed. 2d 876, 110 S. Ct. 1595 (1990). Despite the broad and seemingly unequivocal pronouncements in *Sherbert* and her progeny, the *Smith* Court explained, "[w]e have never held that an individual's religious beliefs excuse him from compliance with an otherwise valid law prohibiting conduct that the State is free to regulate." *Id.* at 878–79, 110 S.Ct. 1595. The *Smith* Court concluded that *Sherbert* and other cases applying strict scrutiny to neutral laws of general applicability constituted narrow exceptions to this general principle. *Id.* at 881–85, 110 S.Ct. 1595.

The *Smith* decision was met with widespread disapproval by those who viewed the decision as a departure from settled free exercise jurisprudence and as a dramatic curtailment of religious freedom. A broad-based coalition of advocates of religious freedom took their cause to Congress which eventually passed the Religious Freedom Restoration Act of 1993 (the "Federal RFRA"), 42 U.S.C. §§ 2000bb *et seq.* The unabashed purpose of the Federal RFRA was to overrule *Smith* and to restore the compelling interest test first set forth in *Sherbert. Id.* at §§ 2000bb(a)(4) & (b)(1).

Four years later, in *City of Boerne v. Flores,* 521 U.S. 507, 536, 117 S.Ct 2157, 138 L. Ed. 2d 624, (1997), the Supreme Court declared the Federal RFRA unconstitutional at least as applied to the states.[9] The Court found that in enacting the Federal [*1281] RFRA Congress had exceeded its enforcement power under § 5 of the Fourteenth Amendment. *Id.*

---

[9] There exists considerable disagreement regarding whether the Federal RFRA is constitutional as applied to the federal government. See, e.g., *Adams v. Commissioner,* 170 F.3d 173, 175 n.1 (3rd Cir. 1999).

In response, advocates of religious freedom took their cause to the state legislatures. In 1998, the Florida legislature passed the Florida RFRA which is modeled after the Federal RFRA and like the federal statute seeks to establish the compelling interest test first set forth in *Sherbert*. *See* Fla. Stat. § 761.01 ("it is the intent of the Legislature of the State of Florida to establish the compelling interest test as set forth in *Sherbert v. Verner* . . .").

2. The Florida RFRA

The Florida RFRA provides in pertinent part:

The government shall not substantially burden a person's exercise of religion, even if the burden results from a rule of general applicability, except that government may substantially burden a person's exercise of religion only if it demonstrates that application of the burden to the person:

(a) Is in furtherance of a compelling governmental interest; and
(b) Is the least restrictive means of furthering that compelling governmental interest.

Fla. Stat. § 761.03(1).

Under the terms of the statute, a plaintiff has the burden of showing that: 1) he or she has engaged in the exercise of religion; and 2) that the government has substantially burdened this religious exercise. If the plaintiff meets this burden, the burden shifts to the government to demonstrate that its action: 1) is in furtherance of a compelling governmental interest; and 2) is the least restrictive means of furthering that compelling governmental interest.

a. Have the plaintiffs engaged in the "exercise of religion" within the meaning of the Florida RFRA?

The Florida RFRA defines the "exercise of religion" as "an act or refusal to act that is substantially motivated by a religious belief, whether or not the religious exercise is compulsory or central to a larger system of religious beliefs." *Id.* § 761.02(3). The plaintiffs contend that any act substantially motivated by a sincerely held religious belief constitutes the exercise of religion under this definition. The Court finds, however, that the plaintiffs' proposed construction is overly broad. A review of the statute's history, its plain language and the application of ordinary rules of statutory construction reveal that the Florida legislature intended to limit the statute's coverage to conduct that, while not necessarily compulsory or central to a larger system of religious beliefs, nevertheless reflects some tenet, practice or custom of a larger system of religious beliefs. Conduct that amounts to a matter of purely personal preference regarding religious exercise does not fall within the ambit of the Florida RFRA.

The historical background of the Florida RFRA provides some insight into the Florida legislature's intent in enacting the statute. As noted above, the Florida RFRA was enacted in response to the Supreme Court's decision in *City* *of Boerne* declaring the Federal RFRA unconstitutional and was modeled closely after the federal statute. While the interpretation of the Federal RFRA in the federal courts was far from uniform, the statute was generally construed to protect only practices which were compulsory or central to an individual's religious tradition. *See, e.g., Mack v. O'Leary,* 80 F.3d 1175, 1178 (7th Cir. 1996) (collecting cases). The Florida RFRA's express admonition that a practice need not be "compulsory or central to a larger system of religious beliefs" in order to fall within the statute's ambit, expresses a clear intent by the Florida legislature to expand the scope of protection afforded to religious practices beyond that provided by the Federal RFRA. The question this Court must resolve is: How far beyond? [*1282] In rejecting the Federal RFRA's "compulsory or central" requirement, the Florida legislature may have been attempting to correct what appears to be a manifest error in the federal courts' interpretation of the federal statute. That is to say, the "compulsory or central" requirement was completely at odds with Congressional intent as reflected in the legislative history of the Federal RFRA. During hearings before the House Judiciary Committee, Representative Stephen Solarz, the original sponsor of the Federal RFRA, stated:

> Were Congress to go beyond the phrasing chosen by the drafters of the First Amendment by specifically confining the scope of this legislation to those practices *compelled or proscribed* by a sincerely held religious belief in all circumstances, we would run the risk of excluding practices which are generally believed to be exercises of religion worthy of protection. For example, many religions do not require their adherents to pray at specific times of day, yet most members of Congress would consider prayer to be an unmistakable exercise of religion.

Hearings on H.R. 2797 Before the House Judiciary Comm., 102d Cong., 2d Sess. 128–30 (May 13, 1992) [emphasis added].

Representative Solarz' testimony, while clearly indicating an intent not to confine the Federal RFRA's coverage to practices which are compelled or proscribed by one's religious tradition, also gives some indication of the intended limits of the federal statute's coverage. In particular, Solarz stated:

> To say that the "exercise of religion" might include acts not necessarily compelled by a sincerely held religious belief is not to say that any act merely consistent with, or not proscribed by one's religion would be an exercise of religion. As I pointed out in my testimony, it would not be reasonable to argue, for example, that a person whose religion did not proscribe the possession of a machine gun had a free exercise right to own one notwithstanding applicable federal laws.

Id. Thus, Solarz' testimony suggests that conduct that is merely consistent with or not proscribed by one's religious tradition does not amount to the "exercise of religion" under the Federal RFRA. In other words, the Federal RFRA was not intended to protect conduct that amounts to a matter of purely personal preference regarding religious exercise. Accordingly, it seems clear that the Federal RFRA was intended to protect conduct that, while not necessarily compulsory or central to a larger system of religious beliefs, nevertheless reflects some tenet, practice or custom of a religious tradition. To the extent the Florida RFRA's rejection of the "compulsory or central" requirement reflects an intent by the Florida legislature to adopt the correct interpretation of the Federal RFRA, the Florida RFRA should be similarly construed.

Moreover, the plain language of the Florida RFRA implies that a practice must be more than a matter of purely personal preference regarding religious exercise in order to fall within the statute's ambit. That is, the fact that the Florida RFRA explicitly states that a practice need not be "compulsory or central to a larger system of religious beliefs" in order to be subject to the protection of the statute, suggests that the practice must have some basis in a larger system of religious beliefs. *See Cassady v. Sholtz,* 124 Fla. 718, 169 So. 487, 490 (Fla. 1936) ("The implications and intendments of a statute are as effective as the express provisions."); *Wolpin v. Philip Morris, Inc.,* 974 F. Supp. 1465 (S.D. Fla. 1997) (*quoting Jones v. Rath Packing Co.,* 430 U.S. 519, 525, 97 S. Ct. 1305, 51 L.Ed.2d 604, (1977) ("Legislative intent may be 'explicitly stated in the statute's language or implicitly contained in its structure and purpose.'"). If the Florida legislature had meant to protect any act motivated by a sincerely held religious belief, it could have easily and more clearly said so.

This conclusion is reinforced by the fact that the plaintiffs' proposed construction [*1283] of the Florida RFRA would render the "compulsory or central" language of the statute mere surplusage and of no effect. It is a fundamental rule of statutory construction that "courts should avoid readings that would render part of a statute meaningless." *Unruh v. State,* 669 So. 2d 242, 245 (Fla. 1996) (*quoting Forsythe v. Longboat Key Beach Erosion Control Dist.,* 604 So. 2d 452, 456 (Fla. 1992)). Moreover, "[s]tatutes should be construed to give each word effect." *Gretz v. Florida Unemployment Appeals Comm'n,* 572 So. 2d 1384, 1386 (Fla. 1991). These principles follow from the presumption that "the legislature does not intend 'to enact purposeless and therefore useless, legislation." *Unruh,* 669 So. 2d at 245 (*quoting Sharer v. Hotel Corp. of America,* 144 So. 2d 813, 817 (Fla. 1962)).

If any act motivated by a sincerely held religious belief were protected under the Florida RFRA, then it adds nothing to the meaning of the statute to say that the act need not be compulsory or central to a larger system of religious beliefs. It is only where the act is presumed to have some basis in a larger system of religious beliefs that the qualification that the act need not be compulsory or central to such a system has any meaning. In short, in order to give effect to all the statutory language, the "exercise of religion" must mean conduct that, while not necessarily compulsory or central to a larger system of religious beliefs, nevertheless reflects some tenet, practice or custom of a larger system of religious beliefs.

The plaintiffs' proposed construction of the statute is unpersuasive for the additional reason that it would lead to absurd results. It is a settled rule of statutory construction that an interpretation of a statute which would lead to an absurd or unreasonable result should be avoided where possible. *See, e.g., Amente v. Newman,* 653 So. 2d 1030, 1032 (Fla. 1995) ("If possible, the courts should avoid a statutory interpretation which leads to an absurd result."). On the plaintiffs' view, neutral laws of general applicability would have to yield to practices reflecting any individual's singular yet sincerely held religious beliefs unless the law was narrowly tailored to achieve a compelling governmental interest. Because the strict scrutiny standard adopted by the Florida legislature is the most rigorous test in constitutional law, few laws would survive its application. *See, e.g., Smith*, 494 U.S. at 888, 110 S.Ct. 1595 (noting that few laws survive strict scrutiny). In the context of the Cemetery's Regulations, the plaintiffs' proposed construction of the Florida RFRA would lead to cemetery anarchy. For example, reasonable size and height limitations on grave decorations would have to yield to sincerely held religious beliefs that grave decorations should be larger than the prescribed limitations. Moreover, the Cemetery's operating hours would have to yield to sincerely held religious beliefs that grave sites should be visited outside the Cemetery's operating hours. The Court does not believe that the Florida legislature intended such a result.

Thus, the Court concludes that in order to establish a cognizable claim under the Florida RFRA, a plaintiff must demonstrate a substantial burden on conduct that, while not necessarily compulsory or central to a larger system of religious beliefs, nevertheless reflects some tenet, practice or custom of a larger system of religious beliefs. Conduct that reflects a purely personal preference regarding religious exercise will not implicate the protections [of] the Florida RFRA.

b.   Does the Court's construction of the Florida RFRA violate the First Amendment?

Having determined the scope of the protection afforded by the Florida RFRA, the Court turns to the problem of developing a workable test for deciding whether a particular practice reflects some tenet, custom or practice of a larger system of religious beliefs or whether the practice reflects a [*1284] matter of purely personal preference regarding religious exercise. In embarking on this task, the Court is cognizant of the plaintiffs' concern that the Court's interpretation of the Florida RFRA involves the courts in the "unacceptable" business of evaluating the relative merits of differing religious claims.'" *Smith*, 494 U.S. at 887, 110 S.Ct 1595 *(quoting United States v. Lee*, 455 U.S. 252, 263 n. 2, 102 S. Ct. 1051, 71 L.Ed.2d 127, (1982) (Stevens, J., concurring)). However, the Court believes that the plaintiffs' concerns are overstated.

It is true that the Supreme Court has repeatedly held that "[i]t is not within the judicial ken to question the centrality of particular beliefs or practices to a faith, or the validity of particular litigants' interpretations of those creeds." *Smith*, 494 U.S. at 887, 110 S.Ct. 1595 *(quoting Hernandez v. Commissioner*, 490 U.S. 680, 699, 109, S. Ct. 2136 ,104 L.Ed.2d 766, 109 (1989)); *Thomas*, 450 U.S. at 716, 101 S.Ct. 1425 ("Particularly in this sensitive area, it is not within the judicial function and judicial competence to inquire whether the petitioner or his fellow worker more correctly perceived the commands of their common faith. Courts are not arbiters of scriptural interpretation."). *See also Presbyterian Church in United States v. Mary Elizabeth Blue Hull Memorial Presbyterian*

Church, 393 U.S. 440, 450, 89 S. Ct. 601, 21 L.Ed.2d 658 (1969) (holding that the First Amendment forbids civil courts from interpreting particular church doctrines and the importance of those doctrines to a religion). The danger, of course, is that "courts will find themselves taking sides in religious schisms if they must opine on matters of religious obligation." *Mack*, 80 F.3d at 1179.

Under the Court's construction of the Florida RFRA, however, courts are not required to interpret and weigh religious doctrine to determine the centrality of a particular practice to a religious tradition. Nor are courts required to determine whether a particular practice is compulsory or prohibited by a religious tradition. Rather, a court's inquiry is extremely limited and purely factual: Does the practice in question reflect some tenet, custom or practice of a larger system of religious beliefs? Accordingly, the risk of courts taking sides in religious controversies is minimized.

Moreover, the Supreme Court has sanctioned such limited inquiries into religious doctrine. For example, in *Gonzalez v. Roman Catholic Archbishop of Manila*, 280 U.S. 1, 16, 50 S. Ct. 5, 74 L.Ed. 131 (1929), the Court held that civil courts may review the decisions of church tribunals "on matters purely ecclesiastical" for arbitrariness. *See also Presbyterian Church*, 393 U.S. at 447–451, 89 S.Ct 601 (reaffirming that *Gonzalez* delineates the scope of permissible inquiry into religious doctrine). A determination of whether a particular ecclesiastical decision is arbitrary necessarily requires a minimal inquiry into whether the decision has some basis in religious doctrine. Similarly, a court's inquiry under the Florida RFRA is limited to whether a particular practice has some basis in the doctrines, traditions or customs of a religious tradition. Accordingly, the Courts finds that its construction of the Florida RFRA does not violate the First Amendment.

c.   Does the maintenance of vertical grave decorations on grave sites reflect some tenet, custom or practice of the plaintiffs' religious traditions or merely the plaintiffs' personal preference with regard to decorating graves?

During the course of the trial, the Court heard testimony from several experts in theology. It was generally agreed that the significance of a particular practice within a religious tradition can be ascertained by a consideration of the religion's sacred texts, doctrines, traditions and customs. *See, e.g.*, Pl.s' Ex. 46 at 1 (Expert Report of Dr. Winnifred Fallers Sullivan) ("Religion scholars would also largely agree that authentic religious practices include both those founded in textually based doctrine taught by institutional hierarchies as well as in folk traditions and customs passed down through families and communities."). Moreover, Dr. Daniel L. Pals, a professor and former Chair of the Department of Religious Studies at the University of Miami, developed a workable framework for determining the place of a particular practice within a religious tradition. *See* Def.'s Ex. 51.

Under Dr. Pals' framework, a court should consider four criteria in order to determine the place of a particular practice within a religious tradition. In particular, a court should consider whether the practice: 1) is asserted or implied in relatively unambiguous terms by an authoritative sacred text; 2) is clearly and consistently affirmed in classic formulations of doctrine and practice; 3) has been observed continuously, or nearly so, throughout the history of the tradition; and 4) is consistently observed in the tradition as we meet it in recent times. If a practice meets all four of these criteria, it can be considered central to the religious tradition. If the practice meets one or more of these criteria, it can be considered a tenet, custom or practice of the religious tradition. If the practice meets none of these criteria, it can be considered a matter of purely personal preference regarding religious exercise.

The plaintiffs contend that marking graves and decorating them with religious symbols constitute customs or practices of their religious traditions. Moreover, the plaintiffs contend that the display of such markers and religious symbols vertically has some independent significance in their religious traditions. The Court finds that while marking graves and decorating them with religious symbols constitute customs or practices of the plaintiffs' religious traditions, the particular manner in which such markers and religious symbols are displayed—vertically or horizontally—amounts to a matter of purely personal preference which is not protected under the Florida RFRA.

Applying Dr. Pals' test, it is clear that marking graves and decorating them with religious symbols constitute customs or practices of the Jewish and Christian traditions. In the Jewish tradition, grave markers have traditionally been used to demarcate graves and prevent people from walking on them. *See* Pl.'s Ex. 39 at 4 n. 7 (Expert Report of Rabbi Michael J. Broyde). The use of grave markers is identified in at least two of the four of the criteria noted above. In particular, while the Jewish sacred text and doctrines make little mention of grave marking, the practice of marking graves has been observed consistently throughout the history of the tradition and in recent times. *Id.* at 1–2.

In the Christian tradition, graves are customarily decorated with religious symbols in order to foster the community's awareness of the deceased as well as to give testimony to the deceased's commitment to the Christian life. *See* Def.'s Ex. 52 at 3. (Expert Report of Dr. Nathan Katz). The decoration of graves with religious symbols can be found in at least one of the four criteria described above. In particular, the decoration of graves with religious symbols has become a common practice in recent times. *Id.*

While the plaintiffs have established the significance of marking graves and decorating them with religious symbols, they have failed to demonstrate that their religious traditions accord any independent significance to the "verticality" of grave markers or religious symbols. For example, plaintiffs' expert Rabbi Broyde failed to identify any significance in the Jewish tradition to the manner in which grave markers are displayed. *See* Pl's Ex. 39 at 5. In fact, Rabbi Broyde concluded that a government regulation which required horizontal rather than vertical markers would not violate Jewish law. *Id.*

Plaintiffs' expert Dr. John A. McGuckin did testify to the importance of standing crosses on grave sites in the Christian faith and concluded that it would be sacrilegious to display a cross horizontally. *See* Pl.s' Ex. 44 at 6. However, Dr. McGuckin provided no objective basis for his opinion [*1286] and, therefore, the Court accords his testimony little weight.

Defendant's expert Dr. Pals provided the most comprehensive and systematic review of the significance of vertical grave markers and religious symbols in the Jewish and Christian traditions. *See generally* Def.'s Ex. 51. Dr. Pals' careful study concluded that neither the Jewish nor the Christian traditions accord any independent significance to the "verticality" of grave markers or religious symbols. *Id.*

Dr. Pals' study begins with a consideration of the significance of vertical grave markers in the Jewish tradition. First, Dr. Pals found that the use of vertical markers is neither asserted nor implied in the Torah, the Hebrew Scripture. *Id.* at 5–6. In fact, the Torah is virtually silent with regard to the issue of grave markers, and those few passages which discuss grave markers do not attach any importance to the type of marker used let alone to whether such markers are displayed vertically or horizontally. *Id.*

Second, a study of the classic commentaries of ancient rabbis found in the Talmud revealed that the use of vertical grave markers is not clearly and consistently affirmed in classic formulations of doctrine and practice. *Id.* at 7–8. In particular, the Talmudic commentaries suggest that use of grave markers is optional and do not accord any significance to the manner in which such markers are displayed. *Id.*

Third, Dr. Pals found that vertical markers have not been used continuously throughout the history of the tradition. *Id.* at 8–9. In fact, archeological evidence suggests that ancient Jewish grave sites were often simply painted white to demarcate them. *Id.* at 6.

Finally, Dr. Pals found that vertical grave markers have not been used consistently in recent times. *Id.* at 9–10. While many Jews of Ashkenazic heritage do place a vertical marker of sorts on the graves of family members, Sephardic and Ashkenazic Jews in Israel make almost exclusive use of horizontal rather than vertical grave markers. *Id.* at 9.

Dr. Pals then considered the significance of decorating graves with vertical religious symbols in the Christian tradition. First, he considered the Bible, the authoritative sacred text of Christianity, and found that the issue of decorating graves with religious symbols is not directly addressed. *Id.* at 10–13. Moreover, the Bible's passing references to grave decorations do not attach any significance to the manner in which such decorations are displayed. *Id.*

Second, Dr. Pals studied the writings of Christian theologians and found that they attached little significance to the form of burial memorials. *Id.* at 13–14. In particular, "they left no mandate that graves be universally marked in any one particular fashion, let alone with a vertical marker or monument." *Id.* at 14.

Third, Dr. Pals found that the practice of decorating graves with vertical religious symbols has not been observed continuously throughout the history of the Christian tradition. *Id.* at 14–16. In fact, historically most Christians were buried in common graves with no memorial whatsoever. *Id.* at 15–16.

Finally, Dr. Pals found that while the practice of decorating graves with religious symbols has increased in modern times, there is no significance to the manner in which such symbols are displayed. *Id.* at 16–18. In fact, the Catholic Archdiocese often uses horizontal grave decorations in its own cemeteries.

In sum, nowhere in the sacred texts, doctrines, traditions or customs of either the Jewish or Christian faiths can the principle be found that grave markers or religious symbols should be displayed vertically rather than horizontally. The primary objective of grave markers in the Jewish tradition—to demarcate and prevent the grave from being walked upon—can be achieved with either horizontal or vertical grave markers. Similarly, the primary objectives of decorating graves with religious symbols in the Christian tradition—to foster the community's awareness of the deceased and to give witness to the deceased's Christian life—can be achieved [*1287] with either horizontal or vertical religious symbols. Therefore, the Court concludes that while marking graves and decorating them with religious symbols constitute customs or practices of the plaintiffs' religious traditions, the plaintiffs' desire to maintain vertical grave markers and religious symbols reflects their personal preference with regard to decorating graves.

> d.   Does the City's prohibition on vertical grave decorations substantially burden the plaintiffs' practices of marking graves and decorating them with religious symbols?

Having established that the plaintiffs have a protectable interest in marking graves and decorating them with religious symbols, the Court must next consider whether the City's prohibition on vertical grave decorations "substantially burdens" the plaintiffs' religious practices within the meaning of the statute. The Court finds that the prohibition does not substantially burden the plaintiffs' religious practices.

The Florida RFRA's "substantial burden" language is identical to the language in the Federal RFRA after which the state law was modeled. Under the Federal RFRA, a law substantially burdens a religious practice if it prohibits or significantly constrains the practice. *See, e.g., Werner*, 49 F.3d 1476 at 1480 ("To exceed the 'substantial burden' threshold, government regulation must significantly inhibit or constrain [religious] conduct or expression. . . ."). However, "[t]he government does not need to justify conduct that merely makes a particular religious practice inconvenient." *Muslim v. Frame*, 897 F. Supp. 215, 219 (E.D.Pa. 1995).

The City's Regulations do not prohibit the plaintiffs from marking graves and decorating them with religious symbols. Rather, the Regulations permit only horizontal grave markers. These markers may be engraved with any type of religious symbol. Moreover, out of consideration for mourners vertical grave decorations are permitted for sixty days after the date of burial and for a few days around certain holidays. Aside from these times, however, vertical grave decorations are not permitted in the Cemetery.

The Court finds that these restrictions on the manner in which religious decorations may be displayed merely inconvenience the plaintiffs' practices of marking graves and decorating them with religious symbols. Accordingly, the Court finds that the prohibition on vertical grave decorations does not substantially burden the plaintiffs' exercise of religion within the meaning of the Florida RFRA.[10]

For the foregoing reasons, the Court finds that the plaintiffs have failed to establish that the City's Regulations violate the Florida RFRA. Judgment will be entered in favor of the City as to count I of the plaintiffs' amended complaint.[11]

[*1288] B. Count II–The First Amendment

In count II of their amended complaint, the plaintiffs allege that the prohibition on vertical grave decorations violates their First Amendment rights to the free exercise of religion and freedom of speech. The Court will consider the plaintiffs' free exercise and free speech claims in turn.

1. The Free Exercise Claim

The Free Exercise Clause of the First Amendment, which applies to the States through the Fourteenth Amendment, *see Cantwell v. Connecticut*, 310 U.S. 296, 303, 60 S. Ct. 900, 84 L.Ed. 1213 (1940), provides that "Congress shall make no law respecting an establishment of religion, *or prohibiting the free exercise thereof*..." U.S. CONST. amend. I. [emphasis added]. "The protections of the Free Exercise Clause pertain if the law at issue discriminates against some or all religious beliefs or regulates or prohibits conduct because it is undertaken for religious reasons." *Church of the Lukumi Babalu Aye, Inc. v. City of Hialeah*, 508 U.S. 520, 532, 113 S. Ct. 2217, 124 L.Ed.2d 472 (1993).

---

[10] The plaintiffs have established that removing markers from a grave constitutes a serious offense in the Jewish faith. See Pl.s' Ex. 39 at 5. The plaintiffs contend, therefore, that even if a prospective prohibition on vertical grave decorations does not substantially burden their religious exercise, removal of existing grave decorations would amount to a substantial burden. The Court disagrees. The plaintiffs placed vertical grave decorations on their cemetery plots in violation of the Regulations. The Court cannot construe the Florida RFRA to reward the plaintiffs for not complying with the Regulations.

[11] Because the Court finds that the plaintiffs have not established a cognizable claim under the Florida RFRA, the Court need not address the statute's constitutionality. The Court does note, however, that the statute, which operates to exempt religious but not secular conduct from compliance with neutral laws of general applicability, evidences a preference for religion that arguably runs afoul of the Establishment Clause of the First Amendment. *Cf., City of Boerne*, 521 U.S. at 536, 117 S.Ct. 2157 (Stevens, J. concurring). ("In my opinion, the [Federal RFRA] is a 'law respecting an establishment of religion' that violates the First Amendment to the Constitution.") Additionally, separation of powers concerns could be implicated to the extent the Florida RFRA is an attempt to expand the scope of the Florida Free Exercise Clause through legislation. See, e.g., *Marbury v. Madison*, 1 Cranch 137, 178, 2 L.Ed. 60 (1803). ("It is emphatically the province and duty of the judicial department to say what the law is.")

Thus, if the object of a law is to infringe upon or restrict practices because of their religious motivation, the law is invalid unless it is justified by a compelling governmental interest and is narrowly tailored to advance that interest. *Id.* at 533, 113 S.Ct. 2217. However, a neutral law of general applicability does not implicate the Free Exercise Clause even if the law has the incidental effect of burdening a particular religious practice. *Id.* at 531, 113 S.Ct. 2217; *Smith*, 494 U.S. at 876–77, 110 S.Ct. 1595 ("We have never held that an individual's religious beliefs excuse him from compliance with an otherwise valid law prohibiting conduct that the State is free to regulate.").

The Regulations at issue in this case are clearly neutral laws of general applicability. They prohibit vertical decorations of any kind—secular or religious—in the newer sections of the Cemetery. Moreover, contrary to the plaintiffs' allegations, there is no evidence that the Regulations were crafted to suppress religious expression. Accordingly, the Free Exercise Clause affords the plaintiffs no basis for challenging the City's Regulations.[12]

The Court's conclusion that the City's Regulations do not violate the Free Exercise Clause is bolstered by the Supreme Court's decision in *Lyng v. Northwest Indian Cemetery Protective Ass'n*, 485 U.S. 439, 108 S. Ct. 1319, 99 L.Ed.2d 534 (1988). In *Lyng*, three Native American tribes in northwestern California challenged the United States Forest Service's decision to permit forest harvesting in, and construct a road through, a portion of a National [*1289] Forest used by the tribes for religious worship. *Id.* at 442–43, 108 S.Ct.1319. The evidence put on at trial established that the government's action would seriously impair the tribes' use of the forest for religious practices. *Id.* at 443–44, 451, 108 S.Ct. 1319. *See also Northwest Indian Cemetery Protective Ass'n v. Peterson*, 565 F.Supp. 586, 594 (N.D.Cal.1983). Nevertheless, the *Lyng* Court concluded that the tribes did not have a cognizable claim under the Free Exercise Clause.

---

[12] In *Smith*, 494 U.S. at 881–82, 110 S.Ct. 1595 the Supreme Court explained *in dicta* that an individual may be relieved of the obligation to comply with a neutral law of general applicability where free exercise concerns are implicated along with other constitutional protections such as freedom of speech and of the press. The plaintiffs contend that *Smith* requires strict scrutiny in such cases and that because this case implicates not only religious conduct but also religious speech, the prohibition on vertical grave decorations is subject to strict scrutiny. The Court disagrees.

Initially, it is not clear whether the *Smith* Court's pure free exercise versus hybrid claim distinction is tenable. See *Church of the Lukumi Babalu Aye*, 508 U.S. at 567, 113 S.Ct. 2217 (Souter, J. concurring). ("[T]he distinction *Smith* draws strikes me as ultimately untenable. If a hybrid claim is simply one in which another constitutional right is implicated, then the hybrid exception would probably be so vast as to swallow the *Smith* rule, and indeed, the hybrid exception would cover the situation exemplified by *Smith*, since free speech and associational rights are certainly implicated by the peyote ritual.") In any event, the Court does not read *Smith* to require strict scrutiny whenever a plaintiff presents a hybrid claim. Rather, the fact that the City's Regulations burden speech as well as religious exercise means only that the City's Regulations must be analyzed under the Free Speech Clause as well as under the Free Exercise Clause.

The basis for the Court's holding was that:

> The Free Exercise Clause simply cannot be understood to require the Government to conduct its own internal affairs in ways that comport with the religious beliefs of particular citizens . . . The Free Exercise Clause affords an individual protection from certain forms of government compulsion; it does not afford an individual a right to dictate the conduct of the Government's internal procedures.

Lyng, 485 U.S. at 448, 108 S.Ct. 1319. The Court concluded that the Free Exercise Clause "does not divest the Government of its right to use what is, after all, its land." *Id.* at 453, 108 S.Ct. 1319. *See also Miccosukee Tribe v. United States*, 980 F.Supp. 448, 464–65 (S.D.Fla.1997) (holding that the government did not violate the Free Exercise Clause by failing to prevent flooding on Native American lands). In *Lyng*, the government took action to improve its National Forest. The fact that the action burdened the tribes' religious practices did not implicate the Free Exercise Clause. Similarly, in this case the City enacted Regulations to improve its Cemetery. The fact that these Regulations may interfere with the plaintiffs' religious practices does not implicate the Free Exercise Clause.[13]

The fact that the plaintiffs in this case, unlike the plaintiffs in *Lyng*, have a limited property interest in their Cemetery plots does not alter the foregoing analysis. It is well settled that "one who purchases and has conveyed to him a lot in a public cemetery does not acquire the fee to the soil, but only a right of burial therein which has been variously designated as an easement or as a licence or privilege." 14 AM. JUR.2d *Cemeteries* § 25 (1964) (and cases cited therein). The plaintiffs' right of burial is subject to the express limitation in their Certificate of Ownership that the right "be used only in conformity with the Cemetery Rules and Regulations as they may be from time to time adopted or amended." Def.'s Ex. 7. Moreover, the Certificate of Ownership clearly states that the plot "shall forever remain under the exclusive control of the [City] for the purposes of care and maintenance." *Id.* Thus, the Cemetery is clearly government property which the City may manage as it sees fit. *Cf. Miccosukee Tribe*,

---

[13] The Court recognizes that the fact that the City's Regulations affirmatively prohibit conduct in the cemetery may be a significant distinction in the case at bar. The *Lyng* Court did state that: "The crucial word in the constitutional text is 'prohibit'; 'For the Free Exercise Clause is written in terms of what the government cannot do to the individual, not in terms of what the individual can exact from the government." *Lyng*, 485 U.S. at 451, 108 S.Ct 1319. However, it is not clear what difference it makes whether the government in administering its land directly prohibits conduct through regulation or merely makes such conduct more difficult or impossible through its own action. For example, if the City, rather than prohibiting vertical grave decorations, had a policy of regularly removing structures that interfered with the aesthetic and maintenance requirements of the Cemetery, the "prohibitive effect" would be identical, and *Lyng* would clearly bar a free exercise challenge. Thus, to the extent *Lyng* stands for the proposition that the Free Exercise Clause cannot be used to challenge the government's administration of its own land, *Lyng* bars the plaintiffs' free exercise challenge.

980 F.Supp. at 465 (applying *Lyng* analysis to tribes' free exercise challenge where tribes' property rights in land were subject to the government's lawful authority to manage the land). Accordingly, the plaintiffs' free exercise challenge fails under *Lyng*.[14]

[*1290] 2. The Free Speech Claim

The Free Speech Clause of the First Amendment, which applies to the States through the Fourteenth Amendment, *see Gitlow v. New York*, 268 U.S. 652, 666, 45 S. Ct. 625 , 69 L.Ed. 1138 (1925), provides that "Congress shall make no law . . . abridging the freedom of speech." U.S. CONST. amend. I. "Private religious speech, far from being a First Amendment orphan, is as fully protected under the Free Speech Clause as secular private expression." *Capitol Square Review & Advisory Bd. v. Pinette*, 515 U.S. 753, 760, 115 S. Ct. 2440, 132 L.Ed.2d 650 (1995). *See also Chabad-Lubavitch of Georgia v. Miller*, 5 F.3d 1383, 1387 (11th Cir.1993) ("Religious speech enjoys sanctuary within the First Amendment."). Moreover, the Eleventh Circuit has held that the display of religious symbols constitutes protected speech under the First Amendment. *Id.* (holding that the display of a Chanukah menorah constitutes religious speech under the First Amendment). Therefore, there can be no doubt that the display of religious symbols such as crosses and stars of David on grave sites constitutes religious speech protected independently under the Free Speech Clause.

a.   Sections IX(2) and XIV(2)

The plaintiffs contend that §§ IX(2) and XIV(2) of the Regulations which prohibit vertical grave decorations in the Cemetery violate the Free Speech Clause by unduly restricting religious expression. The Court disagrees.

It is well settled that the government need not permit all forms of speech on property that it owns and controls. *See Int'l Soc. for Krishna Consciousness v. Lee*, 505 U.S. 672, 678, 112 S. Ct. 2701, 120 L.Ed.2d 541 (1992). The Supreme Court has adopted a "forum-based" approach for assessing the constitutionality of restrictions the government seeks to place on the use of its property. *Id.* Under this framework, regulation of speech on government property that has traditionally been available for public expression (i.e., a "public forum") or that has been designated by the government for public expression (i.e., a "designated public forum") is subject to strict scrutiny. *Id.* at 678–79, 112 S.Ct. 2701. Such regulations will survive only if they are narrowly tailored to achieve a compelling governmental interest. *Id.* at 679, 112 S.Ct. 2701. Regulation of

---

[14] As noted above, the Federal RFRA was enacted in response to the Supreme Court's holding in *Smith*. The Florida RFRA was enacted in response to the Supreme Court's holding in *City of Boerne* declaring the Federal RFRA unconstitutional as applied to the states. To the extent the Florida RFRA is an attempt to codify pre-Smith free exercise jurisprudence, *Lyng*, decided two years before *Smith*, might compel a reading of the Florida RFRA that exempts the government's administration of its own land from the operation of the statute.

speech on all other government property (i.e., a "nonpublic forum") is subject to much more limited review. *Id.* These regulations need only be reasonable and viewpoint neutral. *Id.*

A public forum is government property that has as "a principal purpose . . . the free exchange of ideas." *Cornelius v. NAACP Legal Defense and Educational Fund, Inc.*, 473 U.S. 788, 800, 105 S. Ct. 3439, 87 L.Ed.2d 567 (1985). Residential streets and parks have long been considered public fora because they have "immemorially been held in trust for the use of the public and . . . have been used for purposes of assembly, communicating thoughts between citizens, and discussing public questions." *Lee*, 505 U.S. at 679, 112 S.Ct. 2701. Other government property such as airport terminals are not considered public fora because their principal purpose is not to promote the free exchange of ideas but rather to facilitate passenger air travel. *Id.* at 682, 112 S.Ct. 2701; *Iskcon Miami Inc. v. Metropolitan Dade County*, 147 F.3d 1282, 1286 (11th Cir.1998).

The Court is aware of no case considering whether cemeteries are public or nonpublic fora for purposes of free speech claims. *But cf. Koehl v. Resor*, [*1291] 296 F.Supp. 558, 563 (E.D.Va. 1969) (upholding regulations which barred Nazi Party's political demonstrations as well as signs, placards, banners, and other expressive conduct in Culpeper National Cemetery). Nevertheless, it seems quite obvious that cemeteries are nonpublic fora. It certainly cannot be said that cemeteries have traditionally been used for assembly and the free exchange of ideas. The primary purpose of cemeteries is not to facilitate the free exchange of ideas but, rather, to provide a place for citizens to bury and honor their dead. Accordingly, the Court concludes that the Cemetery is a nonpublic forum for First Amendment analysis.

Having determined that the Cemetery is a nonpublic forum, the Court must consider whether the City's prohibition on vertical grave decorations is viewpoint neutral and reasonable. A regulation is viewpoint neutral as long as it is "not an effort to suppress the speaker's activity due to disagreement with the speaker's view." *Lee*, 505 U.S. at 679, 112 S.Ct. 2701. Moreover, a regulation "need only be reasonable; it need not be the most reasonable or the only reasonable limitation." *Id.* at 683, 112 s.Ct. 2701 [internal citations and quotations omitted].

Sections IX(2) and XIV(2) of the Regulations are clearly viewpoint neutral. They prohibit all vertical decorations—religious or otherwise—in the newer sections of the cemetery. Thus, these Regulations cannot be considered an attempt to stifle religious expression.[15]

Moreover, the Regulations are a reasonable way of promoting their primary objectives; namely to: 1) maximize the use of available Cemetery space; 2) allow ready access to all grave sites for burials and disinterments; 3) ensure

---

[15] The plaintiffs suggest that the Regulations are not viewpoint neutral because they apply to a place where the only foreseeable kind of expression is religious in nature. The Court disagrees. Expression on grave sites is often secular in nature. For example, graves are often decorated with flags or war memorials as an expression of patriotism.

ease of grounds maintenance; 4) ensure the safety of grounds keepers and visitors; and 5) maintain a uniform appearance and aesthetically pleasing environment in the Cemetery. As noted above, the use of vertical grave decorations would permit fewer grave sites in the Cemetery, impede access to the grave sites, make grounds maintenance more difficult and dangerous for grounds keepers and visitors, and create visual clutter. The City's prohibition on vertical grave decorations is reasonable because it minimizes these concerns without wholly foreclosing the plaintiffs' ability to express themselves. The plaintiffs are free to express themselves through religious symbols or otherwise on the horizontal grave markers permitted by the Regulations.

The plaintiffs rely heavily on *City of Ladue v. Gilleo*, 512 U.S. 43, 114 S. Ct. 2038, 129 L.Ed.2d 36 (1994), in support of their free speech challenge. In *Gilleo*, a homeowner challenged a city ordinance which prohibited all residential signs except those falling within one of ten exemptions. *Id.* at 46, 114 S.Ct. 2038. The Court found that the ordinance violated the Free Speech Clause because it prohibited too much speech by completely foreclosing "a venerable means of communication that is both unique and important." *Id.* at 55, 114 S.Ct. 2038. The Court explained that "residential signs have long been an important and distinct medium of expression . . . [that] may have no practical substitute." *Id.* at 55–57, 114 S.Ct. 2038. Moreover, the Court emphasized that a "special respect for individual liberty in the home has long been part of our culture and our law." *Id.* at 58, 114 S.Ct. 2038.

The plaintiffs' reliance on *Gilleo* is misplaced for two reasons. First, the *Gilleo* Court made clear that its holding was based on the notion that expression in the home is accorded special respect. *Id.* In fact, the Court explained that the government has broader power to regulate expression on public property. *Id.* ("Whereas the government's need to mediate [*1292] among various competing uses, including expressive ones, for public streets and facilities is constant and unavoidable, its need to regulate temperate speech from the home is surely much less pressing.") [citations omitted]. *See also Members of City Council of Los Angeles v. Taxpayers for Vincent*, 466 U.S. 789, 811, 104 S. Ct. 2118, 80 L.Ed.2d 772 (1984) (upholding city ordinance that prohibited the posting of signs on public property but noting that a "private citizen's interest in controlling the use of his own property justifies . . . disparate treatment."). As noted above, the Cemetery is government property and, therefore, *Gilleo* is inapposite.

Second, unlike in *Gilleo*, the prohibition on vertical grave decorations does not foreclose an entire medium of expression. The Regulations do not prohibit all symbols on grave sites. Rather, they only prohibit vertical symbols. The plaintiffs are free to express themselves by placing any symbol they wish on the horizontal grave markers permitted by the Regulations.

For the foregoing reasons, the Court concludes that §§ IX(2) and XIV(2) of the Regulations do not violate the Free Speech Clause of the First Amendment.

b.   Section XVI(1)

The plaintiffs also contend that Section XVI(1) of the Regulations violates the
First Amendment by vesting the Cemetery Manager with unbridled discretion
to allow temporary exceptions to the prohibition on vertical grave decorations.
The Court agrees.

It is well settled that:

> an ordinance which . . . makes the peaceful enjoyment of freedoms which
> the Constitution guarantees contingent upon the uncontrolled will of an
> official—as by requiring a permit or license which may be granted or
> withheld in the discretion of such official—is an unconstitutional censor-
> ship or prior restraint upon the enjoyment of those freedoms.

Miami Herald Publ'g Co. v. City of Hallandale, 734 F.2d 666, 673 (11th Cir.1984)
(*quoting Shuttlesworth v. City of Birmingham*, 394 U.S. 147, 151, 89 S.Ct. 935,
22 L.Ed.2d 162 (1969). Moreover, an exception or variance is the equivalent of
a license under this analysis. *See Lady J. Lingerie, Inc. v. City of Jacksonville*, 176
F.3d 1358, 1361 (11th Cir.1999).

Such prior restraints are impermissible because they give "a government official or agency substantial power to discriminate based on the content or viewpoint
of speech by suppressing disfavored speech or disliked speakers." *Lakewood v.
Plain Dealer Publ'g Co.*, 486 U.S. 750, 759, 108 S.Ct. 2138, 100 L.Ed.2d 771
(1988). Thus, in order to survive a First Amendment challenge, a licensing or
variance scheme which gives public officials the power to decide whether to permit expressive activity must: 1) contain precise and objective criteria for decision-
making; and 2) require prompt decisions. *See Lady J. Lingerie*, 176 F.3d at 1361.

The City's Regulations, while enacting a virtual blanket prohibition on vertical grave decorations, also provide:

> The Cemetery Manager, after consultation with the Recreation Services
> Department Director, reserves the right to make temporary exceptions, sus-
> pensions and modification [*sic*] of any rule or regulation, *when in the Ceme-
> tery Manager's discretion, such modification seems advisable.* Such temporary
> exceptions, suspensions and modifications shall in no way be construed
> as effecting [*sic*] the general enforcement of these rules and regulations
> nor as eliminating the authority of the City Council in approving or disap-
> proving all permanent changes in the rules or policies of the Cemetery/
> Mausoleum.

Regulations § XVI(1) [emphasis added]. The plain language of this Regulation
vests the Cemetery Manager with unbridled discretion to allow temporary
exceptions to the prohibition on vertical grave decorations. The Regulation
provides no objective criteria for granting a temporary exception. Nor does
the Regulation provide [*1293] a time frame during which the Cemetery Manager must make a decision. Thus, the Regulation provides the Cemetery Manager with the power to discriminate on the basis of content. For example, a
Cemetery Manager partial to the Christian faith could allow an exception
for crosses while refusing an exception for stars of David. This opportunity to

discriminate is prohibited by the First Amendment.[16] *See Forsyth County v. Nationalist Movement*, 505 U.S. 123, 133 n.10, 112 S. Ct. 2395, 120 L.Ed.2d 101 (1992) ("The success of a facial challenge on the grounds that an ordinance delegates overly broad discretion to the decision maker rests not on whether the administrator has exercised his discretion in a content-based manner, but whether there is anything in the ordinance prohibiting him from doing so."). Accordingly, the Court finds that § XVI(1) of the Regulations is unconstitutional as applied to the prohibition on vertical grave decorations.

If an unconstitutional provision of a statutory scheme is severable, a court should not invalidate the entire scheme. *See Regan v. Time, Inc.*, 468 U.S. 641, 652, 104 S. Ct. 3262, 82 L. Ed. 2d 487 (1984) ("[A] court should refrain from invalidating more of the statute than is necessary."). "In determining whether to sever a constitutionally flawed provision, courts should consider whether the balance of the legislation is incapable of functioning independently," *United States v. Romero-Fernandez*, 983 F.2d 195, 196 (11th Cir.1993), and whether partial invalidation of the statute "would be contrary to legislative intent in the sense that the legislature would not have passed the statute without the invalid portion." *Smith v. Butterworth*, 866 F.2d 1318, 1321, (11th Cir.1989), *aff'd*, 494 U.S. 624, 110 S. Ct. 1376, 108 L.Ed.2d 572 (1990).

Section XVI(1) is clearly severable from the remainder of the Regulations. Absent this provision, the Regulations flatly prohibit vertical grave decorations subject only to the exceptions expressly provided for in § IX(2). Moreover, the City would undoubtedly have enacted the prohibition on vertical grave decorations without the invalid portion of the Regulations.

Accordingly, the Court finds that § XVI(1) of the Regulations is unconstitutional as applied to the prohibition on vertical grave decorations. The Regulations are otherwise valid under the First Amendment. Partial judgment will be entered in favor of the plaintiffs as to count II of the amended complaint.

C. Count III—The Due Process Clause of the Fourteenth Amendment

In count III of their amended complaint, the plaintiffs contend enforcement of the challenged Regulations would deprive them of a property interest in maintaining vertical grave decorations on their Cemetery plots in violation of the Due Process Clause of the Fourteenth Amendment. The Court disagrees.

The Fourteenth Amendment provides that "[n]o State shall . . . deprive any person of life, liberty or property without due process of law." U.S. CONST. amend. XIV, § 1. "The Fourteenth Amendment's . . . protection of property is a safeguard of the security of interests that a person has already acquired in specific benefits." *Board of Regents of State Colleges v. Roth*, 408 U.S. 564, 576, 92 S. Ct. 2701, 33 L.Ed.2d 548 (1972). The *Roth* Court explained that:

> To have a property interest in a benefit, a person clearly must have more than an abstract need or desire for it. He must have more than a unilateral

---

[16] The fact that the Regulations only grant the cemetery manager the discretion to allow temporary exceptions to the prohibition on vertical grave decorations does not alter

expectation of it. He must, instead, have a legitimate claim of entitlement to it . . . Property interests, of course, are not created by the Constitution. Rather they are [*1294] created and their dimensions are defined by existing rules or understandings that stem from an independent source such as state law—rules or understandings that secure certain benefits and that support claims of entitlement to those benefits.

Id. at 577, 92 S.Ct. 2701. *See also Bishop v. Wood,* 426 U.S. 341, 344, 96 S. Ct. 2074, 48 L.Ed.2d 684 (1976) ("the sufficiency of the claim of entitlement must be decided by reference to state law.").

The plaintiffs do not have a property interest under Florida law in maintaining vertical grave decorations on their Cemetery plots. To the contrary, as noted above, the plaintiffs' limited property interest in their plots is subject to the express limitation in their Certificate of Ownership that the plots be used only in conformity with the Regulations which expressly prohibit vertical grave decorations.

The plaintiffs contend nevertheless that a constructive property interest arose by virtue of the fact that they were permitted to maintain vertical grave decorations in violation of the Regulations for several years. The plaintiffs testified that they either: 1) received permission from the Cemetery Manager to maintain vertical grave decorations; or 2) were told by the Cemetery Manager that the prohibition on vertical grave decorations was never enforced. The plaintiffs contend that in light of the City Managers' conduct, the City is estopped from applying its Regulations.

It is well settled in Florida that no property interest arises from the unauthorized acts of municipal officers. *See Miami Shores Village v. Brockway Post No. 124 of American Legion,* 156 Fla. 673, 24 So.2d 33, 35 (Fla. 1945), *overruled on other grounds by Sakolsky v. City of Coral Gables,* 151 So.2d 433 (Fla. 1963) ("Generally speaking, a permit issued . . . in violation of law confers no right or privilege on the grantee."). *Cf. Brett v. Jefferson County,* 123 F.3d 1429, 1434 (11th Cir.1997) (holding that a property interest contrary to state law cannot arise by informal custom). Accordingly, "no estoppel can be sustained against a municipality under such circumstances." *Enderby v. City of Sunrise,* 376 So.2d 444, 445 (Fla. 4th DCA 1979) (*quoting United Sanitation Services, Inc. v. City of Tampa,* 302 So.2d 435, 438 (Fla. 2d DCA 1974). To the extent the Cemetery Manager permitted the plaintiffs to maintain permanent vertical grave decorations on their Cemetery plots, he did so in violation of the Regulations. Accordingly, the plaintiffs have no property interest in maintaining vertical grave decorations in the Cemetery, and the City is not estopped from enforcing the Regulations.

The plaintiffs, relying on *Buccaneer Point Estates, Inc. v. United States,* 729 F.2d 1297 (11th Cir.1984), also contend that enforcement of the Regulations would result in a "manifest injustice." The plaintiffs' reliance on *Buccaneer Point* is misplaced.

In *Buccaneer Point,* a developer completed 80% of a project to build 200 residences, proceeding on the written assurances of the Army Corps of Engineers

---

the foregoing analysis. A temporary constitutional violation is nevertheless a constitutional violation.

and upon existing regulations which provided that the work could proceed. *Id.* at 1298–1299. Thereafter, new regulations were adopted which impeded the project. *Id.* The developer brought an action for declaratory and injunctive relief, and the Eleventh Circuit held that the retroactive application of the regulations to the developer's project would result in a "manifest injustice" because it would interfere with the developer's justified reliance on existing regulations. *Id.* at 1299–1300. In this case, however, the plaintiffs violated the existing Regulations at the time they placed the vertical decorations on their Cemetery plots. Moreover, while the City did agree to postpone enforcement of the prohibition on vertical grave decorations for several years while the Regulations were being studied, the City at all times made clear that the stay on enforcement was temporary, and the plaintiffs were on notice that unless the City chose to change its policy regarding vertical grave decorations, [*1295] the Regulations would eventually be enforced. Accordingly, the plaintiffs do not have a justified reliance interest in maintaining their vertical grave decorations, and no "manifest injustice" will result from requiring the plaintiffs to comply with the Regulations which have governed the Cemetery since before the plaintiffs bought their plots. Thus, the plaintiffs have failed to establish a due process claim. Judgment will be entered in favor of the City as to count III of the plaintiffs' amended complaint.

D. Count IV—The Florida Constitutional Claims

In count IV of their amended complaint, the plaintiffs contend that the prohibition on vertical grave decorations violates their guarantees under the Florida Constitution to freedom of religious exercise, freedom of speech and due process of law. *See* FLA. CONST. art. I, §§ 3, 4 & 9. Florida courts have generally construed their state constitutional guarantees to be coextensive with their federal counterparts. *See, e.g., Florida Canners Ass'n v. State Dept. of Citrus,* 371 So.2d 503, 513, 517 (Fla. 2d DCA 1979), *aff'd sub nom, Coca Cola Co. v. State Dept. of Citrus,* 406 So.2d 1079 (Fla.1981) (applying federal standard to state due process and free speech claims). Accordingly, for the reasons provided above, the Court finds that the City's prohibition on vertical grave decorations does not violate any provision of the Florida Constitution. However, § XVI(1) of the Regulations is unconstitutional as applied to the prohibition on vertical grave decorations. *See* § B(2)(b) *supra.* Partial judgment will be entered in favor of the plaintiffs as to count IV of the amended complaint.

III. CONCLUSION

On the basis of the foregoing, the Court concludes that the Rules and Regulations of the Boca Raton Municipal Cemetery which prohibit vertical grave decorations on Cemetery plots do not violate the plaintiffs' federal or state guarantees of freedom of religious exercise, freedom of speech or due process of law. However, § XVI(1) of the Regulations violates the Free Speech Clauses of both the federal and Florida Constitutions as applied to the prohibition on vertical grave decorations. Final judgment will be entered by separate order.

Notes

Introduction

1. While U.S. administrations have at various time in U.S. history stressed the importance of religious freedom as an element of foreign policy, in 1998, Congress passed, and President Clinton signed into law, the International Religious Freedom Act (IRFA), which requires the president to take action to enforce religious freedom around the world. 22 U.S.C. 6401ff. To review annual country reports required by IRFA, see www.state.gov/g/drl/irf/

2. *Warner v. Boca Raton*, United States District Court for the Southern District of Florida. West Palm Beach Division. Case No. 98-8054-CIV-/CIV-KLR.

3. The current rough division of U.S. First Amendment legal scholars and legal practitioners into two camps with respect to the religion clauses—the separationists and the accommodationists, and its public "culture wars" relative—is the result in part, I would argue, of a failure actually to talk about religion, the real religion of ordinary people—a failure to take seriously the religious history and anthropology of Americans and of law's own role in that history. The exegesis of this trial illustrates the problem of how religious and cultural differences modulate the universal language and claims of rights talk, not in the context of an inflammatory issue like female circumcision, but in the context of the lives of ordinary middle-class Americans. How can modern secular law find ways to take account of the messiness of a cultural fact such as religion? How can the law also come to terms with its own religious formation?

4. *Warner v. Boca Raton*, Trial Transcript, p. 904. Hereinafter I will simply refer to the record of the testimony at trial as "Transcript."

5. It is my experience that scholars and lay people use the word "theology" quite differently. Scholars of religion often draw a sharp line between "theology" and "religious studies." "Theology" is understood by most scholars to be an apologetic discipline that investigates religion as an insider, a discipline that may be in dialogue with the wider academic community but that usually has commitments to the religious life of a particular religious community, while "religious studies" is understood by scholars to be a discipline that investigates religion as an outsider, a discipline that answers to the evidentiary standards of the academic community. While there are philosophical and sometimes ideological reasons for which scholars insist on this distinction, there are also semantic ones. "Theology" implies that religion must always be "theistic," must always be oriented toward a god, while there is ample evidence of religion that is not theistic. Theology also implies a unity to the study of religion, a unity once defined by its presence in medieval universities, a unity that is now lacking. "Religious studies" is a more open term, one that delineates a field of study bringing together scholars from different disciplines,

historians, philosophers, sociologists, anthropologists, and others, to study the human social and cultural phenomena termed "religion." Laypeople often do not draw these distinctions, seeing the two words as interchangeable. I believe Judge Ryskamp was at times using "theology" in an expansive sense, to mean roughly what many scholars mean by "religious studies." But his frame of reference was, in many ways, quite "theological," in the narrow sense of the word. There is a recent Supreme Court decision partly addressing this definitional problem in the context of publicly funded scholarships. *Locke v. Davey*, 124 S.C t.1307 (2004).

6. See, for an overview, Malcolm D. Evans, *Religious Liberty and International Law in Europe*.

7. *Cantwell v. Connecticut*, 310 U.S. 296 (1940); *Reynolds v. U.S.*, 98 U.S. 145 (1878); *Wisconsin v. Yoder*, 406 U.S. 205 (1975); *Lyng v. Northwest Indian Cemetery Protective Association*, 485 U.S. 439 (1988).

8. The fabled "I know it when I see it" standard was first articulated in the concurring opinion of Justice Stewart in *Jacobellis v. Ohio*, 378 U.S. 184 (1964). Commenting on the difficulty of arriving at a shorthand description of hard-core pornography, Justice Stewart wrote, ""I know it when I see it, and the motion picture involved in this case is not that," 378 U.S. at 197.

9. Transcript, pp. 902–903.

10. Much has been written about sincerity as a standard of behavior. In his *Formations of the Secular*, for example, Talal Asad discusses (p. 52) sincerity as a Victorian religious value. For a discussion of sincerity as a standard in religion cases see: Kent Greenawalt, "Judicial Resolution of Issues about Religious Conviction." Sincerity as a social value is famously satired by Oscar Wilde in *The Importance of Being Earnest*.

11. The roots of these contemporary political commitments are complex, and their full delineation is far beyond the scope of this book. They can surely be traced to much earlier times but the conventional account would place their modern inception in what are called the Reformation and the Enlightenment. Useful general accounts can be found in Malcolm D. Evans, *Religious Liberty and International Law in Europe*, and John D. van der Vyver and John Witte Jr., eds. *Religious Human Rights in Global Perspective*. For an argument that finds these origins in religious rather than political thought, see Georg Jellinek, *The Declaration of the Rights on Man and of Citizens*. (For better and worse, the modern history of these ideas is European in origin and this author is limited in her knowledge of non-Western religio-political histories, so this book will not attempt a review of the relationship between law and religion outside this context. For a useful introduction to other traditions of religion and law, see "Law and Religion" articles in the *Encyclopedia of Religion*, 2d edition, forthcoming from Macmillan.)

12. For a useful summary description of these changes, see Eugene Rice and Anthony Grafton, *The Foundations of Early Modern Europe, 1460–1559*.

13. Martin E. Marty and R. Scott Appleby, eds., *Fundamentalisms Observed*.

14. And appropriately so, some would say. Casanova, for example, at pp. 211–34, speaks approvingly of the liberal conditions under which religion enters the political arena today.

15. To use protestant and catholic as categories is to invite a host of rebuttal testimony. I do so advisedly. The categories highlight both the early modern European antecedents of the religio-political problems here discussed as well as the political and legal significance of anti-Catholicism in the United States.

16. It is quite striking to many who study First Amendment law in the United States how often religious groups seem to need the permission, even the "blessing" of the courts and legislatures to do what they say they are compelled to do for religious reasons. Legitimacy is understood to be conferred by the secular, not the religious authority. A former colleague who studies the Jewish communities of contemporary Russia recounted to me her experience of being at a ritual circumcision in which the ritual expert demanded proof from the parents of the baby that they were in fact Jewish. Acceptable evidence was their Soviet identity papers. Her ethnography of her study of a Moscow Synagogue: Sascha L. Goluboff, *Jewish Russians*. See also, Curry, *Farewell to Christendom*.

17. I use the word "ethnographic" somewhat loosely here. I refer to an academic method of investigation involving what is sometimes called participant observation, and subsequent "interpretation" of a community, in real time, a kind of specialized "living with" events, of "being there," in Clifford Geertz's words. Clifford Geertz, *Works and Lives*. I was at the trial as a scholar of religion and as a lawyer. I claim the kind of knowledge that my expertise in those two fields allowed me in my short and limited stay. My time in Boca Raton was too limited, however, to support the epistemological claims made by anthropologists who live for an extended time in the communities they write about. For one discussion of the advantages and limitations of "field work," see Clifford Geertz, *Available Light*.

18. For a helpful overview of recent philosophical reflection on this problem, see Stewart Motha and Thanos Zarthaloudis, "Law, Ethics, and the Utopian End of Human Rights."

19. *Sasnett v. Department of Corrections*, 891 F. Supp 1305 (1995).

20. The constitutional basis for the differences between these kinds of religion cases is discussed in detail below.

21. *Sasnett*; Lloyd Burton, *Worship and Wilderness*; *Chaplaincy of Full Gospel Churches v. Johnson*, 276 F. Supp. 2d 82 (2003); *King v. Richmond Co.*, 331 F. 2d 1271 (2003); *Americans United for the Separation of Church and State v. Prison Fellowship Ministries*, United States District Court for the Southern District of Iowa, Central Division, Nos. 4:03-CV-90074, 4:03-CV-90447, 4:03-CV-90101.

22. Michael McConnell, "The Problem of Singling Out Religion," p. 5.

23. Federal Rules of Evidence 702. In other countries experts are often employed by the court. See, for example, discussion in Gary Edmond, "After Objectivity: Expert Evidence and Procedural Reform," *Sydney Law Review* 25:131–63 (2003).

24. See, for example, Sanja Kutnjak and Valerie P. Hans, "Jurors' Evaluations of Expert Testiomony"; Gary Edmond, "After Objectivity"; and the well-known, if controversial, Peter W. Huber, *Galileo's Revenge.*

25. See, for example, Lawrence Rosen, "The Anthropologist As Expert Witness"; James Clifford, "Identity in Mashpee."

26. For a careful consideration of the more general problem of objectivity in anthropological work, see Johannes Fabian, *Time and the Other.*

27. Recent studies of this issue include Mark Lilla, *The Reckless Mind*; Russell T. McCutcheon. *Critics Not Caretakers.*

28. The Federal Rules of Evidence permits a judge to exclude a witness from listening to the testimony of other witnesses. F.R.E. 615. Judge Ryskamp, at Jim Green's request, gave permission for me to sit through the entire trial. Transcript, p. 14.

CHAPTER 1

1. Donald W. Curl and John P. Johnson, *Boca Raton.* There are other stories of the origins of the name "Boca Raton." One is that the name actually described a different inlet on the Florida coast and was mistranscribed by an early mapmaker. See also Cynthia Thuma, *Images of America, www.ci.boca-raton.fl.us/* and *www. bocahistory.org/*

2. The surviving native peoples of southeastern Florida are Seminole Indians. The Seminole community was formed from members of Creek tribes from Georgia who migrated to Florida (then very sparsely populated) at the invitation of the Spanish in the seventeenth century. The remaining Seminoles today are those who prevented (through famously successful armed resistance and hiding in the Everglades) their forcible removal to Oklahoma. Some Seminole Indians today live on reservations established in the twentieth century. Brent Weisman, "Archaeological Perspectives on Florida Seminole Ethnogenesis" in Bonnie G. McEwan, ed., *Indians of the Greater Southeast.*

3. Yamato is the plain around Osaka. It is the richest agricultural region of Japan. Interestingly, these immigrants to Boca Raton were Christians. *The History of Boca Raton,* a video produced by the News Group.

4. See Caroline Seebohm, *Boca Rococo: How Addison Mizner Invented Florida's Gold Coast.*

5. *Bibletown, U.S.A. v. Sproul,* 212 So.2d 780 (1968).

6. 212 So. 2d at 781.

7. *Jerusalem Post,* March 22, 1991.

8. See Arthur S. Evans, *Pearl City, Florida.*

9. See *www.ci.boca-raton.fl.us/* (This cite was accurate on 4/15/04. Boca Raton has since redesigned the website.) and *www.bocahistory.org.*

10. The City was the target of a successful lawsuit by local property owners in the late 1970s challenging the cap on density established by amendment of its char-

ter. *City of Boca Raton v. Boca Villa Corp.*, 371 So.2d 154 (1979). In March 2003 the City was sued for its effort to restrict the location of halfway houses. See *www. soberhouses.com*

11. Cemetery employees testified at trial that access to grave sites was necessary for removals as well as for new burials.

12. *www.ci.boca-raton.fl.us/parks/cemetery%20history.html*

13. Transcript, p. 670.

14. *www.ci.boca-raton.fl.us/parks/cemetery%20history.html*

15. Katz Report (found in Appendix B).

16. A "sexton" is defined by the *American Heritage Dictionary of the English Language* as follows: "An employee or officer of a church who is responsible for the care and upkeep of church property and sometimes for ringing bells and digging graves." See also *Oxford English Dictionary.* Interestingly, no "secular" or industry definition is given in either source although this term is the one used by the Boca Raton Cemetery.

17. Deposition of Olan Young, pp. 58–59.

18. Transcript pp. 495–96.

19. 64 F. Supp at 1275, and see Section vi of "Rules and Regulations of the Boca Raton Municipal Cemetery and Mausoleum" (1996) (hereinafter "Rules")

20. 64 F. Supp. 2d at 1275.

21. Rules sec. 1.

22. Ibid., p. 13.

23. Young Deposition, pp. 62–63.

24. Emma Trelles, "Grave Injustice."

25. *Death Care Business Adviser* October 9, 1997.

26. Transcript, p. 804.

27. 64 F. Supp. 2d at 1279.

28. The results of the survey were quoted by Judge Ryskamp in his opinion. 64 F. Supp. 2d at 1278.

29. Eliot Kleinberg, "Boca to Vote on Cemetery's Clutter Rules," p. 1B.

30. Judge Ryskamp certified the case as a class action on August 17, 1998. The city councilors were later dropped from the case.

31. A case may be moved to federal court by motion of one of the parties if the federal court has jurisdiction. The *Warner* case stated a cause of action in the U.S. Constitution and was therefore within the jurisdiction of the federal district court. U.S. Constitution. Article III.

32. The First Amendment to the Constitution of the United States provides: "Congress shall make no law respecting an establishment of religion or prohibiting the free exercise thereof; or abridging the freedom of speech, or of the press; or of the right of the people peaceably to assemble, and to petition the Government for a redress of grievances." The first sixteen words of the first amendment are known as "the religion clauses." Section 3 of Article I of the Florida Constitution provides: "There shall be no law respecting the establishment or prohibiting or penalizing

the free exercise thereof. Religious freedom shall not justify practices inconsistent with public morals, peace or safety. No revenue of the state or any political subdivision or agency thereof shall ever be taken from the public treasury directly or indirectly in aid of any church, sect, or religious denomination or in aid of any sectarian institution." Both the First Amendment to the U.S. Constitution and Section 3 of Article I of the Florida Constitution are reproduced in Appendix A.

33. Florida Statutes §761.03.

34. The following states have RFRA statutes: Alabama (Alabama Const., Amend. 622 [2003]), Arizona (A.R.S. § 41-1493 [2003]), Connecticut (Conn. Gen. Stat. § 52-571b [2003]), Florida (Fla. Stat. § 761.01 [2002]), Idaho (Idaho Code § 73-402 [2003]), Illinois (775 ILCS 35/5 [2003]), New Mexico (N.M. Stat. Ann.§ 28-22-1 [2003]), Oklahoma (51 Okl. St. § 251 [2002]), Pennsylvania (71 P.S. § 2401 [2003]), Rhode Island (R.I. Gen. Laws § 42-80.1-1 [2002]), South Carolina (S.C. Code Ann. § 1-32-10 [2002]), and Texas (Tex. Civ. Prac. & Rem. Code § 110.001 [2003]).

35. (§761.02 [3]).

36. 64 F. Supp. 2d at 1281.

37. Subsequent published decisions interpreting the Florida RFRA include: *First Baptist Church of Perrine v. Miami-Dade Co.*, 768 So.2d 1114 (2000); *Sabir Abdul-Hagg v. Singletary et al.*, 766 So.2d 1197 (2000); *Abbott et al. v. Ft. Lauderdale*, 783 So.2d. 1213 (2001), *Toca v. Florida*, 834 So.2d 204 (2002); *Konikov v. Orange Co.*, 302 F.Supp 1328 (2004); *Yasir v. Hancock* et al., 868 So.2d 670 (2004).

38. For a historical introduction to the First Amendment religion clauses, see Thomas J. Curry, *The First Freedoms*; and Mark deWolfe Howe, *The Garden and the Wilderness*. For a doctrinal summary of the history of their interpretation, see John Witte, *Religion and the American Constitutional Experiment*, and Thomas Berg, *The State and Religion in a Nutshell*.

39. See, for example, Stephen D. Smith, *Foreordained Failure*.

40. See, for example, John T. Noonan, Jr., *The Lustre of Our Country*.

41. A significant exception is *Reynolds v. U.S.*, 98 U.S. 145 (1878), which originated in a territory of the U.S. Territories are governed by federal, rather than state, law. In the *Reynolds* case, a Mormon man challenged his prosecution under anti-polygamy laws on the ground that the First Amendment entitled him to an exemption. Mr. Reynolds was unsuccessful. The Supreme Court found that the First Amendment protects only religious *beliefs* unconditionally, while religious *acts* were protected only in so far as they were not offensive. The court described polygamy to be an "odious" practice, foreign to civilized countries.

Furthermore, while there were few cases in the Supreme Court interpreting the religion clauses before the mid–twentieth century, religious freedom as legal and political doctrine does have a history between the end of the eighteenth and the middle of the twentieth centuries. Both state and federal courts decided many cases about religion, and popular ideas about religious freedom were influential in politics. See Mark deWolfe Howe, *The Garden and the Wilderness*, for an outline of the historical sweep of judicial attention to religion, and Philip Hamburger, *Separation of Church and State*, for a history of changing popular attitudes. State constitutions also enshrined disestablishment and religious freedom as fundamental commitments and were litigated during that period.

42. *Cantwell v. Connecticut*, 310 U.S. 296 (1940).

43. The Fourteenth Amendment provides: "All Persons born or naturalized in the United States, and subject to the jurisdiction thereof, are citizens of the United States and of the State where they reside. No State shall make or enforce any law which shall abridge the privileges and immunities of citizens of the United States; nor shall any state deprive any person of life, liberty, or property, without due process of law; nor deny to any person within its jurisdiction the equal protection of laws." U.S. Constitution, Amendment 14, Section 1 (also reproduced in Appendix A). Incorporation is not uncontroversial. See, for example, Raoul Berger, "Incorporation of the Bill of Rights: Akhil Amar's Wishing Well."

44. See *Everson v. Board of Education*, 330 U.S. 1 (1947). For a discussion of the Incorporation Doctrine and the Fourteenth Amendment, see Howe (cited above in note 38); J. R. Pole, *The Pursuit of Equality in American History;* and Joseph Tussman and Jacob tenBroek, "The Equal Protection of the Laws."

45. 494 U.S. 872 (1990).

46. The Native American Church was incorporated in 1918 in Oklahoma as a deliberate strategy to ensure constitutional protection of a Native American religious practice involving the veneration of the peyote cactus. Sam D. Gill, *Native American Religions*, 169.

47. 374 U.S. 398 (1963). *Sherbert* involved the denial of unemployment compensation to a Seventh Day Adventist who refused to work on Saturday for religious reasons. The Court found the denial an unconstitutional burden on her free exercise rights.

48. Gill, pp. 167–71.

49. *Smith v. Employment Div.* 307 Ore. 68 (1988). The United States Supreme Court subsequently granted certiorari. The Supreme Court's decision in the case may be found at 489 U.S. 1077 (1989).

50. 494 U.S. 872, 890.

51. 98 U.S. 145 (1878). See description of case above at note 41.

52. 494 U.S. at 878–79.

53. 494 U.S. at 890.

54. Ibid., at 902.

55. For example, she did the same thing in *Lynch v. Donnelly*, 465 U.S. at 687–94.

56. *Church of the Lukumi Babalu Aye v. City of Hialeah* 508 U.S. 520 (1993). In this case, Santeria practitioners brought an action against the city government for banning animal sacrifice. The high court held that the city had no reason for the particular legislation in question other than outlawing the practices of a disfavored religion.

57. *Lyng v. Northwest Indian Cemetery Protection Association*, 485 U.S. 439 (1988).

58. 42 U.S.C. §§2000bb et seq (1993).

59. The Federal RFRA is reproduced in Appendix A. For discussion of the Act and its history, see Marci A. Hamilton, "Religion and the Law in the Clinton Era."

60. "Remarks on Signing the Religious Freedom Restoration Act of 1993," 29 *Weekly Comp Pres. Doc* 2377 (November 16, 1993). Quoted in Hamilton (cited in note 55 above).

61. See Winnifred F. Sullivan, "Die neuen US Geseze zu 'Charitable Choice' und die Regelungen zu den 'Faith-based' Organisationen," for a discussion of Bush administration politics of religion.

62. 521 U.S. 507 (1997).

63. See David P. Currie, "Reflections of *City of Boerne v. Flores:* RFRA." RFRA may be constitutional with respect to the federal government because the application of the First Amendment to the Oregon statute was by way of the Fourteenth Amendment, which addresses the states.

64. 521 U.S. at 536.

65. H.R. 4019.

66. 42 U.S.C.S. § 2000cc (2004). The constitutionality of RLUIPA has been unsuccessfully challenged in a number of cases.

67. See above at note 34.

68. For a discussion of this issue of definition, see, for example, Witte, *Religion and the American Constitutional Experiment.*

69. *Mack v. O'Leary,* 80 F.3d.1175 (7th Cir., 1996).

70. 80 F. 3rd at 1178.

71. Ibid. at 1179.

CHAPTER 2

1. *http:www.crpc.org/2000/*

2. See *www.calvin.edu* for information about Calvin College and *www.pba.edu* for information about Palm Beach Atlantic University.

3. *Campbell v. Acuff-Rose,* 510 U.S. 569 (1994).

4. Steve Ellman, "14-yr Fight on Behalf of Sugar Cane Cutters in Palm Beach County May Be Entering Last Phase."

5. In fact, we worked long into each evening preparing for the next day.

6. Jim Green testified against Judge Ryskamp in the Senate Judiciary Committee hearing on his nomination to the Eleventh Circuit Court of Appeals. Valerie Greenberg Itkoff, "Rejected Judge Branded 'Unfair': Rights Plaintiffs May Ask Ryskamp to Bow Out."

7. Transcript, p. 896.

8. Ibid., p. 892.

9. *Palm Beach Post* January 20, 1998, p. 4B.

10. Transcript, p. 8.

11. Ibid., p. 12.

12. During the discovery phase of a case, before the trial, lawyers for each party

formally interview the witnesses for the other side. A court reporter transcribes these interviews. These interviews provide the basis for any pretrial motions, allow the parties to present their evidence in court in as concise and informed a manner as possible and allow them to anticipate the concerns of the other side. The depositions also serve as a source checking the witnesses' testimony, so that witnesses are occasionally cross-examined on the basis of this previous evidence given in the case. F.R.Civ.Pro. 27. When witnesses are unavailable, which happened in a couple of cases in this trial, parts of depositions are read aloud and substitute for live testimony.

13. A recent French Catholic Encyclopedia contrasts the two theological understandings of suicide before, and after, Vatican II: "Dans la perspective précédente, on semble admettrre que les raisons de se donner la mort sont simples et conscientes et on ne paraît pas douter de la responsabilité morale du suicidé par rapport à son acte. Les approches récentes de type explicatif ou descriptif ont contribué à mettre en relief la complexité du phénomène et à en dégager différentes formes." s.v. suicide, *Catholicisme Hier Aujourd'hui Demain.* (Translation: "From the former perspective, the reasons for committing suicide were understood to be simple and conscious and no doubt was admitted as to the suicide's moral responsibility for the act. More recent explanatory and descriptive approaches have placed in relief the complexity of the phenomenon.")

14. Transcript, pp. 18–19.

15. Ibid., p. 20.

16. s.v. "Sacred Heart, Devotion to," *New Catholic Encyclopedia.*

17. s.v. "Sacred Heart, Iconography of," *New Catholic Encyclopedia.*

18. For an ethnographic study of American ethnic Catholic practice and its tension with the institutional Church, see, for example, Robert Orsi, *The Madonna of 115th St.* See also Andrew M. Greeley, *The Catholic Imagination* (Berkeley: University of California, 2000); Thomas J. Ferraro, ed., *Catholic Lives,* Contemporary America. Durham: Duke University Press, 1997; and Charles R. Norris, *American Catholic: The Saints and Sinners Who Built America's Most Powerful Church* (New York: Times Book, 1997.)

19. Transcript, pp. 22, 20, 22–23.

20. Ibid., p. 30.

21. Ibid., p. 32.

22. Ibid., p.98–99.

23. Ibid., pp. 102–03.

24. Ibid., p. 103.

25. Religion tied to freedom from political oppression is noted by sociologist of religion José Casanova as one of the key characteristics of modern religion, modern religion that has persisted in a time of widespread secularization. It is, he says, religion connected with political power that is vulnerable in the modern period. Thus, in Europe, for example, in Poland and Ireland where the Church was, until recently, aligned with the people against a hostile political regime, the Soviets in one case, the British in the other, Catholic piety persisted and was more vigorous

than in France and Italy, where the church was associated with oppressive political power. For some Cubans, Catholic piety has played a role to that in Ireland and Poland. José Casanova, *Public Religions in the Modern World.*

26. Transcript, pp. 104–105.

27. Ibid., pp. 101, 100.

28. Ibid., pp. 36–37, 40.

29. Ibid., pp. 36–38, 40.

30. s.v. "Magen David," *The Blackwell Dictionary of Judaica.*

31. Transcript, pp. 38–39.

32. Ibid., pp. 46–47.

33. Ibid., p. 44.

34. Ibid., pp. 78, 79.

35. s.v. "Priests and Priesthood," *The Encyclopedia of the Jewish Religion.*

36. Transcript, pp. 78, 80–81.

37. Ibid., pp. 125–26.

38. Ibid., p. 180–81.

39. See, Colleen McDannell, *Material Christianity*, for a discussion of the use of objects by American Christians.

40. Transcript, p. 180.

41. This expression comes from the third chapter of the Gospel of John, where Jesus tells the religious leader Nicodemus: 'Except a man be born again, he cannot see the Kingdom of God' John 3:3. See also Joel A. Carpenter, *Revive Us Again.*

42. Transcript, p. 197.

43. Ibid., pp. 201, 206–207.

44. Ibid. p. 199.

45. Ibid., p. 202. Mr. Karram here paraphrases from the account in the Gospel of John of his conversation with Martha during the story of the raising of Lazarus. John 11:24–26.

46. Transcript, pp. 203–204.

47. Ibid., p. 211.

48. Ibid., pp. 212–13.

49. Ibid., p. 232.

50. Ibid., pp. 233, 237.

51. Ibid., pp. 237–38.

52. Ibid., p. 241–43.

53. Ibid., pp. 245, 48.

54. Ibid., pp. 397–99.

55. Ibid., pp. 401–403.

56. Ibid. pp. 403, 409.

57. Ibid., p. 405.

58. *http:nl.newsbank.com/nojavascript.html* "*Menorah* planned in Sanborn Square" Siobhan Morrissey.

http:nl.newsbank.com/nojavascript.html "*Boca*, Religious leaders find holiday-symbol compromise: Menorahs, trees could share private site.

59. *Jerusalem Post*, February 12, 1991. See also Winnifred Fallers Sullivan, *Paying the Words Extra*, discussing *Lynch v. Donnelly*, 465 U.S. 668, the 1983 Supreme Court decision concerning the constitutionality of the public display of a crèche.

60. Transcript, p. 576.

61. Ibid., p. 577.

62. See John Bossy, *Christianity in the West*, and Ann Taves, *The Household of Faith*, for discussion of the importance of the extended family for Catholic devotional practice.

63. Transcript, pp. 583–84, 575, 578.

CHAPTER 3

1. Transcript, pp. 60–75.

2. Ibid., pp. 232–348.

3. Ibid., pp. 390–92.

4. Ibid., pp. 565–66.

5. Ibid., pp. 567–71.

6. The Federal Rules of Evidence regulate the filing of expert reports in federal court. Expert reports take the form of sworn affidavits which are a formal part of the record in the case. F.R.E. 702.

7. The plaintiffs' experts were, as is customary, all paid an hourly wage for their work, both in preparation for and at trial. The amount of the wage is required to be disclosed in the reports, although some of the experts may have discounted that time, given that the plaintiffs were being represented free of charge by the ACLU.

8. Michael Broyde, *The Pursuit of Justice*; *Human Rights in Judaism*.

9. A *bet din* is a court of Jewish law. Their origins are traced to the time of Moses. Since the modern legal emancipation of European Jews, many matters formerly considered in Jewish courts are now considered in secular courts. Bet dins continue to exist all over the world, however. These courts rule on questions of Jewish religious practice. s.v. "bet din" Geoffrey Wigoder, ed., *The New Encyclopedia of Judaism*.

10. Broyde Report, p. 1.

11. Ibid., p. 5.

12. Since the destruction of the Temple in Jerusalem by the Romans in 70 C.E., the teaching of what is known as Rabbinic Judaism has guided Jews who have lived, for the most part, in the diaspora, that is outside Israel. That guidance involves both rulings on Jewish religious practice and on the practice of Jews with respect to non-Jewish legal regimes. For an overview of this history, see Robert M. Seltzer, *Jewish People, Jewish Thought*, especially pp. 245ff. See also Natalie B. Dohrmann, "Analogy, Empire and Political Conflict in a Rabbinic Midrash."

13. Broyde Report, pp. 1–2.

14. Transcript, pp. 127–28.

15. See, for example, Louis Jacobs, *A Tree of Life*.

16. Each of the experts teaches and writes in the context of ongoing academic debates about how best to understand and describe religion. Those debates shadow the testimony of these experts in this trial, but the details of those debates are beyond the scope of this book. As for Jewish legal practice, I am particularly grateful to Hillel Gray and Jane Kanarek for helping me understand Jewish legal practice.

17. "So Rachel died, and she was buried on the way to Ephrath (that is, Bethlehem), and Jacob set up a pillar upon her grave; it is the pillar of Rachel's tomb, which is there to this day." Genesis 35:20 (RSV).

18. Talmud is a third century written collection of rabbinic teachings interpreting Torah, still considered the prime source of authoritative teaching by many Jews today. Seltzer, p. 252.

19. Broyde Report (found in Appendix B).

20. Transcript p. 130.

21. Ibid., p. 135.

22. Ibid., p. 134. This practice is interestingly analogous to the Catholic practice with respect to the consecrated elements of bread and wine. Once consecrated, they cannot be disposed of in an ordinary way. Often they are buried. Canon 1367 of the Code of Canon Law provides penalties for those who "throw away" the consecrated species.

23. Transcript, pp. 125, 130.

24. Ibid., pp. 124–25.

25. Ibid., pp. 143–45.

26. Ibid. p. 149.

27. Ibid., p.158–59.

28. Ibid., p. 591. Romanian Orthodoxy is one of the inheritors of the Eastern traditions of Christianity. What is today Romania was probably evangelized by Roman soldiers in the fourth century C.E.. It later came under the ecclesiastical rule of Constantinople. The Romanina Orthodox Church today is the national church of Romania. s.v. "Romania, Christianity in," *The Oxford Dictionary of the Christian Church*.

29. John A. McGuckin, *Standing in God's Holy Fire, St. Gregory of Nazianzus*.

30. Transcript, pp. 591–98.

31. *www.saintmarymagdalen.com/eileen/*

32. *2001 New York Times Almanac*.

33. A new study by the National Opinion Research Center in Chicago suggests that the U.S. Protestant majority is fading. *New York Times* 7/21/04.

34. See, for example, Philip Hamburger, *Separation of Church and State*.

35. Distinguishing Protestant and Catholic religious forms is a tricky business. For one introduction to the distinctive nature of Roman Catholic religiosity in the U.S., see Catherine L. Albanese, *America*, pp. 77–85.

36. Very roughly speaking, to be a faithful Jew is to follow the Mosaic law, as interpreted by the sages. Christianity emerged in part out of a critique of legalistic ways of being religious, although law continued to play a role in Christianity, and

particular churches have developed internal institutional law with which to govern their administration. See s.v. "law and gospel," Van A. Harvey, ed., *A Handbook of Theological Terms.*

37. McGuckin Report, p. 1.

38. Pals Report, p. 12.

39. McGuckin Report, pp. 2–3.

40. Transcript, pp. 605–606.

41. Ibid., pp. 663–65, 615–16.

42. s.v. "dead, prayers for the," *The Oxford Dictionary of the Christian Church.*

43. McGuckin Report, p. 4.

44. Transcript, pp. 601–607.

45. For one delineation of a theology of the cross see, see Alexandra R. Brown, *The Cross and Human Transformation.*

46. s.v. "cross," *The Harper Collins Dictionary of Religion.*

47. A contemporary account of Constantine's vision was given by Eusebius.

48. Transcript p. 607.

49. Ibid., pp. 606–609.

50. "When the theology of the sacraments was defined and their number limited to seven [baptism, confirmation, eucharist, penance, last rites, ordination, and marriage] in the W. church in the 12th cent., analogous religious practices not held to have been instituted by Christ, came to be known as 'sacramentals.'" s.v. "sacramentals," *The Oxford Dictionary of the Christian Church.*

51. McGuckin Report, pp. 2–3.

52. Transcript, pp. 607–608.

53. Ibid., p. 630.

54. Ibid., pp. 630–631.

55. Ibid., pp. 610, 629–30.

56. Ibid., pp. 601–602.

57. Ibid., pp. 644–45.

58. Ibid., p. 603.

59. Ibid., pp. 352–58.

60. Ibid., p. 351–372.

61. Ibid., pp. 493.

62. Ibid., p. 496. See Colleen McDannell, *Material Christianity*, for a description of the rural cemetery movement and the religious sensibility therein expressed, pp. 103ff.

63. Transcript, pp. 496–97.

64. See Mircea Eliade, *The Myth of the Eternal Return*, for an influential, although much criticized account of a religious understanding of history.

65. See, for example, Transcript, p. 869.

66. Transcript, pp. 539–40.

67. Katz Report, p. 8.

68. Nathan Katz, *Who Are the Jews of India?* and *A Jewish King at Shingly.*

69. Katz Report, p. 1.

70. An English language translation of the Code of Canon Law of the Roman Catholic Church, prepared by the Canon Law Society of Great Britain and Ireland, is published as *The Canon Law: Letter & Spirit*.

71. Mr. Villaronga is now apparently a lay minister in Charlotte, NC, according to their website. *www.charlottediocese.org*.

72. *Associated Catholic Cemeteries Memorial Policy* (cited in Katz Report at n. 8).

73. Katz Report, p. 1.

74. *The Catholic Cemetery: A Vision for the Millenium* (National Catholic Cemetery Association, 1997).

75. Katz Report, p. 3.

76. Ibid., pp. 3–4.

77. On cross-examination at trial, Mr. Green asked Katz about the source of the opinion on Protestantism. Katz responded, "Yes, I did slip up there. I let one of the footnotes fall through my word processor." Transcript, p. 463.

78. See, for example, Paul Giles, *American Catholic Arts and Fictions*.

79. Maurice Lamm, *The Jewish Way in Death and Mourning*. Michael Broyde, in his testimony at the trial, criticized Katz for relying on Lamm's English-language summary of Jewish law, rather than going to the Hebrew sources. Transcript, p. 166.

80. Katz Report, pp. 4, 6.

81. Ibid., p. 6.

82. Transcript, p. 436.

83. Katz Report, p. 7.

84. Robert Redfield, *The Little Community and Peasant Society and Culture*.

85. Report, p. 7.

86. Transcript, pp. 437, 440.

87. Ibid., p. 452.

88. Katz Report, p. 4.

89. Transcript, p. 453.

90. Ibid., p. 454.

91. Ibid., pp. 463–64.

92. Ibid., pp. 471–72.

93. Ibid., p. 482–83.

94. Ibid., pp. 482–84.

95. Daniel L. Pals, *Seven Theories of Religion*.

96. Pals Report, p. 2–4.

97. Ibid., p. 4.

98. Ibid., p. 5.

99. Transcript, p. 768.

100. Pals Report, p. 9.

101. s.v. "Ashkenazim," in Geoffrey Wigoder, ed., *The New Encyclopedia of Judaism*.

102. Pals Report, p. 10.

103. Ibid., p. 11.

104. For one discussion of this historical probem, see Jonathan Z. Smith, *Drudgery Divine.*

105. Pals Report, p. 12, 14.

106. Ibid., p. 17.

107. Transcript, pp. 732, 739.

108. Ibid., pp. 768–9.

109. Ibid., p. 775.

110. Winnifred Fallers Sullivan, *Paying the Words Extra.*

111. Sullivan Report, p. 1.

112. Ibid., p. 2.

113. Ibid., pp. 2–3.

114. Ibid., p. 2.

115. Ibid., p. 3.

116. Transcript, p. 842.

117. Ibid., pp. 920–21.

118. 64 F. Supp 2d at 1287, n.11.

119. Transcript, p. 813.

120. Ibid., pp. 813–15.

121. Ibid., pp. 818–19.

122. Ibid., pp. 835–37.

123. Ibid., pp. 842–43.

Chapter 4

1. Transcript, p. 865.

2. Ibid., p. 869.

3. Ibid., p. 880.

4. Ibid., pp. 892–94.

5. Ibid., p. 896.

6. Ibid., p. 897–98.

7. *Lyng v. Northwest Indian Cemetery Protective Association,* 485 U.S. 439 (1988).

8. Helpful discussions of the connection between religion, law, and private property, particularly in the context of the Native American cases, can be found in the following: Lloyd Burton, *Worship and Wilderness*; Williams, Robert W. *The American Indian in Western Legal Thought*; and Kathleen Sands, "'A Property of Peculiar Value."

9. Transcript, pp. 902–903.

10. Ibid., p. 905.

11. Ibid., p. 910.

12. This lack of legal recognition is in marked contrast to many countries in Europe, for example, where clerics are often licensed, even paid, by the state. The closest analogy in this country would be the hiring of chaplains for the armed services and for correctional facilities.

13. Transcript, p. 912–13.

14. Ibid., p. 913.

15. Ibid., p. 921–24.

16. Ibid., p. 930.

17. See Sullivan, *Paying the Words Extra*, pp. 94–109, for a discussion of the Japanese Supreme Court's deference to the "rights" of government entities.

18. *Warner v. Boca Raton*, 64 F. Supp. 2d 1272 (1999).

19. 64 F. Supp. 2d at 1283.

20. Ibid., at 1282.

21. The briefs on appeal discuss at length the rules of statutory construction that govern such a clause, a "whether or not" clause.

22. 64 F. Supp. 2d at 1283.

23. See, for example, *Mack v. O'Leary*, 80 F. 3d. 1175 (1996).

24. Hearings on H.R. 2797 before the House Judiciary Comm. 102d. Cong., 2d sess, 128–30 (May 30, 1992), quoted by Ryskamp, 64 F. Supp. 2d at 1282.

25. Ibid.

26. 64 F. Supp. 2d at 1282.

27. Ibid., at 1282–83.

28. Ibid., at 1284.

29. Ibid., at 1286–87.

30. Among several books and many articles on legal matters, Mr. Laycock is a member of the committee that produced "God Alone Is Lord of the Conscience: Policy Statement and Recommendations Regarding Religious Liberty" for the Presbyterian Church U.S.A. in 1989.

31. *Warner v. Boca Raton*, 267 F.3d 1223, 1227 (2001). On September 2, 2004, after this manuscript had gone to press and three years after the Eleventh Circuit's certification, the Supreme Court of Florida responded to the Eleventh Circuit's questions. *Warner v. Boca Raton*, 2004 Fla LEXIS 1449 (2004). The Florida Court answered the first question in the affirmative while it rephrased the second question as follows: "Whether the City of Boca Raton Ordinance at issue in this case violates the Florida Religious Freedom Restoration Act (FRFRA)?" In an opinion with a skeletal summary of the facts favoring the City's point of view, the Florida Supreme Court announced that the appropriate test under the FRFRA is that "a substantial burden on the free exercise of religion is one that either compels the religious adherent to engage in conduct that that his religion forbids or forbids him to engage in conduct that his religion requires" (2004 Fla. LEXIS at 1478). Applying this test to the Warner case, the Florida Court concluded that plaintiffs had failed to meet that standard because the plaintiffs were permitted to engrave flat markers with religious symbols and were permitted to install temporary vertical grave decorations on anniversaries, finessing the question addressed in this book as to how any plaintiff might prove that they did what their religion "requires." The Eleventh Circuit Court of Appeals has yet to act in response to this decision. The Eleventh Circuit

is expected to address the federal constitutional questions as well as the questions of Florida law.

32. Among a vast number of such articles in law reviews, an influential law-review article attempting such a definition is Kent Greenawalt, "Religion As a Constitutional Concept."

33. The word "religion" appears in many statutes and regulations, including the Internal Revenue Code.

34. *Hernandez v Commisioner,* 490 U.S. 680, 699 (1989).

35. *Thomas v. Review Board,* 450 U.S. 707, 716 (1981).

36. *Mack v. O'Leary,* 80 F. 3d 1175, 1179 (1996).

37. *U.S. v. Ballard,* 322 U.S. 78, 86 (1944).

38. *United States v. Seeger,* 380 U.S. 163 (1965); *Welsh v. United States,* 398 U.S. 333 (1970). These cases also illustrate the difficulties that arise from simply reading religion to mean conscience. See Phillip E. Hammond, *With Liberty for All,* for an argument that the religion clauses ought to be read as protecting conscience, rather than religion.

39. *Gillette v. U.S.* 401 U.S. 437 (1971).

40. 380 U.S. at 180.

41. Ibid., at 180–83.

42. He also wrote a book about the experience: *Creationism on Trial.*

43. *Africa v. Pennsylvania,* 662 F. 2d 1025, 1033 (1982). The Third Circuit considered three factors in applying its analogy test: "First, a religion addresses fundamental and ultimate questions having to do with deep and imponderable matters. Second, a religion is comprehensive in nature; it consists of a belief system as opposed to an isolated teaching. Third, a religion can often be recognized by the presence of certain formal and external signs." 662 F. 2d at 1032.

44. See, for example, Daniel Pals, "Is Religion a *Sui Generis* Phenomenon?" and the following debate in the "Responses and Rejoinders" section of the *Journal* (v. 59:703–13).

45. It is interesting to note that the great German sociologist of religion, Max Weber, is missing from this list.

46. Pals, 270, 282–83.

47. Asad and others have pointed to the difficulties of assigning religious motivation to terrorists. Asad, p. 11.

48. See discussion below.

49. Pat Dunningan, "Constitutional Rights Standing for Religion?" *Broward Daily Business Review* 43:5 2:A17.

50. 494 U.S. at 909.

51. 98 U.S. at 161.

52. 485 U.S. at 442.

53. Initial Brief of Amicus Curiae, Florida League of Cities, Inc. in the Supreme Court of Florida, p. 3. *Warner v. City of Boca Raton,* Case No. SC01-2206.

54. Florida Statutes, §761.02 (3).

55. *The American Heritage Dictionary of the English Language* defines "substantial" as follows: "ADJECTIVE: 1. Of, relating to, or having substance; material. 2. True or real; not imaginary. 3. solidly built; strong. 4. Ample; sustaining: a substantial breakfast. 5. Considerable in importance, value, degree, amount, or extent: won by a substantial margin. 6. Possessing wealth or property; well-to-do."

56. Defendant's Response in Opposition to Plaintiffs' Motion for Summary Judgment. Case No. 98-8054-Civ-Ryskamp (U.S. District Court for Southern District of Florida).

57. Defendant's Response, pp. 5–6.

58. 494 U.S. 872 (1991).

59. Similar arguments were made in an amicus brief filed by Liberty Counsel in the Florida Supreme Court. Amicus Brief of Liberty Counsel in Support of Plaintiffs-Appellants in the Supreme Court of Florida. *Warner v. Boca Raton.* No. SC01-2206. The president of Liberty Counsel, Matthew Staver, drafted the Florida RFRA. For a discussion of *Antigone* and the law, see Costas Douzinas and Ronnie Warrington, "Antigone's Law: A Genealogy of Jurisprudence" in Costa-Douzinas, Peter Goedrich and Yifat Hachamovitch, *Politics, Postmodernity and Critical Legal Studies: The Legality of the Contingent*, Routledge, 1994.

60. Jeb Bush Brief at 6.

61. Harris Deposition, pp. 55–57, 91, 93–94.

62. "Latin" was to be distinguished for McGuckin, I think, from "Greek," as opposed to another frequent usage in which "Latin" Catholicism refers to "Mediterranean" Catholicism and its colonial and postcolonial outposts and is opposed to "Northern European." "Latin," for McGuckin, denominated the religious sensibility of the "Latin" West, the Roman Catholic Church, while "Greek" denominated the religious sensibility of the Orthodox churches.

63. In *Paying the Words Extra*, in a related exercise, I considered different religious sensibilities among the justices of the Supreme Court with respect to each's interpretation of the significance of a crèche displayed in a civic Christmas display.

64. Transcript, pp. 17–18.

65. Ibid., pp. 27–30.

66. Monier deposition, pp. 18–21.

67. Cavedoni deposition, pp. 10–12.

68. Transcript, p. 101.

69. Ibid., pp. 176–77.

70. Transcript, p. 194.

71. Ibid., pp. 189–90.

72. Ibid., pp. 394–95.

73. Ibid., pp. 402–403, 407, 409.

74. Danciu Deposition, pp. 15–17.

75. Transcript, pp. 35–36.

76. Ibid., p. 39.

77. Ibid., p. 641.

78. M. Warner Deposition, p. 12.

79. R. Warner deposition, pp. 14–15.

80. Ibid., pp. 16–17.

81. Ibid., pp. 17–18.

82. Ibid., pp. 27–28.

83. B. Payne Deposition, pp. 17–18.

84. Ibid., p. 26.

85. Ibid., pp. 18–19.

86. Ibid., pp. 29–30.

87. Ibid., p. 41.

88. Transcript, p. 230.

89. Ibid., pp. 231–32.

90. Ibid., pp. 284–86.

91. Ibid., pp. 286–87.

92. Ibid., pp. 287–89.

93. I. Payne deposition, pp. 21–23.

94. The significance of custom in Jewish religious practice is an interestingly complex issue. There are times when custom has the force of law or even when it supersedes law. A friend told me a story about his father. His father led a Sephardic Jewish congregation in Philadelphia. It is the custom in Sephardic Jewish communities for prayers for the dead to be offered at the afternoon service, rather than the morning service. (Ashkenazic communities, in contrast, often say such prayers at morning services.) One day a member of the congregation asked my friend's father to say a prayer at the morning service for my friend's grandfather who had recently died. My friend's father refused. The congregant threatened to resign from the congregation, but my friend's father held firm. To emphasize the point he later told my friend, then a young boy, that even had the congregant asked him to eat a ham sandwich, he would have done that rather than violate Sephardic custom. (Private communication from Jacob Corré about his father, Rabbi Alan Corré, retold with his permission. Rabbi Corré has a website at *www.uwm.edu/~corre.*)

95. Transcript, pp. 611–13.

96. Ibid., pp. 636–37.

97. Ibid., pp. 614–15.

98. Ibid., p. 156.

99. Ibid., pp. 652–54.

100. Ibid., p. 837.

101. Ibid., pp. 659–60.

102. Ibid., p. 780.

103. Ibid., pp. 446–47.

104. Ibid., p. 658.

105. Ibid., p. 168

106. Ibid., pp. 168–71.

107. Ibid., pp. 172–73.

108. Ibid., pp. 617–19.

109. Ibid., p. 460.

110. 64 F. Supp. 2d at 1287.

CHAPTER 5

1. Danièle Hervieu-Léger, "'What Scripture Tells Me.'"

2. Jeb Bush Brief at 18.

3. In the early federal period, state aid to religion was common. Such religion was therefore able in some measure to resist the erosive effect of congregational dissent. It has also been possible from time to time in various places for small insular religious communities to construct coercive and homogeneous religious regimes that have a high degree of ability to compel orthodox practice. Finally, sacralized aspects of government activities are able to compel adherence.

4. See French, "Shopping for Religion."

5. See, for example, Hall, ed., *Lived Religion in America*.

6. "The term 'Immaculate Conception' designates the belief that the Virgin Mary was free from ORIGINAL SIN from the very beginning of her life, i.e., from her conception." Although long discussed by theologians, it was defined as dogma by Pope Pius IX in 1854. s.v. "Immaculate Conception," *New Catholic Encyclopedia*. Devotion to the Immaculate Conception was intensified by the 1858 apparitions attested to by St. Bernadette, a fourteen-year-old girl at a spring in Lourdes, France. According to Bernadette, Mary appeared on a number of occasions, calling for penance and urging the construction of a chapel. On one of these occasions she told Bernadette, "I am the Immaculate Conception." Lourdes is one of the most popular Marian pilgrimage sites in the world, s.v. "Lourdes," *New Catholic Encyclopedia*.

7. Hall pp. 3–5.

8. Ibid., p. 5.

9. McDanell, Colleen. *Material Christianity*.

10. Ibid., p. 272. See also Daniel Miller, ed., *Unwrapping Christmas*.

11. McDannell, p. 274.

12. Transcript, p. 645.

13. Orsi, pp. 4–5.

14. Thomas J. Curry, *Farewell to Christendom*. Thomas Curry is an auxiliary bishop in the Archdiocese of Los Angeles (and titular bishop of Kells, Ireland), and a well-respected historian who has written one of the best books on the historical context for the passage of the First Amendment: *First Freedoms: Church and State in America to the Passage of the First Amendment*.

15. See Rebecca French, "From Yoder to Yoda" and "Shopping for Religion."

16. Curry, p. 84. *Lyng*, 485 U.S. at 458 (Justice O'Connor, writing for the majority).

17. Christian Smith, *American Evangelicalism*, 99.

18. Sidney Mead, *The Lively Experiment*, p. x.

19. Ibid., p. x.

20. Ibid., p. 14. J. Hector St. John Crévecoeur was a French soldier who wrote of his experience in the early republic. *Letters from an American Farmer,* and *Sketches of Eighteenth-Century America.*

21. Katz Report, p. 6.

22. Feminists would, of course, have a field day with Katz's typology.

23. Pals Report, p. 5.

24. The *Warner* trial brought together five scholars of religion (expert witnesses in the case) to opine on a very simple question: Is what people in the United States do at cemeteries today, in remembrance of deceased relatives, "religion" or an "exercise of religion" in the words of the statute? The answers given by all of the experts, although interestingly varied, were, by and large, singularly unhelpful to the court and to the parties. As a discipline, we did not enlighten. Were the definitions and explanations wrong? Is the failure limited to the litigation context or is the failure an index of broader issues in religious studies?

25. You can argue, and people have, that modern disestablished religion, particularly in the United States, is not religion. See, for example, Harold Bloom, *The American Religion.*

26. Robert Bellah, "Civil Religion in America."

27. Brian Barry, *Culture and Equality.*

28. See, for example, Witte, p. 232.

29. J. R. Pole, *The Pursuit of Equality in American History;* Winnifred Fallers Sullivan, "Neutralizing Religion or What Is the Opposite of Faith-Based?"

Some have argued that religion should be narrowly defined for the purposes of the establishment clause and broadly defined for the purposes of the free exercise clause. Such a scheme would, it is suggested, acknowledge that it is government coercion in matters religious that is the primary concern in both kinds of cases. In other words, under such a plan, courts would be concerned about possible establishment clause violations only when persons are coerced to participate in publicly financed religion. Mere accommodation of religion by legislative and administrative bodies would not be unconstitutional. And courts would take a broad brush with respect to the free exercise clause, concerning themselves only when laws actively contribute to coerce nonreligionists. Such a scheme would also acknowledge that, while the two are in a sense two sides of the same coin, they also present interesting differences in the judicial context. An establishment clause case focuses on "separation." Defining religion is believed necessary in such cases in order to contain it, in order to keep government from forcing religion on its citizens through a favoring of religion in general or a particular religion. Free exercise cases focus on "exemption." Defining religion is necessary in these cases, it is said, to facilitate its flourishing. Establishment clause cases are brought by those who fear religion in public life. Free exercise cases are brought by those who claim special privileges for religiously motivated action. Establishment cases are about government. Free exercise cases are about the individual. Appealing as this approach is, I am not clear that it does not just double the problems addressed by this book. Two line-drawing exercises would then have to be undertaken, exercises that would only conceal the judgment of value being made in each case.

30. Howe, *The Garden and the Wilderness*; p. 148.

31. *Boerne v. Flores*, 521 U.S. at 536–37, Stevens, J., concurring.

32. Political support for "faith-based" initiatives are based, in part, on this conviction. See Winnifred Fallers Sullivan, "Die neuen US Geseze zu 'Charitable Choice' und die Regelungen zu den 'Faith-based' Organisationen."

33. See Hammond, *With Liberty for All*.

34. U.S. Constitution Amendment XIV, see Appendix A. While the reach of that guarantee is much debated, I will speak here of the more general principle of equality originally first expressed in the Declaration of Independence and also there embodied rather than the current limitation of that guarantee as it has recently been interpreted by U.S. courts.

35. A project with which many "believers," perhaps often unwittingly, conspire. See, for example, Stephen Carter, *The Culture of Disbelief.* Carter divides Americans into believers and nonbelievers, arguing that believers are discriminated against and misunderstood. Interestingly, at this moment in U.S. history, all groups seem to feel victimized, atheists and religiousts, whether they occupy a majority or a minority position in society.

36. See W.A.R. Shadid and P. S. van Koningsveld, eds. *Religious Freedom and the Neutrality of the State*.

37. For a discussion of differentiation and the secularization thesis, see José Casanova, *Public Religions in the Modern World.*.

38. See Susanne Rudolph and James Piscatori, eds. *Transnational Religion and Fading States*.

39. See, for example, Casanova, *Public Religion in the Modern World*. Talal Asad has recently come at the task of understanding contemporary culture from an effort to articulate what he calls "an anthropology of the secular." In one of his essays in *Formations of the Secular,* Asad discusses the views of the development of secular consciousness of two early twentieth-century thinkers, Paul de Man and Walter Benjamin. Favoring Benjamin's understanding of the working of allegory in the baroque period as a key to understanding the secular, Asad insists that, "what the emblems have to teach is more authoritative than *purely personal preferences.* The interweaving in such communication of what today many would separate as the sacred and the profane remains for Benjamin an essential feature of allegory [emphasis supplied]." Secular consciousness is characterized for Asad not by an insistence on the real as opposed to the sacred but by an uneasy anxiety about the real expressed most characteristically in allegory, a literary form that, unlike classical tragedy, aims to instruct. Asad, like others, returns here to early modern artists and thinkers in order to reinterpret the modern. The modern he describes is not one governed entirely by reason.

40. With apologies to Donald R. Kelley, *The Human Measure: Social Thought in the Western Legal Tradition*, Harvard, 1990, p. 283, the last sentence of which ends

"King Nomos still rules." See also Winnifred Fallers Sullivan, "Religious Freedom and the Rule of Law."

41. See Peter Fitzpatrick, *The Mythology of Modern Law*; Peter Goodrich, *Oedipus Lex*; Tim Murphy, *The Oldest Social Science?*; and Sullivan and Yelle, "Law and Religion: Overview" *Encyclopedia of Religion*, 2d. ed.

42. For a review and evaluation of sociological theories of secularization, see José Casanova, *Public Religions in the Modern World*.

43. Michael Rosenfeld, "The Rule of Law and the Legitimacy of Constitutional Democracy."

44. It is interesting to note that religion was regulated as a private association by Roman law. Onno M. van Nijf, *The Civic World of Professional Associations in the Roman East*.

45. " Virginia Statute for Religious Freedom," drafted by Thomas Jefferson in 1777 and adopted by the Virginia Legislature in 1786. For a full discussion of the Statute, see Merrill D. Peterson and Robert C. Vaughan, eds., *The Virginia Statute for Religious Freedom*.

46. See, for example, Franklin I. Gamwell, *Democracy on Purpose*.

47. Nancy T. Ammerman, "Golden Rule Christianity."

48. See Tim Murphy, *The Oldest Social Science?*

49. See Stewart Motha and Thanos Zarthaloudis "Law, Ethics and the Utopian End of Human Rights."

50. Richard A. Schweder, Martha Minow, and Hazel Rose Markus, *Engaging Cultural Differences: The Multicultural Challenge in Liberal Democracies*.

51. See Motha and Zartholoudis, p. 260, 259.

52. John R. Bowen, *Islam, Law and Equality in Indonesia*. See also W. F. Sullivan, "Normative Pluralism: Religion and Law in the Twenty-first Century," *Religion* (forthcoming 2005).

53. The journal *First Things* is dedicated to the promotion of this position. For a discussion of the political debates leading up the passage of the religion clauses, see Thomas J. Curry, *The First Freedoms*.

54. See Motha and Zartholoudis.

55. In an article reviewing recent thinking on human rights, Stewart Motha and Thanos Zartholoudis argue that for recent human rights theorists attempting to integrate a philosophical critique of human rights, "[t]he existential integrity of each person is held together by a fantasy of completeness which allows each particular being to create 'fragile narratives of biographical coherence out of the many "subject positions" and disconnected fragments of their existence'" (pp. 260–61). In this sense, the modest struggles of the *Warner* plaintiffs might be compared to the struggles of others trying to retain their dignity in a legal context. Without RFRA or the religion clauses of the first amendment, the *Warner* plaintiffs would have to depend on local politics and on the claim that the City, through the regulations of its cemetery, failed to give equal protection of the law to all residents of Boca Raton.

Bibliography

Legal

Abbott v. Ft. Lauderdale, 783 So. 2d. 1213 (2001).

Africa v. Pennsylvania, 662 F. 2d 1025, 1032 (1982).

Americans United for the Separation of Church and State v. Prison Fellowship Ministries, United States District Court for the Southern District of Iowa, Central Division, Nos. 4:03-CV-90074, 4:03-CV-90447, 4:03-CV-90101.

Bibletown, U.S.A. v. Sproul, 212 So.2d 780 (1968).

Boerne v. Flores, 521 U.S. 507 (1997).

Campbell v. Acuff-Rose, 510 U.S. 569 (1994).

Cantwell v. Connecticut, 310 U.S. 296 (1940).

Chaplaincy of Full Gospel Churches v. Johnson, 276 F. Supp. 2d 82 (2003).

Church of the Lukumi Babalu Aye v. City of Hialeah, 508 U.S. 520 (1993).

City of Boca Raton v. Boca Villa Corp., 371 So.2d 154 (1979).

Employment Division v. Smith, 494 U.S. 872 (1990).

Everson v. Board of Education, 330 U.S. 1 (1947).

First Baptist Church of Perrine v. Miami-Dade Co., 968 So. 2d 1114.

Gillette v. U.S., 401 U.S. 437 (1971).

Hernandez v. Commissioner, 490 U.S., 699 (1989).

Jacobellis v. Ohio, 378 U.S. 184 (1964).

King v. Richmond Co., 331 F. 2d 1271 (2003).

Konikov v. Orange Co., 302 F. Supp 1328 (2004).

Locke v. Davey, 124 S. ct. 1307 (2004).

Lynch v. Donnelly, 465 U.S. 668 (1983).

Lyng v. Northwest Indian Cemetery Protective Association, 485 U.S. 439 (1988).

Mack v. O'Leary, 80 F.3d.1175 (7th Cir.,1996).

Reynolds v. U.S., 98 U.S. 145 (1878).

Sabir Abdul-Hagg v. Singletary et al, 7th S. 2d 1197 (2000).

Sasnett v. Department of Corrections, 891 F. Supp. 1305 (1995).

Sherbert v. Verner, 374 U.S. 398 (1963).

Smith v. Employment Division, 307 Ore 68 (1988).

Smith v. Employment Division, 489 U.S. 1077 (1989).

Thomas v. Review Board, 450 U.S. 707, 716 (1981).

Toca v. Florida, 824 So. 2d 204 (2002).

U.S. v. Ballard, 322 U.S. 78 (1944).

U.S. v. Seeger, 380 U.S. 163 (1965).

Warner v. Boca Raton, 64 F. Supp. 2d 1272 (1999).

Warner v. Boca Raton, 267 F. 3d 1223, 1227 (2001).

Welsh v. U.S., 398 U.S. 333 (1970).

West Virginia State Bd. v. Barnette, 319 U.S. 624 (1943).

Wisconsin v. Yoder, 406 U.S. 205 (1975).

Yasir v. Hancock et al, 868 So. 2d 670 (2004).

CONSTITUTIONS, STATUTES, AND RULES

U.S. CONST. Art III, amend 1, 14.

FLA. CONST. art. I, §§ 3, 4 & 9.

Virginia Statute for Religious Freedom, Va Const Art I § 16.

F.R.Civ.Pro 27.

F.R.E. 615, 762

Religious Freedom Restoration Act, 42 U.S.C. §§ 2000bb et seq (1993).

Florida Religious Restoration Freedom Act of 1998, Fla. Stat. § 761.01 *et seq.*

Hearings on H.R. 2797 Before the House Judiciary Comm., 102d Cong., 2d Sess. 128–30 (May 13, 1992).

International Religions Freedom Act. 22 U.S.C. 6401 ff.

Religious Liberty Protection Act, H. R. 4019.

Religious Land Use and Institutionalized Persons Act, 42 U.S.C. §§ 2000 cc (2004).

"Rules and Regulations of the Boca Raton Municipal Cemetery and Mausoleum" (1996).

BOOKS AND ARTICLES

Agamben, Giorgio. *Homo Sacer: Sovereign Power and Bare Life.* Translated by Daniel Heller-Roazen. Palo Alto: Stanford University Press, 1998.

Albanese, Catherine L. *America: Religions and Religion.* 2d Edition. Belmont: Wadsworth Publishing, 1992.

American Heritage Dictionary of the English Language, s.v. "sexton," "substantial."

Ammerman, Nancy T. "Golden Rule Christianity: Lived Religion in the American Mainstream" in David T. Hall, ed. *Lived Religion in America: Toward a Theory of Practice.* Princeton: Princeton University Press, 1997.

An-Na'im, Abduallahi. *Toward an Islamic Reformation: Civil Liberties, Human Rights, and International Law.* Syracuse: Syracuse University Press, 1990.

Asad, Talal. *Formations of the Secular: Christianity, Islam, Modernity.* Palo Alto: Stanford University Press, 2003.

Associated Catholic Cemeteries Policy

Barry, Brian. *Culture and Equality : An Egalitarian Critique of Multiculturalism* Cambridge: Harvard University Press, 2001.

Bellah, Robert. "Civil Religon in America." *Daedalus* 117:97-118 (1998).

Berg, Thomas. *The State and Religion in a Nutshell.* St. Paul: West Group, 1998.

Berger, Raoul. "Incorporation of the Bill of Rights: Akhil Amar's Wishing Well." *University of Cinncinnati Law Review* 62:1–36 (1994).

Berman, Harold. *Law and Revolution: The Formation of the Western Legal Tradition.* Cambridge: Harvard University Press, 1983.

Bloom, Harold. *The American Religion: The Emergence of the Post-Christian Nation.* New York: Simon & Schuster, 1993.

Bossy, John. *Christianity in the West: 1400–1700.* Oxford: Oxford University Press, 1985.

Bourdieu, Pierre. (1986). "La Force du droit: Elements pour une sociologie du champ juridique" and "Habitus, Code et Codification" *Actes de la recherche en sciences sociales* 64: 3–19 (1986).

Bowen, John R. *Islam, Law and Equality in Indonesia: An Anthropology of Public Reasoning.* Cambridge: Cambridge University Press, 2003.

Brown, Alexandra R. *The Cross and Human Transformation: Paul's Apocalyptic Word in 1 Corinthians.* Minneapolis: Fortress Press, 1995.

Broyde, Michael. *The Pursuit of Justice and Jewish Law: Halakhic Perspectives on the Legal Profession.* Hoboken, N.J.: KTAV Publishing House, 1996.

Broyde, Michael and John Witt, eds. *Human Rights in Judaism: Cultural Religion and Political Perspectives.* Northvale, N.J.: Aronson Publishing House, 1998.

Burton, Lloyd. *Worship and Wilderness: Culture, Religion and Law in the Management of Public Lands and Resources.* Madison: University of Wisconsin Press, 2002.

Canon Land Society of Great Britain and Ireland. *The Canon Law: Letter and Spirit.* Collegeville: The Liturgical Press, 1995.

Carpenter, Joel A. *Revive Us Again: The Reawakening of American Fundamentalism.* New York: Oxford University Press, 1997.

Carter, Stephen. *The Culture of Disbelief: How American Law and Politics Trivialize Religious Devotion.* New York: Basic Books, 1993.

Casanova, José. *Public Religions in the Modern World.* Chicago: University of Chicago Press, 1994.

Catholicisme: Hier Aujourd'hui Demain (1996), s.v. "Suicide."

Clifford, James. "Identity in Mashpee." *The Predicament of Culture: Twentieth-Century Ethnography, Literature, and Art.* Cambridge: Harvard University Press, 1988.

Clinton, William. "Remarks on Signing the Religious Freedom Restoration Act of 1993," 29 *Weekly Comp Pres. Doc* 2377 (November 16, 1993).

Comaroff, John L., and Simon Roberts. *Rules and Processes: The Cultural Logic of Dispute in an African Context.* Chicago: University of Chicago Press, 1981.

Cover, Robert. "Foreword: *Nomos* and Narrative" *Harvard Law Review* 97:4–68 (1983).

Crèvecoeur, J. Hetor St. John. *Letters from an American Farmer.* Oxford: Oxford University Press, 1997.

Curl, Donald W., and John P. Johnson. *Boca Raton: A Pictorial History.* Boca Raton: The News, 1988.

Currie, David P. "*Reflections on City of Boerne v. Flores: RFRA.*" *William and Mary Law Review* 39:637–44 (1998).

Curry, Thomas J. *Farewell to Christendom: The Future of Church and State in America.* Oxford: Oxford University Press, 2001.

271

————. *The First Freedoms: Church and State in America to the Passage of the First Amendment*. Oxford: Oxford University Press, 1987.

Dale, Elizabeth. *Debating and Creating Authority: The Failure of a Constitutional Ideal in Massachusetts Bay, 1629–1649*. Burlington, VT: Ashgate, 2001.

Daly, Mary. *Gyn/ecology: The Metaethics of Radical Feminism*. Boston: Beacon Press, 1978.

Darian-Smith, Eve, and Peter Fitzpatrick, eds. *Laws of the Postcolonial*. Ann Arbor: University of Michigan Press, 2001.

The Oxford Dictionary of the Christian Church, s.v., "dead, prayers for the."

Death Care Business Advisor (10/9/97), p. 34.

Demerath, N. J. III, and Rhys Williams. *A Bridging of Faiths: Religion and Politics in a New England City*. Princeton: Princeton University Press, 1992.

Dohrmann, Natalie B. "Analogy, Empire and Political Conflict in a Rabbinic Midrash," *The Journal of Jewish Studies* 53:273–98 (2002).

Doniger, Wendy. "Why Did They Burn?: Religious Sacrifice or a Misogynist Crime: The Missing Voices of Hindu Widows." *Times Literary Supplement* 9/14/01 pp. 3–4.

Douzinas, Costas, Peter Goodrich, and Yifat Hachamovitch, eds. *Politics, Postmodernity and Critical Legal Studies*. London: Routledge, 1994.

Douzinas, Costas, and Ronnie Warrington, "Antigone's Law: A Geneology of Jurisprudence." In Costas Douzinas, Peter Goodrich and Yifat Hachamovitch, *Politics, Postmodernity and Critical Legal Studies: The Legality of the Contingent*. New York: Routledge 1994.

Dunningan, "Constitutional Rights Standing for Religion?" *Broward Daily Business Review* 43:5 2:A17.

Durham, W. Cole, Jr. "State RFRA's and the Scope of Free Exercise Protection." *University of California at Davis Law Review* 32:665–724 (1999).

Durkheim, Émile. *The Elementary Forms of Religious Life*. Translated by Carol Cosman. New York: Oxford University Press, 2001.

Edmond, Gary. "After Objectivity: Expert Evidence and Procedural Reform." *The Sydney Law Review* 25:131–63 (2003).

Eliade, Mircea. *The Myth of the Eternal Return: Or, Cosmos in History*. Princeton: Princeton University Press, 1954.

Ellman, Steve. "14-yr Fight on Behalf of Sugar Cane Cutters in Palm Beach County May Be Entering Last Phase." *Palm Beach Daily Business Review* (April 22, 2003), p. A1.

Engel, David. "Law in the Domains of Everyday Life: The Construction of Community and Difference." *Law in Everyday Life*, ed. Austin Savat and Thomas R. Kearns. Ann Arbor: University of Michigan Press, 1995.

Eusebius, *Conversion of Constantin*. Library of Nicene and Post Nicene Fathers, 2d series (N.Y.: Christian Literature 1990, vol. I:489–91.

Evans, Arthur S. *Pearl City: A Black Community Remembers*. Boca Raton: Florida Atlantic University Press, 1990.

Evans, Malcolm D. *Religious Liberty and International Law in Europe*. Cambridge: Cambridge University Press, 1997.

Fabian, Johannes. *Time and the Other: How Anthropology Makes Its Object*. New York: Columbia University Press, 1983.

Ferraro, Thomas J. *Catholic Lives, Contemporary America*. Durham, N.C.: Duke University Press, 1997.

First Things: A Monthly Journal of Religion and Public Life 1990– .

Fitzpatrick, Peter. *The Mythology of Modern Law*. New York: Routledge, 1992.

French, Rebecca. From Yoder to Yoda: Models of Traditional Modern, and Post-modern Religion in United States Constitutional Law," *Arizona Law Review* 41:49–92 (1999).

———. "Shopping for Religion: The Change in Everyday Religious Practice, and Its Importance to the Law," *Buffalo Law Review* 51:127–99 (2003).

Gamwell, Franklin I. *Democracy on Purpose: Justice and the Reality of God*. Washington: Georgetown University Press, 2002.

Garnot, Benoît. "Justice, infrajustice, parajustice et extrajustice dans la France d'Ancien Regime." *Crime, History and Societies* 4:103–120 (2000).

Gauchet, Marcel. *Le Désenchantement du monde: une histoire politique de la religion*. Paris: Gallimard, 1985.

Geertz, Clifford. *Available Light: Anthropological Reflections on Philosophical Topics* Princeton: Princeton University Press, 2000.

———. "Local Knowledge: Fact and Law in Comparative Perspective," in *Local Knowledge: Further Essays in Interpretive Anthropology*. New York: Basic Books, 1983.

———. *Works and Lives: The Anthropologist As Author*. Stanford: Stanford University Press, 1988.

Giles, Paul. *American Catholic Arts and Fictions*. Cambridge: Cambridge University Press, 1992.

Gilkey, Langdon. *Creationism on Trial: Evolution and God at Little Rock*. Minneapolis: Winston Press, 1985.

Gill, Sam D. *Native American Religions: An Introduction*. Belmont: Wadsworth Publishing, 1982.

Glendon, Mary Ann. *Abortion and Divorce in Western Law*. Cambridge: Harvard University Press, 1987.

"God Alone Is Lord of the Consciences: Policy Statement and Recommendations Regarding Religious Liberty," Presbyterian Church USA 1989.

Goluboff, Sascha L. *Jewish Russians: Upheavals in a Moscow Synagogue*. Philadelphia: University of Pennsylvania Press, 2003.

Goodrich, Peter. *Oedipus Lex: Psychoanalysis, History, Law*. Berkeley: University of California Press, 1995.

Greeley, Andrew, M. *The Catholic Imagination*. Berkeley: University of California Press, 2000.

Greenawalt, Kent. "Judicial Resolution of Issues about Religious Conviction." *Marquette Law Review* 87:461–72 (1998).

273

———. "Religion As a Concept in Constitutional Law." *California Law Review* 72:753–816 (1984).

Greenhouse, Carol. *Praying for Justice: Faith, Order, and Community in an American Town.* Ithaca: Cornell University Press, 1986.

Habermas, Jürgen. *Between Facts and Norms: Contributions to a Discourse Theory of Law and Democracy.* Translated by William Rehg. Cambridge: MIT Press, 1996.

Hackett, Rosalind, and Winnifred Fallers Sullivan. "Religion, Law, and Human Rights." Special issue of *Culture and Religion* 6:1 (forthcoming 2005).

Hall, David D., ed. *Lived Religion in America: Toward a History of Practice.* Princeton: Princeton University Press, 1997.

Hamburger, Philip. *Separation of Church and State.* Cambridge: Harvard University Press, 2001.

Hamilton, Marci A. "Religion and the Law in the Clinton Era: An Anti-Madisonian Legacy." *Law and Contemporary Problems* 63:101–132 (2000).

———. "The Religious Freedom Restoration Act: Letting the Fox into the Henhouse under Cover of Section 5 of the Fourteenth Amendment." *Cardozo Law Review* 16:357–88 (1994).

Hammond, Phillip E. *With Liberty for All: Freedom of Religion in the United States.* Louisville: Westminister John Knox, 1998.

Hart, H.L.A. *The Concept of Law.* London: Clarendon Press, 1961.

Harvey, Van A. *A Handbook of Theological Terms: Their Meaning and Background Exposed in Over 300 Articles.* New York: A Touchstone Book, 1964.

Hatch, Nathan. *The Democratization of American Christianity.* New Haven: Yale University Press 1989.

Hervieu-Léger, Danièle. "'What Scripture Tells Me': Spontaneity and Regulation within the Catholic Charismatic Renewal" in David D. Hall, ed. *Lived Religion in America: Toward a History of Practice.* Princeton: Princeton University Press, 1997.

History of Boca Raton, The. Video produced by the News Group, Delray Beach, FL (2000).

Holy Bible Revised Standard Version.

Howe, Mark deWolfe. *The Garden and the Wilderness: Religion and Government in American Constitutional History.* Chicago: University of Chicago Press, 1965.

Huber, Peter W. *Galileo's Revenge: Junk Science in the Courtroom.* New York: Basic Books, 1991.

Huxley, Andrew. *Religion, Law and Tradition: Comparative Studies in Religious Law.* London: Routledge/Curzon, 2002.

Itkoff, Valerie Greenberg. "Rejected Judge Branded 'Unfair': Rights Plaintiffs May Ask Ryskamp to Bow Out." *Legal Times* (April 29, 1991), p. 9.

Jacobs, Louis. *A Tree of Life: Diversity, Flexibility, and Creativity in Jewish Life.* London: Littman Library of Jewish Civilization, 2000.

Jacobsohn, Gary Jeffrey. *The Wheel of the Law: India's Secularism in Comparative Context.* Princeton: Princeton University Press, 2003.

Jellinek, Georg. *The Declaration of the Rights on Man and of Citizens: A Contribution to Modern Constitutional History.* Translated by Max Farrand. Westport: Hyperion Press,1979.

Jerusalem Post (March 22, 1991) (February 12, 1991).

Joyce, James. *Dubliners.* New York: B.W. Huebsch, 1916.

Kahn, Paul. *The Cultural Study of Law: Reconstructing Legal Scholarship* Chicago: University of Chicago Press, 1999.

Katz, Nathan. *A Jewish King at Shingly: The Story of the Jews of Cochin.* Delhi: Manohar, 2004.

———. *Who Are the Jews of India?* Berkeley: University of California Press, 2000.

Kelley, Donald R., *The Human Measure: Social Thought in the Western Legal Tradition.* Cambridge: Harvard University Press, 1990.

Kippenberg, Hans. *Discovering Religious History in the Modern Age.* Translated by Barbara Harshaw. Princeton: Princeton University Press, 2002.

Kleinberg, Eliot. "Boca to Vote on Cemetery's Clutter Rules." *Palm Beach Post* (June 10, 1997).

Kurland, Philip. *Church and State: The Supreme Court and the First Amendment.* Chicago: University of Chicago Press, 1975.

Kutnjak, Sanja, and Valerie P. Hans. "Jurors' Evaluations of Expert Testimony: Judging the Messenger and the Message." *Law and Social Inquiry* 28:441–82 (2003).

Laderman, Gary. *The Sacred Remains: American Attitudes toward Death, 1799–1883.* New Haven: Yale University Press, 1996.

Lamm, Maurice. *The Jewish Way in Death and Mourning.* New York: Jonathan David Publishers, 1994.

Laycock, Douglas. "Formal, Substantive, and Disaggregated Neutrality toward Religion." *DePaul Law Review* 39:993–1018 (1990).

Levinson, Sanford. *Constitutional Faith.* Princeton: Princeton University Press, 1988.

Lilla, Mark. *The Reckless Mind: The Intellectual in Politics.* New York: New York Review of Books, 2001.

Luckmann, Thomas. *The Invisible Religion: The Problem of Religion in Modern Society.* New York: Macmillan, 1967.

McConnell, Michael. "The Origins and Historical Understanding of Free Exercise of Religion." *Harvard Law Review* 103:1409 (1990).

———. "The Problem of Singling Out Religion," *DePaul Law Review* 50:1–47 (2000).

McCutcheon, Russell T. *Critics Not Caretakers: Redescribing the Public Study of Religion.* Albany: State University of New York Press, 2001.

McDanell, Colleen. *Material Christianity: Religion and Popular Culture in America.* New Haven: Yale University Press, 1995.

McGreevy, John T. *Catholicism and American Freedom: A History.* New York: Norton, 2003.

McGuckin, John Anthony. *Standing in God's Holy Fire: The Byzantine Tradition.* Maryknoll: Orbis Books, 2001.

————. *St. Gregory of Nazianzus: An Intellectual Autobiography*. Crestwood: St. Vladimir's Seminary Press, 2001.

Maine, Henry. *Ancient Law: Its Connection with Early History of Society and Its Relation to Modern Ideas*. New York: Holt, 1864.

Marty, Martin E., and R. Scott Appleby, eds. *Fundamentalisms Observed*. Chicago: University of Chicago Press, 1991.

Mead, Sidney. *The Lively Experiment: The Shaping of Christianity in America*. New York: Harper and Row, 1963.

Melissaris, Emmanuel. "The More the Merrier: A New Take on Legal Pluralism." *Social and Legal Studies* 13:57–79 (2004).

Merback, Michael B. *The Thief, the Cross and the Wheel: Pain and the Spectacle of Punishment in Medieval and Renaissance Europe*. Chicago: University of Chicago Press, 1999.

Merry, Sally. *Colonizing Hawai'i: The Cultural Power of Law*. Princeton: Princeton University Press, 2000.

Messick, Brinkley. *The Calligraphic State: Textual Domination and History in a Muslim Society*. Berkeley: University of California Press, 1993.

Miller, Daniel, ed. *Unwrapping Christmas*. Oxford: Oxford University Press, 1993.

Mir-Hosseini, Ziba. *Marriage on Trial: A Study of Islamic Family Law: Iran and Morocco Compared*. New York: I. B. Tauris, 1993.

Morris, Charles. *American Catholic: The Saints and Sinners Who Built America's Most Powerful Church*. New York: Times Books, 1997.

Motha, Stewart, and Thanos Zarthaloudis. "Law, Ethics and the Utopian End of Human Rights," *Social and Legal Studies* 12:243–68 (June 2003).

Murphy, Tim. *The Oldest Social Science?: Configurations of Law and Modernity*. Cambridge: Clarendon Press, 1997.

Nader, Laura. *Law in Culture and Society*. Chicago: Aldine, 1969.

National Catholic Cemetery Association. *The Catholic Cemetery: A Vision for the Millenium*. 1997.

New Catholic Encyclopaedia (2003). s.v., "Immaculate Conception," "Lourdes," "Sacred Heart, Devotion to," and "Sacred Heart, Iconography of."

New York Times Almanac 2001.

Niehaus, Isak. *Witchcraft, Power and Politics: Exploring the Occult in the South African Lowveld*. London: Pluto Press, 2001.

Nijf, Onnon N. van. *The Civic World of Professional Associations in the Roman East*. Amsterdam: J. C. Gieben, 1997.

Noll, Mark. *American Evangelical Christianity: An Introduction*. London: Blackwell, 2001.

Noonan, John T., Jr. *The Lustre of Our Country: The American Experience of Religious Freedom*. Berkeley: University of California Press, 1998.

————. *Persons and Masks of the Law: Cardozo, Holmes, Jefferson, and Wythe As Makers of the Masks*. New York: Farrar, Straus and Giroux, 1976.

Nussbaum, Martha. "Capabilities and Human Rights." *Fordham Law Review.* LXVI:273–300 (1997).

———. "Religion and Women's Human Rights" in *Religion and Contemporary Liberalism.* Edited by Paul J. Weithman. Notre Dame: University of Notre Dame Press, 1997.

Obiora, Leslye. "The Issue of Female Circumcision: Bridges and Barricades: Rethinking Polemics and Intransigence in the Campaign Against Female Circumcision." *Case Western Reserve Law Review* 47:275–378 (1997).

Orsi, Robert. *The Madonna of 115th St.: Faith and Community in Italian Harlem 1880–1950.* New Haven: Yale University Press, 1995.

Oxford English Dictionary, s.v., "Sexton."

Pals, Daniel. "Is Religion a *Sui Generis* Phenomenon?" and "Responses and Rejoinders." *Journal of the American Academy of Religion* 55:259–82, 703–13 (1987).

———. *Seven Theories of Religion.* New York: Oxford University Press, 1996.

Pathak, Zakia, and Rajeswari Sundar Rajan. "Shahbano." *Signs: Journal of Women in Culture and Society* 14:558–82 (1989).

Peterson, Merrill D., and Robert C. Vaughan, eds. *The Virginia Statute for Religious Freedom: Its Evolution and Consequences in American History.* Cambridge: Cambridge University Press, 1988.

Pocock, J.G.A. *Barbarism and Religion.* Cambridge: Cambridge University Press, 2000.

Pole, J. R. *The Pursuit of Equality in American History,* rev. ed. Berkeley: University of California Press, 1993.

Poulter, Sebastian. *Ethnicity, Law, and Human Rights: The English Experience.* Oxford: Clarendon Press, 1998.

Rawls, John. *The Law of Peoples.* Cambridge: Harvard University Press, 1999.

Redfield, Robert. *The Little Community and Peasant Society and Culture.* Chicago: University of Chicago Press, 1956.

Rice, Eugene, and Anthony Grafton, *The Foundations of Early Modern Europe, 1460–1559.* New York: W.W. Norton and Co., 1994.

Rose, Gillian. *Mourning Becomes the Law: Philosophy and Representation.* Cambridge: Cambridge University Press, 1996.

Rosen, Lawrence. "The Anthropologist As Expert Witness." *American Anthropologist* 79:555–78 (1977).

———. *The Anthropology of Justice: Law As Culture in Islamic Society.* New York: Cambridge University Press, 1989.

———. *The Culture of Islam: Changing Aspects of Contemporary Muslim Life.* Chicago: University of Chicago Press, 2002.

Rosenfeld, Michael. "The Rule of Law and the Legitimacy of Constitutional Democracy." *Southern California Law Review* 74/1307 (2001).

Rouland, Norbert. *Anthropologie juridique.* Paris: Presses universitaires de France, 1998.

Rudolph, Susanne, and James Piscatori, eds. *Transnational Religion and Fading States*. Boulder: Westview, 1997.

Sands, Kathleen. "'A Property of Peculiar Value': Land, Religion and the Constitution," in *Culture and Religion*, forthcoming 2005.

Schweder, Richard A., Martha Minow, and Hazel Rose Marcus, eds. *Engaging Cultural Differences: The Multicultural Challenge in Liberal Democracies*. New York: Russell Sage Foundation, 2002.

Seebohm, Caroline. *Boca Rococo: How Addison Mizner Invented Florida's Gold Coast*. New York: Clarkson Potter, 2001.

Seltzer, Robert M. *Jewish People, Jewish Thought: The Jewish Experience in History*. New York: Macmillan, 1980.

Shadid, W.A.R., and P. S. van Koningsveld, eds. *Religious Freedom and the Neutrality of the State: The Position of Islam in the European Union*. Leuven: Peeters, 2002.

Singer, Isaac Bashevis. *In My Father's Court*. New York: Farrar, Straus and Giroux, 1962.

Smith, Christian. *American Evangelicalism: Embattled and Thriving*. Chicago: University of Chicago Press, 1998.

Smith, Jonathan Z. *Drudgery Divine: On the Comparison of Early Christianities and the Religions of Late Antiquity*. Chicago: University of Chicago Press, 1990.

———. *Imagining Religion: From Babylon to Jonestown*. Chicago: University of Chicago Press, 1982.

———. *Map Is Not Territory: Studies in the History of Religions*. Leiden: E. J. Brill, 1978.

Smith, Stephen D. *Foreordained Failure: The Quest for a Constitutional Principle of Religious Freedom*. New York: Oxford University Press, 1995.

———. "Reflections on *City of Boerne v. Flores:* Losing Jerusalem—RFRA and the Vocation of the Legal Crusader." *William and Mary Law Review* 39:907–24 (1998).

Soloveitchik, Haym. "Rupture and Reconstruction: The Transformation of Contemporary Orthodoxy." *Tradition* 28:64–130 (1994).

Sousa Santos, Boaventura de. *Toward a New Common Sense: Law, Science and Politics in the Paradigmatic Transition*. New York: Routledge, 1995.

Sullivan, Winnifred Fallers. "Die neuen US Geseze zu 'Charitable Choice' und die Regelungen zu den 'Faith-based' Organisationen" in Hans G. Kippenberg and Gunnar Folke Schuppert, eds. *Die verkörperte Religion. Der Öffentlichleisstatus von Religionsgemeinschaften* (in process).

———. "Neutralizing Religion or What Is the Opposite of 'Faith-based'?" in *History of Religions Journal* 41:4 (2002).

———. "Normative Pluralism: Religion and Law in the Twenty-first Century," *Religion* (forthcoming 2005).

———. *Paying the Words Extra: Religious Discourse in the Supreme Court of the United States*. Cambridge: Harvard University Center for the Study of World Religions, 1994.

———. "Religious Freedom and the Rule of Law: A Modernist Myth in a Post-modern World," in Brigite Luchesi and Kocku von Stuckrad, eds. *Religion in Cultural Discourse: Essays in Honor of Hans G. Kippenberg on the Occasion of His 65th Birthday.* Berlin: Walter de Gruyter, 2004.

Sullivan, Winnifred Fallers, and Robert A. Yelle, "Law and Religion: Overview," *Encyclopedia of Religion* 2d. ed. (in process).

Taves, Ann. *The Household of Faith: Roman Catholic Devotions in Mid–Nineteenth Century America.* South Bend: University of Notre Dame Press, 1986.

Taylor, Charles. *Multiculturalism and "The Politics of Recognition."* Princeton: Princeton University Press, 1992.

———. *Varieties of Religion Today: William James Revisited.* Cambridge: Harvard University Press, 2002.

Thuma, Cynthia. *Images of America: Boca Raton.* Charleston: Arcadia Publishing, 2003.

Tierney, Brian. *Religion, Law and the Growth of Constitutional Thought, 1150–1650.* Cambridge: Cambridge University Press, 1982.

Trelles, Emma. "Grave Injustice" *New Times* (November 4, 1999), n.p.

Tussman, Joseph, and Jacob ten Broek. "The Equal Protection of the Laws." *California Law Review* 37 (1949): 341–81.

Twining, William. *Globalisation and Legal Theory.* Evanston: Northwestern University Press, 2000.

Vyver, John D. van der., and John Witte, Jr., eds. *Religious Human Rights in Global Perspectives.* The Hague: Martinus Nijhoff Publishers, 1996.

Alan Watson. *The State, Law and Religion: Pagan Rome.* Athens: University of Georgia Press, 1992.

Weber, Max. *Sociology of Religion.* Translated by Ephraim Fischoff. Boston: Beacon Press, 1963.

Weisman, Brent. "Archaeological Perspectives on Florida Seminole Ethnogenesis" in Bonnie G. McEwan, ed. *Indians of the Greater Southeast: Historical Archaeology and Ethnohistory.* Gainesville: University Press of Florida, 2000.

White, James Boyd. *The Legal Imagination: Studies in the Nature of Legal Thought and Expression.* Boston: Little, Brown, 1973.

Wigoder, Geoffery, ed. *The New Encyclopaedia of Judaism.* New York: New York University Press, 2002.

Wilde, Oscar. *The Importance of Being Earnest.* London: L. Smithers and Co., 1899.

Williams, Robert W. *The American Indian in Western Legal Thought: The Discourses of Conquest.* Oxford: Oxford University Press, 1990.

Witte, John, Jr. *Religion and the American Constitutional Experiment: Essential Rights and Liberties.* Boulder: Westview Press, 2000.

Wuthnow, Robert. *The Re-Structuring of American Religion: Society and Faith Since World War II.* Princeton: Princeton University Press, 1988.

Yelle, Robert. *Explaining Mantras: Ritual, Rhetoric, and the Dream of a Natural Language in Hindu Tantra.* New York: Routledge, 2003.

Websites

www.bocahistory.org
www.calvin.edu
www.charlottediocese.org.
www.ci-boca-raton.fl.us
www.crpc.org/2000/
www.pba.edu
www.saintmarymagdalen.com/eileen/
www.soberhouses.com
www.state.gov/g/drl/irf/
www.uwm.edu/ncorre

Index

abortion, 3

aesthetic, religious, 2, 15–21, 33, 54, 73–74, 106

Africa USA 14

Africa v. Pennsylvania, 101

American Civil Liberties Union (ACLU), 22, 32, 33

Americanness, 4–7, 10, 28, 34, 46, 61, 69, 80, 85–88, 92, 100–101, 105, 111, 115, 118–119, 137, 141, 142, 148–150, 156, 264 n.3; in attitudes toward religion and the state, 4, 6, 28, 46, 61–62, 85–88, 100–101, 111, 115, 118–119, 148–50, 156; of legal practices, 34; of religious practices, 5, 7, 10, 61–62, 69, 80, 85–88, 92, 137, 142–148, 217–218

Amish, 4, 27, 101

Arlington National Cemetery, 54

atheism, 60, 133

Bellah, Robert, 148

Beth Din of America, 56

Bible, the, 6, 19, 39–40, 47, 58, 62–64, 66, 79, 81, 92, 104, 126–127, 133, 134; Christian, 19, 47, 62–64, 66, 79–81, 104, 133, 208–214; Hebrew, 6, 58, 92, 126–127, 134; New Testament, 39–40

Bibletown Community Church, 14

Bibletown, USA 14

Bill of Rights, 25, 27, 158

Black, Galen, 26

Blackwell Dictionary of Judaica, 42

Boca Raton, city of: Cemetery, 14–22, 34, 37, 40–45, 48–55, 70, 86–88, 89–91, 110, 119, 128, 142, 219–221; City Council of, 20, 21, 48, 52, 222–224; city officials of, 5, 18, 20, 22, 40, 48, 50, 52, 54, 69–72, 106; history of, 13–14, 248 n.1; other lawsuits involving, 14, 52, 248 n.10; and *Warner* case, 2–3, 11, 31, 32–38, 41–53, 74, 89–91, 94, 103–104, 108–111, 114, 138

Boca Raton Cemetery, Rules and Regulations of, 16–17, 20–23, 34, 35, 41, 48, 54, 56, 65, 69, 89–90, 166–179, 219

Boca Raton Mausoleum Co., 16

Boerne v. Flores, 28–30, 137, 226

"born again" Christianity, 18, 46, 254 n.41

Bowen, John, 158

Brown v. Board of Education, 150

Broyde, Michael, 45, 56–60, 67, 68, 69, 77, 84, 86, 92, 93, 118, 128, 130, 133–135, 180–184

Buddhism, 73

burial practices, 2, 9, 15, 16, 21, 69–70, 71–72, 83–84, 86, 93, 194–200, 208–214, 215–218; Eastern Orthodox, 46, 62–65, 68, 197; Evangelical Christian, 46–48, 74, 80; Jewish, 43–45, 49, 56–60, 74, 76, 80, 119–128; Muslim, 74; Roman Catholic, 37–38, 41, 45, 51–53, 63–68, 73, 112–119

Bush, George W., 28, 29

Bush, Jeb, 110, 139

Calvin College, 32

canon law, 73

Cantwell v. Connecticut, 25

Casanova, José, 152, 247 n.14, 253 n.25, 266 n.39, 267 n.42

casket, 70

Catholicism, 8, 38–41, 45, 52–53, 61–62, 63–64, 68, 73–74, 77, 81, 83, 85, 93, 110, 112–119, 128–129, 135–136, 139, 140–141, 148, 151, 185–187, 217, 247 n.15, 253 n.18, 255 n.62, 256 n.22, 257 n.35; Polish, 52, 112

Catholics, 2, 28, 104, 106

Cavedoni, Barbara, 18, 37, 39, 40, 41, 112–119

China, 1

citizenship, 4, 7, 8

Clark, Tom, 101

Clinton, William Jefferson, 28

cloning, 3

cofferdam, 69, 70

Cogley, Joseph, 21, 54, 69

"compelling interest" test, 23, 26, 35, 55

Congress, U.S., 24, 28, 29, 70, 71, 96

conscientious objection, 101

Constantine, 7, 62, 64–65, 85

Constitution of the United States: generally, 22, 78, 85, 148, 155; religion clauses of First Amendment of, generally, 24–29, 90, 91, 94, 95, 96, 99–101, 106, 109, 148–151, 161, 228, 230–231, 249 n.32; —, establishment clause, 9, 24–25, 33, 91, 137, 150; —, free exercise clause of, 9, 33, 90, 91, 99, 104, 150, 235–238;—, free speech, 238–241; Thirteenth Amendment, 25; Fourteenth Amendment, 25, 29, 150, 161, 221, 251 n.43, 266 n.34; —, "due process" clause of, 25, 242–244; Fifteenth Amendment, 25

Constitutions, state, 25

Coral Ridge Presbyterian Church, 32

crèche, 52, 82

Crèvecoeur, J. Hector St. John, 145, 265 n.20

cross, display of, 2, 10, 18, 37, 40, 42–51, 63–66, 68, 72, 105, 106, 108, 199

Cuba, 18, 37, 39, 46, 112

Curry, Thomas, 143–144, 156, 265 n.14

Danciu, Charlotte, 36, 52, 115

Danciu, Eleanor, 18, 52, 53, 117–119

Danciu, Emil, 18, 52–53

Davis, Daniel, 50, 51

Davis, Joanne, 18, 50–52, 112–119, 132

death, 5, 81, 83, 87, 89, 110

Death Care Business Advisor, 20

diaspora, religion of the, 2, 152, 153

discrimination, 9, 12, 33, 101, 102, 143, 149, 150, 158

disestablishment, 7, 84, 95, 138, 143, 146, 154

Dominguez, Larry, 37, 41, 112, 115

Driscoll, Donna, 54

Durkheim, Émile, 103

Eliade, Mircea, 103

Emory University, 56

Employment Division v. Smith, 22, 26, 27, 28–29, 90, 104, 109, 149, 226, 251 n.49

Enlightenment, 86, 151

Episcopalians, 63, 153

epitaphios, 63, 64

equality, 25, 138, 149, 150, 157, 159

Ethical Culture Movement, 101

ethnography, 8, 247 n.17

Europe, religion in, 1, 7, 8, 30, 62, 80, 85, 144, 145, 146, 151

euthanasia, 3

Evangelical Christianity, 5, 6, 7, 10, 46, 61, 144

Evans-Pritchard, E. E., 103

"exercise of religion," 23, 26, 30, 31, 35, 36, 55, 72, 82, 96, 97, 107, 109, 127

expert witnesses: for defendants in Warner case, 5, 7, 16, 70–81, 92–94, 102–103, 108, 111, 128–136; generally, 9–10, 35, 255 n.7, 256 n.16, 265 n. 24; for plaintiffs in Warner case, 5, 7, 11, 45, 55–59, 82–88, 92–94, 102–103, 111, 128–136

faith-based initiatives, 3, 246 n.32

Florida, state of, 2, 3, 13–15, 32, 33, 128; Constitution of, 22, 161, 244, 249 n.32; Federal District Courts in, 4, 61; statutes of, 22–24, 29, 31, 95, 98–100, 105; Supreme Court of, 99, 104, 110, 139

Florida Atlantic University, 13, 21

Florida International University, 72

Florida League of Cities, 104

folk religion, 2, 38, 74, 75, 130, 140

France, 1, 3, 156

Francis, St., devotion to, 53, 108, 117, 118

Frazer, J. G., 103

Freud, Sigmund, 103

fundamentalism, 7

Geertz, Clifford, 103, 247 n.17

Georgia, 10

Germany, 144

Gilkey, Langdon, 101

God, references to, 4, 38, 41, 47, 51, 60, 62–63, 69, 104, 108, 112, 116, 117

Greece, 1

Green, James, 9, 32–34, 36, 39, 44, 55, 65, 67, 71, 76, 77, 82, 84, 85, 86, 89, 90, 123, 129, 132, 133, 252 n.6
Guatemala, 75

Hall, David, 140, 144
Hanukkah, 52, 125
Harris, Curtis, 69, 70
Hassan, Camille, 30, 51, 117
Heathrow College, 61
Hervieu-Léger, Danièle, 139
hijab, 1, 3
Holocaust, 44
Holy Sepulchre, Church of the, 65
homosexuality, 3
Howe, Mark deWolfe, 150, 250 nn.38, and 41
Hutchinson, Anne, 139

IBM, 13
Immaculate Conception, the, 118, 140, 264 n.6
Incorporation Doctrine, 25
International Religious Freedom Act (IRFA), 245 n.1
Iowa, 11
Islam, 1, 3, 8, 30, 46, 51, 66, 72, 73, 74, 149, 151, 158, 189
Israel, State of, 43, 65

Jackson, Robert, 27
Jacob, 57, 92, 133
Japanese Americans, 13, 15
Jehovah's Witnesses, 1, 4, 25, 27
Jordan, Kevin, 42, 48, 49, 69, 70
Judaism: burial practices in, 42–45, 48–50, 83, 84, 98–99, 102, 104, 106, 180–184, 204–208; generally, 11, 19, 30, 52, 62, 66, 67, 72, 79, 81, 83, 109, 217, 247 n.16, 255 n.12; law in, 56–60, 72, 74, 76–77, 80, 92, 133–135, 180–184, 187, 255 n.9, 257 n.36, 263 n.94

Karram, Pamela, 47
Karram, Souhail, 18, 40, 46–47, 48, 50, 64, 66

Katz, Nathan, 69, 72–78, 79, 80, 82, 83, 84, 92, 129–130, 132, 136, 146–147, 148, 185–193; and theory of "high traditions and little traditions," 74–75, 77, 80, 82, 129–130, 146–147, 189–190
Kennedy, Anthony, 29

Lamm, Maurice, 74, 80, 187–189, 207, 258 n.79
land, 10, 28, 29, 91
law: definition of, 3, 138, 153; and religion 3, 4, 10, 85, 102, 138, 146, 148, 153, 158
Laycock, H. Douglas, 99, 260 n.30
"least restrictive means" test, 23, 35
Lebanon, 18, 46, 66, 68
Leo XIII, 38
liberalism, 7, 155
liturgical sensibility, 62, 65, 68
"lived religion," 2, 3, 140, 143
Lourdes, 140
Lutherans, 63
Lyng v. Northwest Indian Cemetery Protective Association, 28, 91, 104, 143, 236

Mack v. O'Leary, 30, 228
Marx, Karl, 103
McDannell, Colleen, 141–142, 144
McGuckin, Eileen, 61
McGuckin, John, 54, 60–69, 72, 81, 84, 86, 93, 112, 117, 118, 119, 128, 129–132, 133, 135–136, 142, 144, 193–200
Mead, Sidney, 144–146
Mecca, 72
memorial garden, 70–71, 86
Mennonites, 101
Metzler, John, 54
Miami, city of, 19, 73
Minersville v. Gobitis, 27, 226
Mizner, Addison, 13
modernity, 7, 106, 109, 139, 154
Monier, Caridad, 18, 37–40, 112–119
monuments and memorials, 2, 15, 17–19, 20–22, 35, 37–38, 42, 45, 48–49, 50–53, 54–59, 65–68, 71–74, 80–83, 86, 98, 106, 115, 130
Mormons, 4, 26, 104
MOVE, 101

Mt. Auburn, 70
Muzzey, David, 101

National Catholic Cemetery Association, 73
nation-state, 7, 152
Native Americans, 1, 4, 10, 26, 28, 91, 104,
    248 n.2, 251 n.46, 259 n.8
Nazis, 43, 44, 50, 77, 152
New Catholic Encyclopedia, 38
New York University, 56
Nova Southeastern University Law School,
    32

O'Connor, Sandra Day, 27, 251 n.55
Oregon, 26
Orsi, Robert, 140–141, 142, 143, 144, 146
Orthodox Christianity, 61, 63, 64, 65, 66,
    68, 85, 93, 109, 110, 128, 135, 136
orthodoxy, 6, 7, 10, 29, 38, 60, 85, 92
Ottoman Empire, 46, 66
"outlaw religion," 13, 18, 82

Palm Beach Atlantic University, 32
Palm Beach County, 13, 14, 19, 22, 32, 71
Palm Beach Post, 19, 21–22, 33, 71
Pals, Daniel, 62, 63, 64, 65, 66, 67, 72,
    78–82, 83, 84, 85, 93–94, 103, 130, 132,
    147, 201–215
Pals Test, 79, 94, 98, 99, 104, 147, 148,
    203–204, 231–234
Paul, 62, 64, 81
Payne, Bobbie, 18, 48–49, 50, 59,
    121–129
Payne, Ian, 18, 48–50, 59, 121–129
Pearl City, 14
Peter, St., 108
peyote, religious use of, 26, 90, 104
Pius XI, 38
Pius XII, 38
pluralism, religious diversity and, 2, 19, 20,
    71, 89, 139, 148, 151, 153, 158
popular piety, 68, 140
Posner, Richard, 30
Presbyterian Church in America, 32
Prisons, religion in, 9, 30, 101
Protestantism: burial practices in, 47–48,
    74, 77, 106, 187, 208–214; generally, 2,

7–8, 47, 61, 64, 67, 73, 83, 92, 93, 130,
    133, 138–139, 217, 247 n.15, 257 n.33
public property, 91, 93
"purely personal preference," 35, 69, 77, 81,
    87, 94, 95, 97, 98, 99, 104, 105, 108, 109

rabbi, 56, 45, 56, 57, 92
Rachel, 58, 77, 133, 256 n.17
Reagan, Ronald, 32
Redfield, Robert, 75
Reformation, the, 7–8, 61, 62, 63, 64, 85,
    86, 136, 138–139
religion: academic study of, 5, 7, 8, 9, 10,
    11, 57, 61, 62, 72, 83, 84, 102, 152; de-
    fined by academy, 9, 101–106; defined by
    believer, 5–6, 36, 43, 86–87, 104–105,
    110, 142–143; defined by civil law, 9,
    29–31, 100–101, 110, 146–147, 153–155,
    261 nn.32, 33, 38, and n.43, 265 n.29;
    defined by custom (tradition), 40–44,
    56–57, 67, 79, 105, 146; defined by per-
    sonal preference, 35, 43, 69, 72, 77, 79,
    87, 94–95, 97, 103, 108–109; defined by
    religious law (dogma), 36, 56–57, 79, 92,
    111, 146; defined by sincerity, 6, 7, 92,
    104; lived religion, 2, 105, 140–143
religious authority, 6, 7, 35–36, 41, 57, 58,
    60, 65, 67, 77, 83, 84, 88, 93, 103, 104,
    109, 111, 114, 133
religious freedom, 1, 4, 5, 7, 8, 12, 21, 25,
    28, 37, 40, 66, 79, 86, 102, 108, 123,
    138, 143, 151, 152, 153, 154, 155, 157,
    158, 159
Religious Freedom Restoration Act (RFRA):
    federal, 23–26, 28, 29, 30, 31, 79, 90,
    95–97, 102, 109, 129, 143, 162–164,
    226–228, 252 n.63; of Florida, 22, 23,
    24, 29, 31, 35, 53, 72, 76, 78, 82, 83, 84,
    85, 90, 94–97, 98, 99, 100, 102, 104, 106,
    107, 109–110, 137, 139, 164–165,
    201–203, 225–231, 250 n.37; of other
    states, 23–24, 29, 50 n.34
religious identity, 4, 7, 8, 35, 111, 112, 114,
    120, 125, 142
*Religious Land Use and Institutionalized Per-
    sons Act* (RLUIPA), 29
Religious Liberty Protection Act (RLPA), 29

Reynolds v. U.S., 27, 104, 225, 250 n.41
Riccobono, Maria, 18, 45, 112–119
Robinson, John A. T., 101
Rogow, Bruce, 32–34, 39, 43, 55, 59, 60, 71, 83, 84, 86, 87, 89, 90, 95, 99, 104, 112, 114, 116, 118, 120, 129, 130, 131, 136, 141, 142
Roman Catholic Church, 7, 38, 52, 53, 65, 73, 112, 115, 153
Romania, 61
Romanian Orthodox Church, 60, 61
Rome, 63, 67, 132
Royal Historical Society, 60
Royal Society of the Arts, 60
"rule of law," 153, 154, 155, 157
Russia, 1
Ryskamp, Kenneth L., 3–7, 24, 31–34, 41, 60, 61, 64, 76, 78, 84, 85, 89, 91–95, 96–99, 104, 110, 133–137, 138, 141, 143, 147, 148, 219–244, 252 n.6

sacramentality, 62, 63, 65, 104, 112
Sacred Heart of Jesus, devotion to the, 18, 19, 37, 38, 41, 42, 106, 112, 118
Sakai, Joseph, 13
Scalia, Antonin, 26–27, 90
Schaff, Philip, 144–146
secularism, 63, 67, 106, 108, 109, 153, 199, 266 n.39
Selective Service Act, 101
separation of church and state, 5, 6, 62, 106, 143, 154
sexton, 20, 34, 42, 69, 110, 249 n.16
Sherbert v. Verner, 23, 26, 28, 226, 227, 251 n.47
Sikhs, 1
Simon, Howard, 33
sincerity, 6, 7, 35, 53, 77, 92, 96, 97, 99, 104, 107, 108, 110, 246 n.10
Sloane, Lawrence, 69, 70, 71
Smith, Alfred, 26
Smith, Christian, 144
Society of Jesus (Jesuits), 61
Solarz, Stephen, 96, 97, 98, 228
South Africa, 77

Star of David, 2, 18, 19, 40, 42–45, 49, 105, 106, 119–128
statuary, religious, 2, 18, 37, 40, 44, 63, 67, 68, 83, 86, 114–117
Stevens, John Paul, 137
St. Joan of Arc Church, 15, 37, 45, 52, 116, 118
"substantially burdened," 9, 22, 23, 26, 30, 31, 35, 36, 55, 79, 83, 84, 87, 90, 94, 107, 108
suicide, 18, 41, 115, 135, 253 n.13
Sullivan, Winnifred Fallers, as witness, 10–12, 54, 55, 67, 69, 82–88, 89, 93, 131, 215–218
Supreme Court of the United States, 4, 5, 24–25, 26, 27, 28, 32, 82, 90, 91, 99, 101, 133, 143, 150
synagogue, 79, 119, 122, 123, 124, 126, 127, 146

Talmud, the, 57, 58, 80, 134, 256 n.18
Ten Commandments, 11
theology, 4, 5, 6, 37, 61, 64, 67, 104, 136, 137, 245 n.5
Tillich, Paul, 101
Torah, 77, 92, 133
Turkey, 3, 65
Tylor, E. B., 103

Union Theological Seminary, 60, 130
United Kingdom, 49, 58, 61, 122, 124, 126, 127, 128
United Nations Declaration of Human Rights, 155, 157
United States Courts of Appeal: Third Circuit, 101; Eleventh Circuit, 99
University of Chicago, 75, 82
University of London, 60
University of Texas, 99
U.S. v. Seeger, 101

Vatican II, 101
vault, 69, 70
verticality, 90, 98, 99, 104, 108, 114, 127
Verzilli, Andrew, 54, 55
Villaronga, Frank, 73

Virgin Mary, devotion to the, 18, 19, 50, 51, 52, 53, 68, 117, 118, 128, 140

Warner, Miriam, 18, 41, 42, 43, 44, 59, 119–128

Warner, Richard, 18, 41, 44, 119–128

Warner v. Boca Raton: appeals in, 260 n.31; complaint in, 22; opinions in, 219–244; plaintiffs in, 5, 6, 11, 12, 17, 18, 20, 21, 22, 25, 29, 32, 33, 35, 36, 41, 43, 45, 47, 50, 53, 62, 64, 67–71, 79, 83–111, 120, 128, 132, 133, 138–146, 156, 222; references to, 2–9, 11–17, 19–25, 29–36, 55, 57, 66, 88, 95, 97, 100–103, 110, 138, 141, 146, 158

Washington and Lee University, 82

Waxman, Lynn, 36, 37, 39, 123

Weber, Max, 152, 261 n.45

West Virginia v. Barnette, 27

Wisconsin, 9, 10

World Trade Center, 18

World War II, 13, 19, 25, 80

Yamato, 13, 248 n.3

Yeshiva University, 56

Young, Olan, 16, 19